England's Landscape

East Anglia

Collins

England's Landscape
East Anglia

Tom Williamson

Series Editor Neil Cossons

ENGLISH HERITAGE

First published in 2006 by Collins, an imprint of
HarperCollins*Publishers*
77–85 Fulham Palace Road, London W6 8JB

www.collins.co.uk

10 9 8 7 6 5 4 3 2 1
10 09 08 07 06

ISBN 10 – 0 00 715571 9
ISBN 13 – 9 78 0 00 715571 2

British Library Cataloguing in Publication Data
A CIP catalogue record for this book is available from the
British Library.

Map on previous page:
The regions: the red lines bound the general area covered by
each volume.

Publisher & Commissioning Editor Myles Archibald
Production Director Graham Cook
Edited by Catherine Bradley
Designed by D & N Publishing, Hungerford, Berkshire
Indexed by Sheila Seacroft

Printed in Italy by LEGO SpA, Vicenza

ACKNOWLEDGEMENTS

SERIES EDITOR
Sir Neil Cossons OBE
Chairman, English Heritage
President, Royal Geographical Society
The series editor would like to acknowledge the contribution of
the following people:

EDITORIAL BOARD:
Professor David Cannadine
Queen Elizabeth the Queen Mother Professor of British History,
University of London

Professor Barry Cunliffe
Professor of European Archaeology, University of Oxford

Professor Richard Lawton
Professor Emeritus, Department of Geography, University of
Liverpool

Professor Brian K Roberts
Professor Emeritus, Department of Geography, University of Durham

ENGLISH HERITAGE EXECUTIVE EDITORS:
Dr Paul Barnwell, *Head of Medieval and Later Rural Research*
Dr Martin Cherry, *Former Chief Buildings Historian*
Humphrey Welfare, *Northern Territory Director*
Graham Fairclough, *Head of Characterisation*

ENGLISH HERITAGE PROJECT MANAGERS:
Val Horsler, *former Head of Publishing*
Adele Campbell, *Commercial Publishing Manager*

All new ground and air photography was taken specifically for
this series. Thanks to: Damian Grady, Senior Investigator of
English Heritage Aerial Survey and Investigation Team, and to the
photographic and dark-room teams in Swindon; Steve Cole,
Head of Photography, and the staff of the English Heritage
Photography team. Archive material from the National
Monuments Record was researched by the Enquiry and Research
Services teams led by Alyson Rogers (Buildings) and Lindsay
Jones (Archaeology/Air Photos). Graphics lists were managed by
John Vallender and Bernard Thomason. Graphics were produced
under the management of Rob Read of 3's Company
(Consultancy) Ltd, by Steve Cheshire and Deborah Hibbitt. All
other images were researched by Jo Walton and Julia Harris-Voss.

Contents

Acknowledgements

This book owes everything to the 19 years I spent at the Centre of East Anglian Studies, University of East Anglia, Norwich. Various colleagues, and a succession of research students, have provided inspiration, information and encouragement. Particular thanks must go to Brian Ayers, Keith Bacon, Gerry Barnes, Sara Birtles, David Brown, Edward Bujak, Steven Cherry, Jim Collin, Fiona Cowell, Jon Finch, Christopher Harper Bill, Sarah Harrison, Rik Hoggett, Rosemary Hoppitt, Andrew Hutcheson, Rob Liddiard, Adam Longcroft, Michael Medlar, Peter Murphy, Jo Parmenter, Tim Pestell, Elise Perciful, Ann Reeves, Ivan Ringwood, Andrew Rogerson, Kate Skipper, Janet Sleep, A Hassell Smith, Anthea Taigel, Jenni Tanimoto, Jonathan Theobald, Susanna Wade-Martins, Mavis Wesley, Susie West, Nicola Whyte, Sally Wilkinson, Richard Wilson, Shirley Wittering and Nigel Wright. Friends and associates outside the Centre, in the wider region, have also proved immensely helpful over the years: I would like to mention in particular Chris Barringer, Stewart Bryant, Bruce Campbell, Brian Cushion, John Davies, Alan Davison, Eric de Saumarez, Derek Edwards, Cain Hegarty, Peter Holborn, Graham King, Sarah Newsome, Anne Rowe, Norman Scarfe and Peter Wade-Martins. And, as ever, thanks must go to my family – Liz Bellamy and Matt and Jess Williamson – who have indulged for so long my obsession with all things East Anglian.

Foreword

The landscape of England evokes intense passion and profound emotion. This most loved of places, the inspiration for generations of writers, poets and artists, it is at once both the source of the nation's infatuation and the setting for grievous misunderstanding. For people who visit, the view of England offers some of their most lasting images. For exiles abroad the memory of the English landscape sustains their beliefs and desire for a homecoming.

But for those who live in England the obsession is double edged. On the one hand we cherish the unchanging atmosphere of a familiar place, and on the other make impossible demands of it, believing that it will always accommodate, always forgive. Only in the last half century or so have we started to recognise the extreme fragility of all that we value in the English landscape, to appreciate not only that it is the metaphor for who we are as a people, but that it represents one of our most vivid contributions to a wider culture. At last we are beginning to realise that a deeper understanding of its subtle appeal and elusive character is the key to a thoughtful approach to its future.

The unique character of England's landscape derives from many things. But nowhere is the impact of human intervention absent. If geology and topography set the scene, it is the implacable persistence of generations who since the end of the Ice Age have sought to live in and off this place that has created the singular qualities of the landscape we have today. Not, of course, that the landscape before people was in any sense a static thing; on the contrary, the environment untouched by mankind was and is a dynamic and constantly changing synthesis. Every layer of that complex progression can still be found somewhere, making its own peculiar contribution to the distinctiveness of today's England. It is a compelling narrative. Through this series of regional studies our distinguished contributors – as authors and editors – have distilled something of what has created today's England, in order to decode that narrative.

Unique is an overused term. But it has a special resonance for the landscape of England, both urban and rural. What we hope readers of this series will begin to feel is the nature of the qualities that define the English landscape. Much of that landscape has of course been inherited from cultures overseas, as conquest and migration brought here peoples who have progressively occupied and settled Britain. They created what might be called our shared landscapes, defined as much by what links them to the wider world as through any intrinsically native characteristics. The peoples whose common bonds stretched along the Atlantic seaboard have left a legacy in Cornwall more akin to parts of north-west France or Spain than to anywhere else in England. There are Roman roads and cities and medieval field systems that have their closest parallels in the European plains from whence they derived. Great abbeys and monasteries reflected in their art and architecture, their commerce and industry, a culture whose momentum lay outside these islands. And when disaster came it was a pan-European epidemic, the Black Death, that took away between a third and a half of the people. England's are not the only deserted medieval villages.

And yet, paradoxically, much of what today we would recognise as the quintessential England is only some two or three centuries old. Parliamentary enclosure, especially of the English lowlands, was itself a reaction to an even greater economic force – industrialisation, and the urbanisation that went with it. It has given us a rural landscape that epitomises the essence of Englishness in the minds of many. The fields and hedgerows surrounding the nucleated villages of the pre-existing medieval landscape are of course quite new when set against the timescale of human occupation. Indeed, when the first railways came through there remained, here and there, open fields where the rows of new hawthorn hedges were still feeble whips scribing lines across a thousand years of feudal landscape.

As Britain emerged to become the world's first industrial nation, its astonishing transformation was at its most visible in the landscape, something new, indigenous and without precedent. It fuelled the debate on the picturesque and the sublime and was a source of wonder to those who visited from overseas. But in its urban and industrial excesses it soon came to be detested by aesthetes, social commentators and a burgeoning class opposed to the horrors of industrial capitalism. What was perhaps the most decisive contribution of Britain to the human race provoked a powerful counteraction reflected in the writings of Ruskin, Morris, Octavia Hill and the Webbs. It was this anguish that a century ago energised the spirit of conservation in a growing band of people determined to capture what was left of the pre-industrial rural scene.

Today the landscape of England is, as ever, undergoing immense change. But, unlike the centuries just past, that change once again draws its energy and inspiration from forces overseas. A new form of global economy, North American in flavour, concept and style carries all before it. The implications for the long-term future of the landscape and the people who live in it are difficult to predict. The out-of-town shopping malls, the great encampments of distribution warehouses crouching like so many armadillos across the rural shires, the growth of exurbia – that mixed-use land between city and country that owes nothing to either – are all manifestations of these new economic forces. Like the changes that have gone before, they have become the subject of intense debate and the source of worrying uncertainty. But what is clear is that a deeper understanding of the landscape, in all its manifestations, offers a means of managing change in a conscious and thoughtful manner.

This was the inspiration that led to this new regional landscape series. To understand the language of landscape, to be able to interpret the way in which people make places, offers insights and enjoyment beyond the ordinary. It enables us to experience that most neglected of human emotions, a sense of place. These books set out to reveal the values that underwrite our sense of place, by offering an insight into how the landscape of England came to be the way it is. If understanding is the key to valuing and valuing is the key to caring, then these books may help to ensure that we can understand and enjoy the best of what we have, and that when we make our own contribution to change it will not only reinforce that essential distinctiveness but will also improve the quality of life of those who live there.

Neil Cossons

1

Frameworks

This book has a very definite purpose. It does not set out to provide a general history of the English landscape, using examples drawn from East Anglia. It is solely, and unashamedly, about the landscape of East Anglia itself, and it seeks to answer a simple question: what makes its countryside and towns different from those of neighbouring regions of England? What combination of environmental circumstances, and social and economic processes – of natural and of human history – have given East Anglia its distinctive character? How has the region's particular history shaped the landscape we see today?

'East Anglia' is a problematic term, and the region discussed here – embracing the Fens and extending across most of Essex and much of Hertfordshire, as well as including parts of Cambridgeshire – is considerably larger than the old Anglo-Saxon kingdom of the East Angles, which comprised only the land of the North Folk (Norfolk) and the South Folk (Suffolk), together with parts of the fens (Fig. 1.1). Nevertheless, it does have a certain coherence in terms of social and economic history: a coherence born, above all, of shared environmental circumstances. Key ingredients are: muted topography; soils which, while varying greatly in character, are for the most part at least moderately fertile; a dry, continental climate; and a lack of good building stone, and of the kinds of minerals which, in post-medieval times, might have encouraged large-scale industrialisation. Today, these factors ensure that the region, its southern margins excepted, remains remarkably rural. It has a comparatively low population density, lacks large conurbations, has relatively few 'A' roads and only a single motorway – the M11. Agriculture remains a major industry. Yet the region was not always a backwater. The factors that have, in modern times, engendered rural tranquillity made this the most populous and most economically precocious area of Britain in the medieval centuries.

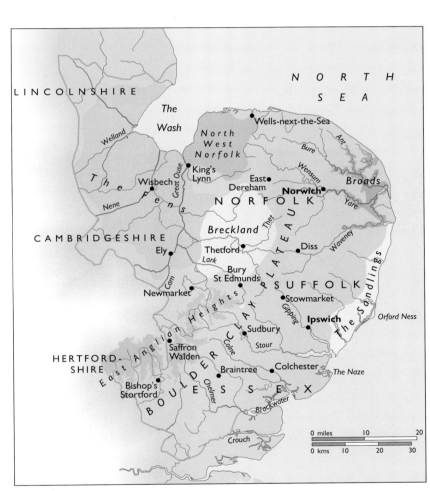

Fig. 1.1 East Anglia and the Fens: principal towns and major rivers.

FRONTISPIECE OPPOSITE:

Turf Fen Mill on the River Ant, Norfolk. *Large areas of East Anglia comprise low-lying wetlands, drained by man.*

Fig. 1.2 East Anglia and the Fens: solid geology (by permission of the British Geological Survey).

	Norwich Crag, Red Crag and Chillesford Clay	NEOGENE
	Coralline Crag	
	Barton, Bracklesham and Bagshot beds	PALAEOGENE
	London Clay	
	Oldhaven, Blackheath, Woolwich & Reading and Thanet beds	
	Chalk, including Red Chalk	CRETACEOUS
	Upper Greensand and Gault	
	Lower Greensand	
	Ampthill and Kimmeridge Clay	JURASSIC
	Corallian Limestone	
	Oxford Clay and Kellaways Beds	

However, the character of a region does not simply arise from soils, topography and climate. It is also a consequence of patterns of contact with other areas: of how easy, or how difficult, it has been for people, goods and ideas to move into and through it. And here East Anglia's position on the eastern edge of England, on the margins of the North Sea basin, is critical. It has always been a region peculiarly open to foreign influences, and to foreign settlement.

THE NATURAL INHERITANCE: GEOLOGY AND TOPOGRAPHY

We will begin with the real foundations of landscape – geology – and with the vital distinction between solid geology, the great masses of rock lying beneath us, and the thinner and more recent deposits that mask them, the superficial or drift geology. Chalk is the dominant underlying rock of the region (Fig. 1.2). Only in the west, beneath the Fen basin and along its margins, are older formations present – most notably Gault Clay, Greensand and Kimmeridge Clay.[1] The chalk was formed between 100 and 70 million years ago on the floor of a warm ocean. Its Upper and Middle Divisions contain the hard irregular rocks called flints, made from the silica of sponges and various microscopic creatures. The chalk underlies most of western and central Norfolk and Suffolk, north-west Essex and eastern Hertfordshire, but it dips towards the south-east and becomes buried ever deeper beneath more recent deposits. For the most part these lie 'unconformably' with the chalk – that is, their deposition did not follow immediately, but only after the rocks laid down in the intervening millennia had been eroded. They are the so-called Crag deposits, a varied collection of clays, gravels and shelly sands, dating from the late Pliocene and early Pleistocene periods – between *c.* 3.5 and 1.6 million years ago. These form the main solid geology of east Norfolk and much of eastern Suffolk. To the south and east the intervening deposits have survived erosion, and form the main solid geology for south Suffolk, central Essex and south-east Hertfordshire. These are various sands and clays of Tertiary date, the most important of which is the London Clay. The solid geology of the region is thus varied, but all the formations are, in geological terms, relatively young and relatively soft, and are thus eroded with relative ease by water and ice.

Only in two main areas is this solid geology exposed. From west Norfolk and north-west Suffolk into north-west Essex and north-east Hertfordshire, the chalk forms a low escarpment, a north-easterly continuation of the Chiltern Hills: its more dramatic section, in south Cambridgeshire and

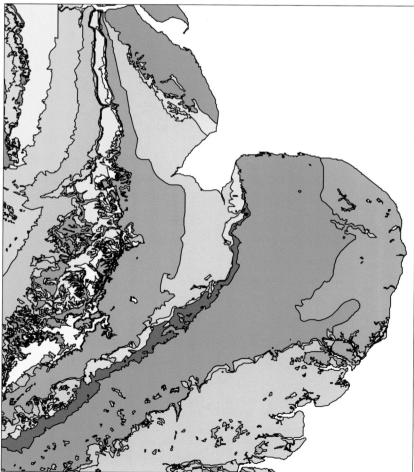

north-west Essex, is dignified by some geographers with the unlikely term 'East Anglian Heights'. In Norfolk, some of the rocks *underlying* the chalk, a complex mixture of clays, sandstones and sands, also outcrop, in a narrow band running along the Fen edge. And along the coastal margins of Suffolk, in the district called the Sandlings, Crag deposits are sporadically exposed. These exceptions aside, East Anglia is the quintessential region of glacial deposition (Fig. 1.3). Indeed, the successive Pleistocene sequences of glacials and interglacials were largely worked out here, and the different phases mainly carry names derived from East Anglian type sites.

The warm Cromerian Interglacial – which saw the formation of the famous Cromer Forest Beds, so rich in plant and animal remains, along the north Norfolk coast – began around 750,000 years ago.[2] Finds of Acheulian hand axes leave little doubt that the first humans were already exploiting the local environment at this time. However, around 480,000 years ago the most extensive of the glaciations, the Anglian, began.[3] Ice approaching

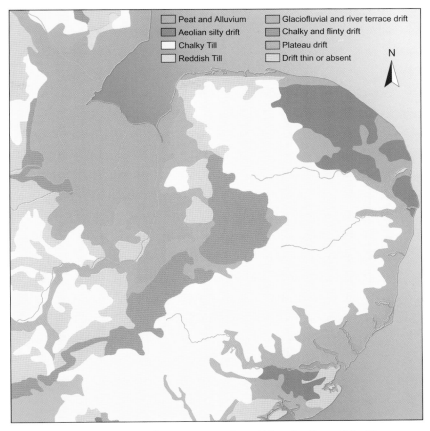

Fig. 1.3 East Anglia and the Fens: drift geology.

Legend:
- Peat and Alluvium
- Aeolian silty drift
- Chalky Till
- Reddish Till
- Glaciofluvial and river terrace drift
- Chalky and flinty drift
- Plateau drift
- Drift thin or absent

N

across the North Sea deposited the sandy brown formation known as the Norwich Brickearth across north-east Norfolk. A more important lobe of ice, coming from the north-west, deposited the so-called Lowestoft Till over a very wide area of south Norfolk, central Suffolk, north Essex and east Hertfordshire. This forms, in effect, a single, extensive plateau, dissected by later valleys and tilting gently, imperceptibly, towards the south and east. The most important component of this till is the so-called 'boulder clay', formed from a wide range of detritus – especially Kimmeridge Clay and chalk – dragged up by the ice as it moved across northern England and through the Midlands. This varies greatly in character, generally being more sandy in northern and central Norfolk, more like clay in south Norfolk and Suffolk and more calcareous (partly because it is thinner, and therefore more mixed with the underlying chalk) in Essex and Hertfordshire. Where the two lobes of ice met in north Norfolk, the underlying ground surface was heaved and contorted to form, in particular, the dramatic ridge that runs between the towns of Cromer and Holt.[4]

The Anglian glaciation ended around 400,000 years ago and was succeeded by the Hoxnian Interglacial, named after the famous site at Hoxne in north Suffolk. Here, in 1797, the antiquary John Frere noticed flint tools and animal bones in the bottom of a clay pit and, in a letter to the journal *Archaeologia*, boldly suggested that they indicated the existence of humans long, long before the earliest date allowed by conventional religious chronology: 'the situation in which these weapons were found may tempt us to refer them to a very remote period indeed, even before that of the modern world'.[5] Although the site gave its name to the interglacial, recent research suggests that the tools and other remains may in fact date from a shorter warm period – an interstadial – within the next glacial phase, the Woolstonian. This began around 200,000 years ago, and ended some 50,000 years later. This time the

ice probably only came as far as the north Norfolk coast, but it has nevertheless left behind one of the most impressive pieces of glacial morphology in the eastern counties. A subglacial stream, flowing near to the front of the ice sheet, deposited pebbles and shingle in a deep crevasse. When the ice eventually melted, this material was left as a steep-sided ridge, the famous Blakeney esker, some 15m high and 3.5km long (Fig. 1.4). A similar feature exists some 30km to the west, in Hunstanton Park. The various plateau heaths along the north Norfolk coast are probably outwash plains from this same glaciation – that is, they represent light sandy and gravelly material deposited by streams flowing out of the ice front. It is possible, however, that some or all of these features were in fact formed during the final glaciation, the Devensian, which began around 110,000 years ago, after a further warm interglacial called the Ipswichian.

Once again, ice did not advance far, if at all, beyond the fringes of the North Sea, but the Devensian nevertheless had a profound effect upon the landscape.[6] The high winds blowing close to the ice fronts deposited a thin layer of silty material called loess across much of the region. This makes for particularly fertile and tractable soils, most notably in north-east Norfolk and in a scatter of

Fig. 1.4 The Blakeney esker, looking east. *The long, sinuous ridge, rich in gravel, has been quarried in many places.*

places between Colchester and Ipswich.[7] It was once more widespread, having been much eroded through natural forces and agriculture in the remote past. The winds also deposited large quantities of sand, and while some of the sandy heaths so characteristic of East Anglia occupy outwash plains, others are formed from aeolian (wind-blown) material. The extensive sandy deposits in the area called Breckland, in south-west Norfolk and north-west Suffolk, were probably formed in this way.[8]

Permafrost conditions during the Devensian had other effects. On light land, especially in Breckland, so-called 'patterned ground' is often found, where stripes or polygons defined by diminutive chalky 'ridges' are separated by narrow 'valleys' filled with sandy material (Fig. 1.5). When the areas in question were tundra, the surface was covered with a metre or so of saturated, frost-shattered rock, mainly from the underlying chalk, overlying a permanently frozen subsoil. In the winter, as the surface froze, this material expanded, and in the summer it melted again and contracted. Under these pressures the watery 'slurry' was cast into ridges which were fossilised when warmer conditions returned at the end of the Ice Age, and the depressions between came to be filled with wind-blown sand. Patterned ground appears not only on heathland (where the different bands of soil carry sharply contrasting vegetation), but also in arable areas (where crops growing on the alternating bands show marked differences in colour).[9]

Pingoes are another East Anglian speciality. They are distinctive pits which often occur in substantial 'shoals', as many as a hundred together, each pit surrounded by a noticeable bank. Good examples can be seen on East Walton Common, Gayton Thorpe, Foulden Common, Thompson Common and Chippenham Fen (Fig. 1.6). Pingoes look man-made, but they are not: they result once again from permafrost conditions. Pockets of water, fed by springs or seepage from adjoining higher ground, were trapped beneath the frozen ground surface and formed mounds of ice. In the summer months the frozen soil melted and slipped sideways from the mounds, producing the 'banks' surrounding the pits which were left when the ice block finally melted.[10]

Such incidents of topography make interesting features in the landscape, but of far greater importance are the more general effects of the glaciations. They provided the raw materials for most of the region's varied soils, ranging (often in a very short distance) from heavy clays to acid, dry sands. And they smoothed and smothered the soft, older rocks, creating the muted landforms so characteristic of the region. It is, in particular, thanks to the Anglian ice that the northern and eastern extension of the Chiltern Hills in the region is such a diminutive escarpment. William Gilpin in the 1760s complained that even the 'Gog-Magog-hills … so little deserve the name of hills, that we should not have observed them, unless they had been pointed out to us'.[11] The ice created,

Fig. 1.5 'Patterned ground', *caused by periglacial conditions in the last Ice Age, at Hillington in Norfolk.*

Fig. 1.6 A shoal of 'pingoes', *the distinctive pits left by the melting of ice wedges, at Gayton Thorpe, Norfolk.*

especially in the north of the region, a landscape in which rivers had gentle gradients and in which there were extensive, low plateaux with slight concavities – a landscape from which water drained slowly and which contained many areas of permanent or seasonal waterlogging (*see* p.2).

However, we should not push the idea of East Anglia as a 'topographically uneventful' region too far. Its popular image as a flat and featureless land is largely based on the rather tedious experience of driving across the Fens, or of boating holidays on the Norfolk Broads, both areas which are indeed quite level. The claylands of north Suffolk and south Norfolk, and parts of north-east Norfolk, are also relatively flat. But elsewhere the topography is at least gently rolling, especially in the south and west (Fig. 1.7). Western Essex and eastern Hertfordshire contain much quite hilly countryside, where deep hollowed lanes, plunging steeply into the valleys and shaded by arches of hedgerow vegetation, seem like tunnels. Even where the terrain is less dramatic, it is usually varied enough to provide extensive panoramas. The famous 18th-century landscape designer Humphry Repton, a native of Suffolk but for long resident in north Norfolk, described how the latter area was endowed with numerous low hills which, though ascended 'with an almost imperceptible egravity, terminate with a prospect of twenty, some thirty miles distant'.[12]

All this said, it remains true that even the hilliest parts of East Anglia *are* topographically muted in comparison with most other regions. This has influenced its economic development in numerous ways (Fig. 1.8). Relative relief is a much neglected factor in history and landscape history, largely because its effects are often indirect and subtle. In particular, low relative relief ensures that, with some notable exceptions in the south of the region and in west Norfolk, most of the major rivers of the region follow lazy, sluggish courses. In consequence, the floors of the larger valleys – in the north of the region especially – are occupied by deposits of peat, or mixtures of peat and clay, rather than alluvium or gravel: and this, as we shall see, made it difficult to manage them as hay meadows, with major effects on the development of medieval farming and settlement. Equally important is the fact that slow-moving rivers with low gradients do not provide much water power. Water-mills were used on a large scale from medieval times for grinding grain and fulling cloth, but there was insufficient flow to provide the power required for factories when the production of textiles, in particular, became

Fig. 1.7 Dane End, Little Munden, Hertfordshire. *The landscape of eastern Hertfordshire and north-west Essex consists of rolling clayland countryside, with areas of heavier soils on the higher ground, often occupied by ancient woods, and with lighter clays or exposures of chalk in the numerous valleys.*

increasingly industrialised in the second half of the 18th century. This is one of the main reasons why East Anglia remained an agricultural land – why the Industrial Revolution largely passed it by – although a number of other environmental factors also contributed to this. There are no coalfields in East Anglia, for example, nor mineral ores to be mined and processed.

In this sense we might say that both geology and geomorphology dealt the inhabitants of East Anglia a poor hand. And in other ways, too, they provided challenges rather than opportunities. The region lacks good building stone, with the exception of small areas in west Norfolk, where hard chalk and carrstone are available, and parts of coastal Suffolk, where the hard coralline Crag has been sporadically quarried. Instead, East Anglia is characterised by an abundance of flint, which occurs both in the underlying chalk and in much of the glacial drift. The irregular nodules of this brittle, silaceous material cannot be easily shaped, and to make corners and openings for buildings it has to be combined with freestone, brought in from outside the region, or with brick. In this manner it was extensively used for just about every parish church in the region, and for some domestic buildings. Flint had other uses – in early prehistory it was the only material available in southern Britain for making edge tools, and the best quality flint in the region was mined and exported on some scale. Flint is a powerful, almost ubiquitous theme in the region's landscape – both in buildings and on the surface of the ground, for it occurs in almost every field, the wetlands and some of the sandy heaths excluded.

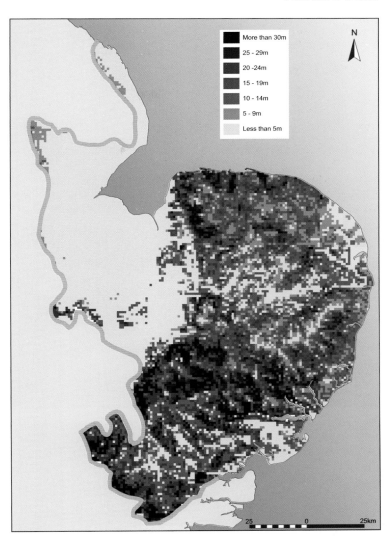

Fig. 1.8 East Anglia and the Fens: relative relief, mapped by kilometre square. *This is a map of how hilly the landscape is, rather than of how high different parts are. The figures refer to the difference in height above sea level between the lowest and the highest points in each square. The lighter the square, the flatter the land. The map shows that in spite of East Anglia's reputation as a flat land, much of the region is in fact pleasantly undulating.*

Most early domestic buildings in the region were not constructed of flint, however, due to the expense involved in obtaining freestone from a distance, to say nothing of the time it took to raise rubble walls course by slow course. Instead, most were built of oak frames, infilled with wattle and daub and roofed with thatch. The heavy clay soils grew prodigious quantities of oak, for even after the wild woodlands had been cleared managed woods were locally abundant, and hedges, thickly studded with timber, could be found in many districts. However, the clay could itself be used in buildings, when fired to form bricks and tiles. The latter were widely used in the south of the region even in medieval times; brick came into use at elite level from the 14th century, much earlier than elsewhere in England, although it was only more widely employed, for farm houses and farm buildings, from the later 17th century.

The soft and easily eroded nature of the region's geological formations – both 'solid' and 'drift' – have ensured that its coastline is peculiarly mutable. Popular mythology tends to exaggerate the rate of coastal erosion, but the soft mud cliffs of north-east Norfolk, or Suffolk, are constantly falling into the sea (Fig. 1.9). To the south of Southwold, the town of Dunwich has disappeared beneath the waves; to the north, the parish of Easton Bavents has been almost entirely lost and Covehithe has been greatly reduced in area. In north-east Norfolk, the parish church of

Eccles is now represented only by the stump of its round tower, exposed on the foreshore at high tide (Fig. 1.10). However, the fate of the eroded material is of far more importance in the making of the landscape than erosion *per se*. It is moved southwards down the east coast, and westwards along the north coast, by currents and by longshore drift, forming mobile 'spits' of sand and shingle which block harbours and estuaries (Fig. 1.11). One particularly notable example is the great 'Ness' at Orford, which diverts the outfall of the Alde for more than 12km to the south (Fig. 1.12).

Changes in the coastline have other, more complex causes. During the glaciations, much water was locked up in ice fields and glaciers, and global sea levels were low. As warmer conditions returned, sea levels rose. Yet the effects of these changes were complicated by isostatic recovery. The weight of ice, especially across the north of Britain, lowered the height of the land masses, effectively pushing the lighter surface formations into the heavier rocks found at depth. As melting occurred, they tended to rise once again relative to sea levels, at times bringing neighbouring areas with them, at others forcing them to sink in compensation. The interaction of all these processes over time meant that water levels sometimes rose and sometimes fell, relative to those of the land, and this complexity was further compounded by local changes in the configuration of the shoreline caused by the formation and destruction of shingle spits. In most areas of England, the effects of all this on the landscape were negligible. But in East Anglia, with its muted topography and extended coastline, they were immense, ensuring that large areas of land are today occupied by post-glacial deposits: by silts, peats and clays formed in valleys and coastal basins.[13]

TOP: ***Fig. 1.9 Soft mud cliffs near Sheringham*** *on the north Norfolk coast.*

ABOVE: ***Fig. 1.10 The village of Eccles*** *in north Norfolk has been largely destroyed by the sea: only the stump of the church tower remains on the beach.*

At the end of the last glaciation, around 10,000 years ago, the southern parts of East Anglia were connected to Europe by low lying ground. But sea levels rose steadily, and by around 6,000 BC the coast lay close to its present line. The drainage of fresh water along the lower reaches of the main river valleys was gradually impeded by the rise in sea levels and deposits of peat built up – that is, acid organic material formed by swampy vegetation whose decay has been retarded by waterlogged, anaerobic conditions. In the great basin now occupied by the Fens, these deposits include the bog oaks – trunks of ancient trees, preserved by the peat –

LEFT: **Fig. 1.11 The marshes to the south of Walberswick, Suffolk.** *The growth of a shingle spit in the late medieval period deflected the mouth of the Dunwich river to the north; extensive areas of peat fen developed in the lee of the spit, which were reclaimed and improved in the 17th, 18th and 19th centuries, before being largely abandoned to fen once more in the 20th. The area is now an important nature reserve. A 19th-century drainage mill can be seen in the centre of the picture, beside the old course of the Dunwich river.*

BELOW: **Fig. 1.12 Orford Ness,** *on the Suffolk coast, is the largest of the great mobile 'spits' of sand and gravel along the East Anglian coast. The 'Ness' is still growing, deflecting the mouth of the River Ore ever further to the south.*

that are still sporadically ploughed up by farmers. The continued rise in sea levels up to around 4,500 BC, however, covered many of these deposits with layers of silty clay. There then followed a period in which different areas of the coastline appear to have experienced diverse conditions. In some areas of coastal marsh the sea was excluded, allowing further deposits of peat to accumulate, as a consequence of large spits of sand and gravel forming over the mouths of estuaries. But during the Iron Age (after *c.* 700 BC) the sea asserted itself once more, and further deposits of silty clay were laid down. In some areas, most notably the northern Fens, the resultant deposits stood high enough to be colonised and farmed during the Roman period. Elsewhere, as in Broadland, estuarine conditions continued into the 4th or 5th centuries AD. The immediate post-Roman period saw a further phase of marine transgression, and further deposition of silt and clay in many coastal areas. But in later Saxon times relative sea levels fell once more, and large-scale colonisation and reclamation of coastal wetlands took place – reclamations which had to be defended from the 12th century onwards, as water levels began to rise again (Fig. 1.13).

Fig. 1.13 The Roman 'Saxon Shore' fort at Burgh Castle, *Suffolk, beside the River Waveney. When the fort was first constructed in the late 3rd century the Halvergate Marshes, on the opposite side of the river, formed an extensive estuary. This silted up after a great shingle spit built up across its mouth, and was subsequently converted to grazing marsh, although parts are now artificially flooded for the benefit of wading birds. The spit is now occupied by the town of Yarmouth.*

Traditionally, however, this name was only given to the peat areas occupying the southern and western parts of this extensive tract, which were mainly reclaimed from the 17th century. The silts and clays lying to the north and east, beside the Wash, were settled from early medieval times and contain ancient villages and great parish churches. In Norfolk this area was traditionally known as Marshland; in Lincolnshire, as the 'townlands', lying within the district of Holland.

SOILS AND THEIR USES

Farming was the main activity that moulded the region's landscape over several centuries, influenced above all by climate and soils. The character of the former is determined, like so much else, by East Anglia's proximity to Europe and its low relief. Lying far from the moderating effects of the Atlantic and sheltered from the prevailing wet westerly winds, average rainfall is low, but daily and monthly temperature ranges are high. The Fens, and the lower parts of central Essex, receive less rain than the relatively high ground of north-west Norfolk – less than 600mm per annum, as opposed to over 700mm. The most hostile climate is that of Breckland, the extensive tract of sand in south-west Norfolk and north-west Suffolk, compounding the problems posed to cultivators by acid and infertile soils. Here, frosts have been recorded in every month of the year.[14] But on the whole the climate is a good one for farmers, especially for those producing cereal crops. Low summer precipitation, in particular, means that crops ripen safely and can be harvested dry – circumstances less certain in the west of the country, and crucial in the long-term development of the region's society and economy.

The region's soils are highly complex, but we may begin by making a broad distinction between those formed in low lying, peaty and alluvial deposits; those formed in clays; and those developed over light, freely draining deposits (Fig. 1.14).[15] The main factors in the distribution of peat and alluvial soils will be apparent from the earlier discussion. Alluvial soils are most extensive in 'Marshland', but can be found in pockets all along the coast, behind spits and in the lower reaches of estuaries, most notably in the Halvergate Marshes to the west of Great Yarmouth (the town itself stands on a spit which has blocked this former estuary of the Bure, Waveney and Yare rivers). Silty, alluvial soils also occur in the flood plains of many river valleys, especially in the south of the region. These soils provide excellent grazing and make good hay meadows, but they can also produce good crops of grain if drained. Peat soils, in contrast, occupy the southern and western parts of the Fen basin (or rather used to do, before intensive farming eroded large areas, exposing the silts beneath), the upper reaches of the Broads valleys and the floors of most major river valleys in the north and east of the region. These areas are damper and in their natural state often produce only reeds, sedge and poor marsh hay. But, when effectively drained, they make good grazing and, in many cases, the most fertile arable land in all England.

Light, freely draining soils are characteristic of three main areas. Firstly, a broad band of very varied character – in places calcareous and moderately fertile, elsewhere poor and acidic – extends along the northern and western coasts of Norfolk, down through west Suffolk and south-eastern Cambridgeshire, and on into north Hertfordshire. It includes the district in north-west Norfolk described, since the 18th century, as the 'Goodsands'; the harsh, desert-like Breckland; and the muted chalk escarpment of the East Anglian Heights. A second area of light land, more uniformly sandy and acid in character, extends in a patchy band from Norwich northwards to the sea. A third, again sandy and infertile, extends all along the Suffolk coast – the area traditionally known as the 'Sandlings' – and on intermittently into north-east Essex.

Light soils presented early farmers with both opportunities and problems. On the one hand, they were generally easy to cultivate, and before the Roman period, and again in Anglo-Saxon times, they often formed core areas of settlement. But on the other hand they are comparatively infertile, or at least soon became so as clearance and cultivation removed any thin layers of more fertile, windblown loess which they possessed. The light soils formed in sands soon became highly acidic in character, as lime leached away through the porous subsoil. In many places soils called podzols developed, in which grey upper levels, leached of humus and iron, overlie hard, impervious layers called 'pan' where these have been redeposited. These were the characteristic soils of the heathlands which, prior to the late 18th century, covered vast tracts of East Anglia.

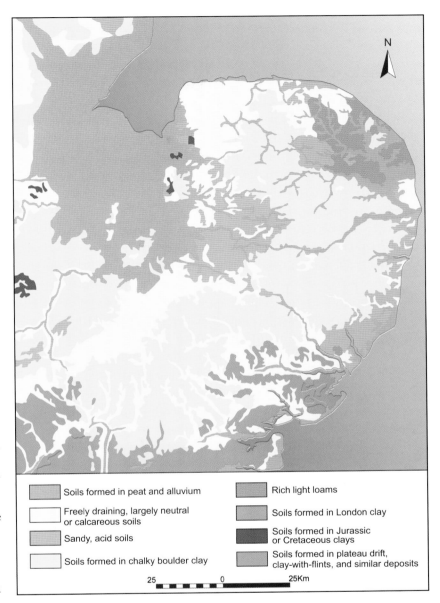

Soils formed in peat and alluvium

Freely draining, largely neutral or calcareous soils

Sandy, acid soils

Soils formed in chalky boulder clay

Rich light loams

Soils formed in London clay

Soils formed in Jurassic or Cretaceous clays

Soils formed in plateau drift, clay-with-flints, and similar deposits

25   0   25Km

Fig. 1.14 East Anglia and the Fens: principal soil types.

Soil acidity reduces cereal yields by enhancing the solubility (and hence the availability) of certain harmful elements, such as aluminium and manganese; some crops, such as turnips, are liable to fail completely on particularly sour land.[16] But it was not only, or even primarily, lime deficiency that made light soils relatively infertile, for even those formed in the chalk of the East Anglian Heights and north-west Norfolk only ever produced relatively modest yields. They were all, to use the parlance of farmers through the ages, 'hungry' soils, from which nutrients were constantly leached. The maintenance of their fragile fertility was the central element in the various farming systems that developed in these districts over the centuries.

Sheep were the most important form of livestock kept on the light lands, although some cattle were always required to supply milk and to pull ploughs. Providing water for these – especially the cattle – as well as for human consumption was a major concern. Settlements were generally located close to springs or in major valleys, but in some places water could also be obtained from ponds called 'meres' occupying deep pits created where the underlying chalk has been dissolved by percolating rain water. Those in Breckland are the largest and best known: their depth fluctuates considerably, with a chronology largely independent of the immediate weather conditions. Instead, the water level rises and falls with that of the underlying chalk aquifer (Fig. 1.15).[17]

Fig. 1.15 Three of the strange fluctuating 'meres' in Breckland: Langmere (right), Fenmere (centre) and Ringmere.

The central parts of East Anglia comprise a low boulder-clay plateau characterised by soils which, while very varied, are all at least moderately fertile, although difficult to cultivate with primitive technology. All, to varying degrees, are stiff and hard to work, and suffer from seasonal waterlogging. This is 'cold' land, which dries out and warms up only slowly in the spring, delaying both cultivation and germination. The more level areas could only be successfully cultivated when heavy ploughs, equipped with mouldboard and coulter, came into use during the later Iron Age, allowing a furrow to be cut which exposed the soil to the weathering effects of the winter frosts. Drainage was assisted by field ditches and, in post-medieval times, by the widespread adoption of under-drains – that is, drains of brushwood or tile, dug beneath the surface of the field. Before this latter development many of the dampest areas could only be used as woodland or grazing, and in some periods extensive areas of the claylands as a whole were under pasture. But the plateau was everywhere cut by valleys, especially numerous towards the south and west, on the sides of which the land was more freely draining and in the deepest of which lighter soils, formed in underlying rocks, were found. The earliest and the largest settlements, and the most extensive areas of arable, were always located here. But when population rose and cultivation expanded onto the drift-covered plateau, settlement could disperse freely, unhindered by restrictions on water supply. Water could be obtained everywhere, from the perched water table, simply by sinking a shallow well. My own house in south Norfolk is supplied with excellent drinking water solely from a well no more than *c*. 7m. It has never yet run dry.

Soils formed in peat and alluvium, chalk and sand, and boulder clay account for most of the land area of East Anglia. But not all. In particular, in north-east Norfolk, in the area of Suffolk between Yarmouth and Lowestoft, and in small patches around Felixstowe, soils formed in aeolian drift or loess are found, which are well drained, easy to work and phenomenally fertile. These, as we shall see, carried abnormally dense populations in early medieval times – perhaps the densest in all England.

Soils form a vital and central part of our story. However we may choose to map landscapes – whether in terms of settlement forms, field systems or the distribution of semi-natural habitats such as woods or heaths – we find, again and again, that the distributions mirror the maps of the soil scientist with uncanny accuracy. Landscapes are not simply reducible to, or equivalent to, soil regions. But the two are, perhaps not surprisingly, very closely related.

CONTACT AND COMMUNICATION

However, the environment has never been the only determinant of farming patterns or landscape character. Networks of contact and communication were also important: for ways of life, economic activities and styles of architecture or of material culture do not arise simply and directly from geology, soils or climate. Ideas, languages, raw materials and objects can also travel from area to area, either through the physical migration of individuals or social groups, or via trade and other forms of exchange. Patterns of contact also encourage, or discourage, particular forms of farming or industry. To understand the character of East Anglia we thus need to look briefly at how easily (or otherwise) it could be reached from elsewhere, and how patterns of contact or communication within it might be channelled or restricted.

An earlier generation of archaeologists and historians believed that, before the medieval period, the heavier clays had been uniformly occupied by dense forest and the Fenlands by impenetrable swamps. Access to central and northern East Anglia was therefore mainly via the chalk escarpment of the East Anglian Heights, along which a long-distance trackway from Wessex, the Icknield Way, made its way. A series of linear earthworks was erected across its course at various times in the late prehistoric and early post-Roman periods, controlling movement and access (Fig. 1.16). More recent work has questioned much of this. In particular, we now know that the clays were largely cleared of woodland by the Iron Age,

Fig. 1.16 Devil's Dyke, *a Dark Age linear earthwork, runs in a straight line across the chalk escarpment near Stechworth in south-east Cambridgeshire. It may have been constructed to control movement along a trackway that ran along the chalk escarpment, it may have been a territorial boundary. Looking north-east, with the Fens in the distance.*

thus reducing the need for travellers to keep to the band of chalk. Some scholars have gone so far as to suggest that the Icknield Way is itself a medieval myth.[18] But equally important is the fact that, far from constituting a barrier to movement, cutting Norfolk and Suffolk off from the Midlands, the Fens and their network of waterways provided an important nexus of communication.

Indeed, when we think of early communication we need to think first and foremost of the sea and inland waterways. Up until the 19th century these provided the cheapest and fastest method of moving heavy cargoes. East Anglia's long coast line was, before the 18th century, punctuated by numerous minor and several major ports (Fig. 1.17). These were served by coasters, which ran south to London and north to Northumberland and beyond – the latter, from as early as the 13th century, bringing cargoes of coal. From earliest times, however, the sea also allowed easy contact with Europe and this has, over many centuries, been one of the most

*Fig. 1.17 **The harbour of Wells**, on the north Norfolk coast – one of many small ports that once punctuated the East Anglian coast. The quay is approached down a long channel through the saltmarshes. The marshes on the left have been embanked and drained.*

Fig. 1.18 East Anglia in its European context – *viewed from the perspective of those approaching from across the North Sea.*

BELOW: **Fig. 1.19 East Anglia and the Fens: coastal shoals and rivers that are navigable.**

important influences on the development of the region. We are accustomed to seeing seas as barriers, but before the 18th century it was easier to reach Holland by sea with a heavy cargo than Liverpool by land.[19] It is a useful exercise to turn a map of the North Sea upside down, and to consider how the region and its coast might have looked to Anglo-Saxon settlers, Viking raiders or Flemish traders or refugees (Fig. 1.18).

However, the coast was not everywhere equally inviting or accessible, and this too was a factor – of immense importance – in the long-term development of East Anglia's character. Norfolk and Suffolk were, for the most part, easily approached, and estuaries and offshore spits offered safe and welcoming habourage for ships (Figs 1.19 and 1.20). But south of Harwich extensive shoals lying parallel with the shore, and wide mudflats, made approach more hazardous for ships, especially primitive ones with poor tacking capability, coming from the north-east, against the prevailing wind. Safe access was largely restricted to the three main estuaries, the Colne, the Blackwater and the Crouch, and there were no early ports along the coast itself. While we should not exaggerate the extent of this difference, it remains the case that Essex has a much weaker maritime tradition than its northerly neighbours.[20] Of course, the region's long coastline did not only provide opportunities for trade and communication, both with other parts of

England and with the continental mainland. It was in itself a rich resource, and salt-making and fishing were important industries from prehistoric times.

Rivers allowed cargoes brought along the coast, or across the sea, to be taken inland, as well as providing for shorter movements of goods and materials within the region. Again, muted topography played an important role, ensuring that many rivers are navigable for some way inland, although the extent of penetration might change over time as the size of ships increased, and as relative land/sea levels, and patterns of silting and deposition, took their toll. The major Roman administrative centres Camulodunum (Colchester) and Venta Icenorum (Caistor-by-Norwich) both probably stood at what were then the upper limits of navigation, of the Colne and the Tas rivers respectively. The county towns established in late Saxon times – Cambridge, Norwich, Ipswich, Hertford and Colchester – were similarly located at or close to contemporary limits of navigation, and the same is true of many other important early medieval urban centres, such as Beccles and Thetford. Such locations were both strategically and economically important: producers in the surrounding countryside would naturally bring their goods to these inland ports, and elites in all periods strove to control and exploit them; major disputes could occur when the upper limits of navigation were artificially extended or contracted. In 1191 the bridge taking Ermine Street over the River Lea at Ware in east Hertfordshire was 'broken down by the men of Hertford'; around 1210 the bailiff of Hertford erected blocks and chains to obstruct entry to it; while in 1274 the bailiffs of Ware were accused of neglecting the weirs in the town, to prevent boats passing upriver to Hertford.[21]

The Lea was a critical river, giving access to the great markets of London, and in medieval and post-medieval times much of the produce of the south of the region passed along it, via Hertford, Ware, Stanstead and other ports. However,

Fig. 1.20 Harwich Haven, where the rivers Deben (right) and Orwell (left) meet the sea, has always provided an inviting entry to the southern parts of East Anglia. Its past strategic importance is signalled by the presence of Landguard fort, an important post-medieval military installation (foreground); its modern economic significance is clear from the boats and containers of Felixstowe Terminal.

other parts of the region were also well served by navigable rivers. East Norfolk and north-east Suffolk benefited from the Broadland complex – the interconnected waterways of the Yare, Bure, Waveney, Chet, Ant and Thurne – which linked Norwich with the sea at Great Yarmouth. Above all, the Fenland rivers connected Cambridge, Thetford, Wisbech and a host of other minor ports with each other, the Midlands and, via King's Lynn and the sea, with London and distant foreign markets. At a very early date artificial extensions to the Fen waterways were made, most notably the Cambridgeshire 'Lodes' – although it is possible that these were originally designed (perhaps in late Saxon times) to improve drainage, and the quality of the grazing, along the Fen edge.[22] The Fen rivers certainly allowed good quality building limestone, from the quarries at Barnack and elsewhere in Northamptonshire, to be brought into East Anglia with relative ease. River complexes like this could have a radical impact on regional economies, more than compensating for local disadvantages in terms of soils and other resources. Breckland, as already noted, is an area of appalling soils, but the cheap transport afforded by the Fenland rivers ensured that medieval farmers here made a good living by exporting malting barley.[23]

Of course, we should not underestimate the importance of land transport, especially for local trade. Some commodities, especially livestock, were always easier to move by land. Roman military roads such as Ermine Street or the Pye Road cut relentlessly across the natural topography, creating patterns of circulation and movement quite independent of it. Nevertheless, it was only really in the 18th and 19th centuries, with the proliferation of improved turnpike roads and subsequent advent of the railways, that patterns of movement less directly related to the configuration of drainage basins and other topographic imperatives were created. It was also at this point that regional distinctiveness, in building materials especially, really began to break down.

The configuration of rivers and their associated drainage basins is important in our enquiry for other reasons. From the Iron Age through to Saxon times the main settlements, and the principal arable areas, tended to be located within the larger valleys, where good supplies of running water were available, plus well-watered pastures for livestock. Moreover, in the kind of countryside with which we are here concerned, extensively covered by various forms of glacial deposits, the most fertile and easily worked soils tended to be found there. Well-watered areas on spring lines at the foot of escarpments of light soil were also favoured zones. The high interfluves between the principal valleys, in contrast, were usually occupied by the heaviest clays and the poorest sands, and they often lacked dependable supplies of water. When population densities were low, they tended to be occupied by woods and pastures. In the north of the region, in particular, almost all the major areas of woodland recorded in Domesday Book were concentrated on the principal watersheds, most notably that running in an arc through the centre of Norfolk, between rivers draining eastwards and those draining to the north and west.[24]

This essential contrast between valleys and interfluves underlies much of the early history of the region. When population levels were low, the forested uplands were exploited by scattered farms, some perhaps only seasonally occupied. But even when the population rose and they were colonised, they still often remained dependent territory, their inhabitants looking to the neighbouring valleys for their principal social and economic contacts. Watersheds represented cut-off zones between communities, and social territories tended to correspond with drainage basins.[25] Even in the early modern period major towns – where workshops produced distinctive local artefacts and buildings, and where people congregated at market, to meet, make deals and marry – were usually in major valleys, with their hinterlands approximating, in part or whole, to a drainage basin. High watersheds were not, of course, the only feature of the natural topography to channel patterns of contact. Wide, navigable rivers might provide arteries for long-distance trade, but at a more local level they prevented contact, especially in their lower reaches.

The patterns of administration imposed upon the landscape in later Saxon times, which in part at least had much earlier origins, reflect this. Hundred boundaries tend to follow watersheds where these bound the upper parts of drainage basins. Where, in their lower reaches, rivers widen, boundaries leave the watersheds and, crossing lower ground, follow the waterways instead. Topographic patterns channelled movement, trade and contact in almost every period before the 18th century. They thus laid another level of complexity on the rich confusion presented by patterns of soil and other environmental factors.

A LAND OF TWO PARTS

One of the hardest tasks of the landscape historian is to identify which aspects of a region's personality derive from environmental factors – from

Fig. 1.21 The River Waveney near Earsham, with the town of Bungay in the background. Although it forms the county boundary between Norfolk and Suffolk, the river never constituted a significant barrier to movement or formed a major cultural frontier.

soils, climate and topography – and which from cultural factors – from patterns of trade and contact with other regions. For the most part, as I shall argue, the *major* aspects of landscape, such as patterns of settlement or systems of fields, arise from the former. They are largely the consequence of farming systems; and farming, more than any other human activity, must be carried out in close sympathy with the environment. New settlers moving into an area have to adapt their farming strategies to the subtleties of local circumstances, if they are to survive and flourish. The *details* of a landscape, in contrast – aspects of architectural style, for example – are more likely to reflect cultural patterns. But in many cases it is, in truth, very difficult to disentangle 'cultural' and 'environmental' influences, not least because in the final analysis patterns of contact are themselves moulded by the environment, by the disposition of land forms, coastlines, river valleys and the like, so that the two can overlap and interrelate in bewildering ways.

In East Anglia this problem is particularly acute for overriding any local variations is a broad, over-arching division that recurs time and again throughout history. If we ignore for a moment the western Fenlands, the real fault-line running through the region follows a line drawn roughly along the Gipping and Lark rivers, which together form a continuous valley running from north-west to south-east through the middle of Suffolk; or, at times, along the watershed which lies a little to the north of this. The county boundaries, between Norfolk and Suffolk and between Suffolk and Essex, have absolutely no significance in cultural or landscape terms. Even their antiquity as political and administrative divisions is uncertain. At the time of Domesday the Stour and the Waveney still formed rather indistinct boundaries (Fig. 1.21). The Hundred of Diss lay in Norfolk, as we would expect. But Diss itself lay in Suffolk, and several other places were on the 'wrong' side of that river. Bures St Mary lies on the Suffolk side of the Stour, but Mount Bures lies on the Essex side, as does Bures Hamlet – although it is part of the parish of Bures St Mary! There are other confusions and anomalies suggesting that the river did not always form a boundary. Either way, in cultural terms the really significant frontier ran, in almost all periods, diagonally across the middle of Suffolk, from the area around Bury St Edmunds to the environs of Ipswich, and in some senses this county hardly exists. In a great many ways south-west Suffolk is really like Essex, while north-east Suffolk differs little, in most respects, from Norfolk.

In later prehistory, and again in the post-Roman period, social and cultural divisions seem to follow this general line. In the medieval period, too, most of the basic structures of the landscape seemed to respect it. Thus to the north-east the settlement pattern, before the great enclosures of the 18th and 19th centuries, was dominated by loose clusters of farmsteads around large greens and commons, and many parish churches stood – and often still stand – curiously alone in the midst of the wide fields. In the south and west, in contrast, villages of more 'normal' form, clustered around parish churches, were and remain more common features, and dispersed settlements mainly take the form of isolated farms set in their own fields, or tight clusters of dwellings around diminutive greens (or 'tyes', as they are often called, but *only* to the south-west of this line) (Fig. 1.22). Many aspects of architecture also follow this pattern. In the north and east a high proportion of parish churches display that most quintessential East Anglian feature, a round tower. To the south and west these are rare, although not unknown. In the north and east pantiles are the dominant roofing material for vernacular houses; these distinctive ridged tiles were introduced from the Low Countries in the late 17th century. Their distribution terminates fairly abruptly at the Lark/Gipping 'corridor'. There are, as we shall see, many other examples that reiterate this same divide. They do not always follow *precisely* the same line, but they nevertheless combine to create a broad band of discontinuity. It is surprising that this 'border' has not previously received much attention from archaeologists and historians.

To some extent the explanation for this recurrent pattern must be sought in the natural environment. In northern and eastern Suffolk, and in Norfolk, where much of the terrain is particularly muted and extensive, level tablelands occur. To the south and west of the Lark and Gipping rivers, in contrast, there is a greater range of relative relief. The countryside is more dissected by river valleys and the overall 'feel' of the countryside is much more rolling. The rivers here are faster moving, their valley floors characterised by silt and alluvium. To the north and

Fig. 1.22 The village green in Finchingfield in Essex. *Nucleated villages like this, clustering around a parish church, are a more characteristic feature of the south of the region than of the north.*

east of the Gipping, in contrast, they are generally more sluggish, the peat deposits more extensive – all factors which seem to have had an important, if subtle, influence, as we shall see, on the evolution of farming.

But the north-east/south-west division also has a cultural component, which is related to patterns of communication and contact both within the region and between the region and the wider world. In terms of overland communications the north of the region is simply more spatially isolated: you do not pass through north-east Suffolk or Norfolk en route to anywhere else. This area has always looked more to the North Sea, not only towards the Low Countries, but also towards the wilder lands of north Germany and Scandinavia. Its coast was, as we have seen, easily approached, and its interior easily accessed, from this direction. The south, in contrast – south of the Orwell estuary, the outfall of the Gipping – was rather less open to such influences. The configuration of its coast discouraged direct access to the Scandinavian world, and foreign influences and contacts were more likely to come from the south, and often overland, via the great gateway of the Thames. This part of the region has always looked to London, to south-east England, to the Low Countries and, to a lesser extent, to northern France. Both natural topography and patterns of communication thus combine to produce this great division between the south-west and the north-east of the region. But which particular aspects of this division were the consequence of environmentally determined 'cultural' factors and how far – once established – this division was cultural and self-perpetuating, with a momentum of its own, are matters to which we shall return in this book.

And even today East Anglia remains, in many ways, a land of two parts, although the division between them no longer quite follows the Lark–Gipping corridor. In the south of the region London's influence is strong, and growing. Villages are more affectedly 'picturesque' in appearance, roads busier, the countryside more crowded. Life for many is geared around the daily commute to London. The north, in spite of the presence of Norwich and King's Lynn and the growing influence of Cambridge, remains more remote, more determinedly rural.

We have set the stage upon which a complex drama will be played out. Soils and climate, relief and topography, patterns of contact and movement, will together combine and interact to mould the history of a region. But the landscape itself is an actor, not a passive backdrop, in this drama. For as we shall see, the patterns and structures imposed upon the land by successive societies have their own trajectories, their own internal logic, unfolding over many centuries.

NOTES

1   Chatwin 1961; Funnell 1993a; Wymer 1999.
2   Wymer 1999; Spencer 1970; Wymer 1984; Boulton et al. 1984, 103–22.
3   Jones & Keen 1993, 73–7.
4   Funnell 1993b.
5   Reprinted 1800 in *Archaeologia*, **13**, 204–5.
6   Jones & Keen 1993, 148–52, 178–85.
7   Catt 1978; Catt 1977.
8   Jones & Keen 1993, 185.
9   Evans 1972; Rackham 1986b, 284.
10 Ibid, 350–1.
11 Gilpin 1809, 10.
12 Armstrong 1781, **3**, 3.
13 Funnell 1993b; Jones & Keen 1993, 260–1.
14 Hodge et al. 1984, 27–34.
15 Ibid.
16 Robinson 1949, 232.
17 Rackham 1986b, 353–4.
18 Harrison 2004.
19 Carver 1989.
20 Imray et al. 2002, C28, Y6, C1.
21 Kiln & Partridge 1995.
22 Oosthuizen 2000.
23 Bailey 1989.
24 Williamson 1993, 113–14.
25 Everitt 1977; Phythian Adams 1987, 1993.

2

Peopling the Land

EARLY PREHISTORIC SETTLEMENT AND SOCIETY

Even a cursory perusal of the archaeological record reveals that East Anglia lacked a coherent, homogeneous identity in early prehistory. It did not constitute a single, distinct and bounded 'culture' or society. The styles of monuments and artefacts found here during the Neolithic and early Bronze Ages were thus shared, for the most part, with other areas in eastern England or beyond, as far as the Low Countries, while from the later Bronze Age they had distributions which cut across, or subdivided, the region.[1] Yet at the same time the region clearly displayed features that distinguished it from other parts of England.

Much of early British prehistory has been written from a 'Wessex perspective', based on the sites found in the chalklands of southern England. In the course of the Neolithic period, following the establishment of the first farming communities in the 4th millennium BC, Wessex saw the development of increasingly impressive ceremonial monuments and extensive ritual landscapes. Causewayed enclosures

Fig. 2.1 Crop marks of the Neolithic cursus at Fornham, near Bury St Edmunds in Suffolk.

and long barrows were thus gradually supplanted by henges and the long enclosures called cursuses. Concentrations of such monuments, such as those at Avebury or Stonehenge, evidently represent centres of power that continued into the early Bronze Age. The apogee of this 'henge-based society' was, however, followed in the middle Bronze Age by a decline in the construction of large monuments, and for the first time more mundane aspects of life, farms and fields begin to appear strongly in the archaeological record.

East Anglia deviates markedly from this familiar pattern. There is nothing like Silbury Hill or Stonehenge here, nor has there ever been. Notable examples of early ceremonial monuments are, of course, known from the region, such as the Arminghall henge to the south of Norwich or the Fornham cursus, which survives as a crop mark near Bury St Edmunds (Fig. 2.1). A number of Bronze Age barrow cemeteries survive, such as that on Therfield Heath near Royston (Fig. 2.2), and many thousands

ABOVE: *Fig. 2.2 The barrow cemetery on Therfield Heath* near Royston, Hertfordshire, includes a Neolithic long barrow and several Bronze Age round barrows.

RIGHT: *Fig. 2.3 Recent aerial surveys* have revealed a wealth of prehistoric sites in the form of crop marks in the Stour valley, on the border between Essex and Suffolk.

more once existed and have been rediscovered through aerial photography. So, too, have large numbers of long mortuary enclosures, cursuses, long barrows and small, henge-like monuments. The recent National Mapping Programme carried out by English Heritage has revealed particularly important concentrations in the Stour valley, its light soils at this time clearly a core area of settlement rather than, as later, a boundary zone (Fig. 2.3). Nevertheless, nowhere in East Anglia were there ever monuments, or concentrations of monuments, to rival those found in Wessex: their absence is not entirely the consequence of later land use, or of the fact that East Anglia was, in later centuries, more intensively farmed than the Wessex chalklands. More intriguingly, while it lacks a plethora of large monuments, East Anglia can boast some extremely early examples of the more everyday, 'mundane' archaeology of farming and settlement. Late Neolithic fields are now known from Fengate near Peterborough and 'Beaker-period' examples from Sutton Hoo and elsewhere. Indeed, the region has more known settlements of the 'Beaker period' (that is, the period of the late Neolithic/Bronze Age transition) than any other in England, many discovered during the excavation of the round barrows that had been erected above them.

Although much of East Anglia is occupied by the kind of heavy clay soil inimicable to early farmers, there are also extensive tracts of light, well-drained loams. On these, to judge from the evidence of field walking and aerial photography, settlement was widespread by the end of the Bronze Age. One particularly

TOP: **Fig. 2.4 The Neolithic flint mines at Grimes Graves, Norfolk.**

ABOVE: **Fig. 2.5 Grimes Graves:** *a recent geophysical survey by English Heritage clearly reveals the way in which Neolithic miners dug down to, and then followed, the layers of good-quality black flint.*

important resource was extracted and
exchanged across a wide area of lowland
England – flint, from mines in
Breckland, most notably those at
Grimes Graves near Brandon (Figs 2.4
and 2.5). By the middle Bronze Age the
region, and especially the margins of the
Fens, was very wealthy, to judge from
finds of rich metalwork from major
rivers, apparently representing ritual
deposits. Prehistoric East Anglia should
not, therefore, simply be regarded as a
sparsely settled, pale imitation of Wessex
– an insignificant backwater. Its
inhabitants evidently adopted ways of
living which for the most part eschewed
the grand and the monumental.

What is particularly intriguing is that
this pattern continues into the Iron Age,
the period after *c.* 700 BC when iron
came into widespread use for edge tools.
The region has few examples of
hillforts, the large embanked enclosures
common in southern and western
England (Fig. 2.6). Those that exist do
not, as in Wessex, appear to have been
defended settlements forming the
central places for tribal territories.
Indeed, many excavated examples –
including those at Tasburgh, Warham or
Danbury – have revealed evidence for
only sporadic occupation or for no
occupation at all.[2] They were either
temporary refuges or, perhaps,
ceremonial sites. The fact that several,
such as Warham, occupy poorly
defensible locations, or have regular
circular plans, tends to support this
latter interpretation (Fig. 2.7). Others,
such as Burgh or Clare in Suffolk, are
rectangular in shape. Like the rather
smaller (and probably later) rectangular

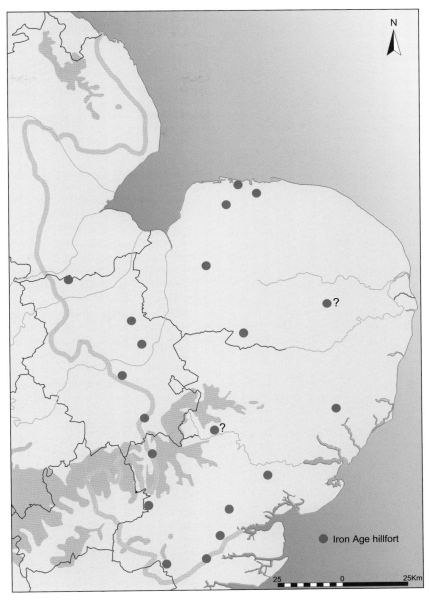

Fig. 2.6 The distribution of Iron Age hillforts in East Anglia.

OPPOSITE PAGE:

Fig. 2.7 The Iron Age 'hillfort' at Warham in north Norfolk. The earthwork in fact occupies a low-lying position beside the River Stiffkey. This, and its precise circular plan, suggests that it may in part have served a ceremonial function.

enclosures surviving only as crop marks at Barham and Foxhall in Suffolk and
in various places across north-west Norfolk, they were perhaps related to
contemporary shrines on the continent of broadly similar size and shape.

But not only are hillforts rare. Small settlements enclosed by banks, ditches or
walls are the commonest form of site across most of Iron Age Britain, but are
unusual in East Anglia (except in the Fens and on the Fen edge).[3] Open,
undefended sites were instead the norm, sometimes loosely concentrated in
particular areas so as to create wide but discontinuous spreads of pottery and other
household debris: open villages like the one excavated at Little Waltham in Essex;
or sprawling, amorphous clusters of undefended farmsteads, as at Sleaford in
Lincolnshire. Why East Anglian settlement should have taken this form is unclear.
It may be that the extensive areas of intractable clay soil, and the relative narrowness
of the bands of lighter, more easily cultivated land, ensured that most communities
retained access to reserves of under-exploited terrain, reducing the fierce

competition for resources which must have affected Wessex, where the light chalk soils were cleared and filled with people at an early date. It is also noteworthy, however, that Iron Age settlements in other regions bordering the North Sea, such as southern Scandinavia, exhibit similar patterns and tendencies.[4] More importantly, this lack of large defended sites is, as we have seen, part of a much longer tradition of eschewing monumental construction. There are hints here of a pattern (which we shall pick up more clearly from early medieval times) of a region in which society was less hierarchical, less stratified and less rigidly organised than in districts further to the west.

THE LATE-PREHISTORIC AND ROMAN PERIODS

From the late Bronze Age there is evidence, in the distribution of different types and styles of artefact, for the emergence of a number of social, cultural and to some extent political divisions within East Anglia. The most important seems to have run through the centre of the region, roughly along the line of the Lark/Gipping valley. It emerges most clearly towards the end of the Iron Age. In this period, largely as a consequence of contacts with the Roman world, larger and more coherent political entities developed across southern Britain.[5] This process went furthest, and fastest, in the south-east of England, and is particularly reflected in the presence of artefacts and sites, which together make up what archaeologists used to describe as the 'Belgic culture': wealthy burials, furnished with grave goods including amphorae from the Mediterranean world and other exotic imports; sophisticated, wheel-turned pottery; the first coinage to be used in Britain; and large, sprawling settlements, often featuring lengths of substantial bank and ditch, which are conventionally termed *oppida* by archaeologists.[6]

In the south of the region the tribal kingdom of the Trinovantes appears to have developed by the middle of the 1st century BC. Its leaders had grown rich through conquest, and through control of exchange with the Roman world. Their principal *oppidum* was at Camulodunum, Colchester, a vast although discontinuous area of settlement, industrial and ceremonial sites enclosed by lengths of bank and ditch (traces of which still survive in the Lexden Road area, especially in Lexden Park, and to the east of Straight Road). One of their leaders, perhaps an individual named Addedomarus, was buried under a great barrow at Lexden, more than 20m in diameter. Other *oppida* existed at Braughing and Baldock, but these were probably associated with another tribal group, the Catauvellauni. They were based outside the region in west Hertfordshire and the Chilterns, but in the period between Caesar's abortive invasion of Britain in 54 BC and the Claudian conquest of AD 43 the Catauvellauni seem to have conquered and absorbed the Trinovantes.

The distribution of coins, wheel-thrown pottery and particular types of metalwork make it clear that Trinovantian/Catauvellaunian power – and the exchange networks with the Classical world with which it was intimately associated – did not extend far to the north and east of the Lark and Gipping (Fig. 2.8).[7] Here, wheel-thrown pottery did not really become current until after the Claudian conquest and true *oppida* probably never developed, although something rather like them may have existed at Saham Tony, Caistor-by-Norwich and elsewhere.[8] Conversely, a whole range of metalwork types – including bridle rings, terret rings and other chariot and horse-riding equipment – is largely restricted to this district, which was, by the time of the Roman Conquest, occupied by a group called the Iceni. These people were evidently less closely linked to the Roman world than their neighbours to the south.

As so often in its history East Anglia was thus divided: the south of the region was tied to exchange networks linking it with south-eastern England and France, to which the north remained peripheral. Yet this did not mean that the elites of northern East Anglia were necessarily impoverished. Far from it, to judge from the great golden torcs found near Snettisham in west Norfolk. Nor was the area's isolation absolute. Coins that began to appear in this region from around 10 BC were copies of Catauvellaunian and Trinovantian types. Their distribution extends westwards into the Fens, now evidently a marginal zone rather than a core one, as it seems to have been in the Bronze Age. However, the restricted distribution of different types of coin, which to some extent mirrors that of different styles of contemporary metalwork, suggests that the Iceni always remained a rather looser political entity than the Trinovantes.[9] They were perhaps always a confederation, dominated by clans or lineages based on Breckland, presumably associated with the great ceremonial centre excavated at Gallows Hill near Thetford, a rectangular, complex site with a strange, concentric arrangement of posts, perhaps intended to imitate a sacred grove.[10] Even after the Conquest the Iceni continued, at least for a while, to be politically marginal. Their dissent from the new order was expressed in the Boudiccan revolt of AD 61, with a savagery vented in equal measure on Trinovantian neighbours as on Roman newcomers.[11]

The late-prehistoric period saw a significant expansion of settlement. Farms and fields were now no longer restricted to light, well-drained loams. Already, by the end of the Bronze Age, settlements had begun to appear on the better-drained clay soils. Field walking surveys suggest that by the eve of the Roman Conquest farms and hamlets were widely scattered across clay plateaux. How far such places were all involved in arable farming, how far they represent ranches for the management of herds and the exploitation of woodlands, remains uncertain. Some, such as that excavated at Silfield near Wymondham in Norfolk, may only have been seasonally occupied.[12] Nevertheless, extensive clearance and settlement had evidently taken place even on these difficult soils, as the analysis of pollen cores from places like Diss Mere in Norfolk makes clear.[13] Large tracts of woodland certainly existed at the start of the Roman period, especially on the high watersheds, but East Anglia was already a well settled landscape, far beyond the pioneer stage.

The Romano-British landscape in most parts of the region was probably not very different from that of the Iron Age, but we can see it more clearly. Roman settlements are easier to identify through field walking surveys because they produce large quantities of highly visible, and highly durable, pottery. Almost everywhere,

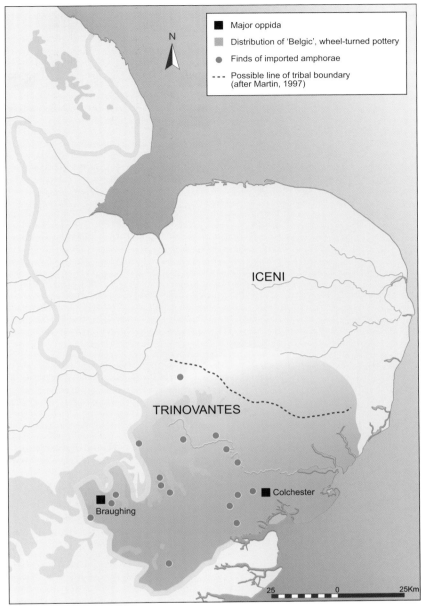

Fig. 2.8 Tribal territories and cultural patterns *in late Iron Age East Anglia.*

Map legend:
- Major oppida
- Distribution of 'Belgic', wheel-turned pottery
- Finds of imported amphorae
- Possible line of tribal boundary (after Martin, 1997)

ICENI

TRINOVANTES

Colchester

Braughing

25   0   25Km

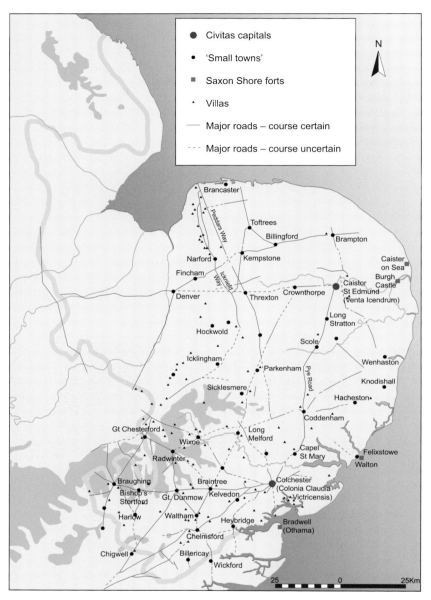

on heavy clays as much as on light loams, aerial photography or field walking surveys reveal a density of between 1 and 1.5 settlement sites per square kilometre and, while not all were necessarily occupied at the same time, the majority were probably in use during the 2nd and 3rd centuries.[14] What all this implies in terms of the relative extent of farmland and woodland is less certain, for it is again possible that some of these sites were specialised settlements, for the exploitation of woods and pastures. Nevertheless, the marked penumbra of stray pot sherds found around most, even on the heaviest clays – presumably reflecting the manuring of arable land – suggests at least a measure of agricultural self-sufficiency.[15]

Field-walking, aerial photography and excavation have revealed significant spatial variations in the character of Romano-British rural settlements. It is clear, for example, that substantial 'villas' – that is, the more sophisticated farms and elaborate 'country houses' – were largely a feature of the lighter soils: of the west Norfolk escarpment, as at Gayton Thorpe; of the valleys running through Breckland, as at Icklingham; beside the light chalk soils on the escarpment of the East Anglian Heights; and in the major valleys cutting through the till plateau of Hertfordshire and Essex, as at Wendens Ambo (Fig. 2.9). On more fertile or heavier soils, settlement mainly took the form of single peasant farms or small hamlets. Overall, the density of villas seems to have been

Fig. 2.9 East Anglia in the Roman period.

lower in the north of the region, perhaps reflecting the relative impoverishment of the local tribal aristocracy in the wake of the Boudiccan revolt.

Most of the region, including the heavier clays, had been opened up for settlement by the end of the Iron Age. Only in the Fens is there evidence for large areas of completely new land being brought into cultivation. In the course of the 2nd and 3rd centuries AD large-scale settlement occurred across the silt soils of Marshland, partly as a consequence of systematic drainage attempts, but mainly as a result of natural changes in land/sea levels. In some areas the intensity of settlement is largely obscured by silt layers left behind by subsequent, post-Roman phases of inundation. But towards the west, in Cambridgeshire and Lincolnshire, this overburden of later deposits is more intermittent, and aerial photographs reveal a complex landscape of fields, drains and droveways. To the south, on the peat, settlements were fewer and largely restricted to the 'roddons' – the beds of old creeks and watercourses, characterised by gravelly soils which stand higher than the surrounding peat, providing firm foundations in this wet and shifting world. Most notable is the long string of sites that follow an old course of the Great Ouse in Welney.[16]

The Roman period saw the development of the first true towns in the region. Major urban centres – defended, and with a range of civic and ceremonial buildings – appeared at Venta Icenorum (Caistor-by-Norwich) and Camulodunum (Colchester): they represented the tribal capitals of the Iceni and the Trinovantes, respectively (Fig. 2.10). At both sites, the remains of the flint perimeter walls survive: those at Colchester, some 3m thick, include an entrance gate, the 'Balkerne Gate'. Colchester Castle is built on the base of the temple of Claudius (Fig. 2.11). It was in such places, and among the indigenous, villa-owning aristocracy that dominated them, that Christianity took the greatest hold after it was declared the official imperial religion in 306. However, its archaeological traces in the region are fairly limited, the most important probably being the 4th-century church, and associated cemetery, discovered outside the walls of Camulodunum.[17] 'Small towns' – nucleated settlements of various sizes, sometimes defended and often with temples, but lacking *fora* and other public buildings – also appeared in many places during the 1st and 2nd centuries. Some, such as that at Braughing in Hertfordshire, developed from pre-Roman *oppida* or other major settlements. Others were entirely new developments. Some probably functioned as the central places and markets for subdivisions, or *pagi*, of the larger tribal groups.[18] But many had industrial functions, for example as centres of pottery manufacture (like Brampton in Norfolk) or iron working (as at Scole in Norfolk). Indeed, we should not

Fig. 2.10 Venta Icenorum, the capital of the Iceni, *stands beside the River Tas some 5m south of Norwich.*

ABOVE: **Fig. 2.11 The Norman castle at Colchester** incorporates the base of the Temple of Claudius, built after the Roman conquest in the colonia of Camulodunum.

RIGHT: **Fig. 2.12 The Roman road called Peddars Way** crossing north-west Norfolk near Houghton.

underestimate the extent of Roman industry in the region, although it has left relatively few above-ground traces; the most noteworthy are perhaps the 'red hills' – mounds of salt-making debris – along the coast of Essex.

Settlements were connected with each other by a network of roads. The familiar 'Roman roads', surveyed and to varying degrees following a straight course, were only one part of this system, equivalent to today's trunk roads and motorways. We should perhaps treat with caution the network presented in Fig. 2.9: some of the routes shown are supported by stronger evidence than others, for only a minority survive entire in the modern landscape. Of particular note are the Pye Road, which forms the modern A140 from near Caistor-by-Norwich to Coddenham in Suffolk; Peddars Way, which runs across west Norfolk in a number of straight alignments; and Worstead Street in south-east Cambridgeshire (Fig. 2.12). The latter two routes exist only as minor lanes and tracks. Quite why these should have survived, when other roads of equal or greater importance have been largely or completely lost, is one of the neglected mysteries of archaeology.

By the end of the 3rd century the region was thus well populated and extensively cleared. But things began to change thereafter. In the Fenland, rising sea levels led to the progressive abandonment of land: by *c.* AD 350 few, if any, settlements here were still occupied. Elsewhere there are signs of deepening recession. The forum at Venta Icenorum was burnt down in the early 3rd century; it was not rebuilt for 50 years, and then on a much smaller scale, while the new defences erected around the same time enclosed only half of the original town and truncated the old grid of streets. 'Small towns', such as Braintree and Chelmsford, similarly contracted during the later 3rd and 4th centuries, and from the mid-4th century the number of coins in circulation, especially in the north of the region, seems to have declined. It is tempting to see these changes as the result of barbarian raiding on the exposed eastern coast, although more general social, economic and political changes may have been equally important. Raiding is certainly indicated from as early as the mid-3rd century by the construction of the imposing fortifications called the Saxon Shore Forts all along the southern and eastern shores of Britain.[19] In the region considered here, only that at Burgh Castle survives in good condition (*see* Fig. 1.13): meagre traces remain at Bradwell-on-Sea, Caister and Brancaster, while the structure at Walton near Felixstowe has been entirely destroyed by the sea. All are positioned close to the mouths of major estuaries, presumably to prevent seaborne raiders penetrating into the interior. In addition to all this, during the 4th century several 'small towns' were defended for the first time, such as Brampton in Norfolk, or supplied with improved defences, as at Great Chesterford in Essex.

AN INVADED SHORE

Recession and insecurity culminated in political and ethnic change. In the early 5th century East Anglia ceased to be a part of the Roman Empire, and over the next 50 years or so it was extensively settled by new peoples from the continent – the Angles, Saxons and others. The scale of that settlement – whether a take-over by a comparatively small warrior elite or a true folk-movement – remains contested. But within a few generations Latin and Celtic ceased to be spoken (only a handful of Romano-British place-names survive in the area) and, so far as we can tell, organised Christianity had disappeared. Indeed, the most archaeologically visible feature of the new settlers are the large 'pagan' cemeteries, containing cremations in decorated urns or inhumations with grave goods, which are such a striking feature of the region's archaeology.

What is particularly interesting is that, following the collapse of Roman power, older cultural patterns seem to re-emerge, but in a new guise. In northern East Anglia – in old Icenian territory – pagan cemeteries are widespread, especially on the lighter soils, and cemeteries dominated by cremations are common. But in

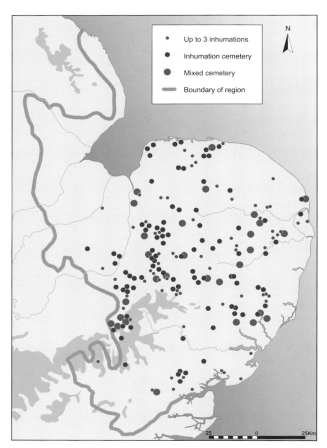

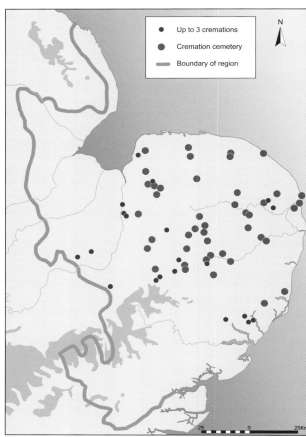

ABOVE: *Fig. 2.13 East Anglia and the Fens: the distribution of early Anglo-Saxon inhumation cemeteries*, and cemeteries in which both cremation and inhumation are represented.

ABOVE RIGHT: *Fig. 2.14 East Anglia and the Fens: the distribution of early Anglo-Saxon cremation cemeteries* in East Anglia.

former Trinovantian lands pagan cemeteries are much fewer in number and cremation cemeteries in particular are virtually unknown (Figs 2.13 and 2.14). Later traditions asserted that the invaders of Norfolk and Suffolk were Angles, from *Angeln* in Schleswig Holstein, while those settling in Hertfordshire and Essex were Saxons from Saxony, and it is thus suggested by some that differences in burial rites reflect ethnicity.[20] A more interesting explanation might be that the broad coincidence of *post*-Roman archaeological distributions and *pre*-Roman polities indicates direct political continuity from the Iceni to the East Angles, from the Trinovantes to the East Saxons. But in all probability systems of contact and exchange, determined by the configuration of coast and river, are the real explanation for this pattern. This is not least because the south of the region, with comparatively few cemeteries and a predominance of inhumations, forms part of a wider zone that extends right across southern England and into northern France. Evidently the south of the region looked, as in earlier centuries, more towards Gaul, former imperial lands settled by (Christian) invaders; while the north asserted contacts across the wild North Sea, with areas in Germany and Scandinavia that had never been under Roman rule.

Certainly, any arguments for political continuity across the 5th and 6th centuries are lessened by the belief of many historians that the immediate post-Roman period saw not only a severe technological and economic recession (coinage disappeared and wheel-thrown pottery ceased to be produced), but also extreme political fragmentation. Effective power is thought to have devolved to tribal groups whose territories extended across tens, rather than hundreds, of square kilometres.[21] The names of some may be preserved in those of the late Saxon administrative divisions called Hundreds: the Cnaveringas (Clavering),

Loddingas (Loddon) and Happingas (Happing) in Norfolk: the Rodingas (Roding) in Essex; and the Brahingas (Braughing) in Hertfordshire.[22] Some of these diminutive territories, including that of the Brahingas, may have been based on Roman towns (in this case Braughing) and may, indeed, have developed from older, indigenous tribal divisions. Many, moreover, seem to have approximated to 'natural territories' based on river valleys and drainage basins, separated from their neighbours by interfluves occupied by heavier soils, from which settlement seems to have retreated in the 5th century.

There is little in the pollen record to suggest massive regeneration of woodland. Demographic decline and contraction of settlement were instead accompanied by an expansion of pasture at the expense of arable.[23] But even on light soils the numbers of settlements seem to have dwindled. At Witton in north-east Norfolk, for example, eight Romano-British settlements were discovered through field walking, but only four areas of early Saxon occupation. Selective excavation and intensive surface collection, moreover, revealed that only one of these was in use throughout the 5th and 6th centuries. One was occupied in the 5th century, one in the 6th, while the third could not be dated accurately. Mobility of settlement was possibly associated with the same regression in agricultural technology which ensured that Saxon farmers shunned the heavier soils. Farms may have drifted across the landscape because, without a mouldboard plough able to bury weeds effectively, fields eventually became so infested that it was easier to break in new land and abandon the old. Whatever the explanation, the evidence for settlement mobility is widespread. At West Stow in Suffolk, for example, a spread of settlement covering some 1.8ha was shown, by careful excavation, not to represent a substantial 'village' but instead to derive from the gradual eastward movement of a single small settlement during the 6th and 7th centuries. The settlement consisted of three timber-built 'halls' with associated clusters of sunken-featured buildings – probably the residences of three family groups.

In the course of the 7th, 8th and 9th centuries East Anglia recovered somewhat from its low population, agrarian recession and political fragmentation. Settlements gradually ceased to migrate around the landscape and became fixed, mainly in locations close to the sites later occupied by parish churches, villages or major manorial sites. The area under cultivation seems to have expanded, and in places the heavier clays began to be settled once again. The plethora of small tribal territories was gradually consolidated, presumably through conquest, so that larger and more centralised kingdoms developed – that of the East Angles in the north and that of the East Saxons in the south of the region. However, the Fens remained for a time debatable territory, still occupied by small, semi-autonomous groups like the tribe called the Gwyre, on the borders with the Midland kingdom of Mercia.

The controlling elites of the two kingdoms and, over time, their subject populations adopted Christianity. In the East Anglian kingdom the Irish monk Fursa established a monastery at Cnobheresburg, probably Burgh Castle, and the Burgundian Felix founded the first bishopric at Dommoc, probably Walton Castle, a Roman fort near Felixstowe, which was destroyed long ago by the sea. In the 680s the East Anglian diocese was divided, with a second bishopric being created to serve the northern parts of the kingdom at North Elmham. The bishopric for the East Saxons lay outside the region studied here, in London. Kings also cultivated forms of long-distance exchange, which they controlled through coastal entrepots or *wics*; these also functioned, at least in some cases, as centres of specialised production.[24] The largest was at Ipswich, where Ipswich Ware – well-made pottery turned on a wheel – began to be made in the early 8th century. The two kingdoms had complex but, after the death of Rædwald, East Anglia's first real king, generally undistinguished political histories. While East Anglia remained more or less independent until 869, Essex was under the domination of the West Saxons by the 820s, and had effectively ceased to be an independent polity.[25]

Contacts between northern East Anglia and Scandinavia, and perhaps significant movements of people, continued through the 6th and 7th centuries.[26] Sam Newton has argued that the Old English epic poem *Beowulf*, which is set in southern Scandinavia, may have been originally composed (as an oral epic) at the court of the Wuffingas, the ruling dynasty of the East Angles – they may indeed be identical to the Danish tribe of the *Wulfingas* mentioned in the poem.[27] The funerary rites practised at their great burial ground – on the heaths at Sutton Hoo overlooking the estuary of the River Deben, the approach to their palace at Rendlesham (Fig. 2.15) – do mirror in some respects those described in that poem. But it was in the 9th century that much of the region, together with north-east England, was wrenched more forcibly into a Scandinavian orbit.

Viking forces attacked East Anglia in 865, and in 869 defeated and killed Edmund, its last king. In 879, according to the *Anglo-Saxon Chronicle*, the Viking army 'went … into East Anglia, and occupied that land, and shared it out', and subsequent entries suggest further settlement.[28] The eastern portion of Mercia, including the Fens, was occupied in 875, but whether the kingdom of the East Saxons, which included east Hertfordshire, was similarly taken into Viking control at this time is less clear. Much of it probably remained under West Saxon dominance. Either way, Viking supremacy was relatively short-lived. In 917 King Edward, Alfred's son, 'went with West Saxon levies to Colchester [and] … many people, both from East Anglia and from Essex, who had previously been under Danish domination submitted to him, and the entire Danish host in East Anglia swore union with him'.[29]

How many Vikings actually settled in the region – whether we are talking about a small elite of warriors or a peasant migration – is again subject to debate.[30] Major Scandinavian place-names are few in number, especially compared to the East Midlands, and are strongly concentrated in certain areas, most notably Flegg, north of Yarmouth (Fig. 2.16). Flegg was effectively an island in this period, surrounded by open water or marsh, suggesting perhaps limited strategic settlement by the indigenous authorities rather than generalised land-grabbing. Yet Scandinavian terms are common in minor place-names. The frequent 'gate' derives from the Danish *gata*, 'street', and, like people in the north of England, we in Norfolk call a stream a 'beck' (after the Old Danish *bekr*).

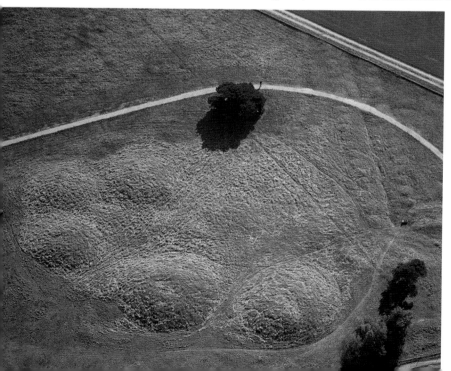

Fig. 2.15 The Anglo-Saxon burial mounds at Sutton Hoo.

Moreover, there have been numerous stray finds of metalwork objects in Scandinavian style, dating from the 9th, 10th and 11th centuries.

Does all this indicate large-scale settlement? Both names and objects may indicate the presence of a powerful immigrant elite, strong trading contacts with Scandinavia at a time when the North Sea basin was becoming a major focus for exchange and the widespread adoption of Scandinavian tastes, much as Britain today adopts so much American popular culture. Significantly, it is *northern* East Anglia – Norfolk and northern and eastern Suffolk – that seems to have been most affected by Danish influence. Most Scandinavian place-names occur to the north and east of the Lark–Gipping corridor, and it is in this area that the majority of Anglo-Scandinavian metalwork finds have been made. Once again, East Anglia emerges, quite clearly, as a land of two parts.

Viking raiding and settlement certainly had no long-term detrimental effects upon the wealth of the region. It may even have stimulated the growth of Thetford and Norwich.[31] East Anglia continued to flourish, moreover, following its reconquest by the West Saxons and absorption into a unified English realm in the 10th century. Major urban centres developed at Norwich, Ipswich and Thetford, and by the time of the Norman Conquest of 1066 this was evidently the richest and most densely settled region in England (Fig. 2.17). Indeed, to judge from the information set out with particular detail in Volume II of Domesday Book ('Little Domesday'), some rural districts in Norfolk and Suffolk probably contained more people in 1086 than in the 19th century. However, and crucially for its later development, this was also – again, to judge from Domesday – the *freest* area in England. Most of England at this time was divided into relatively small estates called manors, usually between one and three per vill, which contained dependent populations of servile cultivators (villeins or bordars) who owed labour services and other obligations to their lord or thegn. In East Anglia, however, vills often contained many manors and a large proportion of the farming population were classed as free men (*liberi homines*) or sokemen (*sochmanni*) (Fig. 2.18). Such individuals enjoyed rights and privileges of an uncertain character, but seem to have had much greater independence from local lords than villeins or bordars. Indeed, it is likely that before the Norman Conquest *liberi homines* were effectively freeholders, and those with large amounts of land were only vaguely distinguished from thegns. This was a complex, uncertain and perhaps highly competitive social world.[32]

Some scholars attribute East Anglia's social idiosyncrasies to the Vikings, not least because they are shared to some extent by the other areas of Scandinavian settlement in the East Midlands.[33] Free men and sokemen, according to this view, represented the descendants of de-mobbed Viking armies, or of Scandinavian peasants who migrated in the wake of conquest. Yet there is little firm evidence for any of this: no real reason to assume that the Danes were lovers of freedom in a way that the English were not. Moreover, the scale of Scandinavian settlement in East Anglia remains contested and was, to judge from the place-name evidence at least, considerably less than in the East Midlands. Once again we face

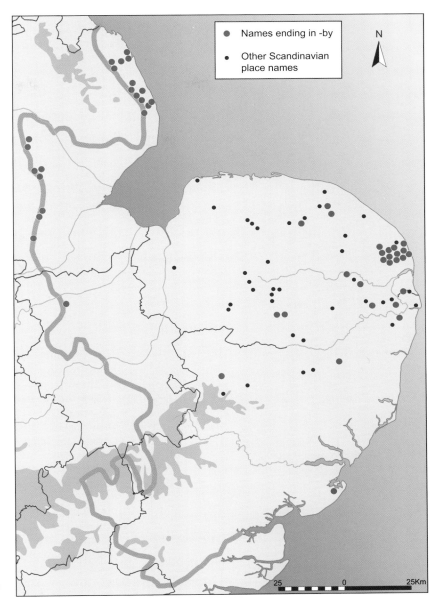

Fig. 2.16 East Anglia and the fens: the distribution of major place-names containing Scandinavian elements (excluding those incorporating the term –thorp, which continued to be used for new settlements into the post-Conquest period).

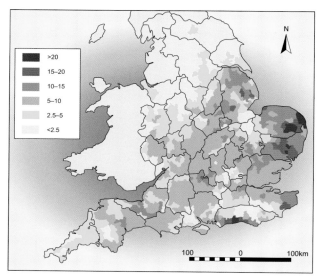

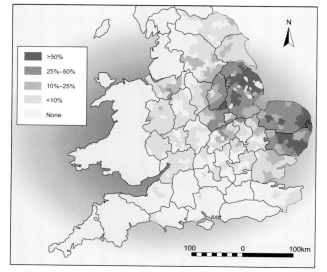

TOP: *Fig. 2.17 Population density in Domesday England: the number of recorded individuals per square mile.*

ABOVE: *Fig. 2.18 The proportion of the population recorded as free men and sokemen in Domesday Book.*

ABOVE RIGHT: *Fig. 2.19 Arable land use in England in c.1940: compare with Figs 2.17 and 2.18.*

the difficulty of deciding whether particular patterns are the consequence of contact and movement – in this case, migration and settlement – or of environmental factors. For while the distribution of the 'free peasantry' in England as a whole may correspond in broad terms to the areas most affected by Viking settlement, it also correlates closely with areas in which the densest populations are recorded by Domesday – and, more generally, with what became, in the course of the 18th and 19th centuries, the main areas of cereal production in England (Fig. 2.19).

These correlations may not be as inexplicable as they first appear. As sophisticated transport systems developed in the modern period, grain growing was increasingly concentrated in those districts in which, thanks to dry summers, the harvest was most dependable and crop yields highest.[34] It is easy to see how, in an earlier age, the same environmental circumstances might have ensured that demographic growth continued with only occasional checks caused by dearth. But they may also have had long-term *social* consequences. Many historians believe that important social changes occurred in the course of the late Saxon period.[35] The tribal kingdoms of middle Saxon times had been divided into large estates, more extensive than medieval manors. Many may have been ancient units, perhaps developing from the independent tribal territories of early Saxon times, or from even earlier roots. Either way, they were used by kings to maintain the members of their warrior entourages, and in time to endow the church. Eventually, according to this model, they fragmented as noble families gained absolute rights over them, and they were divided by sale or inheritance. As a plethora of smaller estates and local lords emerged, the condition of the peasantry declined. Many had formerly been free, subject only to the payment of food rents and services to the king. As estates were alienated from the royal patrimony, however, they were forced by local lords into varying degrees of dependence, and obliged to supply labour to their 'demesnes', or home farms.

The close correspondence between the distribution of late Saxon peasant freedom and population density, and the broader correspondence of both with the principal modern grain growing areas, suggests that this process may have been exacerbated or retarded by environmental circumstances. Favourable climatic conditions evidently encouraged not only population growth, but also the survival and enhancement of peasant freedom as large, ancient estates fragmented. Presumably, to judge from numerous ethnographic parallels, harvest failures encouraged bondage, as cultivators were obliged to fall into dependence on social superiors with greater facilities for the storage of surpluses. We might note in passing how the national distribution of relative peasant freedom indicated by Domesday echoes with uncanny accuracy some of the patterns of prehistory, such as those areas in which, in the Iron Age, defended settlements were rare. Environmental factors could evidently have broadly similar effects on social development across immense periods of time. But in a late Saxon context, other influences may also have been at work. In particular, in this economically buoyant region, tied closely to the engine of North Sea economic growth, a prospering peasantry – especially those colonising new areas of land on clay-covered interfluves – may have been better able to assert or expand their ancient rights against a rising class of thegns than those living in less economically successful areas.

Whether the consequence of invasion and settlement, or of favourable environmental and economic circumstances, tenurial complexity continued to be a striking feature of much of East Anglia throughout the early medieval centuries. Although, in the wake of the Conquest, many free peasants were downgraded to the status of villeins, large numbers survived. Free men were not a feature of all districts, however: where soils were light and poor, especially in Breckland, they were few in number. And both peasant freedom and manorial complexity were less prominent in the southern parts of the region, especially Essex and east Hertfordshire. Here, although numerous free peasants certainly existed, there were also many big manors with particularly large demesnes, up to 120ha or more, which were heavily dependent on labour services. Although the division between 'free' and 'manorial' East Anglia was an imprecise one, and ran some way to the south of the familiar Lark–Gipping line, we can yet again see a marked contrast between the north-east and the south-west parts of the region.

THE LEGACY

By the time of Domesday East Anglia was, with the exception of the Fens, a largely tamed and settled landscape. Even in the Fens settlements existed on major islands such as Ely, and in places on the higher silts towards the Wash, their inhabitants engaged in making salt and exploiting the rich grazing and the reserves of wildfowl and fish. True, Domesday records large areas of wood-pasture on the claylands, but these seldom accounted for more than around 10 per cent of the land surface and they would have been intensively exploited, for wood, timber and grazing.[36]

I have already emphasised the paucity of upstanding, visible monuments left by the remote, pre-Conquest centuries in the East Anglian landscape. There are some striking exceptions, such as the massive Roman burial mounds at Bartlow in Essex, or the barrow cemeteries on Therfield Heath in Hertfordshire or Salthouse Heath in Norfolk. But we seldom find here the earthworks of prehistoric farms and fields of the kind familiar from the chalklands of Wessex. Intense arable land use removed them long ago, and with few exceptions the sites of early settlements are marked only by scatters of pot sherds in the ploughsoil. Perhaps the most striking surviving monuments are the various linear earthworks, especially those running across the low chalk escarpment of the East Anglian Heights. Most seem to have served as territorial boundaries; others may have been intended to control and funnel overland traffic, in order to charge tolls or exact tribute and/or to prevent the movement of

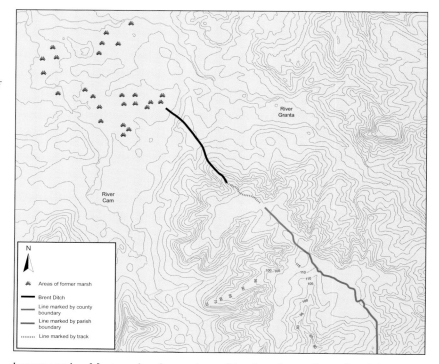

Fig. 2.20 Brent Ditch *is a linear earthwork that runs across the chalk escarpment in south Cambridgeshire. Where it meets the clay plateau to the south-east it ends, but its line is continued by stretches of track and boundary that follow the watershed between the valleys of the two river Cams, or Grantas.*

baggage trains. Most, as already noted, are either Iron Age or Saxon in origin; they vary greatly in scale, ranging from the formidable Devil's Dyke near Newmarket (*see* Fig. 1.16) to some very diminutive Norfolk examples, such as the Panworth Ditch.[37] Some, like the Launditch in Norfolk, vary in scale along their length, and in some cases the line of an earthwork appears to be continued far beyond its recognised termination – the earthwork's recognised course – by stretches of parish or Hundred boundary, marked by no more than a hedge and ditch.

The Brent Ditch in south-east Cambridgeshire is a good example of this phenomenon. Like its neighbours the Fleam Dyke and Devil's Dyke, it lies at right angles to the chalk scarp of the East Anglian Heights, running for some 3km from low, marshy ground near Brent Ditch End in Pampisford to Abington Park Farm in Abington. It lies more or less equidistant between the two River Cams or Grantas, which here flow in a roughly south-east/north-westerly direction, breaking through the line of the chalk escarpment (Fig. 2.20). Beyond the point where the 'official' earthwork ends, where the chalk of the escarpment gives way to the clay of the plateau above, its line is continued for a further 10km by a succession of parish boundaries that follow the watershed between the two river valleys. This 'continuation' is marked by no more than hedge, but there is no reason to believe that it is any younger than the earthwork itself.

Indeed, in many other places on the claylands of East Anglia there is evidence for long, continuous lines of track and hedgeline, closely related to the broad sweeps of the topography, which are followed by parish boundaries and Hundred boundaries established in the late Saxon or early post-Conquest period but which may well themselves be much older. They were first noted by Warwick Rodwell, who discussed a number of examples in Essex.[38] Most striking perhaps is the sinuous line that follows the watershed between the River Roding and various streams draining southwards to the Thames, in the area to the east of Epping. The Roman road from London to Chelmsford follows a straight line that cuts across its sinuous course in two places 'in such a fashion as to leave little room for doubt' that it is a pre-Roman feature. In some places, long tracks and boundaries run up from valley floors to meet these high watershed lines, thus dividing major valleys into roughly rectangular land units – for example, in the Stour and Colne valleys in the area around Colchester.

A number of major boundaries in the region thus appear to be of considerable antiquity. But in some places even quite minor elements of the landscape – local lanes, even individual field boundaries – *may* date back to the pre-Saxon period. During the excavation of the Iron Age settlement at Little Waltham in Essex in the 1970s, Paul Drury discovered that some of the excavated ditches appeared to continue beyond the site as upstanding boundaries. He also noted that, as it approached the site from the north-east, the Roman road from Braintree appeared to cut through the pattern of field boundaries shown on 19th-century maps in a way analogous to a modern by-pass: odd corners and angles suggested that the road had been imposed upon an earlier pattern of land division.[39] These observations were later extended across a wider area, culminating in the suggestion that the structure of the countryside over much of Essex 'was established in the later Iron Age and Roman periods, and has survived because of continuous agricultural usage of the areas concerned'.[40]

More dramatic examples come from further north, in north Suffolk and Norfolk. The Roman Pye Road – the modern A140 – appears to cut obliquely through an organised field system in the area around Yaxley in north Suffolk; northwards, beyond the Waveney, it slights an even more extensive system, in the area around Scole and Dickleburgh (Fig. 2.21).[41] The latter is of 'co-axial' form – that is, like many prehistoric field systems surviving in the form of earthworks or tumbled walls elsewhere in England, it is laid out around a number of sub-parallel, closely spaced axes. These are formed by roads and tracks and alignments of field boundary, which run at right angles to the Waveney valley. Similar patterns, resembling slightly wavy brickwork, can be found across wide areas of Norfolk, north Suffolk and south-east Cambridgeshire,

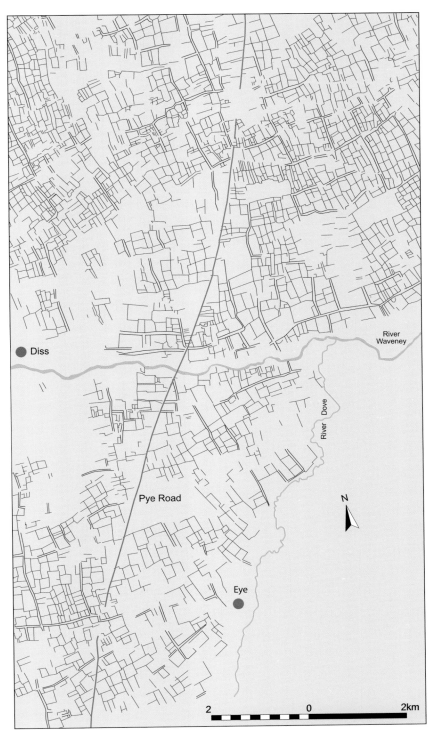

Fig. 2.21 The Roman Pye Road (the modern A140) in south Norfolk and north Suffolk. In a number of places the road appears to cut through the pattern of field boundaries shown on the earliest maps, suggesting that some elements of the modern landscape may have Roman or prehistoric origins.

either in the form of extant fields or in the layout of pre-enclosure furlongs.[42] All are arranged around axes running up from valleys (or, in south Cambridgeshire, the Fen edge) to watersheds. Most, unfortunately, lack the Roman roads that can apparently supply some indication of a prehistoric date, but other evidence often suggests considerable antiquity. Recent excavations at Burnham in north Norfolk seem to show how late Saxon open field furlongs developed within an older, probably late Iron Age, framework of enclosed fields.

Much about these 'relict landscapes' remains contentious. In particular, it is not clear that all their constituent elements are actually of the same date. Many are probably the consequence of the later 'infilling' of an originally much sparser network of lanes and boundaries, related to the division and management of woodland and grazing on the drift-covered plateaux above major valleys. Nor is it clear how far they were planned, rather than developing organically in response to environmental and topographic factors. Indeed, some archaeologists simply do not believe they are ancient at all.[43] On balance, it seems probable that in some parts of the region pre-Saxon landscape features, and systems of land division, did indeed provide the framework within which the medieval and modern landscape developed. Many of the minor boundaries and lanes of East Anglia are probably much older than we usually think.

NOTES

1 Bradley 1993.
2 Hill 1999, 185–207.
3 Ashwin 1999; Martin 1999, 45–99.
4 Hill 1999, 193.
5 Haselgrove 1982.
6 Cunliffe 1995, 58–97.
7 Martin 1999, 83–91.
8 Davies 1999, 14–43.
9 Davies 1996.
10 Gregory 1992.
11 Webster 1978.
12 Ashwin 1996.
13 Wiltshire & Murphy 1999.
14 Williamson 1993, 42–7; Warner 1996; Williamson 2000a, 5–9; Going 1996, 95–108.
15 Williamson 1986.
16 Silvester 1988; Gurney 1986.
17 Crummy 1997, 123.
18 Wickendon 1996.
19 Johnson 1977; Pearson 2003.
20 Whittock 1986, 149; Alcock 1971, 287.
21 Bassett 1989.
22 Williamson 1993, 72, 128–9; Anderson 1934; Bassett 1997.
23 Bennet 1983; Godwin 1968; Godwin & Tallantire 1951; Sims 1978; Peglar et al. 1989.
24 Hill & Cowie 2001; Hodges 1982.
25 Dumville 1992, 1–27.
26 Hines 1992.
27 Newton 1993.
28 Garmondsway 1953, 76.
29 Ibid, 103.
30 Margeson 1996; Hinton 1990, 71; Williamson 1993, 105–10.
31 Margeson 1996, 56.
32 Darby 1971.
33 Stenton 1947.
34 Williamson 2002b, 167–74; Stamp 1950, 85.
35 Faith 1997.
36 Darby 1971, 126–9, 179–82, 232–9; Williamson 2003, 57.
37 Malim 1996; Wade-Martins 1974; Ashwin & Flotcroft 1999.
38 Rodwell 1978.
39 Drury 1978.
40 Drury & Rodwell 1980.
41 Williamson 1987; Williamson 1998b.
42 Harrison 2002; Hesse 1992.
43 Hinton 1997.

3

Making a Living

MEDIEVAL SETTLEMENT

The landscape of East Anglia has deep roots, and some of its features – the location of some settlements and most churches, the layout of some roads and boundaries – were established by the end of the Saxon period. However, the majority of what we see today is the consequence of developments in the centuries following the Norman Conquest, and in some cases of the very recent past. Moreover, fields and settlements, woods, heaths and pastures were all for the most part created by practical activities: by people striving to make a living. Political, social, religious and aesthetic factors were always important, but it was industry and, in particular, agriculture that shaped the basic structures of the physical environment.

The most important feature of East Anglia's settlement pattern is its predominantly dispersed character.[1] Most districts, even those characterised by light and freely draining soils, have long included some outlying farms and hamlets, in addition to the main focus of settlement. That focus, moreover, was itself often more like a collection of contiguous hamlets than a compact village in the usual sense. Indeed, in parts of Norfolk individual 'villages' might be supplied with two or even three separate parish churches (Fig. 3.1). But in most areas, especially where the soils were heavier, there was no real village nucleus at all, only a scatter of small hamlets and isolated farms. There were many variations on this broad theme of dispersal, but, as so often, we can make a broad distinction between areas located roughly to the north-east, and to the south-west, of the Lark–Gipping corridor.

Most areas in the north and east developed in the same idiosyncratic way, largely unparalleled in other parts of England. The stable settlements that had emerged in middle Saxon times continued in place into the 11th century, usually acquiring the parish churches that mark their position today. But, beginning some decades before the Conquest and continuing into the

Fig. 3.1 The village of Barton Bendish in west Norfolk, field-walked by Andrew Rogerson. Like many villages in East Anglia, this seems to have developed through the gradual coalescence of separate but neighbouring Saxon settlements. In common with many Norfolk villages, moreover, Barton Bendish remained divided between three separate parishes.

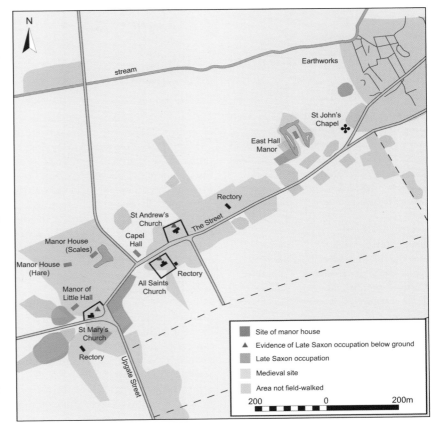

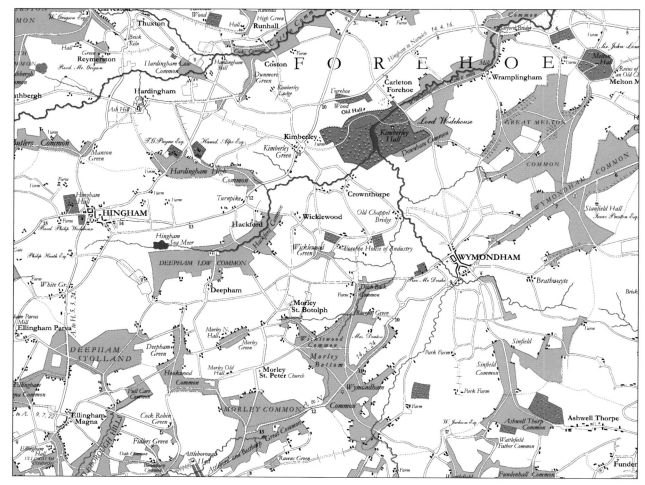

OPPOSITE PAGE:

TOP: *Fig. 3.3 Fritton in Norfolk. The parish church (foreground) was left isolated when the village migrated to the edge of Fritton Common in the early medieval period.*

BOTTOM: *Fig. 3.4 In south Suffolk, Essex and Hertfordshire, large commons were a less prominent feature of the medieval landscape but small greens and 'tyes' formed an important element in the settlement pattern. Many survive, as here at Levens Green, Great Munden, east Hertfordshire.*

12th and 13th centuries, these nucleations were distorted, or disintegrated altogether, as farms moved to new locations beside greens and commons (Fig. 3.2). These occupied the damp, peaty floors of major valleys or, on the claylands, poorly draining concavities in the plateau surface. As a result of this process of settlement drift, churches were often left peripheral to the main concentrations of settlement; in many cases they still stand quite alone in the midst of the fields (Fig. 3.3).[2]

In the south-west of the region, settlement developed in a rather different manner. Most of this area is occupied by the dissected boulder clay plateau and in the principal valleys, and along the muted escarpment of the 'East Anglian Heights', which borders it to the north-west, light and freely-draining soils occur. Most middle and late Saxon settlements were located within or beside these exposures of light soil. These places are usually marked today by parish churches, but some never attained parochial status: many Domesday vills are now represented by isolated manorial sites or small hamlets.[3] Some, such as the settlement excavated at Wicken Bonhunt, were certainly established by middle Saxon times, and many probably have earlier roots.[4] In the course of the 10th, 11th and 12th centuries, cultivation expanded on the heavy soils of the interfluves, but there was no wholesale migration to the edge of greens and commons. Instead, existing settlements grew and coalesced to form irregular nucleations, while the new settlements, spreading out across the clay plateau, took the form of small compact hamlets, sometimes set around diminutive greens (here often called 'tyes') or consisted of isolated farms and sub-manors, often moated, set within their own fields (Figs 3.4 and 3.5).

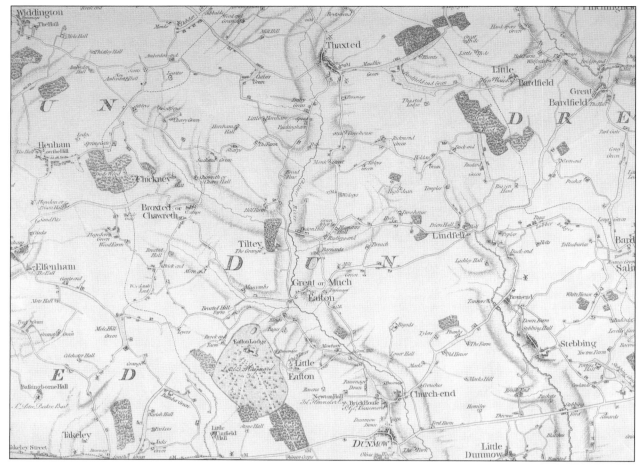

Fig. 3.5 The mixture of small nucleated settlements, *hamlets (many clustered around diminutive greens) and isolated farms typical of southern East Anglia. From Chapman and Andre's map of Essex, published in 1777.*

Both to the north-east and south-west of the Lark and Gipping rivers, the landscape thus developed in ways very different from the Midlands, where settlements, having become fixed in middle Saxon times, simply expanded *in situ*. Farms and hamlets did not disperse widely across the landscape, and the Midlands remained a landscape of villages.

We thus have two things to explain: why East Anglia's medieval pattern of settlement differed so much from that of the Midlands; and why there were broad differences in the character of settlement between the north-east and the south-west of the region (Fig. 3.6). Historians and archaeologists have interpreted such variations in a number of ways. Some have suggested that areas with dispersed settlement were settled at a comparatively late date – that they were sparsely settled, pioneer territory in early medieval times.[5] But as we have seen, Domesday suggests that East Anglia was in fact *more* densely populated than the Midlands, in spite of the fact that it also retained more woodland and, probably, pasture. Others have argued that regional differences were a consequence of 'cultural' or 'ethnic' factors – of the settlement of the region by Friesians or Vikings, or of the survival here of ancient 'Celtic' traditions.[6] None of these theories receives much support from archaeological research and the real explanation probably lies in the more mundane and practical world of farming and the environment.

Both the Midlands and East Anglia are characterised for the most part by clay soils, but these differed in a number of important respects. A higher proportion of the Midland soils are – to use the technical jargon – pelo-stagnogleys: that is, they are clay-like to the surface. Such soils are not only seasonally waterlogged;

they are also particularly prone to
puddling and compaction. When wet,
they form a sticky mass which adheres
to ploughs and harrows; when dry, they
are hard and brick-like. They require
particularly careful, and particularly
carefully timed, cultivation, in order
to make them 'flocculate' – that is,
encourage the microscopic particles of
clay to coalesce in larger grains. If they
are worked in the wrong conditions,
they can become compacted to such
an extent that yields are drastically
reduced or crops fail altogether. In the
spring months, such soils might be
suitable for cultivation for only a few
weeks or even days.[7]

Most of the clay soils in East Anglia
are different. They are less prone to
'puddling', and the drier climate enables
them to be worked over a longer period
of time. The soils that are defined
by the Soil Survey of England and
Wales as the Beccles and Burlingham
Associations have sandy upper horizons
while those of the Hanslope
Association, although stiff and heavy,
are calcareous, and, if treated sensibly,
can be made to 'flocculate' relatively
easily.[8] All this had an important bearing
on the development of settlement, for
peasant cultivators in late Saxon times
generally only possessed two or three
oxen and thus had to combine together
to create the large teams of six or eight
oxen necessary to plough their own
land and that of their lord's demesne.[9]
Where full advantage needed to be
taken of every hour in which the soil

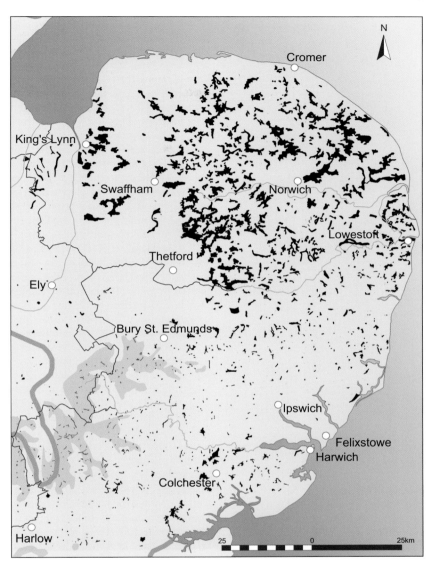

was suitable for ploughing, teams needed to be assembled with particular rapidity,
and this was obviously easier where farms stood in close proximity, in villages,
rather than scattered across the landscape. In areas of dispersed settlement it
might take an hour or more of vital time to send a message to a neighbouring farm
and for the farmer to arrive with his beasts. The broad differences between Midland
settlement patterns and East Anglian may thus in part be explained in terms of
soils, climate and the effects they had on the organisation of joint ploughing.[10]

However, there were other important differences between the Midlands and the
east. Meadow was an important resource in medieval England, providing the hay to
feed the livestock (especially the plough oxen) during the winter months, when grass
does not grow. In the Midlands, large areas of meadow land existed from an early
date: this is clear from Domesday, manorial extents and from such documents as the
Inquisitions Post Mortem. Most vills there seem to have had around a hectare of
meadow for every 10 of arable. The wide valleys of the Nene, Ouse and other
Midland rivers contained extensive areas of alluvial soils which could easily be
managed as meadow simply by keeping livestock off them during the late spring and
early summer months, allowing the grass to grow.[11] In East Anglia, the situation was

*Fig. 3.6 Common edge settlement
in East Anglia and Essex in the 18th
century. The map does not show all
commons, only those which attracted a
significant number of farms and cottages to
their margins. Both the number, and size, of
such commons increases towards the north.*

different. In districts to the south and west of the Lark and Gipping there was less meadow land than in the Midlands, usually only 1ha to every 30 or so of arable, to judge from 12th- and 13th-century documents, and it was widely dispersed, along numerous small, narrow valleys. In most of the districts to the north and east of the Lark–Gipping corridor, in contrast, there was even less. Here the floors of the widely spaced valleys of the slow rivers were often filled with mixtures of peat and clay, giving rise to fen vegetation dominated by reed and sedge, which in their natural state provided only poor, rough hay. In these contexts meadow making was a matter of active creation, involving the digging of drains and, in some cases, the raising of embankments. Even in the early 19th century many valley floors here were still occupied by common fens – surrounded by the usual penumbra of farms and cottages – interrupted only here and there by areas of private meadow.

Hay-making required good weather, abundant labour and the careful timing of farming operations: hence the proverb 'make hay while the sun shines'. Large areas of meadow land thus encouraged the growth of large nucleated villages, in which the work force could be quickly assembled. They also allowed communities to expand their ploughlands at the expense of the woods and pastures as population rose, so that in many Midland vills, by the 12th century, the cultivated land extended all the way to the boundaries of the vill. In contrast, in areas in which meadow was more limited, or more difficult to create, large areas of wood-pasture and other grazing were usually retained by Saxon communities to provide sustenance for livestock late into the autumn. As population rose and cultivation expanded, these came under sustained attack and greater emphasis had to be placed on hay meadows. Where alluvial soils suitable for meadow making were widely distributed, but limited in area, villages often emerged in major valleys, but settlement mainly took the form of scattered farms and hamlets, following thin ribbons of meadow in tributary valleys, while on the interfluves greens provided late grazing into the autumn for the livestock of late settled smallholdings. This was the normal pattern in the south and west of the region, in Hertfordshire and Essex and south-west Suffolk. To the north and east, however, where meadows were created with difficulty and always remained in short supply, the need for late grazing was greater. Common wood-pastures gradually degenerated to open pasture, under the pressure of intense grazing, but vast areas of grazing land were retained, especially in the many places that were difficult to cultivate in this level, waterlogged land: the wide, shallow depressions in the clay plateau, for example, or the damp, peat-filled floors of valleys. Farms clustered around them, to facilitate management of livestock. East Anglia thus had less meadow land than the Midlands, but was always more populous. Indeed, a recurrent theme in its history is this curious contrast between an environment that offers excellent conditions for growing cereals, yet only modest supplies of fodder.

MEDIEVAL FIELDS

The medieval countryside was mainly in the hands of small peasant producers, most of whom held farms of 12ha or less – in some cases, considerably less. Larger enterprises, principally the manorial demesnes, also existed, but probably accounted for less than one-fifth of the total land area. The 12th and 13th centuries were, as already noted, a period of sustained population growth, and the emphasis was firmly on grain production. Animals were essential for fertility and traction, but they were mainly grazed on the arable fields when they lay uncropped and fallow or on common lands, rather than on enclosed pastures.

Most of the arable lay in 'open fields', in which holdings took the form of numerous small, unhedged strips, intermingled with those of other cultivators. The origins of such fields are lost in the distant undocumented past, but they probably developed in part from the successive subdivision of farms between co-heirs; in part from the allocation of land in an equitable and ordered fashion between colonists or freed slaves during the Saxon period; and in part from the division of newly cleared land between the cultivators who had formerly used it as common grazing. Such arrangements could undergo subsequent re-organisation and re-allotment. The layout and organisation of medieval open fields was evidently the consequence of a wide range of social and environmental factors, including patterns of settlement and the character of the local soils.

Open fields dominated the landscape in all areas of light, freely draining soil. They were also extensive on the northern silt fens of Marshland and could be found all over the claylands. The oft-repeated suggestion that the heavier soils of East Anglia were, from earliest times, occupied by enclosed fields is simply wrong. But these fields were not like those in the Midlands, in which holdings were widely and evenly scattered in two or three great fields, across which rigid communal rotations were imposed, with one lying fallow each year, the others being planted with spring- and winter-sown crops respectively. In East Anglia the more scattered pattern of settlement was associated with far less 'regular' field systems.

In the south and west of the region the open arable generally took up only a proportion of the land. It was grouped into numerous small fields, often associated by name with the oldest settlements, located in or beside the major valleys.[12] In Elmdon in north-west Essex, for example, the hamlet of Lea lay on the edge of the clay plateau above Lea Field,[13] while in nearby Chrishall a field book of 1597 shows that the inhabitants of Buildings End held much of their land in the adjacent 10-acre common field called 'Bilden Hill Feylde als Bulls Herne'.[14] Thaxted in Essex had five fields in 1393 – Northefelde, Asshefelde, Worthens, Boxstede and Newefelde – on the slopes of the Chelmer valley, close to the pre-Conquest manors of Thaxted itself, Priors and Yardleys.[15] In most places peasant holdings were not widely scattered, but were instead clustered in the fields close to the farm. Large enclosed demesne farms could also be found in the valleys – the lord's land was less likely to lie in open fields, intermingled with that of his tenants, than in areas to the north and east of the Lark and Gipping. On the heavier, higher ground some small areas of open field could be found, but the landscape was dominated by hedged closes, interspersed with managed woods and deer parks.

In the north and east of the region, where settlement characteristically sprawled in chaotic fashion around the margins of greens and commons, open fields usually took up rather more of the land area. There were fewer enclosed fields, parks or woods, and the demesne land usually lay intermingled with that of the peasants. Field nomenclature was often complex and confusing. In 13th-century Hemsby in north-east Norfolk, for example, surveys make no mention of 'fields' as such, but instead record the location of strips in terms of no less than 100 divisions, of which the largest covered less than 12ha.[16] Here, again, holdings were usually clustered, rather than being evenly and widely spread. Only on the lighter soils of Breckland, in places in north-west Norfolk and sporadically on the patches of very heavy land on the edge of the Norfolk fens were they usually more evenly scattered across the vill, although seldom with the kind of regularity seen in the Midlands.

The ways in which East Anglian open fields were organised also differed markedly from Midland practice. In the south of the region some form of communal rotation, involving a fallow every third year, was generally imposed on the open arable, and sometimes on the enclosed ground, too; but cropping was generally flexible and fallowing was often by discontinuous furlongs, rather than by single continuous blocks or 'fields'. Similar practices were followed further north on the claylands, in south and central Norfolk and north Suffolk, but on the more fertile loams, especially in east Norfolk, virtually no communal controls were maintained. Cultivators planted what and when they wanted, and even fallowing was a matter for informal agreement between neighbours – when it happened at all, for by the 13th century the adoption of a number of innovations, including the widespread cultivation of legumes, had often removed the need for year-long fallows altogether.[17]

Only on the light lands of western East Anglia, and to a lesser extent in the Suffolk Sandlings, could more tightly organised field systems be found. Nutrients were rapidly leached from these porous soils and fertility could only be maintained by grazing flocks of sheep on the heaths or harvest residues by day and closely folding them on the arable by night, when it lay fallow, or before the spring sowing, where they dunged or 'tathed' it. Such 'sheep-corn' systems could be found in most areas of England characterised by light, poor soil, but in East Anglia they often took a distinct form. Many communities in these poor districts were – rather unusually for northern East Anglia – firmly under the control of manorial lords, who took pains to ensure that their land received more than its fair share of the available manure through the institution of the 'fold course'. The manure was a manorial monopoly: the tenants might benefit from the dung dropped as the sheep roamed over the fallows, but they could only enjoy the intensive night-folding in return for a cash payment.[18] The sheep were organised into flocks dominated by the lord's stock and under the care of his shepherd. Because there were usually several manors in a vill, however, each had its defined 'fold course' which included both heath and arable. Often there were only two or three, but sometimes many more: Elveden in Suffolk had 11, Weeting in Norfolk 12.[19] There are signs that fold courses became more rigid and formalised in late medieval times, and that in the 12th and 13th centuries some peasants may have had the right to erect folds, but even then the system had been dominated by manorial lords.[20]

Some medieval fields – those enclosed by hedges, especially on the clays of south Suffolk, Essex and east Hertfordshire – still survive in the landscape, although most have been altered or destroyed over the centuries or amalgamated with their neighbours en masse to form the vast open prairies beloved of modern agriculture. Such areas of ancient enclosures exhibit a variety of forms. In some places they display the kind of co-axial layouts discussed in the previous chapter, but usually they form a more irregular mesh. The region's open fields, in contrast, have left less obvious traces. The earthworks of ridge and furrow – the ridged strips, preserved under grass, which were widespread in the Midland shires until recent agricultural intensification – are rare in East Anglia, largely restricted to some of the Fen islands and to a narrow strip of heavy land in west Norfolk, on the edge of the Fens (Fig. 3.7). Whether East Anglian open fields were seldom ridged, even on the heavier clays, or whether these familiar earthworks have been erased by the intensity of later arable land use remains uncertain.[21] Strip lynchets – the broad terraces formed by ploughing open strips along the contours of steep slopes – are also rare, not surprisingly given the comparatively muted terrain, although some examples exist on the chalk escarpment of the East Anglian Heights and in some of the valleys in north-west Essex, as at Coploe Hill in Ickleton or at Manuden (Fig. 3.8). But if open arable has left few direct signs, many indirect ones remain, in the character of the modern field pattern. It is these which reveal, more clearly than anything, the great extent of open fields in early medieval East Anglia.

Fig. 3.7 Stradsett, Norfolk. Ridge and furrow is rare in East Anglia but some can be found, especially on the heavy soils on the edge of the fens, around Downham Market in Norfolk.

Fig. 3.8 Medieval strip lynchets on Coploe Hill, Ickleton, Cambridgeshire.

THE PROGRESS OF ENCLOSURE

To explain why, and how, we need to move ahead in time, and examine the ways in which open fields and commons came to be removed in the course of the post-medieval period. Enclosure – the replacement of intermixed properties and shared use-rights by physically bounded parcels of consolidated land, owned and managed individually – took place in a bewildering variety of ways, but a broad distinction can be made between *piecemeal* and *general* enclosure.[22] The former involved a series of private agreements – sales and exchanges – which led to the amalgamation, and subsequent hedging, of groups of contiguous open-field strips. The latter, in contrast, involved the community of proprietors acting together to re-allot rights and properties and reorganise the landscape at a stroke. In many East Anglian parishes, general enclosure served to complete a process that had begun in piecemeal form, removing areas of common grazing land that had remained open as the fields around them came to be enclosed – for piecemeal enclosure could not easily deal with areas of shared use-rights, as opposed to intermixed properties. It is often assumed that piecemeal enclosure is earlier than general enclosure – that the one replaced the other. But this is only true in the very broadest sense. Although most piecemeal enclosure did indeed occur in the 15th, 16th and 17th centuries, and most general enclosures took place after this, open fields continued to be enclosed by the former method throughout the 18th and, indeed, into the 19th centuries, often as large estates steadily bought out other landowners in a parish.[23]

General enclosure took a variety of forms. Firstly, where a single individual came to own all the land in a township the common rights were effectively terminated and

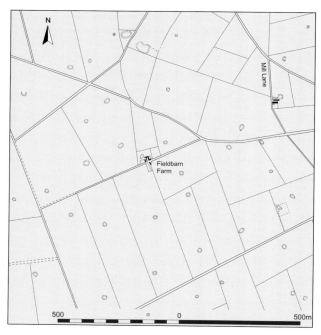

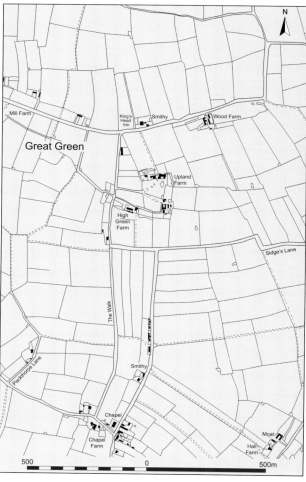

ABOVE: *Fig. 3.9 Highly rectilinear field pattern* created by 18th-century enclosure of open fields and heaths around Great Bircham in west Norfolk, as shown on the First Edition Ordnance Survey map of 1888.

RIGHT: *Fig. 3.10 The sinuous field boundaries characteristic of early piecemeal enclosure*: Denton in south Norfolk, as shown on the First Edition Ordnance Survey map of 1883.

BELOW: *Fig. 3.11 Irregular field pattern* created by direct enclosure from woodland and waste near Sible Hedingham, Essex, in 1881.

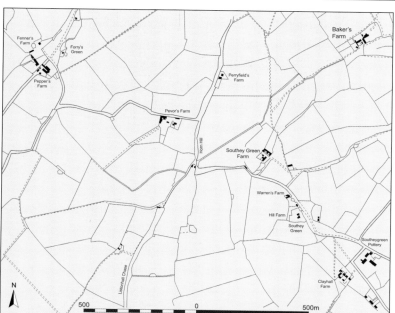

the landscape could be hedged or otherwise rearranged at will. In East Anglia, enclosures of this kind were rare, and generally associated with the contraction or desertion of small settlements in the 15th and 16th centuries. Secondly, there were various forms of enclosure by 'formal agreement', whereby the majority of proprietors agreed to enclose, carried out the appropriate surveys, re-allotted intermixed arable land and divided the commons in proportion to the rights formerly exercised over them.[24] Enclosures of this type occurred mainly in the 16th and 17th centuries, but continued in some places into the 18th century. Lastly, we have Parliamentary enclosure, where landowners petitioned for a Parliamentary act, which was followed by a comprehensive survey of the existing pattern of rights and ownership, and by an award which reorganised the landscape. Here, enclosure required not the agreement of the majority of landowners, but only of those holding a majority of the land – generally three-quarters by value.[25] Parliamentary enclosure was mainly a feature of the post-1750 period, peaking in two great waves – in the 1760s and 1770s, and again during the Napoleonic Wars.[26] It was the latter phase which had the greatest impact upon East Anglia.

The two broad types of enclosure produced rather different kinds of field pattern. General enclosure, and especially Parliamentary enclosure, usually created networks of rectilinear fields largely unrelated to the previous landscape (Fig. 3.9). Piecemeal enclosure, in contrast – because it involved the gradual establishment of hedges along the margins of contiguous groups of strips – tended to preserve older boundary patterns in simplified form. Open-field strips were usually slightly sinuous in plan, having been subtly distorted over the years. Many took the form of a shallow 'reversed S', caused by the way that the ploughman moved to the left as he approached the end of the strip, in order to avoid too tight a turning circle.[27] Others were gently curving, adapted over the long years to the lie of the land. Such shapes were fossilised by piecemeal enclosure. But a more important, more neglected and more subtle sign of this kind of enclosure is the alignment of boundaries. Because strips running end to end seldom came to be enclosed in line by this method, small 'kinks' or dog-legs were produced, where the boundary of one field will run, not to the corner of the next, but to a point some way along the boundary line, a strip or two's distance away (Fig. 3.10).[28] The sinuous parallelism displayed by such field patterns is different, however, from the more irregular arrangements created by direct enclosure from woodland and waste (Fig. 3.11).

We can use these different kinds of field pattern to obtain an approximate idea of the extent of land in the region which, in the Middle Ages, comprised open fields or common land, as opposed to that held as enclosed fields in individual occupancy (Fig. 3.12). I emphasise *approximate*: fieldscapes often have complex histories so that, for example, an area enclosed directly from the waste in medieval times might be comprehensively reorganised by a large landowner in the 18th or 19th centuries in such a way that it now looks like an area enclosed by Parliamentary act. Nevertheless, the whirling, complex constellations of colour in Fig. 3.12 reveal, in particular, the considerable extent of piecemeal enclosure in the region, showing that open fields once dominated the landscape almost everywhere except in the far south-west. Documentary sources – charters, manorial surveys and extents, and court rolls – suggest this. But as so often, it is the landscape itself that is our clearest evidence.

Fig. 3.12 The varying importance within East Anglia of the three main forms of enclosure, as reflected in the modern landscape. Blue represents areas dominated by rectilinear field patterns, indicative of planned general enclosure, mostly by parliamentary act in the 18th and 19th centuries. Red represents areas mainly characterised by early piecemeal enclosure. The white areas are dominated by irregular field patterns, apparently resulting from direct enclosure from the 'waste'. Mapped by kilometre square: where none of these patterns is clearly dominant, this is indicated by the appropriate mixture of colours (eg, purple represents areas in which both piecemeal enclosure, and planned enclosure, are prominent). Yellow represents areas still devoid of field boundaries, mainly heaths and areas of coastal sand.

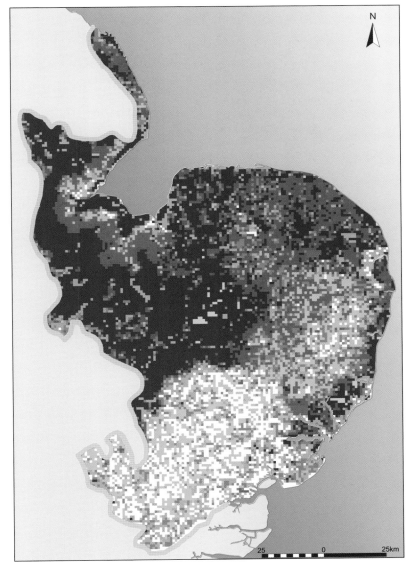

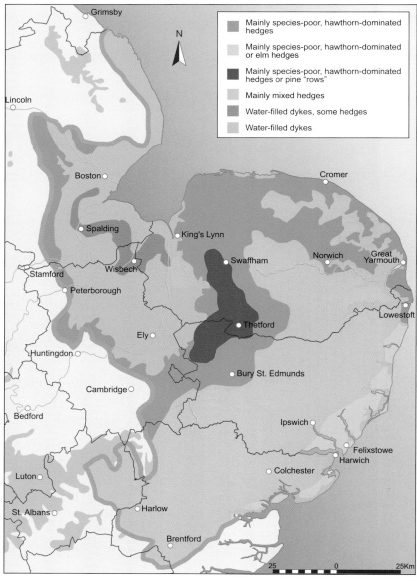

Mainly species-poor, hawthorn-dominated hedges

Mainly species-poor, hawthorn-dominated or elm hedges

Mainly species-poor, hawthorn-dominated hedges or pine "rows"

Mainly mixed hedges

Water-filled dykes, some hedges

Water-filled dykes

THE EARLY MODERN LANDSCAPE

Enclosure was a long and complex process, intimately related to a succession of agrarian changes which began in late medieval times. In the wake of the Black Death there were fewer people, and so average living standards tended to rise. Farms became larger and began to specialise in the production of particular commodities. But these developments were not simply a consequence of demographic factors, for they continued even as population growth resumed in the 16th century. They were part of a wider process, the development of a more complex, market-based economy. By the 16th century this had led to the emergence across England of a pattern of specialised farming regions.

In areas of light soils, the existing 'sheep-corn' farming systems generally persisted. Farmers continued to specialise in grain production, although sheep also increased in importance and manorial lords often exploited their fold course rights to maximise the income from commercial flocks. They thus resisted attempts by farmers to enclose their land piecemeal, because this interfered with the movement of the sheep and reduced the amount of feed available to them. In addition, because in many of these districts field systems were – by East Anglian standards – rather rigidly organised, and the holdings often extensively intermingled, they were anyway difficult to enclose by piecemeal methods. With some notable exceptions, poor light land remained open or 'champion' countryside until at least the 17th century, and enclosure when it came was mainly by general, rather than piecemeal, methods. Most such areas today carry landscapes of rectilinear fields defined by slight hawthorn hedges (Figs 3.13 and 3.14).

Where soils were heavier or more fertile, the story was different. Here field systems were generally of an 'irregular' character and were thus particularly susceptible to piecemeal enclosure – each portion of the arable usually contained the strips of only a few proprietors. Few private deals were required to consolidate holdings, and nobody objected much anyway to the resultant loss of fallow grazing because extensive common pastures also usually existed. By c. 1700 most open fields had disappeared from the claylands, leaving only areas of common grazing to be removed by later, usually Parliamentary, enclosure (Fig. 3.15).[29] As a result, these districts are today characterised by hedges containing a number of shrub species – either because they were planted mixed or because they have been around for so long that they have become colonised by a range of additional plants. In part, the removal of open fields was associated with changes in farming practice. Whereas farmers on the poor light lands continued to make their money from grain crops (especially barley), those on the clays in particular came to specialise in dairying and bullock fattening, and much of the land here was laid to permanent pasture.[30]

Not everywhere fits neatly into this heavy land/light land, woodland/'champion' dichotomy, and there were exceptions to this general pattern. In particular, the Suffolk Sandlings is an area of very poor light soil – sheep-and-corn country – but it experienced much early piecemeal enclosure and has a mixed and complex field pattern. The presence of extensive coastal marshes, and the proximity of heavy clay land to the west, seem to have ensured the development of poorly regulated field systems in medieval times, and the emergence of a mixed economy, with much reliance on dairying and cattle-fattening, in the early modern period. Moreover, in some areas of particularly fertile soil – most notably

OPPOSITE PAGE:

TOP: *Fig. 3.13 'Planned countryside':* *the landscape of straight, flimsy hawthorn hedges created by Parliamentary enclosure on the chalklands of south Cambridgeshire.*

BOTTOM: *Fig. 3.14 The distribution of different kinds of field boundary in East Anglia. Species-poor hedges of hawthorn tend to be characteristic of the late-enclosed areas of East Anglia, while areas of early enclosure have more mixed hedges. The elm hedges of the Suffolk coast, and the pine 'rows' of Breckland, are local specialities reflecting the particularly poor soils of these districts.*

Fig. 3.15 A well-preserved tract of clayland countryside in south Norfolk, near Billingford, with irregularly shaped fields, scattered farms and small woods.

in north-east Norfolk – open fields survived into the 19th century because a plethora of small owners could not agree to enclosure and – such was the money to be made from growing grain on this rich land, largely free from fold courses and communal restrictions on farming – had little incentive to do so. Overall, however, the generalisation contains much truth. The contrast between the landscapes of the poor, light 'fielden' or 'champion' lands, with extensive open fields and heaths, and the more enclosed and bosky 'woodland' countryside of the claylands, with more grass, trees and cattle, was very evident to 16th- and 17th-century writers. It is, moreover, a distinction that has left its mark in other ways.

Specialised arable farming tended to accentuate the existing hierarchical character of the poor, light lands. Small owner-occupiers found it hard to make a living and, already strongly manorialised in medieval times, these areas witnessed the steady development of large estates in the post-medieval period. On the clays, in contrast, more property remained in the hands of small proprietors and minor gentry. This was fertile and therefore expensive land, difficult to acquire in extensive, continuous blocks. Moreover, cattle farming tended to concentrate wealth at a lower level than arable farming: it favoured the medium-sized yeoman farmer rather than the large capitalist producer.[31] Even in the 19th century there were still many farms – tenanted or freehold – of less than 20ha.[32] More and more land in these areas fell into the hands of large landowners in the course of the 17th, 18th and 19th centuries, but generally in the form of splintered rather than continuous estates, interspersed with smaller properties. The clays have, on the whole, more early houses – 'vernacular' buildings – than the poorer, lighter lands. The latter, in contrast, have a higher density of large country houses, surrounded by extensive gardens and parks. Light, acid soils made for aristocratic landscapes: the clays, together with the fertile loams in areas like north-east Norfolk, were more 'peasanty' in character.

It was, most famously, in the post-medieval period that the Fens were drained: not the northern and eastern siltlands which, as we have seen, were settled from early medieval times, but the great tracts of peat lying inland from them. Save for a few limited schemes of reclamation around their margins, these remained as an extensive area of damp common, grazed and cut for peat, reeds and rough hay, until the 17th century. Then, in the 1630s and 1640s, the Dutch engineer Cornelius Vermyden, employed by a consortium headed by the Earl of Bedford, created new watercourses, which served to drain the southern Fens – or the Bedford Level, as it came to be known. Similar schemes were mounted in the Lincolnshire Fens. But this period did not see the creation of the kind of intensive arable landscape that we see here today, with ploughland spreading uninterrupted to the horizon. That came later. The improvers faced continuing problems, for as the peat became drier it tended to waste and contract, falling below the level of the surrounding watercourses and thus becoming waterlogged again. The adoption of drainage windmills remedied this problem to some extent, but it was only in the 19th century that the introduction of steam pumps allowed large-scale arable land use. In the 17th and 18th centuries, as in earlier times, the Fens remained an area that provided fodder, thatching materials and grazing.[33]

THE INDUSTRIAL LANDSCAPE

The 15th, 16th and 17th centuries thus saw the development of a more complex, and more regionally specialised, agrarian economy in East Anglia. However, these centuries also witnessed the emergence of large-scale industry. During the late medieval period major textile industries developed in the West Country and in East Anglia. Woollen cloth, for example, was being produced on a large scale in south Suffolk and north Essex as early as the 13th century, but the industry expanded massively in the course of the later 14th and 15th centuries.[34]

The Stour valley, and especially the towns and villages lying between Clare and East Bergholt, was the principal manufacturing district, but the trade and its various branches – combing, spinning, dying, bleaching, weaving and fulling – was more widely spread across south-western and central Suffolk, and in a broad band down the centre of Essex. Ipswich, Bury St Edmunds and Colchester were also major centres.[35] In the 15th century cloth production also developed in eastern Norfolk, especially in Norwich and the areas around Aylsham and North Walsham. The village of Worstead gave its name to a particular kind of cloth made of high quality yarn spun 'in its oile' from the wool of sheep grazed on the marshes of west Norfolk and the Broads.[36] This was essentially a cottage industry. Clothiers or 'clothmakers' – capitalist organisers – 'put out' the work to a wide range of specialist home workers scattered across the surrounding countryside.

It was not only woollen cloth that was produced. Linen, spun from local hemp, was also manufactured on a large scale. This activity was concentrated in the Waveney valley, but, once again, was thinly spread over a wider area of east Suffolk and east Norfolk. The hemp was grown in small plots, heavily manured, close to farms: such 'hemplands' often feature on early maps. The crop was rotted, or 'retted', in ponds to free the fibre prior to spinning, and many of the small ponds still to be found around settlements in the area were originally used in this way.[37]

Strange as it may seem to modern readers, in the late medieval and early modern periods East Anglia – most of it, at any rate – was thus reckoned an industrial region. Indeed, as late as 1724 Daniel Defoe was able to describe how 'Essex, Suffolk and Norfolk are taken up in manufactures, and famed for industry'.[38] But all this activity has left little obvious trace in the landscape, in the form of specialised buildings or structures, with the exception of a few enclosed industrial courts which survive, in much altered form, in towns such as Long Melford in Suffolk (and fragmentary remains of workshops in what are otherwise domestic buildings). Instead, the wealth generated by textile manufacture, and by its knock-on effects upon the wider economy, is more broadly manifested in the built environment, especially in the Stour valley and surrounding areas, where vast numbers of late medieval and 16th-century houses remain, and where numerous parish churches were flamboyantly rebuilt in the 14th and 15th centuries (Fig. 3.16). In the Norfolk textile areas the legacy of

Fig. 3.16 The picturesque village of Kersey in south Suffolk: the large number of medieval buildings reflects the wealth generated by the textile industry.

Fig. 3.17 The great church at Worstead in north-east Norfolk, like many in East Anglia, was built with wealth derived from textile manufacture.

medieval vernacular buildings is less, but here, too, magnificent late medieval churches litter the landscape, like that at Worstead itself (Fig. 3.17).

The reasons for East Anglia's precocious industrial development are complex. Early industry tended to flourish where population was dense and lordship weak, circumstances that clearly applied to the relevant parts of East Anglia, the 'peasanty' landscapes of the heavy clays and fertile loams already discussed. But the production of woollen cloth required substantial amounts of wool, much of it from sheep grazed on heaths and pastures, rather than solely on the fallows.[39] The textile areas themselves were not, for the most part, districts of sheep husbandry, but they lay close to them. The worstead producers of east Norfolk, as already noted, relied on wool from Marshland and the Broads, while the Suffolk and Essex manufacturers used wool from the Sandlings flocks, and from sheep grazed on the heaths of east Essex. As John Norden observed of Essex in 1594, 'Ther are no great flockes of sheepe in this shire. Yet are ther sundrie places that yealde verie fine woull, but not in the depe countries: the most barren and heathye groundes yelde best woull, and especiallie Kingeswood heath, Lexden heath, Misley heath, about Ardeley, Alresforde, Thurrington, Empsted and Typtree heath'.[40] The juxtaposition of poorly manorialised and populous districts with more thinly populated heaths and marshes specialising in sheep production was a potent combination.

Geography encouraged industrial development in another way. In the 13th century Flanders was the principal cloth-producing area in Europe. But the lower production, transport and trading costs in England, together with freedom from warfare, gave her producers the edge, and by the 1480s English cloth was pouring into the Low Countries. It was purchased, undyed, by Netherland merchants, finished, and then exported throughout the world. East Anglia's proximity to the main European markets was thus an important factor in stimulating industry.[41] However, contacts with the Low Countries took another significant form. From the reign of Edward III, but especially in the later 16th century, successive waves of immigrant textile workers settled in the eastern counties, especially in and around Colchester and Norwich. Many came as religious refugees, and in *c.* 1600 it is possible that as many as one-third of the population of Norwich spoke Dutch or Walloon as their first language. The 'strangers' made a series of innovations that kept the east Norfolk worsted industry at the cutting edge of fashion, producing versions of such continental cloths as fustians, filoselle, Calamanco and damasks, as well as russels (similar to satin) and giving rise to the Norwich 'Stuffs' industry. Never, perhaps, have its close contacts with the continent had such an impact on East Anglia's society and economy as in the late 16th century.

THE AGRICULTURAL REVOLUTION

The rural textile industry declined during the later 18th century and only continued on a large scale in Norwich and its immediate hinterland. The industry could not compete with northern and western Britain, where fast-flowing watercourses, and later an abundance of coal, allowed the development of large-scale factory production. The low gradient of East Anglia's rivers precluded the easy construction of mills with powerful over-shot wheels. In an age of Industrial Revolution, East Anglia de-industrialised. However, the region, and Norfolk especially, was at the leading edge of that other familiar 'revolution' of history text-books – the revolution in agriculture.

The conventional story will be familiar to many readers. In the period after *c.* 1720, but especially after 1760 when – after nearly a century of sluggish demographic growth and low grain prices – the population began to increase rapidly once again, the large landowners and enterprising farmers of Norfolk and neighbouring counties transformed the character of England's agriculture. They increased the production of cereal crops both by extending the arable hectarage – by reclaiming heaths and other 'waste' – and by raising yields, that is, by increasing the amount of grain produced from each cultivated hectare. They achieved all this by using new rotations, imported from the Low Countries, which featured turnips and various 'artificial' grasses such as clover, sainfoin and nonsuch. The most famous of these, the 'Norfolk Four Course', was a four-year cycle of wheat, turnips, barley and clover. Instead of having permanent (and usually poor quality) grazing and areas of permanent arable that were fallowed every third year, all land could now be under regular cultivation. At any one time, half was used to grow nutritious fodder crops that could be fed to sheep in the field or pulled and given to cattle, stalled over the winter in large, modern farmyards (Fig. 3.18). The numbers, and the quality, of livestock were thus improved. More importantly, however, as more manure was now being produced, cereal yields were increased.

There were other changes, too. Open fields were enclosed, farms grew larger and more efficient, and large-scale marling was carried out – pits were sunk through the acidic topsoil, down to the fractured chalk below, which was then spread on the surface to reduce acidity.[42] In the Victorian 'high farming' period after *c.* 1840, these trends were taken further. More sophisticated farmsteads were erected and livestock numbers further increased through the use of imported cattle cake. Even greater volumes of manure meant that crop yields were further increased, and they were boosted even more after *c.* 1850 by the widespread use of artificial fertilisers. Some of the latter were manufactured from

Fig. 3.18 The Great Barn in Holkham Park, Norfolk. Designed by the architect Samuel Wyatt and built in 1792–4, this impressive building served as the venue for the 'sheep shearings' – shows where the latest ideas in agricultural improvement were displayed – which were organised by the landowner, the prominent agriculturalist Thomas William Coke.

Fig. 3.19 Abandoned 19th-century coprolite pits at *Sow-cum-Quy, Cambridgeshire.*

coprolites, phosphatic nodules occurring at the junction of the Gault Clay and the chalk, which were excavated on a large scale in south Cambridgeshire (Fig. 3.19).

There are a number of problems with this familiar account. Recent research suggests that the expansion of the cultivated area in East Anglia – the growth of permanent arable at the expense of pastures, commons and heaths – was on such a scale that the increases in animal numbers, and in manure inputs, resulting from the new rotations probably did no more than keep pace with it.[43] Increases in yields in most of the key 'improving' districts, moreover, do not seem to have been as great as contemporaries asserted, and they may have owed more to other improvements made to the soil, especially through marling. Farms certainly increased in size, but there is little evidence that this made them any more productive; and much of the land reclaimed in this period was of such poor quality that it was abandoned again in the course of the 19th century. Above all, the 'conventional' account really only applies to areas of light soil, to the sheep-corn areas, especially north-west Norfolk and Breckland, with their large estates and big tenant farms. It was only here that extensive tracts of open heathland awaited reclamation, that open fields still survived unenclosed, and that large areas of light, acid soils existed which could be improved by marling and by greatly increasing applications of manure. And these always remained areas of, at best, only moderate fertility. Even after 'improvement', they produced relatively modest yields.

The transformation of the landscape in these districts was certainly considerable. Large areas of heathland and all the remaining open fields disappeared, to be replaced by the classic, straight-sided fields of 'planned' countryside (Fig. 3.20).

Fig. 3.20 Eighteenth- and 19th-century fields and marl pits *in north-west Norfolk.*

However, in agrarian terms the most important changes were taking place elsewhere, on the more productive soils of East Anglia. On the claylands, the area under grass declined rapidly after *c.* 1770, as private pastures were ploughed and commons were enclosed. Land was under-drained on a large scale, areas of woodland were grubbed out, hedgerow timber thinned and hedges removed or realigned on a surprising scale. By 1850 the claylands had ceased to be an area of pasture farming. They had become what they are today, an intensively arable region. And in the Fens, improvements to the arterial drainage system, made in the early 19th century, were followed from 1817 by the construction of powerful steam pumps. Here, too, the pastures fell to the plough, albeit at a slower rate. By 1840, more than half of this fertile land was under the plough; by 1880, more than three-quarters.

This was the real essence of the 'Agricultural Revolution' in East Anglia. It was a complex process of 'arabilisation' which affected the whole of the region, and of which the 'conventional', light land revolution formed only one aspect. The production of cereals had in part been held back by the need to maintain large areas of grazing, a consequence of the paucity of good hay meadows in the region. The widespread adoption of the new fodder crops changed all that. The transformation was, however, only one part of a wider national pattern, the nature and extent of which can be best appreciated by comparing the map of early-modern farming regions produced by the historian Joan Thirsk (Fig. 3.21) with the map of contemporary agriculture produced by James Caird to accompany his *English*

Fig. 3.21 The 'Agricultural Revolution' involved not only the introduction of new crops and farming techniques *but also a radical restructuring of England's agricultural geography. In the 16th and 17th centuries England had comprised a complex mosaic of agricultural regions, and much of East Anglia had wood-pasture, marsh or fen economies in which livestock farming was important (after Joan Thirsk).*

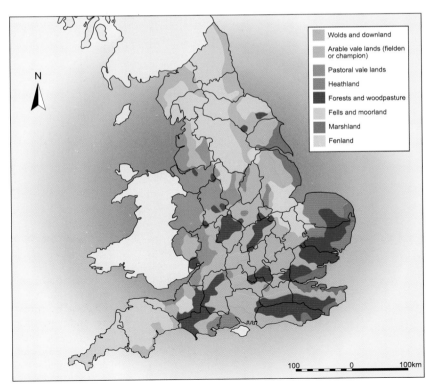

Wolds and downland

Arable vale lands (fielden or champion)

Pastoral vale lands

Heathland

Forests and woodpasture

Fells and moorland

Marshland

Fenland

100   0   100km

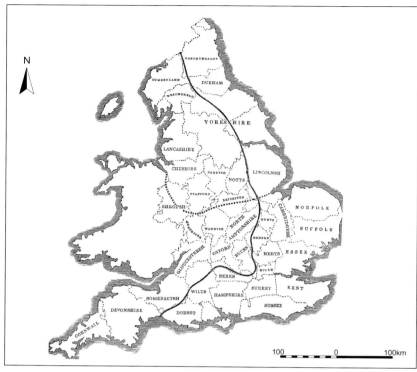

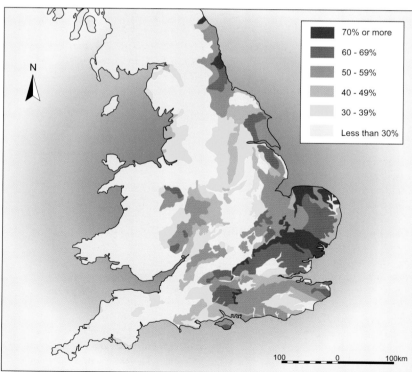

Agriculture of 1851 (Fig. 3.22), or with the patterns of land use revealed by the tithe files of *c.* 1836 (Fig. 3.23).[44] The old, complex pattern of early-modern farming regions, in which some mixed-farming areas could be found in the west of the country and some specialised pastoral areas in the east, was replaced by a much simpler arrangement. Grain production became concentrated in the areas best suited for it, the dry east of the country. It was this development, perhaps more than anything else, which provided the food required by the expanding cities of the Industrial Revolution. It was a development fuelled by improvements in transport infrastructure and by declining wage levels in the arable east, resulting from progressive de-industrialisation. And so it was that East Anglia became what it is today – the bread basket of England, a primarily arable country.

All that grain had to be processed. In popular images of East Anglia windmills feature prominently, towering above the level wheatfields. But such tall, imposing structures are a rather late addition to the landscape. In early medieval times, water mills had been the main method of processing grain – they were already widespread by the time of Domesday – and only from the late 12th century were these supplemented by low, simple forms of windmill called post mills, in which the body of the mill, including the stones, turned on a large post to face the wind (Fig. 3.24).[45] Expanding grain production in the course of the 18th and 19th centuries meant that larger mills, capable of driving two or more sets of stones as well as machinery for cleaning grain and dressing the flour, were required. Tower mills of brick and smock mills of timber framing – in which only the cap was turned to face the wind – were therefore used. These could be made taller and therefore generate more power than post mills.[46] During the late 18th century the fantail came into use, which turned the cap of the mill automatically into the wind, while successive improvements in sails culminated in 1807 with the invention of the 'patent sail' by the Norfolk engineer William Cubitt. In this structure shutters, rather like Venetian blinds,

replaced canvas. They were controlled – via a mechanism called a 'spider' located at the crossing of the sails, a rod passing through the middle of a hollow windshaft (or axle), and a rack and pinion at the rear of the mill – by a chain reaching down to ground level. By hanging weights on this, the miller could match the sails to the strength of the wind while they were in motion. In contrast, a mill with the old 'common' sails, consisting of sheets of canvas, had to be stopped to achieve this.[47]

This was the great age of mill technology in the east. In the period of the 'Industrial Revolution', it was wind power that here stood at the cutting edge of technology. Some of the new mills were huge, such as that at Sutton in Norfolk, *c.* 24m high; or Moulton in Linconshire, *c.* 28m in height and now, restored to its former glory, the tallest mill in Britain (Southdown Mill in Yarmouth, built in 1812 but demolished in 1905, was even taller: at *c.* 31m in height, it was probably the tallest in Europe). Most mills had four sails, but some in the Lincolnshire Fens had more. Those at Alford, Burgh-le-Street and Boston had five, Sibsey Trader still has six and Heckington has no less than eight. This is one of several subtle variations in mill design, which arose from the particular traditions of local millwrights. Most mills in central and eastern Norfolk and north Suffolk have caps like inverted boats, a style probably developed by the Norfolk firm of England's (Fig. 3.25). However, onion-shaped caps predominate in Lincolnshire and Cambridgeshire, and across much of west Norfolk, while in Essex simple caps with curved gables, almost like miniature post mills, are common.

While windmills are particularly characteristic of East Anglia, water mills continued to be employed; these, too, evolved dramatically in the 18th and 19th centuries. Indeed, few earlier examples survive in the region. Wheels became larger and breast-shot wheels, which turned as water filled long 'buckets', often replaced simple undershots, turned by the force of the current hitting the base of the wheel

Fig. 3.24 The earliest windmills were post mills, in which the entire body of the mill could be turned into the wind. Saxstead Green Mill, Suffolk, was built in the late 18th century.

OPPOSITE PAGE:

TOP: *Fig. 3.22 By 1851, when James Caird came to characterise English farming, he presented a rather different pattern. The areas south and east of the dark line – including East Anglia and the Fens – were primarily arable areas, while those to the north and west specialised in livestock husbandry.*

BOTTOM: *Fig. 3.23 Caird's map over-simplified the pattern of 19th-century farming to some extent, but the evidence of the tithe files, compiled in 1836, clearly indicates the extent of arable farming in the east. This map shows the percentage of the land area devoted to arable husbandry.*

ABOVE: *Fig. 3.25 The six-sailed Sibsey Trader windmill near Boston in Lincolnshire*, *built in 1877 and still working today. The late 18th and 19th centuries saw the widespread replacement of post mills by tower mills, and the development of ever larger and more complex forms.*

RIGHT: *Fig. 3.26 As grain production expanded, water-mills also grew larger and more sophisticated: Pakenham Mill, Suffolk, is typical of the kind of large water-mill complex constructed in the region in the late 18th and 19th centuries.*

(as already noted, overshot wheels, powered from above, were always rare because of the gentle gradient of local rivers). These changes necessitated complex schemes of engineering in order to form larger mill ponds. The result was that typical East Anglian sight: a large, weatherboarded mill, often with a projecting 'lucam' or external covered hoist platform, reflected in a large, placid mill pool (Fig. 3.26).

Not all the grain produced in the region was milled, for flour or feed. The good quality barley, grown on the lighter lands, was turned into malt. Before the 18th century there were numerous small malthouses, but rising demand and improvements in transport allowed the development of larger units of production. Many were located beside waterways or on roads providing good access to London breweries. Defoe described in 1720 how the barley from the Cambridgeshire chalklands was 'generally sold to Ware and Royston, and other great malting towns in Hertfordshire, and is the fund from which that vast quantity of malt, called Hertfordshire malt, is made, which is esteemed the best in England'.[48] Remarkable concentrations of maltings – mainly more recent than Defoe's time – can still be seen in Ware (Fig. 3.27) and good examples of 19th-century buildings can be seen in Stowmarket (of flint and local brick with steeply pitched roof), at the head of the Gipping navigation; at Long Melford, some 5km from the Stour navigation; and at Mistley and Snape on the coast – the latter now a concert hall and venue for the Aldburgh Festival. In the late 19th century some really vast complexes, such as the one recently demolished at Beccles in north Suffolk, developed beside railway lines.

The quickening pace of commerce and expanding agricultural production from the late 17th century encouraged major investment in transport infrastructure. Roads were improved, often through the establishment of turnpike trusts. Many of the milestones which the trustees were required by law to erect still stand, neglected and ignored, beside what are now busy arterial roads. Toll-houses can also be found in many places, and the large inns erected to serve travellers (Fig. 3.28).

And improvements were made to waterways. These had long been the most important form of transport and, for the topographical reasons already explained, East Anglia was well endowed with navigable rivers. The 18th century did not see the kind of frenetic canal building that occurred in the Midlands or the north of England, for the absence of heavy industry meant that capital was unavailable for this level of investment. Several rivers were improved, however, extending the reach of shipping deeper inland. The Waveney was thus made navigable between Beccles and Bungay in the late 17th century, the Stour as far as Sudbury in 1709. The Little Ouse was improved to Thetford in 1720, the Nar to Narborough in the 1750s and the Stort in Hertfordshire (after a fashion) in the 1760s, from its confluence with the Lea at Hoddesdon as far upstream as Bishops Stortford. Major improvements were made to the Blyth as far as Halesworth in 1761, to the Gipping to Stowmarket in 1793 and the Chelmer to Chelmsford in 1796. As well as the improvements made to the Waveney above Beccles, other changes were made to the Broadland river system – most notably the creation of the New Cut from Reedham to Haddiscoe in the 1830s (part of a more ambitious scheme to improve navigation to Norwich via Lowestoft), the improvement of the upper Bure in the 1770s and the construction of the North Walsham and Dilham Canal in the 1820s, which extended the navigable section of the Ant for some 8km to the north (Fig. 3.29).[49] Most of these projects involved relatively minor changes, such as cuts across meanders, together with the construction of some locks, especially where mills were bypassed – such as those famously painted by Constable beside Flatford Mill on the Stour navigation (Fig. 3.30). Constable's paintings are often

OPPOSITE PAGE:

TOP: *Fig. 3.28 The 17th-century Scole Inn*, *near the Norfolk/Suffolk county boundary, with its prominent 'Dutch' gables.*

BOTTOM: *Fig. 3.29 Stalham, on the Norfolk Broads, is a well-preserved example of an inland port, with a range of 18th- and 19th-century warehouses.*

Fig. 3.30 **Flatford Mill, *by John Constable (1816–17).*** *Today we read this painting as a lost rural idyll: in reality, the mill was a major piece of industrial plant and the Stour Navigation one of the principal economic arteries of East Anglia.*

viewed today as representations of a lost rural idyll, but many in fact portray a vibrant, intensely commercial world. East Anglia may have missed out on the Industrial Revolution, but it was not an economic backwater.

Railways arrived in the region in 1842 with the construction of the line from London to Cambridge. By the end of the 1850s almost all major towns were on rail lines which connected them, directly or indirectly, with London and the Midlands. Railways had a dramatic impact on the region, although in this relatively level terrain they were built without imposing viaducts or long tunnels and cuttings – except in the south of the region, where the great tunnel at Littlebury in Essex (constructed to hide the railway from Lord Braybrooke's mansion at Audley End) and the magnificent viaduct across the River Colne at Wakes Colne in the same county are notable examples of civil engineering.[50] But they changed the economy, and the landscape, in innumerable ways. They encouraged the more intensive production of livestock within what remained an essentially arable economy – that hallmark of Victorian 'high farming' – by allowing easy movement of fattened animals to market. And, because they permitted rapid transport of a bulky crop, they encouraged a massive expansion of potato cultivation in the Fens. They also led to the expansion of many of those towns and villages provided with stations and stimulated the holiday industry at various points along the coast, as well as on the Norfolk Broads. Above all, they brought about a decline in the use of many traditional building materials. Brick production became increasingly centralised and roofing slates (quite alien to the region) came into widespread use, especially in and around major towns.

RECESSION AND RECOVERY

In the course of the 18th and 19th centuries, East Anglia thus became the bread basket of England. Fens were drained, heaths reclaimed and cereal yields raised to unprecedented levels. But from the late 1870s farming began to slide into depression.[51] The principal cause was the expansion of the American railway network into the prairies of the Mid-West, which meant that Britain was flooded with cheap grain. Prices, rents and land values all fell through the 1880s. After a brief period of stabilisation, a further intense depression occurred in the 1890s, this time also affecting livestock producers, as cheap meat and dairy produce were imported on refrigerated ships from the New World and Australia. Agricultural fortunes revived for a short time during the First World War, but peace brought renewed slump, which continued, on and off, until the start of the Second World War in 1939.

The depression was especially profound in East Anglia for the simple reason that grain prices fell more steeply than those for meat and dairy produce. The area of arable contracted, reversing the trend of the previous century and a half, and in areas of poor light soil some land went out of cultivation altogether. Breckland was particularly badly hit. On the 2,025ha Downham Hall estate in Suffolk in 1923, for example, not a single farm was let and most of the land was derelict.[52] In the 1920s and 1930s large areas of land in Breckland and the Sandlings were purchased and planted by the Forestry Commission, established at the end of the First World War in an effort to maintain the nation's strategic timber supplies and revitalise the depressed economies of the more agriculturally marginal regions of Britain.[53]

Most land, of course, remained in cultivation, producing fodder crops and cereals. But there was some increase in the area under pasture, especially on heavier land, and some diversification. Because prices for fruit and vegetables remained buoyant there was a considerable expansion in market gardening and fruit-growing, especially in the northern Fens. There had been fen orchards earlier, but these 'characteristic' features of the landscape mainly date to the early 20th century. Sugar-beet was widely adopted as a crop from the 1920s, leading to the construction of vast processing plants at Ely, Cantley and Bury St Edmunds. The latter two are still in production and provide striking incidents in the rural landscape.

The long depression had many other effects. Combined with a wider raft of social and political changes, it led to the break-up and sale of many traditional landed estates and the demolition of large country houses, especially on the poorer land, and particularly in the years following the end of the First World War.[54] And in many parts of the region the rural population actually declined. Poverty was widespread: East Anglia became a byword for rural deprivation. Visually, the landscape changed as the neat, manicured and well-managed landscape of 'high farming' was replaced by something rougher and wilder. Hedges grew high and wide and the number of hedgerow trees increased as saplings were left to grow. However, this situation was rapidly reversed with the outbreak of the Second World War.

The war had a direct and immediate impact, for the region stood on the country's front line. Most of the coastal and land defences erected then have left little trace, although pillboxes remain a common sight, and concrete tank obstacles and bases for sprigot guns are still encountered. Such remains are clustered near the coast, but also form internal lines of defence, most notably the 'Eastern Command Line' and the 'GHQ Line', which run diagonally across Essex and Suffolk, and on into Norfolk and Cambridgeshire.[55] But it was East Anglia's role as England's airfield that has left the greatest mark. In 1934 there were only four active air bases in the region. By 1939, as a consequence of the 'expansion' initiative, there were 15, and five satellite landing grounds. By 1945 there were no less than 107, used by fighters and bombers of the RAF and the USAF. Hedges were bulldozed and woods felled on an awesome scale: even today the sites of former airfields announce their presence by a featureless emptiness of the landscape. A handful remain as airports, either military (Marham, Lakenheath, Coltishall, Mildenhall) or civilian (Norwich), but most survive as relict features. In some cases buildings and structures remain, although fewer with every passing year: officer's messes, aircrew quarters (mainly Nissen huts) and sometimes control towers, low two-storey features such as those at Langham or Lavenham. More striking are the water towers, very necessary in a flat countryside where most surrounding villages lacked piped water; and above all the hangers. These come in a variety of forms with arcane names, known only to enthusiasts: 'J' and 'K' type, with their curved, steel plate roofs (good examples at Waterbeach and Swanton Morley); the small 'Blister' hangers, with curved roofs sweeping to the ground, now very rare; the Bellman and various 'T' types, with gabled roofs, like those at Methwold or Newmarket Heath.[56] Even when all these have gone, the basic pattern of the runways often remains. The main runway usually ran in the direction of the prevailing wind, roughly south-west to north-east, and was generally around 2,000m long and 50m wide. Two subsidiary runways formed a triangular pattern and a perimeter track gave access to numerous 'dispersal pans', where the aircraft could be concealed from attack. At Hethel the runway pattern forms the basis for the test track of Lotus Cars, at Snetterton for a racing circuit (the 'T' type hangars still standing on the opposite side of the A11). Elsewhere the runways, once removed, made for such poor agricultural land that they were planted up as shelter belts, or provided firm concrete bases for chicken houses, their layout being strikingly 'ghosted' in this way at

Fig. 3.31 Industrial estate built on a Second World War airfield near Hadleigh in Suffolk.

Langham and Weston Longville in Norfolk. Some redundant airfields have provided suitable places for modern industrial estates (Fig. 3.31).

The war left its mark in innumerable other ways. Many country houses were occupied by the military and Nissen huts can still be found in their grounds (as at Thornham in Suffolk). Occupation often hastened the deterioration of mansions already in severe decline, and the end of the war saw another rash of demolitions. Most dramatically of all, three Breckland villages – West Tofts, Tottington and Stanford, together with the remaining farms in the long-depopulated parishes of Langford, Sturston and Buckenham Tofts – were incorporated into the Battle Training Area. The residents were promised that they could return at the end of the war, but the area is still occupied by the military today.

But above all, the war brought to an end the agricultural depression. The country was blockaded. Land had to be brought rapidly into a high state of cultivation and the cultivated hectarage expanded. And what began in the war continued in the peace. In a world dogged by rationing and food shortages, government policies subsidised production, and new forms of intervention came with Britain's entry into the European Economic Community in 1972. An onslaught on the environment was begun by farmers, now often owner-occupiers rather than the tenants of large estates, who were armed with all the new technologies that had developed during the previous 50 years – tractors, herbicides, JCBs.[57] The arable hectarage expanded dramatically, especially at the expense of heaths and coastal marshes. Ponds were filled in, trees felled and copses grubbed out. Hedges began to disappear at a rapid rate, for they were redundant in a landscape of arable monoculture and got in the way of combine harvesters and other large machinery. In national terms, Essex, Norfolk, Suffolk and Hertfordshire bore the brunt of these developments, for the simple reason that destruction was greatest in the most intensively arable areas. Indeed, by the 1960s many eastern districts had become *completely* arable, with tractors and artificial fertilisers ensuring that farms no longer needed to carry any livestock at all. Holdings also grew steadily in size, so that by the end of the century, on all but the most fertile soils, there were few covering less than 280ha and most were well in excess of 400ha. In landscape terms, all these appalling changes were compounded by the advent of Dutch elm disease in the 1960s, which had particularly severe consequences for the south and east of the region where elm had been particularly common as a hedgerow tree.

The loss of hedges was the greatest change. In Norfolk alone 13,000km – 46 per cent of the total – were destroyed between 1946 and 1970, and although government grants for removal were withdrawn in that year, and the rate slackened, it continued at a lower level into the 1980s. Comparable figures do not exist for Suffolk, east Hertfordshire and Essex, but the extent of destruction was even greater here. Indeed, in parts of Essex there are no longer any 'fields' as such, only vast empty spaces between the public roads, which may have gobbled up 50 or more of the enclosures shown on the First Edition OS 6-inch maps of the late 19th century (Fig. 3.32). The south of the region bore the brunt of 'prairification' because of its earlier enclosure history. As Baird and Tarrant perceptively noted of Norfolk in 1973: 'the greatest amount of field boundary changes ... occur in areas of earliest enclosure. Those parts ... which were affected most by Acts of Parliamentary enclosure in the late 18th and early 19th centuries seem to have undergone relatively few changes'. The large, straight-sided fields found in these districts were better suited to large agricultural machinery than the more intricate patterns created by piecemeal enclosure; while the most complex and irregular field patterns of all, those found in Essex and in parts of Hertfordshire, were particularly inappropriate to the new farming, and were thus removed wholesale. But in addition, the better survival of hedges on the late-enclosed, poorer and lighter lands of East Anglia may reflect the fact that such areas were still in many cases dominated by large landowners, who retained

hedges for sporting and aesthetic reasons in a way that, for example, corporate landowners such as financial institutions would not.

Over the last decade or so the tide of agricultural intensification has turned. The removal of hedges has largely come to an end and in many places they are being re-established, together with small woods and ponds. The explanations are complex. In large measure they are a consequence of changes in the character of government subsidies – now increasingly geared towards environmental conservation, through 'Countryside Stewardship', 'Enviromental Stewardship' and similar initiatives. In part they are the result of legislative changes, especially the passing of the Hedgerow Protection Act in 1997. But these developments are themselves political and institutional manifestations of a wider realisation, on the part of farmers and landowners as much as everyone else, that the need to produce ever-larger quantities of food is no longer the priority that it was in the post-war world of dearth, and that a landscape bereft of trees, hedges and wildlife is not in fact very nice to live in.

Such feelings have been given particular force, however, by radical post-war changes in rural residence patterns. Villages in East Anglia are no longer primarily homes for farmworkers and farmers. Technological changes, increases in farm size and a decline in livestock husbandry have ensured that country dwellers are mainly middle-class commuters, those in the south of the region especially using railways or the M11 (opened in 1982) to make the daily trek to London, others working in the country towns or in the larger cities of Norwich, King's Lynn, Cambridge, Ipswich or Colchester. Such people – quite understandably – want to preserve the rural tranquillity of the environment in which they have chosen to live. They are in many ways a force for good. But in the south of the region especially, the rural idyll they strive to protect is a sham. As house prices soar, the picturesque villages of thatched cottages in the midst of the prairies become middle-class ghettos and local people are obliged to find new homes elsewhere.

Fig. 3.32 The ultimate arable landscape: in some parts of East Anglia the second half of the 20th century saw the effective destruction of the countryside, and its replacement by featureless prairies more reminiscent of the American mid-west than of England.

The landscape thus continues, as it has always done, to be shaped in the first instance by economic and technological factors, mediated through and moulded by the essential frameworks of climate, soils and communication outlined in the first chapter. But the landscape itself, the patterns of fields and settlement inherited from earlier periods of time, could be as important in the development of social and economic forms as any contemporary circumstances. The open fields found in the clayland regions of East Anglia thus disappeared much earlier than those of the light lands not simply because changes in the agrarian economy demanded it, but because of their particular character, forged in the deep medieval past: 'irregular' field systems, as we have seen, were much more amenable to piecemeal enclosure than the more regulated systems found on lighter land. The reader will doubtless have noted other examples, in both this and the previous chapter, of how in East Anglia as elsewhere the landscape was an active, structuring force in human affairs rather than merely a passive reflection of human action.

NOTES

1 Roberts & Wrathmell 1998; Roberts & Wrathmell 2000a.
2 Wade-Martins 1980; Davison 1990; Martin 2001; Williamson 2003, 94–101.
3 Ibid, 101–9.
4 Wade 1980.
5 Roberts & Wrathmell 2000.
6 Homans 1969; Gray 1915.
7 Hodge et al. 1984, 155–8; 285–8, 293–6, 351–4.
8 Ibid, 117–19, 132–5, 209–12.
9 Hill 2000; Langdon 1986, 22–48.
10 Williamson 2003, 140–59.
11 Campbell 2000, 75–8; Williamson 2003, 168–73.
12 Roden 1973; Hunter 1999, 96–106, 115–17, 122–5.
13 Essex Record Office, Q/RD c26.
14 Essex Record Office, Vm 20, fol 18.
15 Newton 1960.
16 Campbell 1981, 16.
17 Campbell 1983.
18 Allison 1957; Postgate 1962, 10, 80–101.
19 Postgate 1973, 315.
20 Bailey 1989, 43–5.
21 Liddiard 1999.
22 Yelling 1977, 11–29.
23 Wade-Martins & Williamson 1999, 34–9.
24 Yelling 1977, 20–8.
25 Mingay 1997.
26 Turner 1980.
27 Eyre 1955.
28 Williamson 2000c.
29 Wade-Martins & Williamson 1999, 16–31.
30 Holderness 1985.
31 Thirsk 1987.
32 Wade-Martins & Williamson 1999, 80–1.
33 Darby 1983.
34 Kerridge 1985, 8–9.
35 Dymond 1999b.
36 Evans 1993.
37 Ibid; Evans.
38 Defoe 1724.
39 Kerridge, 1985, 8–9.
40 Ellis 1840, 9.
41 Kerridge 1985, 13.
42 Beckett 1990; Chambers & Mingay 1966; Ernle, Lord (R E Prothero) 1912; Riches 1937.
43 Wade-Martins & Williamson 1999.
44 Thirsk 1987; Caird 1852; Williamson 2002b, 158–63.
45 Hills 1994, 25–45.
46 Ibid, 50–79.
47 Ibid, 92–108.
48 Defoe 1724.
49 Boyes & Russell 1977; Joby 1993; Robertson 1999.
50 Gordon 1977.
51 Perry 1974, 21–33.
52 Skipper & Williamson 1997.
53 Ryle 1969.
54 Barnes 1984.
55 Kent 1999; Newsome 2003.
56 Bowyer 1979; Freeman 1999.
57 Mabey 1980; Shoard 1980; Baird & Tarrant 1973.

4

Village, Church and Farmstead

CHANGING SETTLEMENTS

The essential features of East Anglia's settlement pattern were established by the middle of the 13th century. However, the morphology and distribution of hamlets and villages have continued to develop up to the present. Moreover, in many ways settlement continued – as in early medieval times – to display unusual, idiosyncratic features. These need to be understood in their own terms, and not simply as manifestations of trends and developments experienced by other regions of England.

In Midland districts many villages disappeared altogether in the later medieval period. Already weakened by the effects of the Black Death, they fell victim to landowners keen to benefit from the opportunities presented by a buoyant livestock market at a time of falling demand for grain. Through the 15th and into the 16th century they turned heavy land over to grazing, or allowed their more ambitious tenants to do so.[1] Farms were amalgamated and many villages dwindled, sometimes withering away altogether. In East Anglia, however, clayland villages replaced by extensive pastures in this way are not common. Examples can certainly be found, as at Pudding Norton or Godwick in Norfolk, both located on particularly poorly draining plateaux (Fig. 4.1).[2] Even on the more rolling and benign clays of east Hertfordshire there are some probable examples, such as Berkesdon or Wakerley.[3] But for the most part the complex tenurial structure of the East Anglian clays – the multiple manors, the large numbers of freeholders – together with the ease with which its 'irregular' open fields could be enclosed and the existence of extensive commons, militated against drastic shrinkage. A less traumatic shift into a grazing economy occurred and in a form that was relatively benign and labour-intensive, capable of sustaining large numbers of small farms.

Fig. 4.1 The ruined church and settlement earthworks of Pudding Norton in Norfolk.

The East Anglian claylands became an area specialising in dairying and bullock-rearing, rather than in the kind of extensive grazing, on large ranches, that came to characterise some Midland districts.[4] Farms certainly disappeared in the course of the 15th and 16th centuries, and hamlets dwindled. But few communities disappeared completely.

Most examples of deserted villages in East Anglia are not in fact found on the heavy clays, but on light, poor land: in north-west Norfolk and, in particular, in Breckland. Well-known examples include Egmere, Waterden, Buckenham Tofts, West Tofts and Lynford. Most are in locations that were both agriculturally and spatially marginal – normally on high, dry interfluves, on plateaus of acid drift away from the more fertile and tractable soils of the principal valleys.[5] Most had developed as villages rather late in the Saxon period, and most had always been relatively small places, firmly under the control of a manorial lord or lords. In most cases decline was gradual and the consequence of a complex interaction of factors. The villages slowly haemorrhaged population as tenants migrated to take up farms in more appealing locations, vacated as a consequence of the late medieval demographic decline. However, organic contraction was usually accelerated by the actions of manorial lords striving to maximise their income from livestock, not by laying land to pasture, but by exploiting their fold course rights. Instead of using these in the traditional manner, to ensure that a disproportionate amount of manure came to the demesne arable, the institution was used as a way of monopolising the grazing afforded by the crop residues and fallow weeds of the open fields: tenants' sheep were now excluded from the flocks. At the same time, commons were frequently overstocked by manorial lords. Under such pressure many copyholders and freeholders left, to take up farms in more congenial places, and communities long dominated by manorial lords now

Fig. 4.2 Earthworks on the edge of Hockwold in Norfolk indicate that the village was once considerably larger than it is today.

fell completely under their control. Over time, copyholds were replaced by leases and farms were steadily amalgamated to produce larger units, ensuring that landlords had fewer expensive buildings to maintain. In smaller villages these processes might mean that only one or two large farms remained, each cultivating 200 or even 400ha, standing within the earthworks of a vanished community – as at Egmere in north Norfolk.

Complete desertions like this were unusual, however. Most communities affected by these kinds of processes diminished in size without disappearing completely. There are many places in western Norfolk – such as Hockwold or Rougham – where villages are flanked by areas of earthworks or scatters of debris and pottery in the ploughsoil, indicating that they were once twice their present size or more (Fig. 4.2). These shrunken settlements generally became what 19th-century commentators described as 'closed' or 'close' villages, in contrast to the larger 'open' villages which could be found nearby, normally on lower and more fertile ground.[6]

In closed parishes there was only one landowner, or a small number of landowners, who strove to control the size of a settlement because, under the terms of the Elizabethan Poor Law, each parish was responsible for supporting its own poor or indigent through a rate levied on the principal owners and their tenants. It therefore made sense to limit the size of the population in order to restrict the number who might come to claim relief, through ill health or ill fortune. Enough labourers to serve the regular needs of the estate farms and the great house would be housed. At busy times of the agricultural year, extra workers could be imported from neighbouring 'open' settlements.

In the latter there were usually several owners and, in consequence, it was less easy to control the size of the population. But in addition there was less incentive to do so, for owners were often petty rentiers, publicans or shopkeepers who stood to gain from a rising population. These settlements tended to maintain their size, or grow larger, in the course of the post-medieval period. They also usually developed a more diversified economic base than 'closed' settlements, with numerous shops and inns, and they often possessed Nonconformist chapels and meeting houses. In closed villages, the parish church was usually the only place of worship. Established landowners mistrusted religious Nonconformity in all its forms, but most especially – in the 19th century – the Primitive Methodists, commonly regarded as the Agricultural Workers Union at prayer. Of course, as a number of scholars have suggested, the reality was more complex than this bald model suggests. It was not simply patterns of ownership that determined the character of rural settlements, but also such things as whether the owner was resident in the parish. Simple statistics of ownership are, moreover, a poor guide to the degree of 'open' or 'closeness'.[7] Castle Acre, a sprawling village with an abundance of shops and chapels, was a notorious open settlement, in which numerous individuals owned property. But the wider parish itself was largely in the hands of, albeit forming a distant, outlying portion of, the great Holkham estate. Nevertheless, on the light lands of north-west Norfolk, Breckland and to some extent on the low escarpment of the East Anglian Heights, the distinction between 'close' and 'open' parishes remains a useful one in understanding the character of post-medieval villages.

Those landlord-dominated villages which lay inconveniently close to great mansions were sometimes dispensed with altogether as large parks and gardens were laid out around them. They were demolished, and a replacement usually provided in the form of a 'model' village, designed by an architect in an ordered or, from the 19th century, a 'Picturesque' form. The earliest example is Chippenham in south Cambridgeshire, probably the first model village in England, which was rebuilt at the park gates in the 1690s (Fig. 4.3). The latest

Fig. 4.3 Chippenham in Cambridgeshire was comprehensively rebuilt at the end of the 17th century when the existing village was cleared to make way for a park. Clustering deferentially at the park gates, it is probably the earliest 'model' estate village in England.

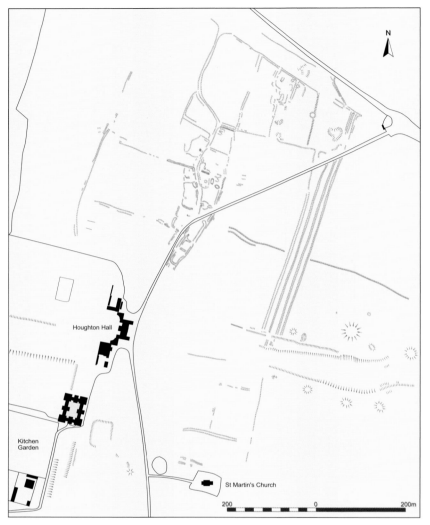

Houghton Hall

Kitchen
Garden

St Martin's Church

200   0   200m

Fig. 4.4 Earthworks in Houghton Park, west Norfolk. *The village, which lay near St Martin's church, was cleared away in the 1720s when the park was expanded, and its site systematically levelled. To the north of the Houghton Hall, however, extensive settlement remains indicate that the village had already experienced considerable contraction. The other earthworks shown represent relict field boundaries, and features associated with the making of the park itself – most notably a substantial cutting made through the low hill to the east of the hall, to improve the prospect.*

example is perhaps Anmer in west Norfolk, finally rebuilt on the margins of the park as late as 1810. Enforced movement usually came at the end of a long period of shrinkage and decline, the consequence of the by now familiar mix of voluntary out-migration, engrossment and the workings of the Poor Law.[8] The village of Houghton, for example, was cleared away in the 1720s when Sir Robert Walpole, first prime minister of England and flush with the spoils of office, expanded the existing park, which had probably been created in the 17th century. Maps show the village ranged along an east–west street immediately to the south of the park, but archaeological survey shows that this was merely the rump of a once much more substantial village, originally 'T' shaped, which extended northwards for more than a kilometre: this area of settlement seems to have declined gradually, in the course of the 15th and 16th centuries (Fig. 4.4).[9]

A visitor in 1731 described how 'Sir Robert has removed about 20 houses of the Village to a considerable distance and he proposes to remove the rest. The new Building they call Newtown'.[10] The new settlement comprised a single north–south street flanked by neat pairs of white, semi-detached cottages. Two substantial farms stood nearby. All were constructed in a simple, stripped-down Palladian style, for the settlement was originally hidden away on a cul de sac some way from the park's entrance and screened by its perimeter belt. It now stands at the gates of the park, on a through road, but this is a consequence of 19th-century changes, of a desire to express a fashionable paternalism in visible form – 'the rich man at his castle, the poor man at his gate' (Fig. 4.5). Similar sentiments, and a taste for the Picturesque, could lead to the use of much more ornamental styles in the design of 19th-century estate housing, most strikingly at Somerleyton in north-east Suffolk (Fig. 4.6). Here, in the 1850s, Sir Morton Peto transformed an existing settlement on the edge of the park in a flamboyant rustic style, to designs by the architect John Thomas. The cottages, complete with thatch and fake half-timbering, are clustered around a green. Older houses stand on another building line, a little way behind them, for the original common was enclosed in 1805 and Peto's village and green were created on the allotment received by his predecessor.[11]

Closed villages and model villages, shrunken villages and deserted villages, have been described at some length, but it is important to emphasise that, although dramatic incidents in the landscape, they are rare and largely restricted to the districts of poor light soil and large estates. However, the post-medieval period saw many other changes in the settlement patterns of East Anglia. Some were the consequence of enclosure in the 18th and 19th centuries. Where, mainly

on the light lands of north-west Norfolk and Breckland, extensive areas of open field and heath were removed by large-scale, planned enclosure, new farmsteads would sometimes be created on new sites, away from existing settlements, in the midst of their newly hedged fields. Once again, we must be careful not to read East Anglian developments in Midland terms, for the migration of farms in this manner was less common here, partly because of the difficulty of obtaining water on the dry expanses of sand and chalk. But examples do certainly exist. Following the enclosure of Snettisham in west Norfolk in 1766, for example, two new farms were built – Inmere Farm and Red Brick Farm, both with large barns and other buildings necessary to service their large, compact holdings.

TOP: *Fig. 4.5 Houghton 'New Town'* *which was built to replace the existing village, cleared in the 1720s when the park was expanded.*

ABOVE: *Fig. 4.6 Somerleyton, Suffolk: the picturesque model village created by Morton Peto on the edges of his park in the 1850s.*

85

Fig. 4.7 High Common, Dickleburgh, *in south Norfolk was enclosed in the early 19th century. The farms which once clustered on its margins now stand unconnected in the middle of the fields. Note the straight roads, laid out at the enclosure.*

However, it was the enclosure of rather more circumscribed areas of common land that brought about more profound changes in settlement. Many East Anglian settlements were, as we have seen, grouped around greens or commons, and their enclosure had two main effects. Where commons were surrounded by a discontinuous scatter of farms, enclosure served in effect to sever settlement from its established context. What had, for centuries, been a girdle of dwellings around an area of open ground now became a scatter of isolated farms and cottages standing alone and unconnected in the fields, each usually reached by a short length of private track from the straight roads laid out across the former common (Fig. 4.7). At the other extreme, where the margins of greens and commons were more closely settled, their area was often more minutely subdivided between larger numbers of commoners following enclosure, and often subsequently built over. Sometimes this occurred quite soon after enclosure, elsewhere the process was more gradual, but the overall effects were the same. A cluster of dwellings around an open space became a much more 'nucleated' settlement. Examples of both these developments – and of the various intermediate stages between them – are particularly common in northern East Anglia, but they can also be found elsewhere. Littlebury Green in Essex, for example, was a large elliptical common with farms and cottages strung around its margins until it was enclosed by parliamentary act in 1816. It was subsequently built over. Typically, the settlement displays two distinct building lines – 'double banking' – with an inner core of 19th- and 20th-century houses along a straight road, laid out at enclosure, and an outer ring of older dwellings.

Enclosure was not the only factor working to transform the old medieval patterns of settlement. The disappearance of individual farms, or even small hamlets, seems to have continued throughout the post-medieval period and even up to the 20th century. In the early 18th century, for example, Stubb Green was a hamlet of six small farms and cottages in the parish of Shottesham in south Norfolk. In 1841 there were still five dwellings here, but by the end of the century only three.[12] Today, only a single house remains. There are many other instances, all largely the consequence of changes in the structure of farming. Farm sizes tended to increase during the 18th and 19th centuries, especially as East Anglia became a more arable economy. Large arable farms were held to be more efficient than small ones because they could benefit from economies of scale. More importantly, landowners were keen to amalgamate tenancies in order to attract more substantial tenants, and to reduce the amount that had to be spent on maintaining a plethora of farmhouses and buildings. Farmhouses rendered superfluous by such amalgamations were sometimes subdivided and converted into farmworkers' accommodation but on occasion, if located in some inconvenient and isolated place, they were simply demolished. Desertion and shrinkage could, however, come from a host of other causes – as population ebbed and flowed, as individuals and families bought and sold property, as particular places became insalubrious or isolated from the main currents of economic and social life.

Fig. 4.8 Thorpness, Suffolk: the holiday village created in the early 20th century by Glencairn Stuart Ogilvie. Note the 'Meare', created out of a natural lake; and the 'House in the Clouds', the village's idiosyncratic water tower. Sizewell nuclear power station lies in the distance.

And villages continued to change into the 20th century. Indeed, in many settlements in the north and east of the region especially, the majority, sometimes the overwhelming majority, of houses are of 20th-century date, either as a consequence of massive expansion or because of large-scale replacement of poor, substandard housing stock – before a greater consciousness of the importance of heritage and conservation ensured that even the most tumble-down old slum seemed worthy of restoration. And, in a few places, entirely new villages have come into existence. One of the most striking is the small seaside resort of Thorpness in Suffolk, developed in the course of 20 years from 1910, with its 25ha lake and neat houses decorated with timber-framing and weatherboarding, echoing in a curious way the paternalistic archaism of Peto's Somerleyton (Fig. 4.8).

THE CHURCH IN THE LANDSCAPE

Landscape historians like to emphasise variations in settlement patterns, but to most people it is the character of the buildings that gives each region its particular character. Space does not allow a full account of the origins and development of East Anglia's churches: instead, I will concentrate on the distinctive features of their location and appearance. First and foremost we must note again the character of available building materials – East Anglia lacks good building stone and, when this was required, it had to be brought in by water from elsewhere. Usually this was from the limestone quarries around Barnack in Northamptonshire, but also, especially in the late 11th and 12th centuries, from the Caen district of northern France. Its use was usually restricted to corners and openings – windows and doors – or, in late medieval times, to decorative work. Almost invariably, the main body of

BELOW: *Fig. 4.9 The parish church of Aythorpe Roding, Essex, with typical 15th-century timber turret.*

BOTTOM: *Fig. 4.10 Ornamental 'flushwork' on the parish church of Glemsford, Suffolk.*

the church was built of flint, usually gathered from fields or beaches but sometimes – and generally only from the 14th century – quarried from the chalk. Other materials, where available, were used but normally in combination with flint, such as the carrstone of west Norfolk or the lower, harder levels of the Crag in the Suffolk Sandlings (the tower of Chillesford church is entirely built of it). Puddingstone was used in north-east Essex and, especially in the same county, brick looted from Roman sites was extensively employed. The absence of good building stone presumably explains the many timber towers and belfries (Fig. 4.9) erected in Essex, including the fine, free-standing example at Margaretting. Most are 14th- or 15th-century although some are earlier: that at Navestock may date from the late 12th century. Timber porches are likewise well represented in the county, as at Radwinter (14th century) and Margaretting (15th). Absence of good stone also presumably explains the remarkably early use of brick – from the 12th century in Norwich churches, but more usually from the 14th and 15th centuries – although the region's close contacts with the Low Countries, where the art of brickmaking was first revived, were also important. Essex has more churches with brick-built features, especially towers but also including the fine nave at St Osyth, than the other counties. Suffolk and Norfolk also have some striking examples, however, such as the remarkable church built by Ralph Shelton at Shelton in Norfolk in the 1450s. A range of other materials was thus employed in the construction of East Anglian churches, but flint always remained paramount, even in the 15th century, when masons found novel ways of using it as carefully cut blocks – often combined as 'flushwork' with brick or freestone to produce complex, striking patterns (Fig. 4.10).[13]

As elsewhere in the country, ecclesiastical provision in the centuries following the conversion in the 7th century was based on large territories or *parochiae*, served by groups of priests operating from churches called minsters, usually located at major estate centres. In the course of the later Saxon period, as large estates disintegrated and local lordships emerged, *parochiae* also gradually split into smaller parishes. Saxon thegns and Norman lords built churches to serve their families and workers, as a mark of prestige (a church was an essential symbol of thegnly status) and

as a source of profit.[14] East Anglia shared in this general pattern, but with significant differences, especially in the areas to the north and east of the Lark–Gipping corridor.

Firstly, the disintegration of the minster system seems here to have begun earlier, and to have progressed faster, than in other parts of the country – presumably a reflection of the region's considerable wealth and dense population. Indeed, it is difficult to discover direct evidence for the existence of minsters, although the locations of some can be deduced from indirect documentary and topographic evidence, or from place-names. Secondly, by the end of the 12th century there was a greater density of parishes than anywhere else in England, and medieval churches are still noticeably thick on the ground. In Norfolk, Domesday records a total of 274 churches, but we know from other documentary or archaeological evidence that many were omitted, and allowing for this there may already have been as many as 600. By the 13th century there were no less than 928 separate parishes.[15] In Suffolk, Domesday seems to provide a more complete record: it mentions around 418 churches (including 12 in Ipswich and three in Dunwich) and there were around 510 medieval parishes. In Essex, only 37 churches are mentioned in Domesday or implied by the presence of a priest: more systematic omission seems to have occurred here, for there were 400 medieval parishes and around 70 non-parochial chapels.[16]

To a large extent this high density of churches is, once again, a simple reflection of the fact that this was both the most populous, and the wealthiest, region of early medieval England. But it may also be a consequence of social factors, for some tiny medieval vills – in terms of both area and population – attained the status of separate parishes: places such as Frenze in Norfolk, covering c. 200ha, or Thorpe Parva in the same county, covering less than 160ha (Fig. 4.11). Moreover, some medieval vills had two or more churches (Shottesham in Norfolk had no less than four). Indeed, as many as 79 Norfolk vills contained more than one church. It is possible that in the complex social world of late Saxon East Anglia, where (as we have seen) the line between free peasant and thegn was not easily or neatly drawn, prospering individuals were particularly keen to erect a church, as a sign that they had 'thrived to thegn-right'. And some may have been built by groups of freemen, related or otherwise, because there was no other way of securing adequate ecclesiastical provision. Domesday records a church at Stonham in Suffolk with 8ha, which nine free-men had given 'for the salvation of their souls', while at various other places it notes how churches were owned by groups of freemen, or shared between freemen and a more substantial landowner.[17]

Another curious feature of East Anglia, and especially of the north and east of the region, is the phenomenon of two (or even three) parish churches built within a single churchyard. Norfolk has, or had, 12 examples; Suffolk four; Cambridgeshire two; and Essex one. In a number of other places churches stand in yards so close that they practically join, as at Gillingham or Kirby Bedon in Norfolk (Fig. 4.12). In almost all cases, the churches in question served named parishes within one vill: Great Melton All Saints and Great Melton St Mary in Norfolk, for example (Fig. 4.13). However, at Reepham in the same county, where three churches once shared a single yard, each served a separate vill – Hackford, Whitwell and Reepham itself, the parish boundaries of the three meeting, in crazy configuration, in the centre of this small town.[18] Once again, the explanation may lie in the idiosyncratic social structure of late Saxon East Anglia. Shared churchyards perhaps reflect the growth and division of free kindreds, each family line maintaining its own church within an ancestral burial ground; or they may result from groups of freemen getting together to found a new church next to an existing one, perhaps as a symbol of their status and their independence from some larger owner. At Stowmarket, Domesday records how four brothers built a chapel on their own land close to the churchyard of the existing church.

Fig. 4.11 The ruined round tower of Thorpe Parva church, Norfolk. *The parish covered no more than 160ha.*

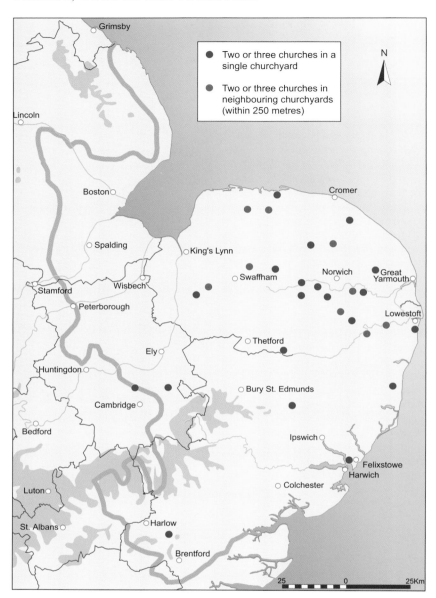

ABOVE: *Fig. 4.12 East Anglia: the distribution of shared and adjacent churchyards.*

ABOVE RIGHT: *Fig. 4.13 Two churches in one yard at Great Melton, Norfolk. All Saints church is still in use, but only the tower remains of St Mary's.*

Pre-Conquest churches in East Anglia were mainly built of timber, but only one has survived, at Greenstead in Essex, and this – with its walls of split trunks – is relatively late and may well be atypical. Only meagre traces of others have been recovered by excavation beneath existing churches, as at Barton Bendish or Guestwick in Norfolk. How many stone – that is, largely flint – churches had already appeared before the Norman Conquest is uncertain, due to the difficulties of distinguishing late Saxon from early Norman construction (not all local masons died at the battle of Hastings). A few unquestionably pre-Conquest structures can be found – such as the tower of Forncett St Peter in Norfolk, with rings of circular windows. But even such things as double-splayed windows, triangular-headed openings or long-and-short work can apparently be found in what are unquestionably post-Conquest buildings.[19]

One important aspect of this problem is the date and significance of the round church towers, which are such a characteristic feature of the region, and

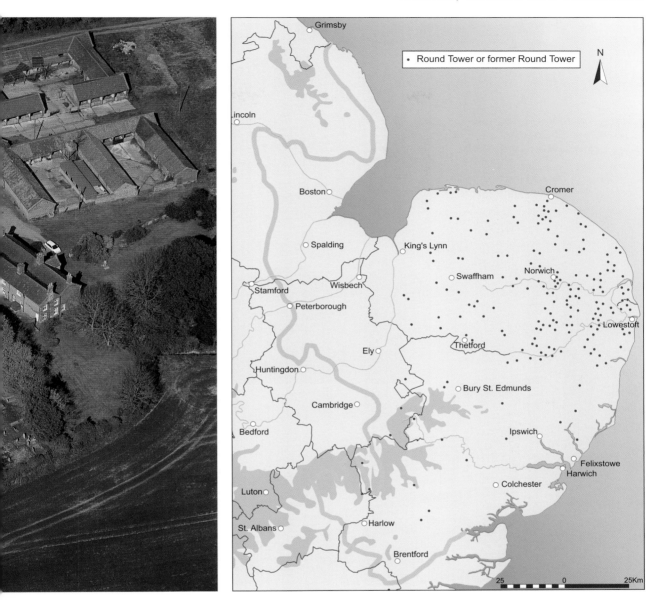

Fig. 4.14 East Anglia: the distribution of round-towered churches.

particularly (once again) of the districts lying to the north and east of the Lark–Gipping corridor (Fig. 4.14). Norfolk has 123 surviving examples, with a further 11 in ruins and 10 that have disappeared completely; the equivalent figures for Suffolk are 38, three and two: they are mainly in the north of the county. Essex has six examples and Cambridgeshire two (Fig. 4.15). The whole of the rest of England can boast a mere eight.[20] Early antiquarians thought that these structures were of Saxon date and perhaps defensive in character, places of refuge from Danish attack, but the overwhelming majority are now considered post-Conquest and some may have been built as late as the 13th century.[21] Most authorities accept that a round shape became fashionable because, as numerous petty landowners erected their churches, it was expensive to obtain the large quantities of freestone needed for openings and corners, and they therefore economised by making the towers circular. This sensible theory has its problems, not least the fact that some square flint towers *were* built without freestone corners, as at Hethel in Norfolk, and

RIGHT: *Fig. 4.15 Hales church, Norfolk,* with round tower and semi-circular apse, is one of the finest Norman churches in East Anglia.

BELOW: *Fig. 4.16 The 15th-century brick church at Shelton, Norfolk.*

some people have suggested that the towers should be seen in a wider cultural context – as a fashion brought to the region from across the North Sea, where similar structures were being built around this time in northern Germany and southern Sweden.[22] In this context we might note again their concentration in the north of the region, and the broad similarity between this and certain other distributions with North Sea connections, which we have examined. The truth probably lies somewhere between these 'practical' and 'cultural' explanations. A lack of good building stone may well have encouraged the adoption of this particular foreign fashion at a time of frenetic church-building.

By no means all 11th- and 12th-century towers, even in the north of the region, are of this unusual and distinctive type. Massive, square Norman towers exist at, among other places, South Lopham in Norfolk. And in general the churches of Norfolk, Suffolk, east Hertfordshire and Essex go through the same styles as those elsewhere in the country – 'early English', 'Decorated' and 'Perpendicular' – patrons and congregations more often adding piecemeal than rebuilding wholesale with the passing centuries. However, we need to be cautious. Both the terminology traditionally employed by students of ecclesiastical architecture, and the neat chronology it implies, are misleading, in East Anglia more than elsewhere. As one recent commentator has observed, in reality the different styles 'all merged imperceptibly with each other and overlapped considerably in time': 'Medieval masons did not recognise periods of architecture'.[23]

To some extent, the structural development of each church – as well as reflecting a succession of doctrinal and liturgical changes – was related to the demographic and economic fortunes of the parish that it served. But the links are complex and often indirect. Apart from the obvious fact that the parishioners paid for the nave and the incumbent (or impropriator) the chancel, building activity often reflected the fortunes of individual families, rather than entire communities, whose wealth might derive from lands or interests elsewhere. Thus the earliest stone churches were usually built by manorial lords, rather than their tenants; and in later periods wealthy individuals might pay for particular additions – towers, porches, even a complete refitting of the nave – as an act of piety and in order to aid the passage of their soul through purgatory. They might even, on occasions, pay for the entire church, as at Shelton in Norfolk, where at the end of the 15th century Sir Ralph Shelton caused the astonishing brick church to be erected (Fig. 4.16).

Nevertheless, some broad geographical patterns can be discerned in the structural history of East Anglian churches. Those that appear mainly of 12th- and 13th-century date tend to survive in small rural parishes, largely untouched by later medieval prosperity. In contrast, churches rebuilt in late medieval times, while sometimes found in out-of-the-way parishes and the work of individual lords, are concentrated in areas where agricultural wealth was growing with particular rapidity in the 14th and 15th century, as at Marshland, where churches such as Walpole St Peter or Terrington St Clement dominate the flat landscape; or, above all, in places of industrial or commercial prosperity.

Soaring Perpendicular churches are indeed one of the great glories of the region. Funded by a peculiarly vibrant local economy, late medieval church builders in East Anglia, perhaps more than anywhere else in England, sought to create impossibly light and airy box-like spaces, without any major structural division between nave and chancel, with walls more glass than stone and with elaborate ceilings lit by lines of clerestory windows. Coastal examples, proclaiming the importance of a parish as a former port, include the long chain running down the Sandlings coast – Lowestoft, Covehithe, Kessingland, Blythburgh, Southwold, Walberswick – as well as Cley, Blakeney, Salthouse and Cromer on the north Norfolk coast. Most major urban churches were largely or wholly rebuilt in this style, often on a vast scale, as at Saffron Walden or Thaxted in Essex, 65m and 60m long, respectively, or at Swaffham in Norfolk. But it is the Stour valley and its hinterland – areas of considerable industrialisation in the later medieval period – that can boast the finest examples, including Cavendish, Long Melford, Lavenham and Clare in Suffolk, and Dedham and Thaxted in Essex (Fig. 4.17). Often described as 'wool churches', they were in reality funded by the manufacture of textiles, and by the wider prosperity that this engendered. The wealthy merchants, industrialists and gentry who paid for their construction are often commemorated in inscriptions or heraldry. The church at Long Melford was rebuilt between *c.* 1460 and 1495, and the progress of construction is clearly reflected in a series of inscriptions:

> *Pray for ye sowl of John Keche, and for his Fad' and Mod' of whose goodis yis arche was made.*

Local people often took neighbouring churches as their models, copying or outdoing them in an expression of individual, familial or communal pride. When the inhabitants of Walberswick on the Sandlings coast engaged masons to build a new tower in 1425, they stipulated that it should be similar in appearance to the tower at nearby Tunstall, and have a west door and windows 'as good as' those of the church at Halesworth.

Late medieval wealth in these economic 'hot spots' – but also, more widely, the ripples of prosperity spreading into agricultural hinterlands – also paid for the stunning 14th- and 15th-century fittings and interiors. These are major features of the region and not to be matched anywhere in England: screens, stalls and the magnificent hammerbeam and double-hammerbeam roofs, many adorned with flights of angels, such as those at Cawston, Gissing, Knapton and Swaffham in Norfolk, and Woolpit, Hopton or Worlingworth in Suffolk. Those at Blythburgh have musket shot imbedded in them, a legacy of the parliamentarian soldiers billeted there in the Civil War.

Even in the late medieval period, the region's ecclesiastical architecture displayed some idiosyncratic features. Except in the Lincolnshire Fens, where the influence of the Midlands was strong and good quality limestone available at no great distance, spires are a rarity. In Hertfordshire and Essex the fleche or 'spike'

Fig. 4.17 Long Melford church, Suffolk.
Like many churches in the textile areas of south Suffolk and north Essex, this was comprehensively rebuilt in the 15th century.

is sometimes found, but there are otherwise few true spires (notable exceptions include Saffron Walden and Thaxted) and they become rarer towards the north and east. In the whole of Norfolk there are only 18 examples. But late medieval towers are often very tall, making a significant impression on the landscape, especially in this more level terrain. They are also often rather plain, and massive, reaching through four or five stages. Many of the largest have no battlements, presenting a curiously austere appearance, as at Cawston and Wymondham in Norfolk or Southwold in Suffolk (Fig. 4.18).[24]

Although the vast majority of parish churches are of medieval date, mention must be made of the relative few that were erected in the post-medieval period. At Gunton and Houghton in Norfolk, and at Ickworth and Euston in Suffolk, churches isolated within parks were treated in effect as garden buildings: that at Gunton was rebuilt in *c.* 1770 to designs by Robert Adam as neat Classical temple, while Houghton was given a new west tower and generally 'Gothickised' in the 1730s (Fig. 4.19).[25] However, the most striking rebuilding was perhaps that

BELOW: *Fig. 4.18 The great tower of Cawston church* dominates the surrounding Norfolk countryside.

BOTTOM: *Fig. 4.19 Gunton, Norfolk.* *The church stands next to the hall and was rebuilt – as a fashionable adornment to the landscape – in the 1770s, to designs by the architect Robert Adam.*

carried out at Booton in Norfolk in the 1870s and 1880s by the rector, Rev Whitwell Elwin, in an extravagant Gothic style, with tall west tower and a central feature almost like a minaret.

The huge number and often large size of East Anglian churches, coupled with the fact that many stand in isolated locations and in level terrain, ensures that they have a greater impact on the landscape than in most regions of England. More subtle is the effect of Nonconformist chapels and meeting houses, structures often neglected by historians of landscape. East Anglia has a long Dissenting tradition, born of its early industrialisation, idiosyncratic social structure and close links with the continent. Holland served as a convenient refuge for the persecuted: Robert Brown slipped away to Middelberg following the suppression of his 'gathered church' in Norwich in 1581, while in the early 17th century many of the Norwich clergy suspended for refusing to read King James *Book of Sports* fled to Holland. Early Dissent has left few clear traces in the landscape, although the Congregational chapel at Walpole in Suffolk may date from as early as 1647, during the Commonwealth years. It was really only after the 1672 Declaration of Indulgence, and in particular following the 1689 Act of Toleration, that purpose-built meeting houses began to appear, one of the first being the Old Meeting in Colegate, Norwich, of 1673. Quakers, Independents, Baptists and Presbyterians erected a number of meeting houses in the late 17th and first half of the 18th century. Some were simple buildings, not dissimilar to

Fig. 4.20 The Congregational (originally Independent) meeting house at Oulton in Norfolk *was opened in 1731. With its double Dutch gables and pantile roof, it is a good example of the kind of meeting house erected by wealthy Dissenting congregations in 18th-century East Anglia.*

vernacular farmhouses – such as the
Presbyterian Meeting House at
Hapton in Norfolk. Others were more
elaborate affairs, large square buildings
with double gables or (more rarely)
hipped roofs, such as the Unitarian
Meeting House at Ipswich of 1700, or
the Congregational chapel built at
Oulton in Norfolk in 1728 (Fig. 4.20).
The period from *c.* 1750 to *c.* 1800 saw
a substantial increase in their numbers.
Some were built by the established
Dissenting groups, but most by the
Methodists, a new breakaway group
from the established church. These
buildings were mainly square in plan
and usually had hipped roofs and
internal galleries: examples built
towards the end of the period, such as
the Little Walsingham Methodist
chapel of 1793, display some
architectural sophistication, with
Classical detailing and half-round
windows and porticoes.[26] Most
meeting houses and chapels erected
before *c.* 1800 were located in the

Fig. 4.21 One of the many diminutive Primitive Methodist chapels built in East Anglia in the 19th century, this example at Besthorpe in Norfolk – erected in 1866 – has, typically, just been converted into a private house.

major market towns, with a sprinkling of rural examples across the fertile loams
of north and east Norfolk, and the claylands of south-central Norfolk and central
Suffolk – areas in which the power of large landowners was muted. Their
congregations were drawn from tradesmen, merchants and prosperous yeomen
farmers. More interesting than the distribution of these buildings, however, is
their location. Most stand within their own burial grounds, but in hidden or
isolated locations, down alleys in towns or, in the countryside, away from major
nucleations of settlement. This pattern may in part reflect the inability of
congregations to raise enough money to purchase more convenient plots, but it
probably primarily indicates an awareness that a discrete rather than a blatant
presence encouraged a grudging toleration on the part of neighbours.[27]

It was only in the 19th century, and in particular from the late 1820s, that the
number of Nonconformist chapels increased to the point where they became a
common feature of the countryside, especially in Norfolk and Suffolk. The
largest number were built by the Primitive Methodists, a group that split from the
Methodists (one of many splits to which this group were prone) in 1809. They
received support from small farmers, petty traders and agricultural labourers in a
way that no earlier Dissenting tradition had done. Other denominations,
including further splinter groups from Methodism, also actively proselytised in
rural areas, and as a result the northern parts of East Anglia, including the Fens,
are peppered with small, brick-built, rectangular chapels with gable ends facing
the road (Fig. 4.21). Most are in a simple Classical style, but some, from the late
19th century, are in a rude Gothic. They usually lack graveyards and are often
separated from the road by light iron railings. Still a common sight, they are now
less commonly used for their original purpose, many having been converted to
private dwellings as congregations have dwindled. By the middle of the 19th
century there were several denominations in many East Anglian villages,
competing keenly for congregations. In Upwell in the Norfolk Fens, for example,
there were three Wesleyan chapels, four Primitive Methodist and three Wesleyan
Reform, as well as a Baptist chapel.[28]

VERNACULAR BUILDINGS

Vernacular buildings – farmhouses, farm buildings and cottages built in local styles and with local materials – are another large subject, and once again it is necessary to concentrate on what is particularly characteristic of the region. Perhaps the most striking feature of its villages and small towns, and especially those in the south, is the great wealth of timber-framed houses. East Anglia falls firmly within the 'box frame' province of England – there are no examples here of true crucks, that is, buildings in which pairs of inclined timbers sweep from floor to the apex of the roof, supporting both walls and roof. Instead, the essential structure of the building and the roof were distinct, although both were raised together, as a series of trusses defining a number of bays, each truss comprising principal posts, principal rafters, ties and collars in a variety of combinations. Between were smaller members or studs, which held the panels of wattle and daub that formed the wall itself. Styles of framing, and plans of houses, both underwent many complex changes over the centuries, and much of the variety apparent in the countryside today is a consequence of regional variations in the chronology of building as much as a manifestation of regional styles *per se.*[29]

Late medieval buildings are most numerous in districts to the south and west of the Lark and Gipping rivers. The largest numbers are to be found in the old textile areas along the Stour and its tributaries, especially in towns such as Lavenham, Hadleigh and Sudbury, or in formerly industrialised villages, for example Kersey. Subtle changes in the character and distribution of late medieval economic activity can still be picked out in the varied styles of timber framing found in this belt of countryside. Houses erected in the late 14th and early 15th centuries have wide gaps between the timber posts and studs, and such buildings are a notable feature of villages such as Kersey. In the late 15th century 'close studding' became the fashion – flamboyant, wasteful displays of upright studs, with so much wood that façades sometimes appear more 'black' than 'white'. This form of framing dominates Hadleigh, Lavenham and similar towns, reflecting changes in the scale and character of textile production to a more urban-based, international industry (Fig. 4.22).[30]

Industrial prosperity generated wealth for rural hinterlands. South Suffolk, northern and central Essex and east Hertfordshire boast a phenomenal concentration of medieval houses, of all conceivable dimensions and evidently the homes of people ranging in status from wealthy capitalist farmers to poor bond peasants. Almost all are built to the standard medieval plan. This comprised a central hall, which formed the main living room and that generally contained the only fire, for warmth and cooking. Because there was no chimney this was open to the roof, the smoke gradually drifting out through the thatch, or through openings in the gables (Fig. 4.23). To one end lay a parlour – a kind of bed-sitting room, the private space of the owner – with a chamber above. At the other were two service rooms, again usually with a chamber above, which were separated from the hall by a cross passage running the full width of the house, with doors at each end. The end of the hall nearer the parlour was the more prestigious part of the room, the 'upper end'. Such plans are remarkably standardised: variations in wealth and status were mainly expressed in the quality of materials, the extent of studding and in the sophistication of carved decoration and internal wall paintings. The larger houses, however, often had their service and parlour ends in separately framed wings, at right angles to the hall range, and in this form they are often still easily recognisable, especially in the hamlets and villages of east Hertfordshire and northern Essex. One or both of these ends is often 'jettied': that is, the upper floor projects slightly beyond the line of the ground floor. This may have been done for structural reasons or to increase the amount of floor space upstairs, but it was probably in the main a stylistic device, which also signalled to the outside observer that these parts of the house were floored.

It is hard to exaggerate the incredible wealth and variety of medieval buildings in east Hertfordshire, north Essex and south-west Suffolk. They are unparalleled in any other region of England, and include numerous non-domestic structures such as religious guildhalls (36 in Suffolk alone), warehouses and enclosed industrial courts behind houses fronting the street, such as those still surviving at Long Melford. The density of surviving late medieval houses thins out to the north, onto the clays of north Suffolk and south Norfolk. On the lighter lands of the Sandlings, Breckland and west Norfolk they are extremely rare, and in the Fens non-existent. In these areas, we may assume, the houses occupied by the farming population, while more than insubstantial shacks, were not so well-built or commodious that they were worth maintaining into later centuries, and subsequent phases of rebuilding swept them away – although the absence of surviving medieval houses in the fertile, industrialised areas of north-east Norfolk remains a

ABOVE: *Fig. 4.22 Medieval buildings, like these at Lavenham*, *reflect the immense wealth of the textile districts of south-west Suffolk in the 14th and 15th centuries.*

BELOW: *Fig. 4.23 Late medieval houses* in East Anglia had a *central open hall, a cross passage, one or more floored ends and, in most cases, a crown-post roof.*

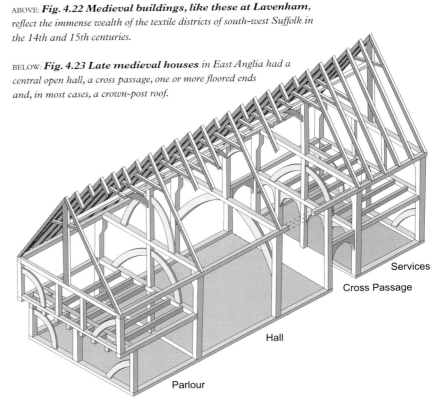

Services

Cross Passage

Hall

Parlour

Fig. 4.24 A 'crown post' in a cottage in Norfolk: a typical feature of medieval houses throughout East Anglia.

mystery. Perhaps the minute partition of holdings in this densely populated district ensured that few large, durable houses were erected.

Medieval houses in East Anglia were of 'single-pile' construction – that is, they were only one room deep – but to gain additional floor space they were often aisled, like barns: a good example is Edgar's Farm, re-erected at Stowmarket Museum in Suffolk. The very earliest had complex roof structures featuring many long braces, but no longitudinal timbers – 'purlins' – running the length of the roof.[31] Why builders should have been so concerned with lateral strength, yet were happy to neglect longitudinal stability in this way, remains unclear. However, by the time buildings able to survive in some numbers to the present were being erected, from the 14th century, roofs with longitudinal stiffening had come into widespread use. They took two main forms, which have, to some extent, a regional distribution. South and west of the Lark–Gipping corridor so-called crown-post roofs are ubiquitous.[32] A tie-beam running the width of the building prevented the walls from pushing apart under the weight of the roof, and from this rose a vertical crown post, often ornately carved, which supported a collar purlin running down the length of the roof. Each pair of rafters was tied together by a transverse collar, and each collar was supported at its centre by the collar purlin (Fig. 4.24). To the north and east of the Gipping, where medieval buildings are generally less numerous, crown-post roofs are likewise common, but queen-post roofs are also found. In the latter, posts rise from the tie beam, each of which supports a purlin set in the plane of the roof.[33]

The textile trade remained important in the Essex/Suffolk borderlands, but declined in relative terms through the later 16th and 17th centuries. Places such as Lavenham were effectively fossilised for many centuries – there was insufficient money to rebuild out-of-date houses in more fashionable style. At the same time, rising general levels of rural wealth after *c.* 1530, reflecting the increasing profitability of farming as population began to grow again after the long, late-medieval demographic slump, ensured that large numbers of new houses were erected throughout the region, replacing less substantial structures. A few can be found even in the light soils of Breckland and the Sandlings, but the densest concentrations are again on the clays, although now in south Norfolk and north Suffolk as well as in districts to the south and west of the Lark and Gipping. These new houses were of a different character to their medieval predecessors. They were still only one room deep and divided into three main sections (services, hall, parlour). But they had chimney stacks, and they were fully floored throughout, instead of having an open hall. Existing houses were modified along similar lines. Once again, however, areas to the north-east and south-west of the Lark–Gipping corridor tended to go their separate ways. In south-west Suffolk, Essex and east Hertfordshire it was usual to place the stack against the cross passage or on a back wall, something which allowed traditional ways of using the hall to be maintained: the end nearest the parlour continued, as before, to be the more prestigious end, while cooking could take place at the 'lower' end, nearest the service rooms (Figs 4.25 and 4.26). In north-east Suffolk and Norfolk, however, stacks were more likely to be placed between the parlour and the hall (Fig. 4.27), an arrangement that disrupted established hierarchies of space but did allow the parlour to be heated – firstly by radiant heat from the rear of the stack, subsequently with a separate fireplace.[34] Again, this hints at important social or cultural differences between the two regions in the early-modern period, differences which do not appear clearly in any documentary sources.

There were other changes. With the hall now floored over, there was little incentive to display elaborate, ornate roof trusses, and both crown posts and queen posts declined in popularity. The former was in any case rendered impractical by the fact that the chimney stack got in the way of the central collar purlin. The roofs that replaced them were simpler structures, featuring purlins that were clasped between the principal rafter and the collar.

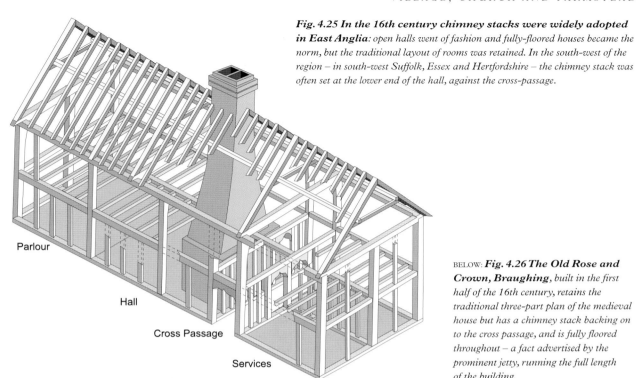

Parlour

Hall

Cross Passage

Services

Fig. 4.25 In the 16th century chimney stacks were widely adopted in East Anglia: *open halls went of fashion and fully-floored houses became the norm, but the traditional layout of rooms was retained. In the south-west of the region – in south-west Suffolk, Essex and Hertfordshire – the chimney stack was often set at the lower end of the hall, against the cross-passage.*

BELOW: **Fig. 4.26 The Old Rose and Crown, Braughing**, *built in the first half of the 16th century, retains the traditional three-part plan of the medieval house but has a chimney stack backing on to the cross passage, and is fully floored throughout – a fact advertised by the prominent jetty, running the full length of the building.*

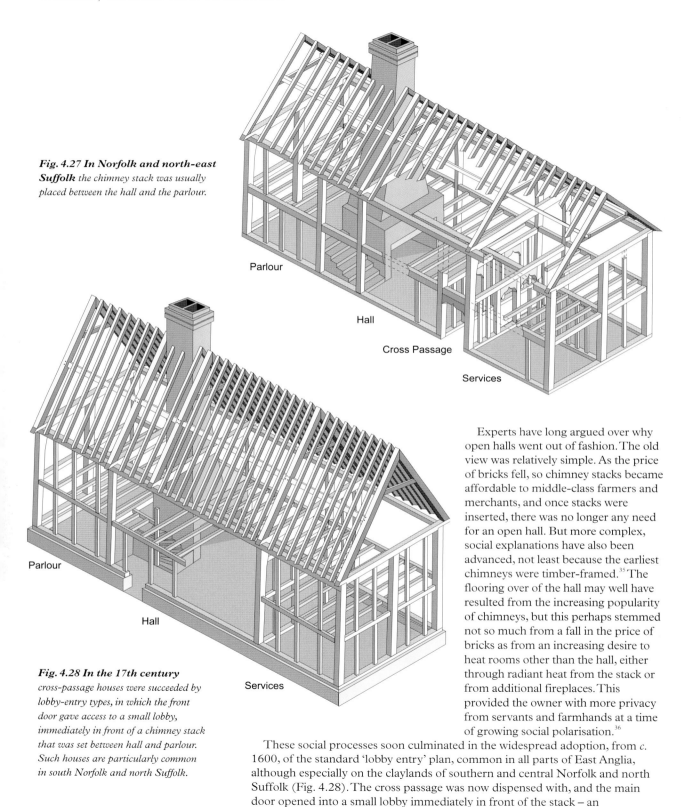

Fig. 4.27 In Norfolk and north-east Suffolk *the chimney stack was usually placed between the hall and the parlour.*

Parlour

Hall

Cross Passage

Services

Parlour

Hall

Services

Fig. 4.28 In the 17th century *cross-passage houses were succeeded by lobby-entry types, in which the front door gave access to a small lobby, immediately in front of a chimney stack that was set between hall and parlour. Such houses are particularly common in south Norfolk and north Suffolk.*

Experts have long argued over why open halls went out of fashion. The old view was relatively simple. As the price of bricks fell, so chimney stacks became affordable to middle-class farmers and merchants, and once stacks were inserted, there was no longer any need for an open hall. But more complex, social explanations have also been advanced, not least because the earliest chimneys were timber-framed.[35] The flooring over of the hall may well have resulted from the increasing popularity of chimneys, but this perhaps stemmed not so much from a fall in the price of bricks as from an increasing desire to heat rooms other than the hall, either through radiant heat from the stack or from additional fireplaces. This provided the owner with more privacy from servants and farmhands at a time of growing social polarisation.[36]

These social processes soon culminated in the widespread adoption, from *c.* 1600, of the standard 'lobby entry' plan, common in all parts of East Anglia, although especially on the claylands of southern and central Norfolk and north Suffolk (Fig. 4.28). The cross passage was now dispensed with, and the main door opened into a small lobby immediately in front of the stack – an arrangement that allowed direct access to the private parlour, without passing through the more public space of the hall. In east Hertfordshire, northern and central Essex and south Suffolk, the majority of houses with this plan evolved from the conversion and alteration of older structures, of medieval or 16th-century date. North and east of the Lark–Gipping corridor, however, while such houses are also common, far greater numbers of newly built examples can be found. Here there were fewer substantial earlier farmhouses to be converted.[37] Rather rarer is the two-cell lobby-entrance house, in which a central chimney stack provided fireplaces in two rooms, one serving as a parlour and one as a combined hall/kitchen. The rise of the lobby-entry house was accompanied by further changes in roof construction. Clasped purlins declined in popularity: purlins were now butted directly into the principal rafters.

The close-studding that was such a feature of late 15th-century buildings in East Anglia continued to be popular through the 16th century – displayed most flamboyantly, perhaps, at Thomas Paycock's House in Coggeshall, Essex. However, from the late 16th century it became more fashionable to cover over

the studs and timbers with plaster and, in south Suffolk and Essex especially, this was sometimes moulded to form the decorative patterns known as pargetting, a quintessential feature of the district.[38] The most striking displays can be found in the small towns, often on inns or other public buildings (Fig. 4.29). Sometimes, and mainly in the south of the region, the outside of the house was clad with horizontal weatherboarding, a tradition more closely associated with the South East of England.[39]

By the early 17th century buildings sufficiently durable to survive to the present were being erected in some numbers not only on the clays of East Anglia, but also on some areas of light soils, especially in north and west Norfolk. Here they were usually constructed not of timber-framing, but of various kinds of stone and rubble, combined with brick. Flint, flint pebbles, hard chalk and carrstone were all locally employed. Many of these

Fig. 4.29 The Ancient House, Clare, boasts a particularly fine display of the ornamental plasterwork, called 'pargetting', characteristic of south Suffolk and north Essex.

houses were of lobby-entry type, but some were provided with stacks in the gable ends, something comparatively easy to achieve where walls were of solid construction. In the middle decades of the 17th century this fashion was sparingly adopted in timber-framed houses, the stacks set in gables built of brick and wrapped around the sides of the building – as at Dairy Farm, Tacolneston, or Quaker's Farm, Wramplingham, both in Norfolk. The latter has stepped gables – 'crow-stepped gables' – which are a common feature of houses in the Low Countries, Germany and parts of Scandinavia. These had been used on many manor houses since the 16th century, but were now increasingly adopted at vernacular level.[40]

By the 1670s brick-built farmhouses were appearing in some numbers throughout East Anglia, and by the middle of the 18th century the larger farmhouses were often of double-pile construction – two rooms deep – rather than single-pile, as all earlier vernacular buildings had been. By this time, however,

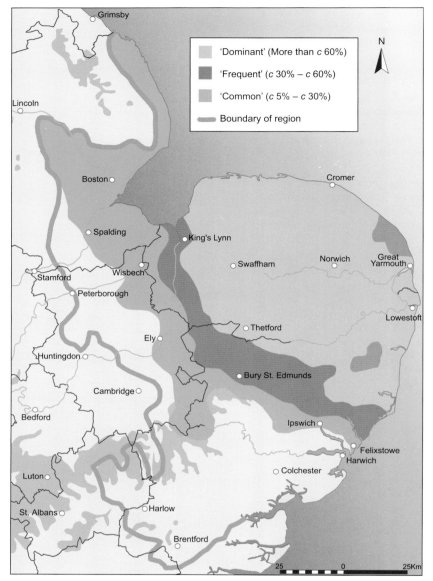

Fig. 4.30 East Anglia and the Fens: the distribution of pantile roofs.

the availability of pattern books was beginning to ensure the increasing standardisation of design, although more humble dwellings continued to be constructed in the vernacular mode. In parts of Essex and Cambridgeshire, light timber-framing continued to be used for the construction of cottages into the 19th century, sometimes covered externally with horizontal weatherboarding. Moreover, while plans and elevations might have become increasingly repetitive, regional distinctiveness in construction materials was often perpetuated even at quite high social levels.

Some vernacular houses, throughout East Anglia, have thatched roofs – mainly of reed in the north of the region, where there were extensive areas of fen, and straw in the south. However, many are roofed with tile and a high proportion of these with pantiles (Fig. 4.30). These distinctive tiles have a section like a shallow 'S'. Unlike 'normal' plain tiles, they are not nailed or pegged into the roof battons, and are laid in such a way that each only overlaps one, rather than two, others. Pantiles were introduced into England from the Low Countries – the Dutch word 'pan' means 'tile'. They were first imported in the late 17th century and were manufactured locally from the start of the 18th: many houses which now carry them were thus originally roofed with thatch.[41] An innovation of the mid-18th century was the glazed tile, usually black: glazing was mainly intended to protect the tile from frost cracking.

Pantiles are absent from the Midlands and the West of England except, rather curiously, for a marked pocket in Somerset. But while they are a distinctive feature of East Anglia they are not confined to this region. Their distribution extends, somewhat intermittently, right up the east coast as far as Northumberland and into eastern Scotland. Nor are they found throughout East Anglia. They are most common in Norfolk and north-east Suffolk and can be found across much of the Fens. However, they are virtually unknown from Essex or Hertfordshire and are rare in south-west Suffolk: their distribution falls off markedly, like so much else discussed in this book, roughly along the line of the Lark–Gipping corridor. One reason may be that by late medieval times tiles were already being used at vernacular level in some of the wealthy and industrialised parts of south Suffolk and north Essex. Pantiles were perhaps only adopted in areas in which, prior to the late 17th century, thatch had been the exclusive roofing material, making little headway in districts where plain tiles were already established. But the fact that their distribution falls off close to the Lark–Gipping corridor indicates that aesthetic preferences may also have been important, and that even in the 18th century this familiar line may have marked some kind of 'cultural frontier' – although if so, it is strange that we get no hint of this in any written source.

More restricted in distribution is another classic East Anglian building material, clay bat or clay lump – large blocks of unfired clay and straw, usually measuring *c*. 10cm by 30cm (*c*. 4 inches by 18 inches) (Fig. 4.31). These are a feature of central and southern Norfolk, north Suffolk and south Cambridgeshire, although their distribution also extends intermittently into south Suffolk and Essex. The material is used for cottages, some farmhouses, farm buildings and – in south Cambridgeshire especially – for garden walls. Lump is vulnerable to damp and needs to be rendered when employed externally. It is often described as a 'traditional' material, but this is only true in the widest sense. Although mud-walled construction seems to have been a feature of poorer buildings in the medieval and early-modern periods, large unfired bricks, mortared together, were probably first used as late as the 1790s, possibly by an enterprising builder from Great Shelford in Cambridgeshire called Joseph Austin.[42] The technique spread through south Cambridgeshire and adjacent areas of Essex in the first two decades of the 19th century, but may only have become common in Norfolk and Suffolk after John Claudius Loudon published an account of it in his *Encyclopaedia* of 1833. Certainly, in 1846 Charles Poppy reported that numerous houses and cottages newly constructed of lump could be seen along the turnpike road (the modern A140) between Stonham in Suffolk and Long Stratton in Norfolk. The technique almost certainly originated in the use of unfired clay bricks for the nesting boxes in 18th-century dovecotes. Clay lump continued to be employed sporadically into the 20th century: in Norfolk, some early council houses were built of it.

Fig. 4.31 This school at Bressingham, Norfolk, erected in the mid-19th century, is constructed of the large unfired clay blocks known as 'clay lump' or 'bat' and has a roof covered with pantiles.

There is no space here to do anything more than mention the various other materials used in the construction of later 17th-, 18th- and 19th-century buildings in East Anglia. Flint continued to be employed, especially in the north and west of the region (its use is especially marked in the Breckland area) and sea-rolled pebbles were used all along the coast, in a band a few kilometres wide. The hard building chalk called clunch was used in north-west Norfolk and Breckland (especially in Fen-edge villages such as Hockwold) and sporadically along the chalk escarpment of south Cambridgeshire. More distinctive is the dark brown carrstone, a Cretaceous formation occurring beneath the chalk, which is exposed dramatically on the cliffs of Hunstanton, but is otherwise reached only by quarries which exist, or existed, at various sites in west Norfolk. It was widely but sporadically used in medieval times for churches and high-status buildings, and in the 16th and 17th centuries for farms and cottages (usually in combination with other materials) in a narrow band, gradually fading in intensity, from Old Hunstanton to near King's Lynn. In the 18th and 19th centuries, however, carrstone was quarried on a larger scale and used across a wide area of west Norfolk for stables, lodges and other estate buildings, and for the housing developments at Downham Market, New Hunstanton and elsewhere. Brick continued to display some local and regional variation, even after brick production became increasingly centralised in the course of the 19th century. In particular, while the dominant brick colour throughout East Anglia is red, light bricks – Suffolk whites, Burwell whites – are found across much of Cambridgeshire and the Fens, and in parts of south-west Norfolk and western Suffolk. Such bricks are the result of mixing the clay with lime, easily available in these districts from the local chalk. They were also widely used in many of the major towns in Suffolk and Norfolk, following the spread of the rail network in the middle decades of the 19th century – something which brought increasingly alien forms of building material, and ever more standardised kinds of construction, to the region. Nevertheless, even in the 20th century some local traditions – most notably, the use of pantiles – were still maintained.

NOTES

1   Dyer 1980; Beresford & Hurst 1971; Rowley & Wood 2000, 16–19.
2   Allison 1955, 31, 116–62; Davison 1988.
3   Rutherford Davis 1973.
4   Holderness 1985.
5   Allison 1955; Davison 1988.
6   Clemenson 1982; Darley 1978; Holderness, 1972.
7   Banks 1988; Way 2000.
8   Williamson 1998a, 132–5.
9   Ibid, 55–7.
10 Markham 1984, 88.
11 Williamson 2000b, 138–40.
12 Shottesham Tithe Accounts, Norfolk Records Office, FEL 480 553; Shottesham Tithe Award Map, Norfolk Records Office, 558.
13 Pevsner 1965; Pevsner 1961; Pevsner & Wilson 2002a; Pevsner & Wilson 2002b; Addison 1982.
14 Blair 1988.
15 Batcock 1991.
16 Darby 1952; Williamson 1993, 149–61; Hunter 1999, 107.
17 Warner 1986.
18 Ibid; Williamson, 1993, 158–61.
19 Pevsner & Wilson 2002a, 43–5; Fernie 1983, 171.

20 Heywood 1993 in Wade-Martins, 56–7.
21 Gage 1831; Goode 1982; Taylor & Taylor 1965.
22 Heywood, 1988.
23 Pevsner & Wilson 2002a, 49.
24 Addison 1982, 118–20.
25 Yaxley 1994.
26 Ede et al. 1994, 17–26.
27 Ibid, 15.
28 Ibid, 27–32.
29 Smith 1958; Mercer 1975; Hewitt 1980.
30 Aitkens 2002; Stenning 1996, 136–42; Smith 1992, 31–45.
31 Colman & West 1975; Hewett 1968.
32 Coleman 1999.
33 Coleman & Barnard 1999; Stenning 1996, 137–8.
34 Eden 1968; Mercer 1975, 50–60; Smith 1992, 95–100; Longcroft 2002.
35 Smith 1992, 185–6; Lucas 1993, 24, 18–19.
36 Mercer 1975, 58–9; Johnson 1993.
37 Smith 1992, 97.
38 Sandon 2003, 114–15.
39 Ibid, 117–18.
40 Ibid, 101–3.
41 Brunskill 1978.
42 McCann 1987, 18, 1–16; McCann 1997.

5

Towns and Cities

THE ORIGINS OF EAST ANGLIAN TOWNS

East Anglia, as I have already emphasised, is quintessentially a rural region. There are no sprawling 19th-century connurbations here, of the kind found in the West Midlands or the North West of England, because the Industrial Revolution largely passed it by. However, the region's precocious economic development in the early medieval period and location on the margins of the North Sea ensured the growth of a number of large urban centres, especially in the north and east of the region. Innumerable market towns testify to the importance of the textile industry, as well as to more general levels of medieval and post-medieval prosperity. Towns were the engines of economic growth, and the development of the rural landscape cannot be understood in isolation from them.

The medieval urban network in East Anglia owed something to that of the Roman period. However, there was no direct functional continuity, for urban life disappeared in the course of the 5th century – if it had survived that long. Where medieval towns occupy Roman sites, it is for different and often complex reasons.[1] In some cases, old locations were simply reoccupied as urban life returned in the later Saxon period because they were well placed with regard to communication routes. In others, a Roman site continued to be important through the early and middle Saxon period not as a town, but as a centre of political power – the residence of a tribal king, a major estate or the seat of a bishop. The regular influx of people attending courts, religious meetings or other assemblies ensured that such a site later developed urban functions. Lastly, in later Saxon times, walled Roman towns often provided convenient places in which to place a defended town or *burh*.

The main Roman towns in East Anglia – the *civitas* capitals – suffered differing fates. Venta Icenorum, just to the south of Norwich, was abandoned and remains to this day an empty field surrounded by impressive earthworks and crumbling walls, although the parish church of St Edmund stands suggestively in its south-eastern corner. Its place was eventually taken by Norwich, some 6km downstream: possibly changes in water levels ensured that the latter was now the highest point of navigation for large ships on the River Tas. Camulodunum, while never entirely abandoned as a settlement in the post-Roman period, only re-emerged as the town of Colchester after its circuit walls were used to enclose a *burh* by Edward in the late 9th century.[2] The 'small towns' also experienced diverse fates. Many disappeared entirely; others, such as Braintree, reappeared as urban places in medieval times because they lay at major route centres.[3] Cambridge was re-fortified as a Mercian *burh*; Braughing in Hertfordshire became a major Saxon estate centre and the head of an archdeaconry, and thus developed in time as a small urban centre.[4] A similar pattern of development can perhaps be seen at Ware in the same county, where excavations have uncovered good evidence for 6th- and 7th-century occupation. Ware's urban development, however, probably had more to do with geographical factors. It lay on Ermine Street and – especially once the ruined Roman bridge was rebuilt some time in the 11th or 12th century – was well positioned to function as a transhipment point where cargoes brought by land could be loaded onto boats for the journey to London.[5] Although the Roman legacy, in terms of route networks, central places and walled spaces, was thus an important influence on medieval urban development, there was no direct continuity of town life in East Anglia.

The rebirth of urbanism was itself a complex process. Archaeologists use the term *wic* to describe a certain kind of site that developed in the middle Saxon period. These were coastal entrepots through which tribal kings controlled long-distance exchange, some of which subsequently developed as centres of production.[6] The earliest examples probably emerged in the late 6th century when East Anglia was still a constellation of diminutive polities, and were no more than beaches where boats, coming across the North Sea, would habitually unload their cargoes under supervision. The earliest phase of Ipswich was like this: an open settlement, probably only occupied intermittently, beside the inviting harbour of the Orwell. It presumably served a small territory ruled by the Wuffingas. Its long-term success, and perhaps theirs, may be due to its position at the junction of the two great zones of contact and communication into which East Anglia was divided, the one looking northwards to Scandinavia, the other south towards southern England and France. Other petty rulers in East Anglia presumably possessed similar landing places. A territory centred on Blything, for example, probably had one at Dunwich, and others perhaps existed at Burnham and Bawdsey in Norfolk. As the Wuffingas consolidated their hold over East Anglia, Ipswich became the principal *wic* for the whole of the kingdom, although some of the others continued to function as trading places. It is possible that another major centre existed to serve the kingdom's northern parts at Norwich – the *North Wic* – where large amounts of middle Saxon material have been recovered over the years from various places in the city.

During the later 7th and 8th centuries, occupation at Ipswich spread across most of the area of the present town centre and over the river, into Stoke. By the 720s a special form of pottery was being produced here, Ipswich Ware, which was used throughout the kingdom, and a variety of other goods was manufactured and distributed under royal control. Much of the street system of the town may date back to middle-Saxon times and some of the churches – including St Mildred's and St Augustine's – almost certainly originated then.[7] The kingdom of the East Saxons was served by a *wic* at London – Aldwych – but there may have been others. The sandbanks and shoals that infest the coast to the south of the Stour estuary suggest that the most likely sites would be at or near Maldon on the Blackwater, or perhaps at the evocatively named Harwich, the *here wic* or 'army *wic*'.

Although middle-Saxon Ipswich was recognisably a town, it did not exist within a true market economy. It was a centre for royal import and production, from which prestige goods could be distributed to a favoured elite. A true market economy, in which free exchange of commodities and the use of money were spread widely through society, probably only developed during the 9th century, as part of a general expansion of trade, and especially North Sea trade. A major aspect of this was the creation, following the reconquest of East Anglia and Essex by Edward the Elder, of a number of *burhs* or royal fortresses, some but not all of which also funtioned as market centres. Those created at what became the county towns – Hertford, Colchester, Norwich and Cambridge – certainly functioned as royal markets, and Thetford probably had some urban functions even before the *burh* was founded there. However, the *burhs* at Witham, and perhaps at Maldon, appear to have been no more than forts.

By the time of the Norman Conquest, Norwich was the third largest city in the country, after London and York. Domesday records 1,320 burgesses, implying a population of perhaps 7,500, and there were around 40 churches and chapels. The market place was in the area now called Tombland, to the west of what is now the cathedral precinct. Much of the river bank, which had been consolidated in places with timber and hurdles, was occupied by warehouses. The city was a major port, trading with Scandinavia and the Rhineland, and pottery and other commodities were manufactured on a large scale.[8] Norwich's affluence in the later Saxon period reflects the dynamism of the North Sea economy, of which the spread of Viking influence and culture – and the military success of Scandinavian armies – were other manifestations. Thetford was also a major town, located at the head of navigation for small boats coming up the Little Ouse. It was the main centre for the manufacture of the distinctive pottery to which it has given its name – Thetford Ware. Excavations have shown that settlement was initially concentrated to the south of the river, and that only later did a defensive circuit also take in land to the north. The whole area of the late Saxon town was rather sparsely filled with gravelled streets and timber buildings, set in yards which were interspersed with areas of open ground. Domesday records 934 burgesses, suggesting that it was the sixth largest town in England.[9]

In addition to these early defended *burhs*, a number of other towns and markets came into existence in the course of the 10th and 11th centuries. They appear to have been created under the direction of the king or great lords, lay or ecclesiastical, although some may have developed under their own impetus as local trade expanded and a range of manufactured goods, including pottery, came into wider use. By the time of Domesday there were additional *burhs* at Beccles, Clare, Dunwich, Eye, Sudbury, Ipswich and Stowmarket in Suffolk, while Bury St Edmunds in the same county was clearly a major town – although described as a 'villa', it had a population of about 3,000. Yarmouth is also described as a *burh* and 70 burgesses are recorded there, although it was probably mainly a fishing port rather than a market centre. *Burhs* are also recorded at Colchester and Maldon in Essex, and at Ashwell and Stanstead Abbots in eastern Hertfordshire. In addition, Domesday mentions markets at Blythburgh, Haverhill, Hoxne, Kelsale and Thorney (now Stowmarket) in Suffolk, and at Cawston and Litcham in Norfolk, and implies some kind of urban life at Bungay.

It is also clear that other local markets existed, which are passed over in silence by the Survey, such as Downham Market in Norfolk, referred to in a document of 1050. Newport in Essex, the 'new market', was not recorded as a market or as a borough by Domesday, but was certainly functioning as such within a few decades of the Conquest. And it is noticeable how many of the places that were later to achieve full urban status were already large and important at the time of Domesday, functioning as royal manors or the centre of Hundreds – places such as Hingham, Holt or Aylsham in Norfolk. It is not inconceivable that some had already acquired trading functions, for the regular gatherings of people must have formed a tempting market for traders. One wonders whether the large numbers of bordars and sokemen which Domesday records at many of these places might not, in reality, have been part-time traders. At Aylsham, for example, there were 20 villeins but no less than 104 bordars, as well as 60 sokemen, in 1066.

MEDIEVAL TOWNS AND CITIES

This said, there is no doubt that the century and a half following the Norman Conquest saw a massive expansion of urban life in the region. The largest towns seem to have increased in importance and size after the Conquest. In Norwich, the construction of the massive royal castle destroyed large areas of housing and at least one church, but the extent of new development more than compensated. A new borough, for the 'Frenchmen of Norwich' (continental merchants who came in the wake of the Conquest), was created to the west of the castle, around a new market place – the grid of streets surrounding the present market. The seat of the bishopric was moved to the city from Thetford in 1094, and the construction of the cathedral began two years later. The city continued to grow during the 12th and 13th centuries, with development filling the space between a number of

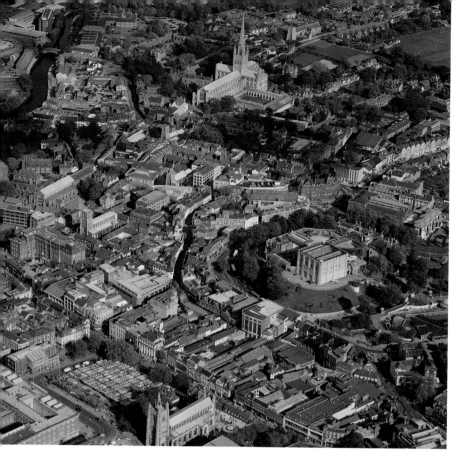

earlier settlement foci. The present defences date from the late 13th century: by this stage, the population had probably passed the 20,000 mark and there were more than 60 churches, as well as a number of monastic institutions.[10] In many ways, Norwich remains the quintessential medieval city in the region. It is still dominated by castle and cathedral, and retains extensive stretches of its (not very imposing) flint walls, although this ancient core is now surrounded on all sides by wide areas of 19th- and 20th-century housing (Fig. 5.1). Similar, if less dramatic, developments occurred at other major late Saxon towns, such as Colchester, which in the late 11th century received a royal castle and two monastic houses: St Botolphs Priory and St Johns Abbey. Both the castle and the Priory survive as striking Norman ruins.

However, as well as witnessing the growth of most existing urban centres, the 11th and 12th centuries – a period of considerable economic expansion – saw the establishment of many new towns. Major landowners were actively involved, for money could be made from renting out burgage plots, as well as from the tolls charged on traders using the market. Lords often granted special privileges to a town – endowing it with a charter, for example, which made it a borough – while the Crown granted the right to hold a market as a mark of favour, or in return for services or cash.[11] In theory, the documentary evidence generated by these formal and legislative procedures should allow us to chart with reasonable confidence the pattern of urban growth within the region, but in practice there are problems. Not all medieval towns ever received a charter, for example. Even quite large places, such as Royston in Hertfordshire, only ever received permission to hold a weekly market. Moreover, many markets were claimed by prescription or 'ancient custom' and never received a formal grant. Above all, a charter or market grant does not necessarily provide a date for the inception of urban development. The town or market in question might have been in existence for many years, the legal documents merely signifying the point at which local lord or central government began to cash in on a spontaneous economic development.[12]

Nevertheless, it is clear that many new towns were encouraged or established by great lords – tenants-in-chief, both lay and ecclesiastical – often close to major centres of power such as castles or abbeys. Many of these were at sites of ancient importance, but some were in entirely new places. Some were attached to castles, and – like Castle Acre, Pleshey or Saffron Walden – encompassed by walls or earthworks that formed extensions of their defences. The greatest 'new town' of the 12th century, however, was probably Lynn in west Norfolk, where Herbert de Losinga encouraged development at what may already have been a small trading and market centre (Fig. 5.2). In 1095 he founded the church and priory of St Margaret, probably laying out the market place, now the 'Saturday Market', beside it. Development soon sprang up throughout the area lying between the Millfleet and the Purfleet, the rather serpentine street pattern reflecting the earlier

Fig. 5.1 Norwich is still dominated by its Norman cathedral and castle keep: *note also the large number of parish churches, reflecting the city's wealth and importance in the early medieval period.*

OPPOSITE PAGE:

TOP: **Fig. 5.2 King's Lynn, Norfolk, one of the most important ports in medieval England.** *Long plots, occupying land reclaimed from the marshes, stretch down to the River Ouse, many still occupied by warehouses. In the middle distance is the Tuesday Market, laid out in the middle of the 12th century. In the foreground is the Customs House, designed by the architect Henry Bell and erected in 1683.*

BOTTOM: **Fig. 5.3 New Buckenham, Norfolk**: *the planned town laid out below the castle in the 12th century is now little more than a village.*

configuration of natural watercourses. A further phase of expansion occurred from the 1150s, when a planned grid of burgage plots and streets was laid out to the north of the Purfleet around a second large market place (the 'Tuesday Market'), beside the new church of St Nicholas.[13] Like Norwich and Yarmouth, King's Lynn had a royal castle and imposing defences.

Towns established before *c.* 1250 possess varying plans, but all had the essential feature of a central market place, onto which fronted plots for shops. In almost every case, the original size of the former has been obscured by infilling as stalls developed into islands of permanent buildings, sometimes leading to severe contraction, and fragmentation, of their original area. The infilling process sometimes began quite early. The 1251 survey of Ely shows that the market place, created soon after the Conquest, was already filling with permanent structures, while recent excavations at Saffron Walden likewise show that the market place was being infilled by the late 13th century.[14] In many East Anglian towns it is, indeed, difficult to ascertain the original extent of the market place, but it is clear that many towns created in the period before *c.* 1200 – including those established in the pre-Conquest period – were supplied with particularly large examples, such as the 'Tuesday Market' at Lynn or the great open space provided at Bury St Edmunds. Most were in the shape of elongated triangles, but some rectangular examples also existed. A number of these early towns also display strikingly regular plans, partly for practical reasons, partly perhaps to demonstrate the power and control wielded by an individual or institution; as we shall see, planned towns could form one element in a wider 'landscape of lordship' in the early medieval period. Notable examples include King's Lynn, Orford in Suffolk, Saffron Walden in Essex and New Buckenham and Castle Rising in Norfolk, but many other places, including Royston, also display some planned elements (Fig. 5.3).[15] At

Saffron Walden, not only the properties fronting on the market place but also the stalls within it, subsequently 'fossilised' by their development into permanent structures, were laid out on a measured grid.[16] The most striking example of planning is Bury St Edmunds, where Abbot Baldwin transformed the existing royal town by laying out a great grid of streets to the west of the abbey in the immediate aftermath of the Conquest. Domesday records an increase of 342 houses in the 20 years since 1066.[17] The grid still forms the basic street pattern of the modern town, but is perhaps best appreciated from the air (Fig. 5.4).

Not all towns created before the mid-13th century could boast large market places or exhibited clear signs of planning. In some, property boundaries appear chaotic and the market place was no more than a simple widening in a major road, or a pre-existing green or common, commandeered for the purpose, as apparently at Wymondham in Norfolk (Fig. 5.5). Most, however, had market places closely associated with the manor house and/or parish church, even in Norfolk, where settlements and churches are often poorly related: examples include Pulham Market,

ABOVE: **Fig. 5.4 Bury St Edmunds, Suffolk.** *From the air the planned grid of streets, laid out in front of the Abbey by Abbot Baldwin soon after the Norman Conquest, is striking.*

BELOW: **Fig. 5.5 Wymondham town and abbey.** *Not all early medieval towns in East Anglia have large market places or other obviously planned components. Many appear to have grown up, or been placed, around greens or commons. Planned or unplanned, medieval towns were often associated with major castles or – as here – with monastic houses.*

established by Ely Abbey some time in the 12th century, and Burnham Market, an enormous green/market place, which had a church at each end.[18] The medieval world was a deeply symbolic one, and the layout of features in the landscape reflected shared values. The physical presence of the church served as a pressing reminder of the need for probity in transactions.

We should avoid creating an impression of uninterrupted and uniform urban expansion through the later 11th, 12th and early 13th centuries. The immediate post-Conquest decades, in particular, saw some change and adjustment in the existing urban network, largely brought about by political and administrative decisions taken by a new and ambitious elite. Domesday thus describes how there had been a Saturday market at Hoxne, but 'William Malet built his castle at Eye and, on the same day as the bishop's market at Hoxne … established another market in his castle. So the bishop's market is spoilt, worth little. Now it is held on Friday, but the market at Eye is on Saturday'. In Essex, the de Mandevilles secured a charter in 1141 to close down the existing market at Newport and establish a new one beside their castle at Saffron Walden.[19] More striking is the fate of Thetford. This initially flourished after the Conquest: it was the site of a major castle, received a planned addition and briefly, between 1071 and 1094, replaced North Elmham as the seat of the bishopric of East Anglia. But it went thereafter into a gradual decline and, while it continued to maintain no less than 12 parish churches and a number of religious houses, never recovered its former greatness.[20] It may have lost ground to King's Lynn, more advantageously situated at the mouth of the Ouse.

Town formation – or perhaps more accurately, town *recognition* – continued into the later 13th and 14th centuries. Indeed, in the course of the 13th century there were no fewer than 47 market grants in Suffolk alone, 33 of which were concentrated in the second half of the century.[21] Many of these relatively late creations had fairly small market places, occupying slight widenings in major roads. Certainly, few seem to have been equipped with the kinds of really spacious market place that graced many earlier foundations. And few display obvious signs of planning, although there are notable exceptions, including Harwich in Essex, if its neat grid of streets was indeed laid out after the granting of a charter in 1318. Moreover, the close association of church and market place, so obvious in earlier towns, is less evident. In the more crowded and cluttered world of the 13th and 14th centuries, it was difficult to create open spaces where none had existed before, in symbolically significant locations. Markets and associated plots thus frequently had to be slotted into any available space, often at some distance from existing settlement, church or manor. Stevenage in Hertfordshire, on the eastern fringes of the region, is perhaps the most dramatic case. A market grant was received in 1281: the market place was located on what was becoming the Great North Road, nearly a kilometre away from what was presumably the site of the Domesday manor, and probable original focus of settlement in the parish, beside the parish church of St Nicholas.[22] At Harleston in Norfolk, the town similarly developed in the 13th century around an area of common land on the fringes of the parish of Redenhall, far from the church (a small church was eventually erected in the market place in the 15th century, but it remained a chapel-of-ease, without burial rights).[23]

These later towns were not, moreover, usually the creations of great magnates and prelates.[24] Town-making was now mainly the work of minor local lords, who often possessed more optimism than sound economic sense. The lord of Popes Hall manor in Buckland, on Ermine Street in east Hertfordshire, for example, obtained the right to hold a market, and a three-day fair, at a place called 'New Chipping' (from the Old English *cieping*, market) in 1252. The enterprise was a failure and Chipping remains today a minor hamlet on the A10. The site had no clear advantages that would draw trade from the well-established town of Royston, only 7km to the north. Whether markets had ceased to be held here before 1258, when the lord of Buckland manor obtained a grant to establish a market a little further north along Ermine Street, in Buckland village, remains unclear, but this attempt similarly met with little success. Instead a town developed at Buntingford, some 11km to the south of Royston, at a point where Ermine Street crosses the River Rib, and is itself crossed by an east–west route leading from Baldock to the Pelhams. No vill of this name appears in Domesday Book; in 1288 the place was described as a hamlet, but by 1292 a chapel to St John the Baptist had been erected here. A market place was created in a widening of Ermine Street and the town prospered, but only later became a separate parish, carved out of Aspenden, Layston, Throcking and Wyddial.[25]

The abortive earlier attempts to create a town on Ermine Street were not unusual: and, compared with towns established before *c.* 1200, relatively few of the places receiving market grants or charters in the 13th or 14th centuries were particularly successful. Settlements such as Codicote or Bygrave in Hertfordshire, or Pettistree and Clopton in Suffolk, always remained as villages. There were exceptions, such as Saxmundham in Suffolk or Bishops Stortford in Hertfordshire (although this may again have been an earlier establishment, only belatedly receiving formal recognition). However, on the whole, later 13th- and 14th-century creations never made the first division of East Anglian towns. The reasons for this are perhaps worth exploring. With the exception of some of the planned settlements associated with castles, most of the older towns, created before *c.* 1200, were organic developments, which grew up in places of ancient importance and/or occupied locations of particular economic significance in the landscape, such as the highest point of navigation on major rivers (Beccles in Suffolk, Ware in Hertfordshire) or the junctions of major routeways (Royston in Hertfordshire). The newer creations, in contrast, were often much more artificial beasts and – like Chipping or Buckland – had to compete with well-established, more advantageously positioned neighbours. In this context it is noteworthy that the more artificial of the pre-13th century creations – especially those laid out at the gates of Norman castles – also often failed to flourish in later centuries. Castle Acre, Castle Rising, Pleshey and New Buckenham were all little more than large villages by the start of the 17th century.

In other words, the fate of towns was shaped by wide economic and geographical factors, not simply by the whims of their founders, and location was the key to success or failure. Waterborne communications were especially important. Yarmouth and King's Lynn thus owed much of their importance to positions on estuaries giving access to major river systems: in the former case, the Broadland rivers, serving fertile and populous east Norfolk and Norwich; in the latter, the network of Fenland waterways reaching deep into Cambridgeshire, Huntingdonshire and Bedfordshire. Lynn's growth may, as already noted, partly explain Thetford's decline. By the

Fig. 5.6 Boston in Lincolnshire: the market place and immense parish church of this important medieval port.

13th century it had become a great
international port, trading with
Scandinavia and the Baltic. The
development of larger sea-going ships in
the course of the 12th and 13th
centuries may have reduced the
economic advantages of other towns
located high up river systems –
Yarmouth thus similarly eclipsed
Norwich as a port in the course of the
13th century, and continued to grow in
importance as the east Norfolk textile
industry flourished, although herring
fishing also remained a key activity. The
relationship of Boston in Lincolnshire,
at the mouth of the Witham, and
Lincoln, lying inland on the same river,
in some ways mirrors the relationship
between Thetford and Lynn. Like Lynn,
Boston became a great international
port, and as early as 1205 it paid a levy
greater than any other port except
London. Few medieval buildings
survive here, but the vast market place is
still dominated by the huge parish
church, with a ground area of more than
20,000 square metres, which was begun
in the early 14th century (Fig. 5.6).

Environmental circumstances could
break as well as make a town. Dunwich
was, in the early medieval period, one

*Fig. 5.7 **Dunwich in Suffolk** is perhaps
the largest settlement in England to have been
destroyed by the sea. Once one of the most
important towns in East Anglia, only its
western margins, including the remains
of the Franciscan friary, now survive.*

of the largest towns in Suffolk. There were 236 burgesses in 1086, with a further
80 living in the 'suburb' of Alneton in Westleton, three churches and a population
that may already have numbered 3,000. By the 13th century there were eight
parish churches, several friaries, town walls and two market places, and the town
rivalled Ipswich. However, the sea's advance was relentless. Domesday records
that land was already being lost to the sea. St Leonard's church was washed away
around 1300; in 1328 storms choked the harbour with shingle and diverted the
mouth of the river northwards; and by 1350 more than 400 houses, together with
shops and windmills, had been destroyed. Shortly afterwards the churches of St
Bartholomew, St Michael and St Nicholas fell into the sea. The following two
centuries saw the loss of almost all the remaining area of the town. All that
survives today is its western fringes, including the wall and gateway of the friary
and the Romanesque leper-chapel dedicated to St James, typically located beyond
the ramparts of the city (Fig. 5.7).

Dunwich is the largest settlement in England to have been destroyed by coastal
erosion.[26] Other East Anglian ports have suffered from less dramatic shifts in the
coastline, however, most notably Blakeney, Cley and Wiveton in north Norfolk,
prosperous trading places in medieval times but gradually reduced in importance
by the relentless accumulation of a shingle spit across the mouth of the River
Glaven. The men of Yarmouth cut six successive channels through the
lengthening spit blocking the outfall of the Yare to the south of the town.

In the larger towns and cities of East Anglia some medieval merchants' houses
survive, from as early as the late 12th century at Bury (most notably the stone-built
Moyses Hall, with its first-floor hall). King's Lynn has a number of important
14th- and 15th-century open-hall houses, including Clifton House, 4–6 St Annes

**Fig. 5.8 Diminutive late-medieval hall-
houses** line the streets of Hadleigh in Suffolk,
once a major textile town.

and Hampton Court, most of them lying to the west of the old market places on
land reclaimed from the tidal Ouse. They have long plots, which stretch down to
the waterfront, some still with the remains of medieval warehouses.[27] There are also
a number of examples in Norwich, although mostly from the 14th and 15th
centuries. Many of these originally had an 'L'-shaped plan with a hall range set
back from, but lying parallel to, the street, and with a service range running at right
angles and fronting on to it, which often served as a shop. As population pressure
built up, a new building line often appeared on the street frontage. This, together
with further piecemeal addition, produced the kind of courtyard plan seen with
particular clarity at Strangers Hall in Norwich. Jetties were widely employed on
street frontages, and in Norwich the early enforcement of fire regulations by the
city authorities led to the emergence of a distinctive form of building, in which the
gable ends and the ground floor were constructed of masonry but the first floor,
which was usually jettied, was of timber framing. Another Norwich speciality is
brick-built undercrofts, which first appeared in the 14th century, but continued to
be constructed into the 17th.[28] Vast numbers of late medieval houses, as already
noted, survive in former textile towns such as Hadleigh or Lavenham – rows of
diminutive hall houses, closely packed together along the streets (Fig. 5.8). Some
served as shops, although the evidence for such a function – characteristic wide
arched openings, two or more in number – is usually obscured.[29]

Some medieval shops and houses can also be found in the smaller market
towns, although their true character is usually concealed by later developments.
In Wymondham in Norfolk, for example, numbers 20–22 Damgate Street once
formed a typical 'L'-shaped urban hall house, while the nearby Green Dragon
public house retains much of what was originally a medieval shop front, with hall
to rear.[30] However, it is only in the larger towns and cities that a variety of other
medieval secular buildings survive, such as the warehouses at King's Lynn
already mentioned or the 14th-century building known as Dragon Hall in
Norwich, with its stunning crown-post roof, which served as a display warehouse
for textiles. Above all, the larger centres are distinguished by their large number

of medieval churches, something which reflects both high populations and social factors – the need for people to find a community focus more immediate than that of the town or city itself. Norwich, not surprisingly, boasts the greatest number – 35 still remain out of a medieval total of perhaps 70. Ipswich comes second, with 21 (13 remaining, but mostly much rebuilt in the 19th century). Other notable expressions of communal identity include the various guildhalls erected by merchants and trade associations, ranging from vast masonry structures such as Guildhall of the Holy Trinity (built in the 1420s) in King's Lynn to the timber-framed examples at Hadleigh and Lavenham in Suffolk or Thaxted in Essex (Figs 5.9 and 5.10).

ABOVE: *Fig. 5.9 The Moot Hall at Hadleigh, Suffolk, a timber-framed guildhall erected in the early 15th century.*

POST-MEDIEVAL TOWNS

The later 14th and 15th centuries saw a significant reduction in the number of markets and a shake-out of urban centres. Some – generally, as noted, the later and more artificial creations – tended to decline to the status of villages, although in Norfolk in particular many places of intermediate status survived, and to some extent still survive. These 'market villages', for want of a better term, include places such as Hingham, in which a market and some permanent shops were maintained in what was otherwise a largely rural community. At the same time,

BELOW: *Fig. 5.10 The timber-framed guildhall at Thaxted, Essex, was built in the late 14th century.*

other urban centres, generally the more 'organic' creations, retained or enhanced their status – in spite of the fact that many, especially Bury St Edmunds and Ely, suffered temporary set-backs when their associated monasteries were suppressed by Henry VIII. Norwich remained by far the largest city in the region; next came the major county towns and great ports of Lynn, Boston, Yarmouth, Bury, Ipswich and Colchester; and below them, the plethora of small market towns such as Hadleigh, Wymondham or Hertford – the latter a county town in name, but eclipsed by the development of neighbouring towns in this hinterland of London.[31] All these places experienced successive waves of rebuilding in the course of the later 16th, 17th and 18th centuries, in which earlier structures were replaced, or altered and re-fronted, in accordance with contemporary needs and fashions. On the edges of towns, houses were free-standing and followed the broad patterns of development exhibited by ordinary rural dwellings (*see* pp.100–3). But in town centres, and especially around market places, they were closely packed together, forming continuous building lines, and a variety of specifically urban forms developed. Where pressure was greatest, three-storey buildings might appear – sometimes by later conversion of the roof space. In overcrowded Norwich, this produced the distinctive, wide-gabled dormer windows often described as 'weavers' accommodation'.

The function and character of urban centres in the region changed in the course of the 17th and 18th centuries. Medieval towns were essentially trading centres, occupied by tradesmen, craftsmen, merchants and their dependants. During the 17th century, however, many began to attract residents whose wealth did not directly derive from commerce: they became fashionable places to live.[32] By *c.* 1720 Daniel Defoe was able to describe Bury St Edmunds as 'the *Montpelier* of Suffolk … it being thronged with Gentry, People of Fashion, and the most polite conversation'.[33] From the late 17th century many large, elegant houses were erected and the bigger towns and cities began to exhibit a measure of social zoning, with areas suitable for the homes of the 'polite' contrasting with areas of increasing poverty. Large town houses might resemble small country houses, although this is not always apparent – most never had spacious grounds, and those that did lost them as the density of housing increased. Norwich has some notable 18th-century examples, such as Churchman House and the imposing dwellings on Surrey Street. Elsewhere, denser packing of properties ensured more distinctly urban forms. Wisbech is an interesting case. The flat Fen landscape did little to encourage wealthy individuals to make their home in the countryside, and fine 18th- and early 19th-century residences – some the homes of local merchants, others of professionals or landowners – are closely packed along 'the Brinks', overlooking the River Ouse. These include Peckover House, now in the care of the National Trust (Fig. 5.11).

The poor lived in small tenements, often built into courtyards or converted from larger houses vacated as their inhabitants moved to more fashionable areas of town. Such mean dwellings were extensively removed, from Norwich and Yarmouth especially, by 20th-century slum clearance programmes. In the larger urban centres, such as Norwich, the process of social segregation had reached

Fig. 5.11 The imposing 18th-century merchants' houses lining the North Brink, Wisbech, Cambridgeshire.

Fig. 5.12 Newmarket lies in Suffolk, *but within a curious salient extending into Cambridgeshire. It became a major centre for racing in the 17th century, and its prosperous 19th-century houses reflect the continuing importance of this industry.*

the point by the end of the 18th century that some members of the urban elite moved out of town altogether into surrounding villages, which became, in effect, middle-class suburbs. Catton, just to the north of the city, was described in 1781 as a 'very pleasant village, and the residence of many opulent manufacturers, who have retired from Norwich, and built elegant houses'.[34] Middle-class flight from the crowded city perhaps explains the noticeable absence of the kinds of elegant Georgian terraces that grace many of the major cities of England. In the smaller towns, however, wealthy individuals continued to live cheek-by-jowl with their poorer neighbours.

To cater not only for their 'polite' residents, but also for those dwelling in their hinterlands, many 18th-century towns were equipped with entertainment facilities. Most notable among these were 'assembly rooms', where people would gather regularly for card playing, dancing and other forms of recreation. Some were no more than rooms in inns (such as the Black Boys Hotel at Aylsham), but many fine purpose-built examples were erected by speculators or subscribers and a number still survive, as at East Dereham (1756), Swaffham (1776–8) and elsewhere. Perhaps the most impressive 18th-century public building is the Town Hall or 'Market Cross' at Bury St Edmunds – a large, Classical structure built between 1774 and 1780 to designs by Robert Adam, which combined the functions of market hall and theatre. Inns proliferated as travel increased, especially in towns on one of the major roads fanning out from London. The inns of Hertford had stabling for over 530 horses in 1756.[35] Some urban churches were extensively rebuilt in fashionable style, most notably St George's at Yarmouth.

Some places developed largely as 'leisure towns' in this period. Newmarket, lying within a curious salient of Suffolk extending out into Cambridgeshire, became a major centre for horse racing in the 17th century. Inigo Jones designed a house here for Prince Rupert (it has not survived, and most of the buildings in the town date to the 19th and 20th centuries) (Fig. 5.12). By the end of the 18th century there were a number of fashionable 'watering places' along the coast, including

Cromer (Fig. 5.13) and Yarmouth in Norfolk (the latter possessed a bath house as early as 1759) and Walton in Essex. Richard Rigby attempted to establish one at Mistley in Essex in the 1770s, with buildings designed by Robert Adam. However, only a square with a central pond and fashionable additions to the parish church (north and south towers and porticoes with Tuscan columns) were ever completed.

While their role as centres of fashionable consumption, recreation and residency might have increased, towns continued to have basic industrial and trading functions. Weekly markets continued to be major events in the local calendar (Fig. 5.14) and many towns had some kind of market house – a committee room standing on columns, beneath which traders could shelter in inclement weather; or market crosses, more diminutive structures. That at North Walsham in Norfolk dates from 1600; Wymondham's was built in 1617–18; Bungay's in 1689 (Fig. 5.15). Probably the latest to be built is the elegant structure at Swaffham – a dome on Ionic pillars – designed by the fashionable architect James Wyatt in 1781 (Fig. 5.16).

TOWNS IN THE 19th AND 20th CENTURIES

Books on landscape history usually concentrate on medieval and early-modern urban developments. Most towns, however, are mainly composed of 19th- and 20th-century buildings, and those in East Anglia are no exception. The greatest growth in this period was experienced by the largest towns and cities – Norwich, Lynn, Yarmouth, Ipswich and Colchester – especially following the arrival of the railways, which allowed faster communication with London and with the industrial areas in the Midlands and the north (Fig. 5.17). For the most part, improved communications maintained or enhanced, rather than overturned, the ancient urban hierarchy.

ABOVE LEFT: *Fig. 5.15 Bungay market place*, *with the 'Butter Cross' of 1689.*

ABOVE: *Fig. 5.16 The Market Cross at Swaffham*, *designed in 1781 by James Wyatt.*

OPPOSITE PAGE:

TOP: *Fig. 5.13 Cromer, painted by James Stark around 1837. The town,* *located on the north Norfolk coast, was already a small but fashionable watering place.*

BOTTOM: *Fig. 5.14 Market places continued to be the centre of urban life throughout the post-medieval period,* *and market days brought in throngs of people from the surrounding countryside: Beccles market place, painted in the early 19th century by an unknown artist.*

Although, as we have seen, the textile industry declined across East Anglia through the late 18th century, it continued to thrive into the 1850s in Norwich, thanks to the adoption of steam-powered spinning and weaving machines. The Albion Mill and the Norwich Yarn works, both built close to the River Yare in the 1830s, still testify to this rearguard attempt at perpetuating an ancient industry (Fig. 5.18).[36] Other industries, notably leather working and brewing, were also important, and the city supplied a wide variety of services to its hinterland. Its population continued to grow, from around 37,000 in 1800 to 68,000 in 1850. By the 1840s it was beginning to expand beyond its medieval walls. Growth initially followed the main roads leading into the city, especially from the south and west, but in the late 19th century general sprawl occurred in all directions (Fig. 5.19).[37] New developments continued to display patterns of social segregation. At one extreme, there were affluent middle-class suburbs, most notably those along the Newmarket Road and Thorpe Road; at the other, large areas of slums, based around insanitary courts, continued to exist within the old walls, especially around King Street and Magdalene Street, until the large-scale slum clearances of the post-war years. In between were the new roads of terraced houses, built for labourers and artisans by speculative builders.

Colchester experienced considerable growth following the arrival of the railway in 1843 and the establishment of the military barracks in 1854–6. Ipswich expanded rapidly after the construction of the Wet Dock in the 1830s and the arrival of the

OPPOSITE PAGE:

TOP: *Fig. 5.17 Thorpe station, Norwich.* *The first station here, erected in 1844, was rebuilt in flamboyant style in 1886.*

BOTTOM: *Fig. 5.18 Jarrold's printing works, Norwich,* *was originally erected as a yarn mill in 1839 – part of a rearguard attempt to perpetuate the city's ancient but ailing textile industry.*

THIS PAGE:

Fig. 5.19 Norwich in 1917 – a photomap prepared by photographers of the Royal Flying Corps. The core of the medieval city, with the castle at its centre, occupies the middle of the picture. The city's three railway stations (now reduced to one) stand just outside the walls. The main areas of 19th-century urban expansion can be seen to the west and south-west of the city, and to the north.

Fig. 5.20 Victorian terraced houses in Norwich.

railway in 1846. The population rose by 30 per cent in the 1840s alone. Here, too, considerable residential zoning is apparent, the middle-class terraces and villas on the Woodbridge Road, or around Christchurch Park, contrasting with the terraces that comprised the majority of the new housing. Much industrial expansion occurred around the docks and the railway stations. This was the home of Ransomes, manufacturers of agricultural machinery and, by the late 19th century, lawnmowers.[38] For the most part, Victorian terraces in East Anglian towns differ little from comparable speculative developments elsewhere in England, but there are some local touches (Fig. 5.20). In Norwich, almost all have roofs of pantiles, continuing local tradition; and pantiles are also common on 19th-century houses in Ipswich (most of the earlier houses here were provided with plain tiles, the pantile 'frontier' running across the region thus moving slightly to the south in this period).

As populations grew and urban government became more sophisticated, provision was eventually made for proper water supply and sanitation in the larger towns and cities. In Norwich, the pumping station at New Mills was constructed in 1868, but revamped in 1897 to use compressed air (supplied by water wheels) to pump the city's sewage to Trowse. The 19th century was also a period of religious revival. Nonconformists built urban chapels on a lavish, flamboyant scale, fuelled by the wealth of local industrial and commercial elites, and the established church followed keenly, erecting new places of worship wherever urban and suburban expansion occurred. The largest Nonconformist chapels were vast affairs, such as Princes Street Congregational in Norwich. After extensive rebuilding in 1869 and 1879 its three floors housed, beside the chapel itself, school rooms, library and various meeting and lecture rooms. Princes Street was designed in a bold Classical style by the important Norwich architect Edward Boardman, a member of the congregation, but from the 1860s Gothic was increasingly adopted by urban Nonconformist congregations (the Union Chapel at King's Lynn of 1859 is one of the earliest examples). The new places of worship erected by the Church of England were invariably in this style.[39]

Most of the smaller market towns also grew in size in this period, so that their original, pre-19th century core is surrounded by a penumbra of Victorian houses. Here, too, new forms of buildings continued to appear, with many towns acquiring chapels and churches and some gaining imposing corn exchanges, usually on or close to the market place, in which farmers could negotiate with merchants the value of their grain (such as that built at Swaffham in Norfolk in 1868). Expansion was almost always greatest where towns lay on major rail routes. However, the arrival of the railways could damage, as well as enhance, a town. The Essex port of Manningtree, for example, flourished after the Stour was made navigable to Sudbury in 1705, but declined sharply in importance when the latter town was connected to the rail network in 1848.[40]

A few entirely new urban centres developed in East Anglia in the middle and later years of the 19th century. On the coast, the arrival of the railways coincided with higher levels of disposable income among the burgeoning middle class and led to the appearance of a number of holiday resorts. New Hunstanton in Norfolk grew up on an entirely new site, a mile from the village now known as 'Old' Hunstanton. The town owes its existence to the arrival of the railway in 1862 and to the entrepreneurial acumen of Henry le Strange, owner of the Hunstanton estate. A new parish church was erected in 1865 and by the 1890s the town – with its tall, distinctive carrstone houses, laid out around a grid of streets – could boast a pier some 245m long, a golf course, town hall and theatre.[41] Similar, if slightly later, was Skegness in Lincolnshire, transformed from a small country town in the 1870s and 1880s. Here, too, a grid of streets was laid out and various hotels and public buildings erected, including the pier of 1881 (Fig. 5.21). The railways likewise ensured the transformation of existing watering places, such as Walton in Essex or Yarmouth and Lowestoft in Suffolk. Some entrepreneurs astutely anticipated the likely effects: at Lowestoft the two piers were begun in 1846, a year before the construction of the railway station. Cromer on the north coast of Norfolk had attracted visitors since the 18th century and had a bath house by 1814. Between 1800 and 1845 its

Fig. 5.21 Skegness, on the Lincolnshire coast, was largely rebuilt as a holiday resort in the 1870s and 1880s.

population doubled, in spite of a disastrous flood in 1837 that destroyed many of its facilities. It continued to develop, but with particular rapidity after the arrival of the railway in 1877.[42] Today, although the core of the old fishing village, with cottages of beach pebbles clustered around the church, is still very evident, the sea front is dominated by 19th-century hotels and guest houses and red-brick, late Victorian houses line streets extending to the west and south-east. The nearby town of Sheringham owes its development almost entirely to the arrival of the railways, as do Clacton and Frinton in Essex.[43] Not all new 19th-century towns were resorts, however. March in the Cambridgeshire Fens originated in medieval times as a small trading centre around a tributary of the Nene, with several small quays and market places. Its trade declined in the post-medieval period and its present appearance as a sprawling 19th-century settlement derives from its location at the junction of a number of major railways leading through the Fens and out of them, into the East Midlands; March eventually became a major marshalling yard.[44] On a smaller scale, the village of Melton Constable in Norfolk, with its rows of Victorian terraced houses, was similarly associated with a locomotive works, that of the Midland and Great Northern Railway.

The first half of the 20th century saw continued expansion. Although East Anglia lacks the kind of extensive inter-war suburbs characteristic of the Home Counties, some ribbon developments of semi-detached houses with fake beams in their gables can be found, for example along the Ipswich by-pass. This same period also saw the construction of the first council estates, especially in Norwich, where they were (and are) of a particularly high standard – a legacy of the city's long history of Labour control. However, development has occurred at a much faster rate since the end of the Second World War, its distribution now determined by patterns of roads rather than railways and by the planning policies of national and local governments. Large areas of Ipswich, Norwich and Colchester comprise post-war development – the precise area is hard to estimate, because much of the growth has taken the form of the expansion and fusion of surrounding hamlets and villages rather than growth of the urban core *per se*. And, once again, most other towns (including quite minor market towns) have significant areas of modern housing, which in many places such as Wymondham vastly overwhelm their historic core. Perhaps most dramatically of all, the ancient town of Thetford was declared an overspill town for London in 1958, and by 1971 had quadrupled in population and gained extensive industrial estates. It was a fate only narrowly escaped by the town of Diss.

Towns and cities are discussed in their own chapter, something easier to do in essentially rural East Anglia – where they generally remain spatially discrete settlements – than in many of the more crowded and industrialised parts of England. However, there are clear dangers in treating the 'urban' as a category too decidedly divorced from the 'rural'. In reality, town and country were always in a complex, symbiotic relationship. They developed together over many centuries in response to both the broad currents of the national and international economy and the more local pulses of regional life, framed and conditioned by the enduring structures of geography. The character of East Anglian towns is firmly embedded in the wider social and economic history of the region. The greatest urban centres thus developed, for the most part, as major ports and trading places, benefiting from their location on major rivers or estuaries giving access to the North Sea – for example, Lynn, Yarmouth, Norwich, Ipswich; or else as major administrative centres. Otherwise, because the region was largely untouched by the Industrial Revolution, it is characterised today by a plethora of small market towns. Many of these are now engulfed by recent developments, although in some – especially in Suffolk and north Essex – the ubiquity of late medieval buildings hints at past industrial greatness.

NOTES

1   Lilley 2002, 2–5; Hill 1998.
2   Eddy 1979, 4.
3   Ibid, 23.
4   Haslam 1982; Williamson 2000a, 107–10, 197, 201; Short 1988.
5   Kiln & Partridge 1995, 72, 108–14, 142–3.
6   Hill & Cowie 2001; Hodges 1982; Wade 1993.
7   Wade 1988; Scull 2002.
8   Ayers 1994, 30–40; Green & Young 1986, 9–11.
9   Dunmore & Carr 1976; Rogerson & Dallas 1984; Penn 1993b.
10 Ayers 1994, 41–53, 63–76; Green & Young 1986, 11–16.
11 Lilley 2002, 42–9.
12 Ibid 47–8.
13 Parker 1971; Owen, D 1980.
14 Andrews et al. 2002, 245–8.
15 Ayers 1993; Wade & Dymond 1999; Andrews et al. 2002; Munby 1977, 78.
16 Andrews et al. 2002, 266.
17 Scarfe 1972, 115–18.
18 Penn 1993a; Smith 1992, 140–2.
19 Hunter 1999, 92.

20 Penn 1993b.
21 Scarfe 1999; Britnell 1981.
22 Munby 1977, 99–100.
23 Lilley 2002, 119–22.
24 Penn 1993a.
25 Munby 1977, 100–1.
26 Scarfe 1986, 129–37.
27 Parker 1971.
28 Ayers 1994, 83–8.
29 Stenning 1985.
30 Pevsner & Wilson 2002b, 803.
31 Patten 1978, 244–95.
32 Smith 1992, 155–6.
33 Defoe 1724, 49.
34 Armstrong 1781, **9**, 15.
35 Smith 1992, 170–4.
36 Edwards 1984.
37 Muthesius 1984.
38 Grace 1999.
39 Ede et al. 1994, 27–30, 38–41.
40 Rowley 1972.
41 Dymond 1985, 176–7.
42 Reid 1986.
43 Dymond 1985, 176–9; Rowley 1972.
44 Taylor 1973, 255–6.

6

Genius of the Place:
Elite Residences and
Designed Landscapes

Great mansions and their grounds are usually studied by art historians as features quite distinct from the working countryside that surrounds them, and primarily as local manifestations of national or international fashions. However, I shall here also be concerned with their social role and significance, as expressions of power and status, and especially with the ways in which East Anglian examples display particular local and regional styles. Such idiosyncrasies are in part a consequence of topographic and environmental circumstances, which in each district presented their own particular opportunities, and challenges, to architects and designers. But in addition, local social and economic histories determined the quantities of money and land available to landowners of different kinds, in different periods, thus ensuring that certain phases or styles of elite architecture or landscape design are better represented in some districts than in others.

CASTLES AND MONASTERIES

The earliest elite residences that have left clear traces in the landscape are the castles established by the new Norman elite in the 12th century. Saxon ealdormen and thegns had had their great halls, in East Anglia as in other parts of England, but nothing remains of them above ground. Unlike North Wales, East Anglia is not an area noted for its castles. In part, this is because the paucity of building stone meant that many were systematically quarried once abandoned. Bishops Stortford and Saffron Walden, for example, lying temptingly within towns, have been reduced to uninspiring flint shells; Bungay in Suffolk has fared little better. More important, however, is the simple fact that relatively few large castles were ever built here.[1] Castles did not form a coherent system of national defence. If they had, we would expect to find them placed with more strategic care, and perhaps with a more coastal distribution. Royal castles existed, especially in the county towns – in Hertford, Norwich, Cambridge and Colchester – the latter raised on the ruins of the Roman temple of Claudius.[2] But most were private possessions, the centres of baronial estates. Their location was determined to some extent by that of earlier Saxon residences, but also by the need to find space for them in what was already a crowded countryside. For, as Robert Liddiard has shown, baronial residences had to be provided with an appropriate 'landscape of lordship', featuring gardens, deer parks, fishponds and – in many cases – monasteries and planned settlements, such as those created in the 12th century at New Buckenham and Castle Rising in Norfolk, or at Orford in Suffolk.[3] Castles and their surroundings were meant for show as much as warfare. Hedingham Castle in Essex is faced with stone brought from the

ABOVE: ***Fig. 6.1 Pleshey, Essex:*** *the 11th-century motte and bailey castle was dismantled and rebuilt in the late 12th century. Around it, within an outer earthwork and wall, lay a defended town. Most of the castle was demolished in the 1620s and used as building material.*

BELOW: ***Fig. 6.2 Castle Rising, Norfolk:*** *the great 12th-century keep of William d'Albini stands within its massive ringwork.*

Midlands, not because this increased its defensive potential, but because it displayed the wealth of its owner. Indeed, defensive capability was sometimes compromised by the needs of display, as at Castle Acre. Here the castle stands on sloping ground, visible for kilometres across the Nar valley but overlooked by, and vulnerable from, the high ground to the north.[4] The need to find space to accommodate castle and associated landscape ensured that great lords developed those parts of their far-flung estates with space to spare – places with few other landowners and extensive areas of heath or woodland. Given that the greatest barons held estates scattered across England, this might on occasions lead them to build outside crowded, difficult East Anglia.[5]

Yet if the region contained few large castles, it was nevertheless at the forefront of new fashions in castle design in the 12th century. Early deviations were made here from the classic Norman motte and bailey form, exemplified by such sites as Pleshey in Essex (Fig. 6.1), towards more sophisticated forms: large keeps set at ground level but surrounded by massive earthwork banks, as at New Buckenham or Castle Rising (Fig. 6.2); or new forms of keep, such as the striking polygonal example built at Orford by Henry II in the 1160s.

As well as these impressive statements of Norman lordship, the region can boast a number of other, smaller castles, small mottes, motte and baileys or simple ringworks, built of earth and timber. These, in contrast to the large stone residences, were intended primarily for defence, and usually lacked associated designed landscapes. They also often lack well-documented histories, but many were probably erected during the 'Anarchy' of Stephen's reign (1135–54). Good examples include the tree-covered mounds at Elmdon in Essex and Denton in Norfolk. The distribution of such sites is curious, for there is a remarkable correlation with a particular variety of boulder clay soils, those of the Hanslope Association (Fig. 6.3). It is possible that on this stiff clay it was simply easier for lesser landowners to construct steep mounds at times of political instability than where soils were of sand, chalk or gravel, or where – as across much of northern East Anglia – the boulder clays contained a higher proportion of sand.

From the early 13th century new forms of castle developed. Keeps disappeared and emphasis was placed instead on the curtain wall, punctuated by numerous towers. Framlingham in Suffolk (c. 1190–1210) is a remarkably early example. More elaborate designed landscapes were now being laid out and Framlingham, as well as possessing two deer parks, had a garden flanked by terrace walks immediately below the main hall range, which still survives as an earthwork.[6] Beyond lies an extensive lake, The Mere, natural in origin but modified by the castle's builders, the Bigod family (Figs 6.4 and 6.5). Fashion now demanded that – wherever possible – a substantial lake should exist near or beside a lordly residence, partly to keep fish in, partly for recreation but also to act as a mirror from which the castle should appear to rise, when viewed from a distance. How far Framlingham was a primarily defensive structure is again open to debate: it never suffered serious attack, and the circuit towers are open and vulnerable at the rear.

In the course of the 13th century, more and more emphasis was given to the gatehouse as the main defensive element, and moats became a more important feature of castle design, as at Mettingham in north Suffolk, built in the 1350s. This style of castle continued in popularity through to the 15th century at such sites as Baconsthorpe in Norfolk, begun in the 1460s by Sir John Heydon.[7] Here the great gatehouse is the only seriously defensive feature: the low circuit walls look as if

Fig. 6.3 *The distribution of medieval castles in East Anglia. Most of the smaller mottes, erected by local lords at times of political crisis, are in areas of Hanslope Association soils. Perhaps these stiff clays were particularly suitable for the rapid construction of steep-sided mounds.*

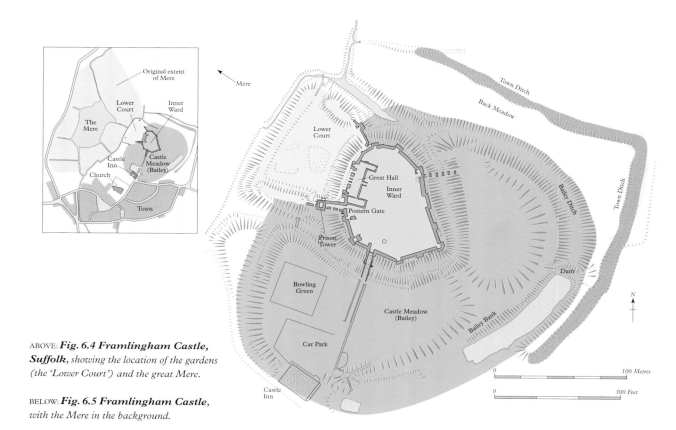

ABOVE: *Fig. 6.4 Framlingham Castle, Suffolk, showing the location of the gardens (the 'Lower Court') and the great Mere.*

BELOW: *Fig. 6.5 Framlingham Castle, with the Mere in the background.*

they are more for show than defence and the moat appears primarily ornamental in character. More impressive, and very different in character, is Caister Castle in east Norfolk, built by Sir John Fastolfe in the 1430s and 1440s, with its regular rectangular plan, corner towers, gunports and soaring tower, over 27m in height. However, the needs of defence were compromised, not least by the large window near the base of the tower, which would have been an inviting target for any attacker. The most striking feature of the building is that it is built of brick – the first really large building in the region to be so constructed.[8]

The early use of brick is, as already noted, particularly characteristic of East Anglia, a consequence of proximity to the continent and lack of good building stone, and from the late 15th century a number of brick mansions were constructed which, although provided with battlements, moats and great gatehouses, were more country house than castle. Examples include Middleton Towers and Oxburgh in Norfolk (Fig. 6.6); Nether Hall in Reydon and Faulkebourne in Essex; and Tattershall in Lincolnshire.[9] Large windows in vulnerable positions, poorly placed arrow slits and an absence of gunports make it clear that defence was not now a serious consideration, even if fashion still demanded a martial appearance. The style continued into the 16th century, although now less overtly military in character, in such buildings as Layer Marney Tower in Essex, the entrance for an otherwise unbuilt mansion, conceived on a grand scale. Other examples have disappeared without trace, including Shelton Hall and Wodehouse Tower at Kimberley, both in Norfolk.[10] We often forget that with elite residences as much as with vernacular houses, what we see today is only a fragment of a once more extensive population, which survived due to a family's subsequent inability to rebuild in more fashionable style. Oxburgh thus exists because the Bedingfeld family's Catholic faith ensured their relative impoverishment throughout the 17th and 18th centuries. By the time the family fortunes had recovered in the 19th century, 'Gothic' buildings were once more in vogue and the house was consequently 'restored', rather than being demolished.

Fig. 6.6 The 15th-century Oxburgh Hall, Norfolk. The house is set within a moat, and has a massive gatehouse, turrets and battlements, but was never intended for serious defence.

Houses like these were ranged, inward-looking, around a central courtyard. This was partly because they were constructed within moats, but also because they were only one room deep – they were 'single-pile' dwellings, like the vernacular farmhouses discussed in Chapter 4. In addition to the familiar 'core' of parlour, hall, cross-passage and service rooms, great landowners needed spacious accommodation for their extensive households, storerooms, chapels and the rest. Rather than creating a long, attenuated line, it made sense to form a square, an arrangement more convenient in terms both of access and security.

Medieval monasteries make a minor impact on the East Anglian landscape, compared with regions such as North Yorkshire. Once again, this is partly a consequence of the fact that they provided useful quarries for a populous region in the aftermath of the Dissolution, as in the case of St Olaves Priory in Suffolk, purchased in 1547 by Sir Henry Jerningham and used to provide materials to build his nearby mansion. Those located within major towns, as with castles, were particularly vulnerable – the great Thetford Priory is now largely reduced to low rubble mounds. But there were a large number of monastic houses in the region – 70 in Norfolk alone, although some were very diminutive institutions, such as Mullicourt, which had only a single monk in 1381 – and they had a major impact on the economy.[11] The largest were generally the earliest: the great pre-Conquest Benedictine houses, which possessed far-flung estates and important legal privileges. There is a marked concentration of such places in areas of peat fen: Ely, Ramsey, Thorney and Crowland all occupy islands in the Fens. Peterborough was located on the western margins of the Fens, while St Benets occupies a low island in the Bure marshes in eastern Norfolk. Most claimed ancient, middle Saxon foundations, but these were largely mythical and most were probably established

Fig. 6.7 St Benet's Abbey, Norfolk.
The site occupies an island in the Broadland marshes. The lower walls of the abbey church survive, together with the gatehouse, into which an 18th-century drainage mill has been inserted. The island is covered with earthworks, including particularly complex systems of fishponds.

following the re-conquest of the region from the Danes in the 10th century, as part of the centralising policy of the West Saxon monarchs.[12] The frequent association with wetlands presumably reflects the desire of noble or royal founders to provide both isolated locations and extensive estates, which were of comparatively little value but which could be improved by careful management and investment.

Established houses continued to acquire land, donated by larger and small landowners alike, after the Conquest. But the new houses established in the post-Conquest period mainly belonged to the new orders, such as the Cluniacs and Augustinians. Two of the largest – both Cluniac houses – were at Thetford and Castle Acre, the former founded by Roger Bigod in 1103–4, the latter by William de Warenne in c. 1090. The distribution of these later foundations is interesting: the greatest concentrations were in areas of strongest lordship, and there were few where freeholders were numerous. They were thus rare in Marshland and on the claylands of south Norfolk and north Suffolk, but common in west

Norfolk, especially in the valley of the River Burn, and to some extent on the edge of the Suffolk Sandlings. Both the founding of new religious houses and the scale of donations to established ones tended to tail off in the late medieval period. The main recipients of popular piety were now the friars, most of whose houses were established in major urban centres.

A few monastic houses have left extensive remains, most notably Castle Acre, where the church, abbot's lodgings, gatehouse and other structures make a particularly impressive and picturesque ruin close to the River Nar. Most are much less striking. St Benet at Holme is in an atmospheric and romantic spot on rising ground beside the River Bure and the earthworks (which include particularly extensive areas of fishponds) are impressive (Fig. 6.7). But the church is reduced to a few low walls and the only substantial survival is the great 14th-century gatehouse, with the ruins of an 18th-century drainage mill built into it. Gatehouses were – as with secular residences – often the most impressive features of monastic complexes by late medieval times. Perhaps the most striking is that at St Osyths in Essex, with its elaborate flushwork, but there are several other examples, including the St Johns Abbey Gate in Colchester (which also displays some fine flushwork) and the Great Gate at Bury St Edmunds – rebuilt after its predecessor was burnt down in a riot in 1327. Together with the 'Norman Gate', this provided access from Abbot Baldwin's planned town (to the west) to the abbey precinct (to the east). The latter survives as a largely open space, although it contains only fragmentary remains of what was one of the four most powerful monasteries in England. At Norwich, too, impressive medieval gates give access to what is still a largely open precinct, enclosed by its medieval walls. However, much more survives here, thanks to the fact that the monastic church also served as the cathedral. The fine cloister thus remains on the south side and fragments of numerous other medieval structures are built into the elegant houses of The Close. At Ely the cathedral was likewise served by a Benedictine monastery, and the cloister and numerous fragments of monastic ranges survive, albeit much altered. Elsewhere monastic churches have similarly survived only where they also served as parish churches, as at Wymondham or Binham in Norfolk, or Ramsey in Cambridgeshire. In a few places monasteries and abbeys were converted to country houses, as at Audley End or St Osyth in Essex. But this does not seem to have been as common in East Anglia as in some other parts of England, and subsequent phases of rebuilding have generally obliterated obvious signs of the monastic legacy.

Because there are relatively few obvious remains, it is easy to underestimate the impact of monasteries on the medieval landscape. The older monasteries, in particular, owned vast territories and were actively involved in fen drainage and in the creation of towns (as at Bury St Edmunds). Some sense of the omnipresence of monastic communities in the landscape is still provided by Ely cathedral, that icon of the Fens, visible for kilometres across the flat surrounding wetlands (Fig. 6.8).

Fig. 6.8 Ely cathedral, *flanked by the much-altered remains of its Benedictine abbey, stands on a former island in the Fens and dominates the landscape for kilometres round.*

RENAISSANCE LANDSCAPES

Great mansions gradually changed in appearance in the course of the 16th century. To begin with, turrets, battlements and gatehouses continued to be important, as at Hengrave in Suffolk, built in the 1520s and 1530s by the London merchant Thomas Kytson (Fig. 6.9). But new political and social circumstances meant that such pretensions to defensibility slowly fell from favour. Instead, great mansions displayed a familiarity with Renaissance culture. 'Gothic' arches were eschewed and greater emphasis was placed on symmetry – initially in terms of external elevation, later with regard to the overall arrangement of spaces within the building.[13] Towards the end of the century some great houses were laid out, following the injunctions of Italian Renaissance architects, to careful ratios, as at Stiffkey in north Norfolk.[14] This, like medieval houses, was built around a courtyard, and most great mansions continued to be arranged like this well into the 17th century – as at Blickling in Norfolk, built by the Hobart family between 1618 and 1629. The largest early 17th-century mansion in East Anglia, however, was Thomas Howard's Audley End near Saffron Walden, which survives only as the large rump of a once much larger building, designed to receive and impress King James I. It was, unusually for East Anglia, built largely of stone: other great mansions were of brick.

Smaller landowners – the local gentry – also rebuilt their homes extensively in this period, often with money derived, directly or indirectly, from the textile industry. The East Anglian countryside is studded with examples. Some were ranged around courtyards, but most were not, for their owners did not require the kind of extensive accommodation that made this kind of arrangement necessary. Instead, they took the form of a main range with cross wings, which – together with a prominent central porch – produced the familiar 'E' plan, as for example at Kentwell Hall in Suffolk. Brick increasingly replaced timber framing and was sometimes employed in striking and exuberant ways, with a profusion of twisting chimneys and finials, as at East Barsham in Norfolk, built in the 1530s. Stepped or 'crow-stepped' gables were extensively used from the early 16th century – a common form, found in a number of countries bordering the North Sea, including Germany, Holland and Denmark. Slightly later are the shaped 'Dutch' gables, popular from the 1580s (as at Spain's Hall at Finchingfield in Essex) into the 18th century. As the term implies, these were also probably a manifestation of the region's close contacts with the European mainland.

Great mansions were accompanied by gardens, and often by deer parks. The latter changed significantly in the course of the late medieval period. Although great castles such as Framlingham had parks in close proximity, on most medieval estates they lay at a distance from the manor house, in relatively remote and marginal locations. They were well-wooded areas, which functioned primarily as venison farms and hunting grounds, rather than as ornamental landscapes. From the 15th century, however, park and mansion were increasingly brought into close proximity, as old parks were abandoned and new ones laid out at the expense of agricultural land, many – as at Long Melford – on the fringes of major textile towns.[15] They became less densely wooded, more 'park-like' in appearance. This was the real beginning of the ornamental park, a phenomenon we usually attribute to the great 'improvers' of the 18th century. Indeed, several noted 18th- and 19th-century parks – including Helmingham and Hengrave in Suffolk, and Hedenham and Hunstanton in Norfolk – had their origins in the 15th or 16th centuries.

Tudor gardens were of a formal, structured character and were enclosed

Fig. 6.9 Hengrave Hall, Suffolk: the cut-down remains of a larger mansion, erected for Sir Thomas Kytson in the 1520s and 1530s.

by walls or fences. They featured knots (geometric patterns of box, grass and gravel), topiary and gravel walks, as well as areas of ornamental woodland called 'wildernesses'. In the 1570s Sir Thomas Kitson of Hengrave bought 'a Dutchman' from Norwich to 'viewe ye orchardes, gardyns and walks', and later paid him for 'clypping the Knotts, altering the alleys, setting the grounde, finding herbes, and bordering the same'.[16] Several such gardens appear on early maps, like that of the Bishop's Palace at Hoxne in Suffolk of 1619 (Fig. 6.10).[17] But little remains on the ground today, even of the 'hard' landscaping. Walled gardens were generally swept away from fashionable façades in the 18th century, but a few survive, for example at Besthorpe or Intwood in Norfolk or Stutton Hall in Suffolk. Their design – like that of the houses they accompanied – often involved flamboyant use of brick. Garden buildings also sometimes remain, as at Bawburgh in Norfolk or Long Melford Hall in Suffolk.

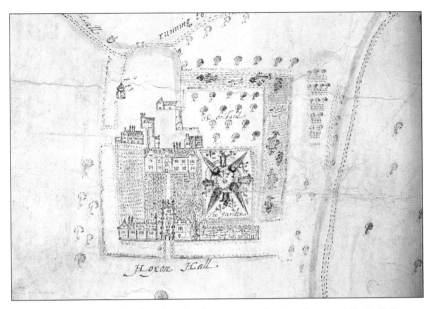

ABOVE: **Fig. 6.10 Hoxne Hall, Suffolk:** *detail from a map of 1619, showing the moat and geometric gardens.*

BELOW: **Fig. 6.11 Raynham Hall, Norfolk:** *an innovative, triple-pile house built for Sir Roger Townshend in the 1620s and 1630s.*

Not all great houses built in the period before the Civil War were of single-pile construction. Raynham Hall in Norfolk was designed in the 1620s by its owner, Sir Roger Townshend, assisted by his 'mason' William Edge (Fig. 6.11). It displays a firm knowledge of the ideas of Italian Renaissance architects such as Andreas Palladio, and of the buildings being erected at the time for members of the royal court by the innovative architect Inigo Jones, including the lost Prince's Lodging at Newmarket. Not only was Raynham highly symmetrical, both in internal organisation and external appearance, it was also a compact 'triple-pile' structure – that is, it was three rooms deep, rather than having a central court. Moreover, its design was carefully integrated with that of the gardens around it, so that – following the injunctions of Italian writers – both were laid out on the same axis of symmetry.[18]

Familiarity with Italian ideas is evident at other places. At Somerleyton in Suffolk, for example, the gardens created in the late 1610s not only shared a single axis of symmetry with the mansion, but also became (as Italian precedent demanded) more irregular in layout with increasing distance from it (Fig. 6.12). The compartment lying furthest from the house comprised an area of woodland, cut by serpentine paths, in which Classical sculptures were displayed.[19] William Edge visited in 1619, reporting to his master how he

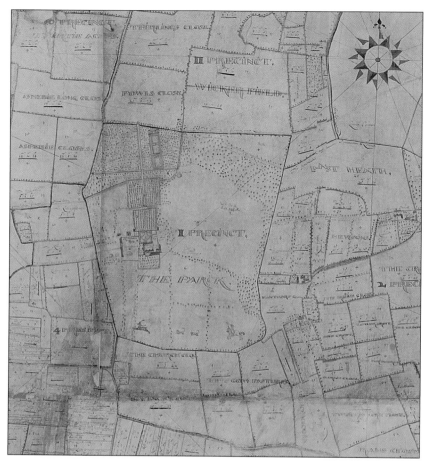

had seen 'the statues both of men and women, settinge uppon several beasts', set upon 'great pillaers made of brickearthe and fyttinge to stand att the meetinge of a crosse walke in a woode or otherwise'.[20] However, houses and gardens laid out along such sophisticated lines were always rare, and more rambling and irregular arrangements remained the norm, even at the highest social levels, up until the time of the Restoration. Most mansions continued to be surrounded by a jumble of enclosed courts containing not only ornamental gardens but also functional and productive areas: orchards, nut grounds, fishponds, dovecotes and farmyards.[21] Indeed, at many gentry residences like Aspenden in Hertfordshire such arrangements persisted well into the 18th century (Fig. 6.13).

At the highest social levels, the Civil War of the mid-17th century marked a watershed in the design of both mansions and their grounds. Many landowners had fled – or had been exiled – abroad during the war, to witness at first hand the houses and gardens of France and the Low Countries. On their return, they were keen to imitate them. This was also the

heyday of the gentleman architect, designing for self and friends rather than for a living, and East Anglia had more than its fair share. Roger North – lawyer, historian and architect – rebuilt Rougham Hall in Norfolk in the 1690s and described his experiences in the *Cursory Notes of Buildings*, a volume that remained unpublished in his lifetime.[22] The house, with an innovative free-standing portico, was demolished in the following century, but survives as a remarkably distinct parchmark in the parkland turf. More important was Roger Pratt, who designed a number of compact double- and triple-pile houses in the region, including the lost Horseheath in Cambridgeshire and his own mansion at Ryston in Norfolk, much altered by Sir John Soane in the late 18th century (Fig. 6.14).[23]

All this was part of a wider shift in taste. After the Civil War great mansions were no longer built in the traditional way, around courtyards. Compact, symmetrical designs, two or three rooms deep, variously influenced by French and Dutch models, were now the norm. Although elements of the old medieval plan with hall, cross-passage and the rest lingered for a while, new and more symmetrical arrangements of rooms soon emerged. The grounds of these mansions, moreover, displayed a number of new features. Avenues had been planted sporadically in East Anglia since the 16th century (Hengrave in Suffolk had one in 1587),[24] but they now became *de rigueur*, spreading out through the adjacent parkland or fields. Most were of lime or sweet chestnut: fine examples survive at Little Glemham in Suffolk and at Rougham and Houghton in Norfolk. Avenues are often described as a French fashion and to some extent they were. But they also expressed power and ownership, for only absolute control over the surrounding land allowed an owner to plant across it. Places such as Melton Constable in Norfolk – typically illustrated by Kip and Knyff, in their famous book *Britannia Illustrata*, from an impossible aerial perspective, in order to display the combined symmetry of house, grounds and wider landscape – expressed the new-found confidence of the landed elite in this post-Revolutionary world (Fig. 6.15). Linear ponds or 'canals', in contrast, were a prime feature of Dutch gardens. They generally doubled as fishponds and are particularly common in East Anglia and especially in Suffolk, with fine examples surviving at Campsey Ash and Abbots Hall,

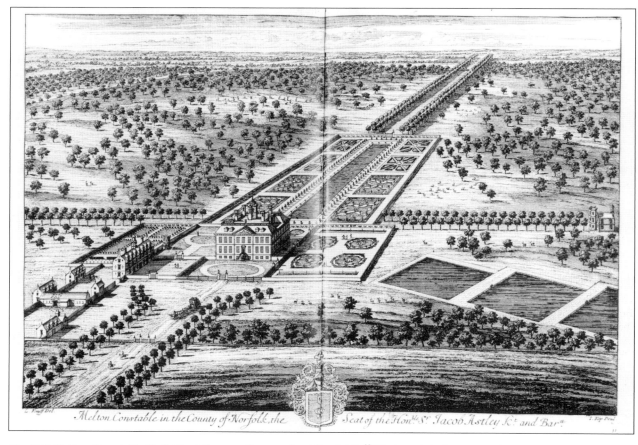

Fig. 6.15 Melton Constable Hall, Norfolk:
*the house, gardens and park, depicted from an
impossible aerial perspective in Kip and Knyff's*
Britannia Illustrata *of 1707.*

**Fig. 6.16 The remains of the early
18th-century gardens at Campsey Ashe,
Suffolk** *include this fine formal canal.*

Stowmarket (Fig. 6.16).[25] Their popularity may again be a consequence of the
region's links with the Low Countries, but may be due in part to
environmental factors. Homestead moats were also a common feature in the
region. Both could be created with relative ease on the heavy East Anglia clays
and it is noteworthy that there was some contemporary confusion between the
two. Roger North, for example, described moats as 'a Delicacy the greatest
Epicures in Gardening court, and we hear of it by the name of Canal'.[26]

PARKLANDS AND PALLADIANISM

The trend towards a more faithful
expression of Renaissance principles
continued into the 18th century.
Architects now turned for inspiration
not to French or Dutch models, but
directly to the works of the Italian
Renaissance architect Andreas Palladio,
and to Inigo Jones, his 17th-century
English interpreter – a taste that was
encouraged by the growing enthusiasm
for the 'Grand Tour' to Italy. In the
1720s and 1730s fashionable country
houses were designed like Italian villas,

with central porticoes, a rusticated basement and – in the larger houses – flanking pavilions. Internally, all trace of medieval arrangements had now gone: two main public reception rooms, ranged one behind the other – hall and saloon – occupied the central axis of the building, with suites of rooms, and further reception rooms, leading off from them. Norfolk has some of the finest and earliest examples of neo-Palladian architecture in the country, most notably Holkham, Houghton and Wolterton. Holkham was built of yellowish grey brick, in imitation of the colour-washed exteriors of Italian villas, but Houghton – the home of the first prime minister of England, Robert Walpole – is of stone, brought at immense expense from quarries in Lincolnshire (Figs 6.17 and 6.18). Both have corner turrets, a firm mark of the new style, which were often added during the 1740s and 1750s to existing

Fig. 6.17 Holkham Hall, Norfolk. The great Palladian mansion, built between c.1735 and 1759, stands in a designed landscape with a complex history. The lake, the great southern avenue, Obelisk Wood, and the obelisk itself, were all part of the first, geometric but rather simple layout, created in the late 1720s and 1730s. The park was expanded and substantially redesigned at the end of the 18th century under Thomas William Coke.

Fig. 6.18 Houghton Hall, Norfolk, from the air. The great avenues were planted by Charles Bridgeman in the early 1730s.

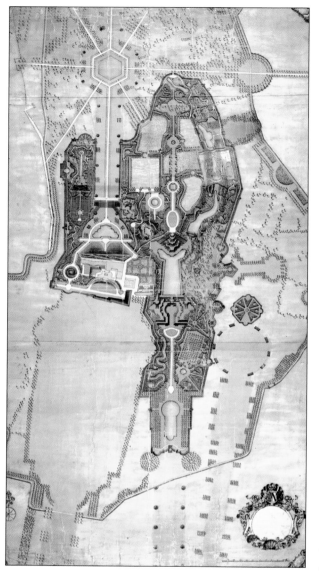

houses, as at Langley and Kimberley in Norfolk.[27] Palladian mansions and 'villas' continued to be built into the late 18th century – notable examples include Robert Taylor's Heveningham in Suffolk (1778), and James Paine's Shrubland Park in Suffolk (1770) and Thorndon in Essex (1764).

The earliest Palladian houses were provided with grounds which were still strongly geometric, albeit simpler and less cluttered than those of earlier periods. Perimeter walls were sometimes replaced by a *fosse* or ha ha – as early as *c.* 1720 at Houghton; fussy parterres gave way to smooth lawns; and clipped hedges and ornamental woods or wildernesses became prominent, the last now brought much closer to the house than in earlier periods and often provided with serpentine as well as straight walks. Such designs have not survived well, but are well documented in illustrations and plans (Fig. 6.19). More radical developments were soon taking place, however, motivated in part by a desire to provide Palladian buildings with an appropriate 'Italian' setting, loosely based on the popular paintings by Nicolas Poussin and Claude Lorraine. William Kent supplied a particularly innovative design for the South Lawn at Holkham in the 1730s. There were no straight lines at all, but instead an irregular prospect, with scattered trees and a small temple – a little slice of the Italian *campagna* improbably recreated on the windswept north Norfolk coast (Fig. 6.20). More evolutionary and less radical, but more common, were the kinds of design promulgated by the great Charles Bridgeman at places such as Houghton or Wolterton in Norfolk, or by Kent at Euston in Suffolk. In these, gardens were simplified still further, the division between garden and park was dissolved by the use of the ha ha, and avenues and other geometric clutter were removed wholesale. The positioning of clumps and the careful framing of vistas continued to provide geometric structure, especially when the landscape was viewed in plan or from above. However, the overall impression was that the house stood in an open, simple setting in which the park had triumphed over the garden.[28]

From *c.* 1760, at the most fashionable residences, this tendency was taken to its logical conclusion and all residual geometry was removed. The 'naturalistic' landscape style of Capability Brown and his contemporaries had arrived. The local gentry, it is true, often hung on to older arrangements until the 1770s, 1780s or even 1790s when – riding on the back of the rising tide of agricultural prosperity – they finally came to rebuild their homes in a simplified, less erudite, stripped-down version of the Palladian style, and reorganised their landscapes accordingly. Rebuilding of mansions and the redesign of their surroundings may have been linked in more complex ways than by a simple availability of funds permitting both. The open, casually irregular landscape

of the park perfectly complemented the compact, elegant form of the Palladian villa, just as the structured gardens bounded by elaborate walls had suited well the brick-built Tudor mansion. Moreover, country houses built after *c.* 1750 had their rooms arranged in a circuit rather than along symmetrical, linear sequences leading off hall and saloon, something which perhaps encouraged a less formal, and more flowing, disposition of their grounds. Either way, by the end of the century enclosed geometric gardens had become unfashionable, and anybody with serious pretensions to gentility had their house set within open parkland.

The new style is firmly associated in the popular mind with the name of Lancelot 'Capability' Brown. He was certainly the most successful of all the 'improvers', and responsible for a number of important landscapes in the region, including Kimberley, Langley and Melton Constable in Norfolk, Heveningham, Ickworth and Redgrave in Suffolk, and Audley End and Thorndon in Essex. But there were other designers who ran national landscaping practices and some of these also worked extensively in the region. Nathaniel Richmond designed the parks at West Wratting in Cambridgeshire; Skreens near Roxwell and Terling in Essex; Sacombe in Hertfordshire; Beeston St Lawrence in Norfolk; and probably Woolverstone in Suffolk.[29] Richard Woods – a man with a number of important Essex connections – worked at Hengrave in Suffolk, and at Wivenhoe, Thorndon and Audley End in Essex (Fig. 6.21).[30] Most parks, however, were the work of

local surveyors or nurserymen, many of whom set up in business after having been employed by one of the more famous 'improvers'. William Gooch, announcing in the *Norwich Mercury* in 1764 that he had 'now arrived from London in Norwich with an intention to undertake New Work in all its branches', typically emphasised that he had been 'many Years Foreman to the eminent Richard Woods, Land Surveyor and Designer of New Work'.[31]

Traditionally, garden historians have emphasised the importance and novelty of the landscape park. But recent research has modified established assumptions. Parks as ornamental landscapes were not entirely new, as we have seen, nor did gardens completely disappear in the course of the 18th century. As François de la Rochefoucauld, a Frenchman who toured through East Anglia in 1784, observed:

Fig. 6.21 Wivenhoe Park – now the campus of the University of Essex – as illustrated by John Constable. The park was designed by Richard Woods, a contemporary of 'Capability' Brown who lived for a time in Essex.

Fig. 6.22 The Tea Bridge in the gardens of Audley End, Essex, *was designed by Robert Adam in the 1760s.*

'near the house ... is what the English call the garden. It is a small pleasure ground, extremely well-tended, with little well-rolled paths ... Flowers planted in them...'.[32] Relatively few 18th-century pleasure grounds survive in good condition, but notable exceptions include those at Great Saxham in Suffolk, located a little way away from the mansion around a small lake, complete with 18th-century 'tea house' and a range of specimen trees. At Audley End in Essex, Richard Woods was responsible for laying out the pleasure grounds, elements of which – including the 'tea bridge' designed by Robert Adam – again survive (Fig. 6.22).

The landscape parks of 18th-century East Anglia were created in two ways. A minority developed from earlier deer parks. Avenues were felled and walled geometric gardens, wildernesses and the rest removed, so that open 'naturalistic' prospects appeared to extend right up to the walls of the house – although in reality an area of mown lawn, separated from the park by a discrete ha ha, formed the immediate setting for the mansion. Most of Brown's creations were like this, as he tended to work for the kind of wealthy landowner who already possessed a park of some kind. The majority of landscape parks, however, were entirely new creations, made at the expense of agricultural land. Formal clutter was removed from around the house and the surrounding fields were thrown together. But as the hedges were grubbed out, hedgerow trees were usually retained in some numbers in order to form an instant sylvan scene, while small copses and woods were often re-used as clumps or to form part of the perimeter belt. William Gilpin perceptively noted in the 1760s how, at Houghton, 'it is easy to trace, from the growth of the woods, and the vestiges of hedge-rows, where the ambition of the minister made his ornamental inroads into the acres of his inheritance.'[33] Most East Anglian parks thus contain trees that were already mature when the park was created, usually ancient pollarded oaks. Particularly impressive collections can be found in the parks at Benacre, Ickworth, Sotterley and Thornham in Suffolk, and at Kimberley and Raveningham in Norfolk (Fig. 6.23). Most are associated with the earthworks of old field boundaries, or hollow ways marking the line of former roads. Indeed, in this intensively arable countryside, parks are among the few places where earthwork remains of the medieval and early post-medieval landscape can survive on any scale.

Some 18th-century parks also contain earthwork traces of lost settlements, but these had often been abandoned long before the park was laid out and only a handful of hamlets and villages in East Anglia were actually cleared to make way for the landscapes of fashion. Most disappeared in the period before *c.* 1750 (Ickworth around 1702, Raynham *c.* 1704, Houghton and Holkham *c.* 1730, Wolterton in the late 1730s), although some examples were later, including Letton in Norfolk in the 1780s and Anmer in the same county as late as 1810 (Fig. 6.24).[34] Sometimes destruction occurred in stages, as at Audley End in Essex, where Lord Howard de Walden removed the hamlet of Audley End, another hamlet to the north of the mansion and a number of properties on the Littlebury side of the Cam, in order to improve the view.[35] The destruction of villages and hamlets was unusual, in part because of the region's dispersed pattern of settlement. Manor houses often lay isolated from, or peripheral to, the main focus of settlement in the parish, and parks could often be created with the removal of only a few dwellings, or none at all. More common, however, was the closure of roads and footpaths. Initially this was achieved by using a parliamentary act, or a writ of *Inquisition ad Quod Damnum*. But from 1773 the much simpler process of Quarter Sessions Road Closure Orders was adopted. The ubiquity of road and footpath closures is one signal that, although usually studied primarily in aesthetic or horticultural terms, 18th-century parks also had a profound social significance. They were landscapes of seclusion, their belts excluding all close views of the local population or their homes and providing their owners with privacy, as well as offering some protection for the game with which the larger parks at least were usually well stocked. The removal of walled gardens, moreover, was also accompanied by the destruction of nutgrounds, orchards, dovecotes, fishponds and farmyards – all the productive clutter with which the gentry had once been happy to associate themselves. This, too, made an important statement: that the owner was distanced from the humdrum practicalities of domestic production, a member of a class quite distinct from the farming and labouring population. Removal of formal gardens also emphasised the superiority of the landed elite over the expanding middle

Fig. 6.23 Ancient hedgerow oaks, *incorporated from the earlier working countryside, in the park at Kimberley in Norfolk.*

Fig. 6.24 Anmer Park in Norfolk: *most of the earthworks shown relate to a settlement cleared away when the park was expanded as late as 1810.*

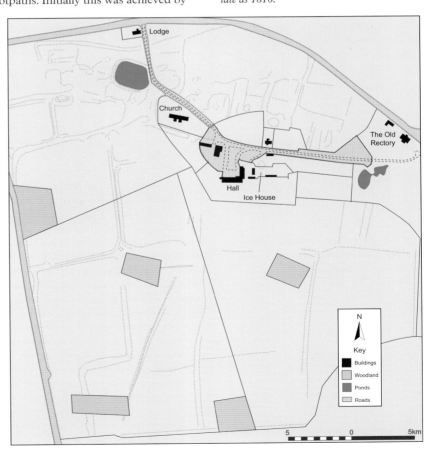

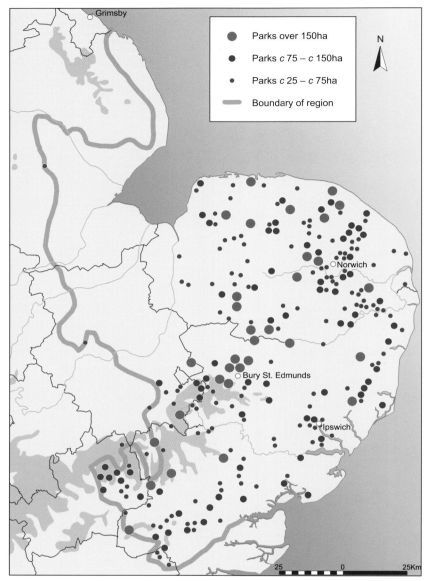

classes, who – of necessity, given the size of the plots at their disposal – continued to lay out structured and often fairly geometric gardens. In a polarised yet socially problematic world, the landscape style flourished because it required the one resource which only the established elite, and those wealthy enough to join it, possessed – land in abundance.

Parks were not distributed evenly across the region (Fig. 6.25). There were hardly any in the Fens, an area characterised by small landowners and splintered estates, where level terrain provided no opportunities for the rolling prospects demanded by fashionable taste in landscapes and in which malaria or 'ague' was endemic (until eradicated by improvements in drainage, and changes in land use, in the course of the 19th century). The central parts of the boulder clay plateau, in south Norfolk and north-east Suffolk, were also sparsely parked. Here a combination of high land values, complex tenurial patterns inherited from the medieval past and a largely pastoral economy had retarded the development of large estates, and most land was again in the hands of small owners or was owned in discontinuous blocks by absentees. Similar economic factors explain the marked lacuna in the distribution on the fertile loams of north-east Norfolk. On the other hand, parks were frequent in areas of poor, light soil – areas of low land values and with a long history of lordly domination – such as Breckland or the heaths to the north of Norwich. But there were also other, more subtle

Fig. 6.25 East Anglia and the Fens: the distribution of landscape parks in the late 18th century.

influences on their distribution. There was a marked 'packing' around the major towns of Norwich, Bury St Edmunds and – in the far south – London. Given the choice, most members of the wealthy elite preferred to reside near to a major urban centre, with all the shops, assemblies and other diversions to alleviate the tedium of rural life. Some of these parks, however, were diminutive creations surrounding the homes of upwardly mobile industrialists and financiers, who had purchased and suitably ornamented farms or minor manors on the outskirts of town, from where they could reach their business interests with relative ease. Also noteworthy is the line of parks down the east of Suffolk, roughly parallel with the coast, following close to the boundary between the clay plateau and the light soils of the Sandlings. The latter region was, by the 18th century, largely in the hands of substantial landed estates, but – open, largely treeless and with light, droughty soils – it provided poor opportunities for park-making. Owners thus chose to live on the western margins of their estates, in old-enclosed country, where the abundance of trees and woods made it easier to create a stylish, 'natural' landscape.

Indeed, where mansions were located – as they often were – within more extensive areas of open, unenclosed countryside, prodigious feats of afforestation had to be carried out to create an agreeable prospect. When the park at Holkham was redesigned and expanded in the 1780s and 1790s by Thomas William Coke, his gardener John Sandys planted well over two million trees in the vast perimeter belt and clumps. Plantations such as these were of economic as well as aesthetic value: growing timber was like money in the bank. A sales catalogue for the West Tofts estate in Breckland described in 1780 how the great perimeter belt contained no less than six hundred thousand trees: 'which, in the course of a few years, will at least be worth a Shilling a Tree, and consequently amount to Thirty Thousand pounds …'.[36]

Park-makers also had to deal with the problems posed by muted topography. Extended, rolling prospects were available across much of Essex and east Hertfordshire, and also in the north and north-west of Norfolk, and in these districts some of the most visibly satisfying creations of the landscape movement can be found – for example, at Holkham, Bayfield or Audley End. But over much of the region extensive, level tablelands and wide flat valleys made it hard to compose a suitably varied scene and, in particular, precluded the construction of adequate lakes. Parks such as Docking in north-west Norfolk are almost completely level and – save for the occasional pond – almost entirely waterless. Even at Houghton, visitors regularly lamented the absence of water, while at Langley – on the level clays of south Norfolk – Brown's proposals for a lake came to nothing. He did make one at Melton Constable, but it had to be in the far south of the park, almost out of sight of the mansion.

Muted topography had another effect, exaggerating a general tendency in parkland design, found in all parts of England, into something approaching a rule. Where, in the absence of rolling landforms, no particular prospect was more appealing than another, park-makers tended to maximise the extent of the view across the park which could be enjoyed from the sunny south side of the house, where the principal reception rooms were located. From this arises the 'north side rule': the larger the park, the nearer to its centre the mansion will stand; the smaller the park, the closer will it be to the northern boundary. This is a particularly noticeable feature of the parks found in the areas of more level terrain, in north Suffolk and south Norfolk.

By the end of the 18th century the smooth, manicured, pastoral landscapes created by Brown and his 'imitators' began to be criticised, most vocally in the 1790s by those famous proponents of 'Picturesque' taste, Uvedale Price and Richard Payne Knight. They demanded more varied settings for mansions, less repetitive and stereotyped, more in tune with the character of the local landscape and with lusher, more varied planting. They also had a strong preference for expansive vistas, tall mountains, cliffs and cascades – all hard to find in East Anglia.[37] Indeed, it is a moot point how influential 'Picturesque' ideas really were anywhere in lowland Britain during the lifetimes of their original proponents. However, a more effective challenge to the Brownian ideal was about to be mounted, one much more closely associated with East Anglia. Humphry Repton was born in Bury St Edmunds in Suffolk, but moved with his parents to Norwich in 1762 at the age of 10. Two years later he was sent to Holland to learn Dutch, presumably to prepare him for a career in the textile trade, for he was subsequently apprenticed to a textile merchant and for a while worked as such. Following his parents' death, however, he bought a small property at Sustead in north Norfolk, where he farmed on a small scale, sketched and socialised. He moved to Hare Street in Essex in 1786, two years before he began to practise as a landscape designer, so Essex perhaps has the best claim on him (although many of his family continued to reside in north Norfolk and Repton is himself buried at Aylsham).[38]

In stylistic terms, Repton stands on the cusp of the 18th and 19th centuries. He built on the principles formulated by Brown, but developed forms which were to

lay the foundations for the Victorian garden. He was not, as some contemporary critics alleged, a slavish copyist of Brown. His designs were more considered, intimate and subtle: he was a make-up artist, not a cosmetic surgeon. And unlike Brown he wrote widely, producing both published books (seven in all) and numerous 'red books', illustrated design proposals for particular sites (he did not provide the actual workforce to carry out the proposed 'improvements', as Brown generally did) (Figs 6.26 and 6.27). From these texts we know that he was acutely aware of the social messages conveyed by landscape. At Honing in Norfolk, he objected to the abrupt right-angle turn made when the grounds were entered because it suggested that the public road continued on 'to some place of greater importance' (Fig. 6.28). At Livermere in Suffolk, he proposed painting all the fences in the village the same colour, to emphasise the fact that the Lee family owned it all. He was most at home with relatively small commissions, and his style worked best with these. When he supplied designs for larger places, as at Holkham, he generally dealt with parts rather than the whole – in this case laying out a pleasure ground around the lake. Both snobbish and paternalistic, his greatest contributions were perhaps the reintroduction of structured gardens across the main façade of the house (something which he advocated as early as 1789 at Shrubland Park in Suffolk) and the development of a style that could be used effectively on quite minor properties, even down to the level of the large suburban villa. Repton worked all over Britain, but East Anglia has more of his commissions than anywhere else, including his first – Catton, just to the north of Norwich – and his last – Sheringham, on the north Norfolk coast (Fig. 6.29).[39] But perhaps the greatest interest lies in the way that his long sojourn in north Norfolk – a district of gentle terrain, densely studded with the diminutive parks of the gentry – seems in many ways to have moulded his social and artistic eye.

THE 19th CENTURY

Country houses continued to be built, and on an increasingly lavish scale, right through the 19th century. However, the dominance of the neo-Palladian style came to an end around 1800. Houses in neoclassical and 'Greek revival' modes – more accurate copies of Classical buildings, reflecting the increasing knowledge of Greek and Roman architecture resulting from excavations at Pompeii and elsewhere – were soon joined by ones in an 'Italianate' style, modelled on the architecture of 17th-century Italian palaces; and, above all, by various forms of Gothic. Some of the latter resemble Tudor mansions, with angle pilasters, projecting porches and prominent gables – such as Dunston Hall to the south of Norwich (now a hotel), built in 1859. Others ape Jacobean manor houses, with shaped gables and a profusion of dormer windows – like Lynford in west Norfolk, designed by William Burn in the 1850s. The largest examples, however, imitated rambling castles, such as the amazing Shadwell Hall in south-west Norfolk, extended and Gothicised in two stages by Edward Blore and S S Teulon.[40] Many of these larger buildings have fared badly. Later generations found their soaring towers and open halls both inconvenient and expensive to maintain, and so the great Costessey Hall to the west of Norwich is now no more than a ruined tower in the middle of a golf course (Fig. 6.30), while Hillington Hall in west Norfolk is just a complex of parch-marks in the grounds of a much reduced house. This latter building was designed by one of the most important East Anglian architects of the 19th century, W J Donthorne, the son of a Swaffham hatter. Like many architects of the time he worked in a variety of styles, but mainly produced various forms of Gothic, most strikingly perhaps at Cromer Hall in north Norfolk.[41]

Although an exuberant Gothic was the preferred style for country houses in East Anglia, the Italianate was also favoured. Here, too, there have been losses, including the vast Haveringland Hall to the north of Norwich, again the

OPPOSITE PAGE:

TOP: *Fig. 6.26 An illustration from Humphry Repton's 'Red Book' for Livermere in Suffolk: before 'improvement'.*

MIDDLE: *Fig. 6.27 An illustration from Humphry Repton's 'Red Book' for Livermere in Suffolk: the anticipated result of the proposed changes.*

BOTTOM: *Fig. 6.28 Honing, Norfolk. The park was redesigned by Repton in 1792; he also made some changes to the house itself.*

THIS PAGE:

ABOVE: *Fig. 6.29 Catton, just north of Norwich, was Repton's first paid commission (in 1788). Now engulfed in the outer suburbs of the city, it is currently being restored.*

BELOW: *Fig. 6.30 Costessey Hall, Norfolk. The massive gothic ranges erected by J C Buckler between 1826 and 1855 dwarf the original, 16th-century manor house (in the foreground).*

Fig. 6.31 Shrubland Hall, Suffolk: the hall has a complex history but in its present form is a huge 19th-century Italianate mansion, flanked by magnificent gardens.

work of Edward Blore, completed in 1852 but completely demolished less than a century later. Bylaugh in mid Norfolk was a magnificent, picturesque ruin, its floors collapsed and trees growing unrestrained within its vast shell, until recently restored. The most striking surviviors are perhaps Somerleyton in north-east Suffolk, designed in a mixed Jacobean/Italianate style by John Thomas, and Shrubland Hall to the north west of Ipswich. Both, typically, have tall, asymmetrically placed towers (Fig. 6.31).

Shrubland is a useful reminder that the larger country houses of the 19th century were not always completely new buildings, but often had long and complex histories.[42] A small Palladian house with two flanking pavilions, designed by James Paine and erected on a virgin site in the 1770s, it was first extended in *c.* 1810 and then, much more extensively, in the years around 1830 for Sir William and Lady Anne Middleton by the architect J P Gandy Deering. His design was in turn soon altered, in the late 1840s and early 1850s, by Sir Charles Barry, who provided the great tower and Italianate detailing, but the core of Paine's original house can still be clearly seen (Fig. 6.32). What is true of Shrubland applies to many other large houses. Somerleyton's 19th-century façade concealed in part the stylish 17th-century mansion of the Wentworth family, while Hamels Mansion in east Hertfordshire has been christened a 'country house chameleon': a house of early 18th-century date, incorporating parts of a building of *c.* 1590, which was modified in the 1760s and again, more drastically, in the 1830s, in fashionable Elizabethan mode.[43]

In the immediate surroundings of such mansions, the trends initiated by Repton were now taken further. Through the middle decades of the 19th century gardens grew larger, more elaborate and more formal in character, and were positioned prominently across the main façades. Bedding plants in geometric parterres, exuberant topiary and splendid collections of plants in ferneries, pineta and arboreta all enjoyed immense popularity, reflecting in part a burgeoning interest in scientific horticulture.[44] The most notable designer of the period was William Andrews Nesfield, who worked at a number of sites in the region, including Henham, Flixton and Woolverstone, creating his hallmark parterres of box, gravel and bedding plants, flanked by raised terraces, urns and topiary.[45] He claimed that their design was closely based on 16th- and 17th-century prototypes, but this was, at best, only partly true. The main difference between Victorian parterres and their supposed models, however, is that whereas the latter had been placed in walled enclosures, the former were separated from the park only by low balustrading. Such was the popularity of the park, and its importance as a marker of status, that it had to be proudly displayed, in full view of house and gardens. The best surviving examples of Nesfield's work in East Anglia are at Holkham, Lynford and above all Somerleyton, where, although the parterres have long been grassed over, the terraces and topiary remain, and the arboretum, ornamental kitchen garden and elaborate maze are maintained in fine condition (Fig. 6.33).

Whether Somerleyton represents the finest Victorian garden in the region is, however, a matter for debate. Shrubland Hall is another contender for that crown, as the transformation of the hall was mirrored by radical developments in the grounds. Lady Anne Middleton, working in close association with the great gardener Donald Beaton, laid out an elaborate chain of gardens at the foot of the escarpment below the house, which included a Swiss garden (complete with substantial chalet) and a maze. Together they experimented with different ways of combining bedding plants, part of a somewhat esoteric contemporary debate about whether smooth transitions of colour, or striking contrasts, should be employed in formal displays. The greatest addition to the gardens came in the early 1850s, however, when Sir Charles Barry, having completed work on the house, created a new parterre garden around it and – developing an idea that had originated with Lady Anne – linked this to the existing pleasure grounds below with a steep 'Descent', vaguely based on the gardens at the Villa D'Este near Rome. This terminated at another magnificent parterre with a fountain and a 'loggia' – surely one of the finest pieces of Victorian landscape design in the country (Fig. 6.34). Running all along the base of the escarpment, moreover, he created the long, straight 'Green Terrace', which served to link together the existing string of gardens, and several new ones, into one vast and elaborate spectacle. More than 80,000 geraniums, verbenas, petunias, lobelias and other plants were required each year for planting-out in the various beds. When completed in the late 1850s, the gardens cost over £2,000 a year to maintain.[46]

Fig. 6.32 Like smaller farmhouses and cottages, many great mansions in East Anglia developed in a series of stages. Shrubland Hall was built on a virgin site in the 1770s, to designs by James Paine (top). It was a modest Palladian villa, with flanking pavilions connected to the main block by curving corridors. The house was extended in c.1808; and again, in c.1830, by the architect J P Gandy-Deering. Charles Barry provided Italianate detailing and a striking asymmetrical tower in 1848–50. Although it is often said that Charles Barry designed Shrubland Hall, the original 18th-century 'core' is still clearly visible.

Gardens such as Shrubland and Somerleyton were, in terms of their scale, exceptional. But everywhere – at great mansions and minor manor houses alike – gardens grew more elaborate, with their creation and maintenance underpinned by the buoyant agricultural economy of the 'high farming' years. As agricultural prices rose, rental incomes boomed, although some East Anglian owners also had access to other forms of income and a few – like Sir Morton Peto, the civil engineer and entrepreneur who created Somerleyton – came from outside the ranks of the established landed elite. Yet while we tend to remember the great gardens of the age, parks, too, continued to be important. Many new ones were created, and the majority of existing examples increased in size. Entrance lodges proliferated (they had been relatively rare before 1800) and planting became more varied, with greater use of exotic conifers (although pines had not been rare in Brown's parks) and a more diverse range of deciduous trees, especially lime, horse chestnut and beech. The region's continental climate has ensured a high rate of loss of the more tender exotics from parks, arboreta and pleasure grounds, but Wellingtonia (*Sequoia giganteum*) in particular often make a great visual impact, most notably at Lynford in Norfolk, where Nesfield planted a magnificent avenue of them. Although we tend to think of parks as essentially 18th-century features, even those which originated in that period normally have a majority of 19th-century trees. Indeed, while I have been discussing designed landscapes as if they belonged to particular periods, most East Anglia examples are a palimpsest, mainly 18th- and 19th-century in date, but often incorporating traces of earlier geometric designs and fragments of the earlier working countryside that the landscape of gentility replaced. It is this complexity that makes them so interesting to study.

The agricultural recession that started in the 1880s, and the great social and political changes of the early 20th century, effectively brought to an end the construction of large country houses with extensive grounds. Leading designers and writers turned their attention to smaller, more intimate 'arts and crafts' houses, in pseudo-vernacular styles and accompanied by relatively small, compartmentalised gardens. In these, an abundance of 'hard' landscaping (in the form of walls, paths and pergolas) was combined with informal, profuse planting, mostly of hardy species and mainly in wide borders. East Anglia can boast comparatively few examples of this type, especially when compared with districts in the immediate hinterland of London. However, some elements of the new style

Fig. 6.34 Shrubland Hall: *Barry's 'Great Descent', constructed in 1852, is the finest piece of Victorian garden design in East Anglia.*

OPPOSITE PAGE:

Fig. 6.33 Somerleyton Hall, Suffolk.
Another 19th-century Italianate mansion that incorporates earlier structures, Somerleyton is most famous for its Victorian gardens, which were mainly laid out by William Andrews Nesfield in the 1850s for Sir Morton Peto. Immediately below the house is Nesfield's terraced gardens, the ornate parterres now long grassed over. Beyond lies the extensive arboretum, and in the distance the vast kitchen garden and the maze.

were adopted in country house gardens; some minor manor houses were acquired and renovated by businessmen and their grounds revamped in a broadly 'arts and crafts' style, as at Stutton in south Suffolk; and a number of new residences wholeheartedly displaying the new taste appeared, largely in coastal locations, serving as holiday or retirement homes for the wealthy. Examples include Detmar Blow's Happisburgh Manor in north-east Norfolk, with its innovative 'butterfly' plan; Edward Lutyen's The Pleasaunce in Overstrand; and Felixstowe Lodge, designed by Robert Schultz Weir, with terraced gardens on the side of the cliff, a large pergola, sunken flower gardens and ornamental dipping well.

Nationally, there were some exceptions to the general trend towards smaller, more compact residences for the rich. In the immediate hinterland of London, in particular, some new country houses were built well into the 20th century with large parks and extensive gardens in the Victorian manner, by wealthy businessmen eager to adopt the trappings of traditional wealth. But in East Anglia the local economy was too firmly tied to agriculture for much money to be available to carry out such ambitious schemes. There were exceptions, and the most striking proves the rule. In the decades around 1900, one Cuthbert Quilter erected a house in an eclectic mixture of styles at Bawdsey on the Suffolk coast. He laid out a park, blew up a martello tower to make a sunken rose garden, and – disappointed by the crumbling mud cliffs – had new ones created, from artificial rock called 'Pulhamite'. But Quilter was no local squire, even if he named his new house 'Bawdsey Manor'. He was an Ipswich businessman who had made his money in the telephone business.

NOTES

1   Rogerson 1993.
2   Brown 1976; Cathcart King 1983.
3   Liddiard 2000a.
4   Ibid.
5   Liddiard 2000b.
6   Brown 1951.
7   Dallas & Sherlock 2002.
8   Barnes & Simpson 1952.
9   Nicolson 1998; Andrews & Ryan 1999.
10 Edwards & Williamson 1999, 4–17.
11 Rickett & Rose 1993; Wilton 1980; Knowles & Hadcock 1971.
12 Pestell 1999.
13 Smith 1992, 46–66; Girouard 1978.
14 Hassell Smith 2002.
15 Hoppitt 1999a; Hoppitt 1992; Williamson 2000b, 19–24.
16 Gage 1822, 17.
17 East Suffolk Record Office HD40 422.
18 Harris 1961; Campbell 1989.
19 Williamson 2000b, 17–19; East Suffolk Records Office, 942.64 Som.
20 Williamson 2000b, 18–19.
21 Williamson 1995, 31–5.
22 Colvin & Newman 1985; Williamson 1996.
23 Silcoxe-Crowe 1985.
24 West Suffolk Records Office, P746/1.

25 Martin 2002.
26 North 1713, 27.
27 Edwards & Williamson 2000, 43–53; Schmidt 1980, 214–17, 298–301; Moore 1996.
28 Williamson 1998a, 46–96.
29 Brown 2001.
30 Cowell 1986a; Cowell 1987; Cowell 1986b.
31 *Norwich Mercury* 4 February 1764.
32 Laird 1999; Scarfe 1988.
33 Gilpin 1809, 41.
34 Davison 1988.
35 Brown 1996, 101.
36 Norfolk Records Office MC 77/1/521/7.
37 Appleton 1986.
38 Daniels 1999.
39 Williamson 1998a, 195–202; Williamson 2000b, 91–105.
40 Girouard 1979.
41 O'Donnell 1978.
42 Williamson 2002a.
43 Rowe 1998.
44 Elliott 1986.
45 Ridgeway 1993; Williamson 1998a, 212–13; Williamson 2000b, 122–42.
46 Williamson 2000b, 122–9.

7

The Claylands

The character of East Anglia as a whole was shaped by location, climate and topography. These factors influenced patterns of contact and trade, determined levels of population and moulded broad aspects of the medieval and post-medieval economy. The most important determinant of individual landscapes *within* East Anglia, however, was unquestionably soil. Different kinds of soil posed particular problems, and presented particular opportunities, to successive generations of farmer. The ways in which people dealt with poor drainage, acidity or infertility, exploiting the environment to take advantage of market opportunities or simply to feed themselves and their families, served, more than anything else, to shape systems of fields and patterns of settlement. While the local environment itself might be relatively stable and unchanging, however, society was not. Population rose and fell, different forms of social and economic organisation developed, then perished; and as they did so the structures created by one group of local inhabitants, to deal with one set of circumstances, often had knock-on effects for later generations. In consequence, each district tended to develop, to a significant extent, in its own particular way – not, of course, isolated from the broader currents of national life, but nevertheless following its own idiosyncratic trajectory. Soils, as we have already noted, do not simply or directly make landscapes. But the boundaries of particular kinds of landscape nevertheless correspond, to a significant degree, with particular kinds of soil.

In East Anglia the range of soil types is considerable, the gradations between and within them immense, and in most places different soils lie interdigitated in complex ways. In a book of this size we must simplify, and in the chapters that follow some important districts will, of necessity, receive scant attention, such as the rich loams of north-east Norfolk or the small area of heavy soils, derived from the Gault Clay, in the area to the east of Downham Market on the Norfolk Fen edge. Instead, I will consider the development of the rural landscape under three simple headings: claylands, meaning the boulder clay districts occupying the central bulk of East Anglia; light lands, derived from chalk, sands and gravels; and wetlands, areas of low lying marshes and fens.

THE CLAYLAND LANDSCAPE BEFORE 1700

The East Anglian claylands have the most complex and the most interesting history of all the region's varied landscapes. The essential pattern of fields and settlements was, in most districts, in place by *c.* 1250, and many of the surviving buildings – especially in the textile-rich south – were erected before 1550. Nevertheless, much of what we see here today is the consequence of relatively recent developments, of changes that have taken place over the last two centuries or so. In some ways the term 'clayland landscape' is misleading, for this extensive tract of land, nearly 8,000 square kilometres, stretching in a great arc from mid Norfolk to east Hertfordshire, comprises a number of quite different landscapes.

Fig. 7.1 *Towards the north, the clayland landscape comprises extensive, level plateaux between wide river valleys. A typical view in north Suffolk: an intensely arable landscape, yet still retaining some ancient woods and hedges.*

Fig. 7.2 **Littlebury Green, Essex**: *the typical landscape of the Hertfordshire and Essex boulder clays, with rolling landforms, much woodland and irregularly-shaped fields – some the result of medieval assarting, some created by the early piecemeal enclosure of small open fields. The green from which the hamlet takes its name was enclosed in 1805, and subsequently largely built over: the original building line is still marked by the older farms and cottages.*

A useful division can, however, be drawn – as so often in the study of East Anglia – roughly along the line of the Lark–Gipping corridor. In topographic terms the clayland areas to the north and east are noticeably flatter, with wide, level tablelands between the principal valleys. To the south and west, in contrast, the valleys are much more closely spaced (seldom more than 4 or 5km apart) and the terrain is often dramatically rolling – the clay 'plateau' as such is here hardly recognisable as a topographic feature (Figs 7.1 and 7.2). The soils, too, differ markedly in character to either side of this line. In north-east Suffolk and southern and central Norfolk the plateau areas are occupied by soils classified today, by the Soil Survey of England and Wales, as the Beccles Association, poorly draining yet slightly sandy in character, while the valley sides are characterised by those of the Burlingham Association, sandier and more freely draining. To the south, the principal plateau soils are the stiff, but calcareous, stagnogleys of the Hanslope Association. These contrast sharply with the various lighter soils, formed in thinner drift mixed with underlying chalk or glacio-fluvial deposits, which are found within the principal valleys.[1]

In the medieval period the main variations in settlement followed this same broad divide. Extensive commons were the key feature in the districts to the north and east of the Lark and Gipping rivers. They formed magnets for settlement which, in the course of the 11th, 12th and 13th centuries, sucked farms away from older sites, so that parish churches often came to stand alone in the midst of the fields (Fig. 7.3). To the south and west, in contrast, while large commons and isolated churches could sometimes be found, individual farms set in their own fields and small clusters of dwellings around diminutive greens were the main consequence of early medieval settlement expansion. Here churches more frequently stood in villages or large hamlets – the older settlements, located in or beside the principal valleys.[2]

Although often considered a quintessential 'ancient countryside', the claylands in the medieval period could boast extensive areas of open fields. To the north and east of the Gipping these were widespread on all soils, but in the south they were more restricted to the valleys, with woods, deer parks, commons and areas of enclosed fields occupying the interfluves between (Figs 7.4 and 7.5). Demesne land – the lord's home farm – was more likely to lie in consolidated blocks in this area, although it sometimes comprised strips, intermingled with the land of the tenants – as for example at Thaxted in Essex.[3] If demesne land lay in enclosed fields, these were sometimes very large. At Cressing Temple in Essex the North Field covered 76 acres (31ha), Bannerley 110 acres (45ha) and Whistocks 300 acres (121ha). The scale of medieval commercial grain production at Cressing is also manifested in the huge, timber-framed barns, of 13th- and 14th-century date, which still stand beside the manor house (Fig. 7.6).[4] Nevertheless, nowhere on the clays would we have encountered the kind of empty, treeless and hedgeless landscapes that characterised some of the open or 'champion'

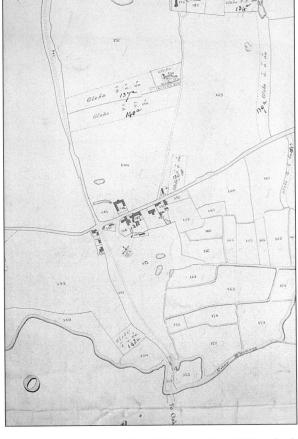

ABOVE: *Fig. 7.3 The parish of Billingford in south Norfolk, as shown on the Tithe Award map of 1839. The church stands isolated from the main areas of settlement, which cluster beside greens and commons. By this time, the open fields had all disappeared through gradual, piecemeal enclosure, but a few glebe strips remained, now lying within hedged fields owned by others.*

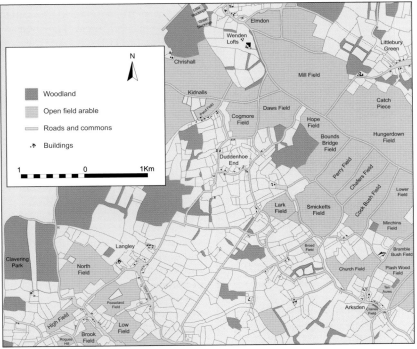

LEFT: *Fig. 7.4 The area around Elmdon, Langley and Littlebury in north-west Essex in the early 19th century. Open fields survived rather later here than in most parts of Essex. They were located on the lighter soils, in the major valleys. The higher ground was occupied by areas of woodland and enclosed fields, some of the former marking the sites of medieval deer parks.*

Fig. 7.5 Morley St Botolph and St Peter in central Norfolk in 1629. *Large areas of open fields still remained in the two parishes, and the configuration of field boundaries indicates that in the medieval period they had been even more extensive, occupying almost all the land other than that taken up by woods, the deer park, and the various commons that formed the main foci for settlement. Typically for northern East Anglia, the parish churches stood isolated in the midst of the fields.*

districts on the poorest, lightest soils of East Anglia. Woods and hedges were everywhere in evidence: even where open fields and large demesne closes dominated the scene, the principal roads and tracks were hedged.

To what extent the clayland landscape was entirely a creation of the medieval period and how far it had much older roots, remain matters for debate. Certainly, settlement was widespread by the end of the Iron Age, and field-walking surveys suggest that across much of the claylands there were between 1 and 1.5 Roman settlements, on average, per square kilometre. The larger and wealthier sites were generally located in or beside the principal valleys (as they were in the medieval period), but smaller, poorer establishments were widely scattered across the plateau and could be found even on the very heaviest clays.[5] As noted in Chapter 2, in a number of places fragments of prehistoric systems of land division appear to form the framework within which medieval fields and furlongs developed. These are mostly arranged in 'co-axial' form around long boundaries and lanes running out of major valleys and up onto watersheds (*see* Fig. 2.21). Nevertheless, extensive tracts of woodland still remained in – or had regenerated by – Saxon times, and the 11th, 12th and 13th centuries were unquestionably periods of expansion, as farms were established

*Fig. 7.6 **The huge medieval barns at Cressing Temple** indicate the scale of demesne grain production on the Essex claylands in the medieval period.*

beside greens and commons or were carved out of woodland in remote corners of parishes.

Archaeological surveys, and such documents as charters and extents, allow us to see the broad outlines of the medieval landscape. Post-medieval maps and surveys provide more detail. By the 16th and 17th centuries, however, important changes had taken place. In particular, the period after the Black Death saw the progressive enclosure of open fields, almost always by informal, 'piecemeal' methods. Large areas of common land remained into the 19th century, but otherwise the clays had, by the start of the 18th, become an enclosed landscape. Enclosure was associated with a steady expansion in the area under pasture, and a concomitant reduction in that under tilth: for the claylands became, in the course of the 15th and 16th centuries, a district that specialised in dairying and bullock fattening.[6] However, the extent of this involvement in pastoral husbandry tended to vary between the north and south of the region, the line of division roughly following, once again, that of the Lark–Gipping corridor. To the north, by the 16th century, pastures were extensive and most farms had only around one-fifth of their land in arable. To the south and west, in contrast, on the more calcareous clay, the proportion of arable was significantly higher. Robert Reyce, writing in the 17th century, noted this distinction as manifested within Suffolk. The farmers in the north and east of the county, he wrote, 'cheifly consist upon pasture and feeding', while the 'middle parts', although 'enjoying much meadow and pasture, yett far more tillage doe from thence raise their chiefest maintenance'.[7]

Early writers often described the claylands as a 'woodland' district, but this term referred less to the density of managed woods (although these were prominent in many areas) as to the large numbers of farmland trees that gave these districts a 'bosky' – that is, well-wooded – appearance. Most hedges were liberally stuffed with trees, which were also scattered across the pasture fields and some of the commons. Data from nine surveys, from farms in Essex, Suffolk and Norfolk, made between 1650 and 1771, suggest an average of around 10 trees per acre.[8] But some places had far more. A survey made at Denham in Suffolk in 1651, for example, suggests that there was an average of 15.4 trees per acre, while another, made in Thorndon in the same county in 1742, implies no less than 29 per acre.[9] Most were oaks, but ash, elm and hornbeam were locally significant. At Langley in Norfolk in the mid-17th century, 70 per cent of the trees recorded in an estate survey were oak and 30 per cent ash; at Thorndon in 1742 67 per cent were oak, 16 per cent ash and 17 per cent elm; while at Buckenham in Norfolk in the 1690s 49 per cent were oak and 44 per cent ash, together with 6.6 per cent elm (and six unspecified 'young' trees).[10] Most trees were managed as pollards: that is, they were repeatedly cut at intervals of 10 to 15 years, at a height of around 2 or 3m – out of reach of grazing livestock – in order to produce a regular supply of straight 'poles' for fuel, fencing and a host of other uses. Only a minority were left to grow as timber trees. This dominance in part reflected the great need for wood (as opposed to timber) on the part of the local population, and in part the importance of freeholders and the strength of tenants in this land of small and splintered estates. Both medieval custom and the terms of post-medieval leases generally stipulated that the tenant had the right to take wood, but not the timber, from the farm, and the temptation to convert any young tree into a pollard was thus overwhelming. Of the trees mentioned in the Thorndon survey of 1742, for example, no less than 82 per cent of the trees recorded were pollards, 13 per cent were classified as saplings and a mere 5 per cent were timber trees.

Although pollarding was mainly carried out to provide large quantities of wood it may also have been practised, especially in medieval times, to produce 'leafy hay' – winter fodder for cattle. As late as the 16th century the agricultural writer Thomas Tusser, an Essex man, advised:

> If frost doo continue, this leson doth well,
> For comfort of cattell the fewell to fell;
> From eurie tree the superfluous bows
> Now prune for thy neat therupon to go browse.[11]

Indeed, some trees appear to have been managed primarily with this in mind. A survey of the manor of Redgrave in Suffolk, made shortly after the Dissolution of the monasteries, described how on the 'seyd mannor and dyvers tenementes there … be growing 1,100 okes of 60, 80 and 100 yeares growth part tymber parte usually cropped and *shred* '.[12] Shredding involved shaving off the side branches of the tree so that it grew to resemble a kind of fuzzy toilet brush, producing an abundance of fresh, leafy growth. Oaks were the most commonly shredded species, although elm, poplar and ash were also managed in this way. In some districts it was customary to group pollards and 'shreds' along the field margins, in 'rows' three or four deep. This was one aspect of a more general phenomenon in these landscapes. Where fields were used as arable, the cropped area frequently did not run right up to the boundary hedge. Instead there was often a 'hedge green', an uncultivated strip on which the plough team could turn, and which was mown for hay or used for grazing tethered cattle.

Post-medieval fields on the claylands varied greatly in size, a consequence in part of the district's complex enclosure history. Where open fields had once existed, and had undergone gradual piecemeal enclosure, fields might be very small indeed. A survey of Diss in Norfolk, made in 1589, describes closes ranging in size from 40 acres (*c.* 16ha) down to 3 rods (0.3ha) or less, while another in the same parish, made in 1771, describes 21 fields with an average size of less than 3 acres (*c.* 1.2ha).[13] But some very large fields, of 30ha or more, could also be found. A few may have been survivors of the great demesne grain-fields of the medieval period, although most of these seem to have been subdivided into smaller parcels as large-scale demesne farming came to an end in the 14th and 15th centuries. Most were large 'grazing grounds', upland wood-pastures reclaimed direct from the 'wastes'.[14]

The scattered settlements of the claylands were linked by a complex and intricate mesh of lanes and tracks. Most of the roads in these districts – together with those now surviving only as 'green lanes' – were in place by *c.* 1300, and many are more ancient still. They generally meander in a perplexing fashion and, in the more undulating southern districts in particular, have often been deeply hollowed by centuries of use and erosion, and are flanked by high hedge banks. The claylands are also distinguished today by a phenomenally high density of footpaths, for they never underwent the kind of wholesale reorganisation by planned, post-medieval enclosure that rationalised route networks in the former 'champion' lands on lighter soils.

This was a prosperous land in the 15th, 16th and 17th centuries, as numerous timber-framed farmhouses testify. Many are accompanied by large late medieval or early-modern barns. These can be found even towards the north of the region, in districts in which agricultural historians often suggest there was only a limited hectarage under tilth, such as the fine example at Dairy Farm, Newton Flotman, Norfolk, of 15th-century date. However, the majority are found to the south and west of the Lark–Gipping corridor, where the economy was more mixed and a more even balance maintained between arable and pasture. Some of the wealth manifested in vernacular buildings derived, as we have seen, from the textile industry. But it also reflected the fertility of the rich clay soil, and the fact that these areas were characterised by prosperous yeoman farmers and remained largely free of the domination of large landed estates.

While the land might be fertile, however, it had to be treated with care. Here, in contrast to the situation on the light lands, the main problem facing arable farmers was not a shortage of soil nutrients – nitrates and phosphates were not rapidly leached away as they were on the poor 'hungry' lands – but seasonal waterlogging. This was 'cold' land: wet soils warm up slowly in the spring and germination and plant growth are delayed.[15] Drainage was a prime concern, and was effected in a number of ways. Where land lay in open fields farmers may have ploughed their land in broad ridges, in the Midland manner, with deep furrows between to carry off the water. But there are only a few scattered examples of the familiar 'ridge and furrow' earthworks on the clays, and while this may well be due in part to the intensity of later land use, it seems that farmers always relied more on the network of deep ditches that surrounded both enclosed fields and the smaller blocks of open arable. These formed, and often still form, a complex mesh of artificial watercourses, flowing with water throughout the winter months, which eventually feeds in to the natural streams and the main rivers. The ditches would be cleared out every five years or so – a particularly unpleasant task, carried out in the winter months – and the excavated material dumped on the adjacent hedge bank, which was thus augmented and strengthened. Surface drainage was sometimes assisted by ploughing narrow impermanent ridges which (unlike those in ridge and furrow) were ploughed out and replaced by new ridges, in different places, every year or every few years. This practice was known as 'stitching' or 'stetching' and was, according to William Folkingham in 1610, a particular feature of East Anglia and Hertfordshire.[16]

THE CLAYLANDS SINCE 1700

The 'Agricultural Revolution' as popularly conceived – the enclosure of open fields and sheepwalks, marling and the cultivation of turnips and clover – was essentially a feature of the light lands of East Anglia. But there were also major changes in the agriculture of the claylands in the 18th and 19th centuries. In particular, the period

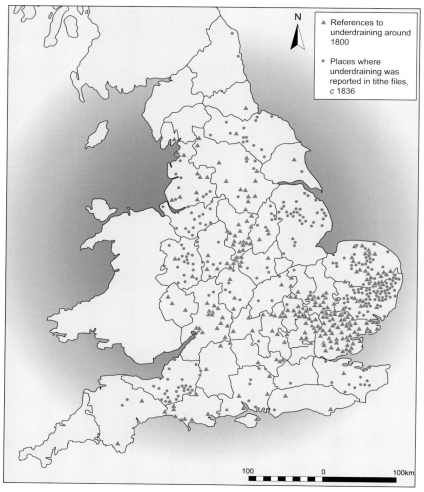

between *c.* 1760 and 1850 saw the extent of pasture decline significantly as the district became what it is today – one of the prime arable areas of England. However, this transformation was accompanied by a number of fundamental changes in the character of the farming environment. The most important was the widespread adoption of new, more efficient modes of drainage. This not only led directly to improved cereal yields, it was also a necessary precondition for the successful adoption of the new rotations, for turnips are particularly susceptible to waterlogging, while the tightly packed nature of clay soils makes it difficult to 'pull' the crop, so that the livestock have to consume it where it grows in the field – something which can itself cause problems, for large numbers of animals (especially if closely folded) serve to compact these soils. The crucial development was the widespread adoption of under-drainage – that is, the use of drains cut beneath the surface of the soil to remove water downwards, beyond the root zone; and then laterally, into the ditches around the edge of the field. In the 19th century this was achieved by using earthenware tiles and pipes, but in the 18th century 'bush' drains were widely employed. These were trenches cut across fields and filled with faggots cut from pollards or woods, capped with straw or furze and then backfilled with soil (Figs 7.7 and 7.8). The drains were generally spaced at intervals of 12 yards (*c.* 12m), were dug to a depth of 24 inches or 26 inches (*c.* 0.6m), and fed into main drains dug to a depth of 28 inches (*c.* 0.7m). Field drains of this kind would commonly last between 10 and 15 years, although they could survive for longer.[17]

The idea of laying single drains, or small groups of drains, to improve particularly damp areas had long been known. However, the practice of 'thorough' drainage – filling a clay field with a dense network of drains – seems to have been first developed in Essex at the start of the 18th century, hence its alternative name, the 'Essex method'.[18] Richard Bradley in 1727 described the practice as 'but a late invention' on the claylands of north Essex, while in 1728 Henry Salmon described how the 'cold and wet lands' of Hertfordshire – the clay soils which occupy much of the south and east of the county – had been 'greatly improved' by the use of under-drains, an innovation that had been introduced 'within twenty years' from the neighbouring parts of Essex.[19] The practice spread slowly at first, but then more rapidly as prices rose (and labour costs fell) in the last decades of the 18th century. By the 1840s one of the contributors to the Raynbirds' survey of Suffolk agriculture felt able to assert that 'at the present time nearly every piece of land in the heavy land district of this county has been drained, and many pieces several times'.[20] In the first half of the 19th century tile drains came into widespread use, but they never entirely displaced bush drains. They were a more 'permanent' improvement – they did not need to be replaced every 10 or 15 years – and were thus often paid for by the landowner, rather than the tenant. But they were probably not much more efficient than the older method.

Improvements to drainage were vital in transforming the agriculture of the claylands in the Agricultural Revolution period. But, in terms of the present appearance of the landscape, other changes that accompanied the intensification of arable farming were of much more importance. New farm buildings were often erected – in particular, shelter sheds built of wood, lump or brick, ranged around yards, were often added to existing timber-framed complexes of buildings, so that cattle could be fattened on turnips and other fodder during the winter, their manure mounting before being taken to the fields and spread in the spring.

A series of Parliamentary enclosure acts, concentrated in the early decades of the 19th century, removed the great clayland commons that still survived across great swathes of southern and central Norfolk.[21] Their locations can still be often identified as islands of neat rectilinear fields, defined by straight hawthorn hedges, which usually contrast sharply with the more irregular patterns around them. Above all, changes were made to the *existing* pattern of boundaries, as the irregular and 'bosky' landscape of the claylands came under sustained attack from improvers keen to maximise cereal yields.

Small and irregular fields were inconvenient for ploughing, while tall hedges and their trees shaded out the crop, robbed the soil of nutrients and took up large areas of potentially productive land. So hedges were often drastically cut back, or completely replanted with hawthorn, and the amount of timber in them was substantially reduced. Pollards were regarded with particular hostility. Their dense heads spread a deep pool of shade, and they were looked on by improvers as relics of backward peasant agriculture (the larger farmers were now increasingly using coal, rather than wood, for their fires). Pollards perhaps offended 'polite' taste because they were as 'unnatural' as the topiaried trees in formal gardens, which were now out of fashion amongst the rich and educated. At the end of the century Anthony Collet described how Suffolk landlords were giving their clayland tenants leave to 'take down every pollard tree that stands in the way of the plough'.[22]

What is particularly striking is that many hedges were grubbed out altogether, in order to create larger, neater parcels of ground more suitable for ploughing. The grubbing of hedges was especially common in the 'high farming' period after *c.* 1830, but in many districts it was occurring on some scale from the late 18th century, together with the removal of small woods and copses. Indeed, a government enquiry into the state of the nation's timber supplies was initiated in 1791 and included the question: 'Whether the Growth of Oak Timber in Hedge Rows is generally encouraged, or whether the grubbing up of Hedge Rows for the enlarging of fields, and improving Arable Ground, is become common in those Counties?'[23] The answers received from the principal groups questioned make it clear that it was generally thought to be 'frequent', 'becoming common' or the 'general practice' in eastern clayland districts. 'The county of Hertfordshire consists chiefly of Land in Tillage, and by clearing the Hedges of all kinds of Trees they admit of plowing to the utmost Bounds of their Land'.[24] Thomas Preston from Suffolk stated that 'Much

OPPOSITE PAGE:

TOP: *Fig. 7.7 The distribution of under-drainage in England in the late 18th and early 19th centuries,* as indicated by references in the General Views *and in the Tithe Files of 1836. Activity was strongly concentrated in East Anglia.*

BOTTOM: *Fig. 7.8 This illustration, from Henry Rider Haggard's* A Farmer's Year *of 1899, shows men laying bush drains in south Norfolk.*

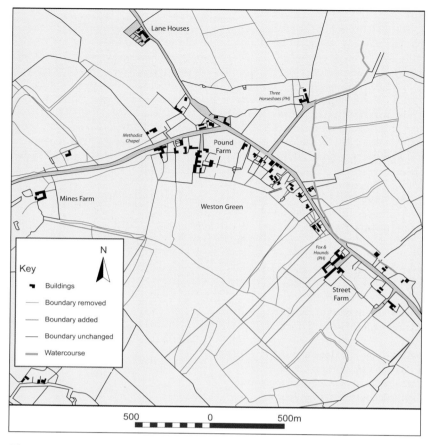

Fig. 7.9 Weston Colville,
Cambridgeshire. A map of 1825 shows
the alterations to the field pattern in this long-
enclosed parish proposed by the landowner,
George Hall. The majority of the changes
were carried out: numerous boundaries
were straightened or removed. Similar
changes occurred in many parts of the East
Anglian claylands during the late 18th and
19th centuries.

Timber and the Improvement of Arable
Land are incompatible. Arable land in
Suffolk is improved, and therefore
timber is lessened'.[25]

> Underwood, particularly
> Blackthorn Bushes, in Hedge
> Rows that spread Two or Three
> Rods wide, is the true nursery
> of Oak Timber, but such Rows
> are a dead Loss and Nuisance
> in a well cultivated Country
> … It is the Improvement of the
> Kingdom … that has brought
> about the very good and
> proper Diminution of Oaks;
> and it is to be hoped that the
> Diminution will continue, for
> if it does not, the Improvement
> of our Soil will not advance.[26]

In some places the transformation of the
old landscape was piecemeal in
character and limited in scale, but on
some of the larger estates in particular it
could be both rapid and extensive.
George Hall, owner of the Weston
Colville estate in south-east
Cambridgeshire, thus drew up a plan
for improvements in 1825, and within a
few years the field pattern over much of
the parish had been completely transformed (Fig. 7.9).[27] The rector of Rayne in
Essex typically observed in his tithe accounts of the 1790s how on one farm in his
parish 'the fields were over-run with wood', but 'since Mr Rolfe has purchased
them, he has improved them by grubbing up the hedgerows and laying the fields
together'. In 1801 one observer in the same county was able to declare: 'what
immense quantities of timber have fallen before the axe and mattock to make way
for corn'.[28] We must be careful not to exaggerate the extent to which the ancient
landscapes of the clays were transformed in the 18th and 19th centuries.
Hedgerows, pollards and sunken lanes survived in abundance. Nevertheless, there
are many areas, especially in south-east Cambridgeshire, western Essex and eastern
Hertfordshire, where – ignoring those bounding public roads – the majority of
boundaries are as recent as those found in areas of Parliamentary enclosure.

The onset of agricultural depression from c. 1880 brought agricultural
intensification to an end, and for the following 70 years or so hedges grew tall and
wide, while the number of farmland trees increased once more. Some land even
returned to pasture. The advent of the Second World War, however, saw a renewed
attack on this ancient countryside, which intensified into an orgy of destruction
through the 1960s and 1970s. Hedges were not only unnecessary in this now
completely arable landscape. They also interfered with the movement of large
machines, especially combine harvesters, and took up valuable ground. They were
removed wholesale, and in some Essex parishes effectively disappeared altogether:
as already noted, the more irregularly shaped fields found in the south of the region
were particularly badly suited to the new, highly mechanised methods of farming.
Today the tide has turned, but too late for great swathes of the claylands, flailed
bare of all life and interest, the prairies extending uneventful to the far horizon.

HEDGES

Although many thousands of kilometres of hedges have thus disappeared in the last four decades or so, they remain an all-important component of the clayland landscapes of East Anglia. Numerous examples of ruler-straight, species-poor, hawthorn-dominated hedges can be found on the clays – where large commons were enclosed in the 18th and 19th centuries, or where large estates and improving farmers rationalised the existing field pattern. However, the majority contain a mixture of shrub species, and in autumn provide a rich riot of colour, dominated in particular by the dark red of dogwood and the vivid yellow of maple, and with occasional flashes

Fig. 7.10 An ancient, species-rich hedge in north Essex, featuring maple, dogwood, hazel, wayfaring tree and much else.

of deep scarlet provided by the berries of spindle. Such hedges, as already noted, often stand on large hedge banks and are flanked by deep ditches (Fig. 7.10).

In some parts of the country, especially the Midlands, hedges were traditionally managed by laying or plashing. At intervals of 10 to 15 years they would be drastically thinned, and the main branches cut part way through and woven through upright stakes in order to form a dense, impenetrable mass. Although occasionally practised, by the 18th century at least plashing was not normal in East Anglia. Instead, hedges were managed by coppicing. The shrubs were simply cut down to within a few centimetres of the ground, at intervals of between 10 and 20 years. Coppicing required less skill than laying and perhaps produced more useable firewood. It demanded careful management, however, for the new growth required protection from browsing livestock for two or three years. Substantial ditches usually protected one side: livestock were excluded from the unditched side for the necessary period, or the hedge might be temporarily protected with hurdles or lines of staked brushwood.

In the 1960s the ecologist Max Hooper carried out a detailed study of hedges in Devon, the East Midlands and East Anglia, and concluded that variations in the numbers of species they contained were broadly related to age.[29] He went so far as to formulate an equation:

Age of hedge = (no. of shrub species in a 30 yard length × 110) + 30 years

or, in simplified form, 'one species = one century of age' (the method excludes climbers such as brambles and honeysuckle). The principal explanation he advanced for this relationship was that hedges, once planted, acquire new species over time, but fairly gradually, and at a roughly constant rate. Hooper believed that the formula could only provide a rough indication of age, but it was over-enthusiastically embraced by many local historians. More recent studies, however, suggest that age and species number are rather poorly correlated, especially in East Anglia. Many hedges in the claylands break Hooper's 'rule' with gusto: one, planted at the enclosure of Denton Common in Norfolk in 1815, contains no less than seven species in each 30m length!

There are a number of reasons for this. Although most 18th- and 19th-century hedges were usually planted with hawthorn, blackthorn or a mixture of both, many older ones seem to have started life with rather more species, for local farmers saw them not merely as a barrier to livestock but also as a source of fuel, timber and perhaps fodder. Thomas Tusser from Essex, writing in 1573, advocated the use of elm, ash, crab, hazel, sallow and holly when planting hedges and, in praising the advantages of 'severall' or woodland countryside over 'champion', emphasised the abundance of fuel and fruit they provided.[30] Arthur Young described in the 1790s how in Hertfordshire the local shortage of firewood had 'induced the farmers to fill the old hedges everywhere with oak, ash, sallow and with all sorts of plants more generally calculated for fuel than fences'.[31] But in addition, rates of colonisation are not standard across the whole of the country; they were fundamentally effected by the character of the local seed supply, and especially by the abundance or otherwise of woodland and hedges. Maple, for example, is generally found only in the very oldest hedges in the Midlands, where the medieval and post-medieval landscape was largely devoid of hedges and trees, yet it is moderately common even in hedges planted in the 19th century on the claylands of East Anglia, where woods and hedges remained abundant.

The hedges of the East Anglian claylands cannot, therefore, be 'dated' in any simple and direct way by counting the numbers of shrub species that they contain. The only relatively clear distinction in terms of species content is between those hedges planted before the mid-18th century, and those after. The latter were established, for the most part, by larger landowners with access to commercial nurseries, and are still dominated by hawthorn, although they generally contain four, five or more other species. These include rapid colonisers such as blackthorn, ash and dog rose, and species originally planted as timber like oak or elm, but also (as already noted) allegedly slow colonisers such as maple or dogwood. The pre-1750 hedges, in contrast, are all usually very mixed and contain five or more species including – in addition to those just mentioned – plants such as hazel, holly, hornbeam, crab apple and spindle. The precise number, and variety, of species present in these hedges is the consequence of a range of factors including location, and what they were originally planted with, as well as their age.

Nevertheless, while pre-1750 hedges tend to form a single, undifferentiated group, the very oldest – those found along roadsides, parish boundaries and former common edges – do sometimes exhibit distinctive characteristics. They can contain great banks of hazel, maple and dogwood; significant amounts of

Fig. 7.11 Dog's mercury, a common plant in clayland woods and hedges.

very slowly colonising species like hornbeam; and, on occasion, trees such as pry (small-leafed lime) and wild service, which do not now set seed easily. Such hedges are similar to the 'woodland relic' hedges identified by Hooper's co-researcher Ernest Pollard, and which he believed originated from direct management of the woodland vegetation around medieval assarts. Most East Anglian examples probably did not begin life like this, but they certainly seem to have first come into existence in a highly wooded environment. Pollard also drew attention to a number of distinctive woodland herbs that were characteristic of hedges of this kind, including wood anemone, primrose, bluebell and dog's mercury (*Mercurialis perennis*) (Fig. 7.11), but on the East Anglian claylands few of these seem to have any real historical significance. Woods and hedges remained so abundant in the district throughout its history that large reserves of these plants always existed, and they spread without difficulty on the damp, fertile soils. Indeed, primrose and dog's mercury can often be found in hedges that were planted when commons were enclosed by Parliamentary acts in the early 19th century.

Many clayland hedges still contain mature trees, although seldom in the numbers present a century or so ago. Their ages are hard to gauge. As a very rough guide, free-standing timber trees (such as oaks) gain around 2.5cm of circumference for each year of growth. Those growing in hedgerows, however, appear to put on girth at a slightly slower rate, largely because of competition with the neighbouring shrubs (especially in the early years of growth). Either way, the majority of timber trees in clayland hedges seem to be less than 200 years old, probably because – before the second half of the 19th century – hedgerow timber was felled as soon as mature, at around 75–100 years. Older hedgerow trees are usually former pollards, and their age is even harder to ascertain. Pollards seem to put on girth at a much slower rate than other trees because the periodic removal of the crown reduced the ability of the tree to grow, until a new one had become established. Some of these trees may be as much as twice the age of free-standing trees of equivalent circumference. Almost all are more than 250, and many are more than 500, years old.

Oak, as already noted, is the characteristic farmland tree of the claylands, but ash is becoming increasingly common in many districts. Elm was also frequent, especially in Essex and south Suffolk, before the devastation of Dutch elm disease in the 1960s and 1970s. Although mature elms are now a very rare sight, elm remains a common shrub in hedges, suckering vigorously and often forcing out other species for long lengths. Only when it begins to grow into a true tree, with fully formed bark, does it fall victim to the elm beetles *Scolytus scolytus* and *Scolytus multistiatus*, which carry the fungus *Ceratocystis ulmi*, the cause of the disease. So long as hedges are kept managed by frequent cutting, the effects of the disease are minimal. Most of the hedgerow elms of the claylands – like those found in adjacent districts of light soil – are of a particular variety, the East Anglian elm (*Ulmus minor* or *carpinifolia*).[32] This has a longer, more pointed leaf and a more vigorously suckering habit than the more normal English elm (*Ulmus procera*), which dominates the landscape of the areas immediately to the south and west of the region – south Essex, central and western Hertfordshire and the Midlands. Our elms cannot reproduce from seed, but only by suckering, and the botanist R H Richens has mapped the extraordinarily restricted distribution of particular clones and attempted – rather less convincingly – to relate them to successive waves of prehistoric and early historic invaders.[33]

WOODS, PARKS AND COMMONS

Domesday Book shows that, in spite of a long history of clearance and settlement, the claylands remained well wooded, especially towards the south-west, in Essex and east Hertfordshire. This woodland was not, however, like the enclosed and intensively managed woods of later medieval times. The fact that Domesday generally measures it in terms of the number of pigs it could support, on the acorns and mast dropped in the autumn, shows that it mostly took the form of 'wood-pasture', in which there were abundant trees but not (as in most later woods) a managed understorey. Instead, grass and other herbage grew beneath the trees, which were regularly grazed by livestock. In the period between the 10th and the 13th centuries, as population increased, much of this woodland was destroyed. Some was enclosed, however, and preserved by manorial lords, in the form of managed woods or as deer parks – in effect, private wood-pastures.

Parks were a common feature of the medieval landscape – even quite minor knights might have one. They were valuable assets and important expressions of social status, although as noted in Chapter 6 most parks lay at some distance from manorial halls, typically towards the boundary of a vill or parish. They might be used for hunting, but most were primarily venison farms, used to produce the elite food *par excellence*; they also provided wood and timber, from areas of enclosed coppice and pollarded trees, carefully preserved from browsing animals and indiscriminate felling. They were surrounded by a stout fence or pale, made of cleft oak.[34]

Ancient woods are one of the great glories of the clayland landscape. All were, until comparatively recently, managed as 'coppice with standards': that is, the majority of trees and bushes within them were cut down to or near ground level on a rotation of between 7 and 15 years, in order to provide a regular crop of 'poles'. The plants then regenerated vigorously from the stump or stool, or suckered from the rootstock. Coppicing was a much easier operation than pollarding, as it did not necessitate the use of ladders and trestles, but the regrowth was vulnerable to browsing livestock and woods were invariably bounded by a substantial bank, flanked by a ditch and topped with a hedge. Hazel – so useful for fencing, and for the wattle and daub used in the walls of timber-framed buildings – and ash – excellent for tool handles and firewood – were common components of the understorey, but a wide range of plants including lime, hornbeam, elm, maple, hawthorn and holly could also be found, their distribution sometimes restricted – for a combination of environmental and historical reasons – to particular districts. The full-grown 'standard' trees were mainly oaks.[35] They were widely spaced, so that they did not shade out the coppice growth, and normally felled at around 80 years of age, when they had reached a suitable size for use in the construction of buildings or – more rarely – ships. Medieval woods, which were invariably the private property of manorial lords, came in a great range of sizes. As well as the more extensive areas there were also numerous tiny groves, springs or *grovetts*, some composed entirely of coppices, which might cover as little as 2,000sq m.

The management of woods changed over time. In particular, the frequency with which they were coppiced gradually declined. In the 13th century most were cut at intervals of six to seven years, but by the 19th century this had lengthened to around 14 years. Most of this increase seems to have occurred in the period from *c.* 1550 but the reasons have never been fully explained. In part, it may be due to changes in the demand for fuel: the shift from open hearths to chimneys increased the demand for larger logs, as opposed to faggots. However, it was also probably because the density of standard trees in woods increased steadily in the course of the post-medieval period from around 17 to 50 per ha), thus reducing the vigour of the coppice understorey.[36] The officials who compiled the documents called the tithe files in 1836, commented on a number of occasions on the poor condition of local coppices, noting at Fulmodestone near Fakenham, for example, that it would have been 'much better if timber was thinned'.[37]

Many clayland woods, especially the smaller examples, were grubbed out and turned over to agriculture during the Agricultural Revolution. However, the majority of the larger woods survived into the 20th century. Then, as the market for coppice poles declined, they became less intensively managed, and from the middle years of the century many were grubbed out altogether and turned over to farmland, or were replanted with commercial conifers (usually with limited success). Only a few continued to be managed along traditional lines. Since the 1960s, however, there has been a significant resumption of coppicing, now carried out by landowners or conservation groups keen to maintain the diversity of flora and fauna produced by this type of management. A number of examples are open to the public, including Wayland Wood and Foxley Wood in Norfolk and Bradfield Wood in Suffolk (Fig. 7.12).

Much of the woodland recorded by Domesday, especially in the north of the region, escaped both enclosure (as managed woodland or deer parks) and conversion to farmland. Instead, it continued to be exploited, for grazing and as a source of wood and timber, by local communities. Such areas did not, however, remain as woodland indefinitely. Most gradually lost their trees and degenerated

Fig. 7.12 Bradfield Woods, west Suffolk: *an area of ancient woodland still managed on traditional lines.*

to open pasture, for as trees fell, or were felled, it was hard for replacements to become established in the face of regular grazing. Indeed, many East Anglian greens and commons have names suggestive of woodland origins: Diss Heywood in the parish of Diss in south Norfolk, for example; Norwood Green in Catfield; or Allwood Green near Mells in north Suffolk. The monks of Bury St Edmunds, given the choice of three different estates by a late Saxon benefactor, chose Chippenhall in Fressingfield because 'it abounded in woods'. In 1066 there was woodland for 160 swine here, according to Domesday, but this had been reduced to sufficient for 100 by 1086. 'By the 18th century there was virtually no woodland at Chippenhall, but there was, and still is, a fine green, with the partial ghost of another green close by'.[38] Even in the 17th century many wooded commons remained, such as Hook Wood in Morley in Norfolk, and some clayland commons can still boast a few pollards – such as those at Fritton Common in the same county. But most commons now retain no evidence of their former wooded character. Moreover, most medieval parks were destroyed in the course of the 16th, 17th and 18th centuries. As a result there are now very few examples of wood-pastures remaining on the East Anglian claylands. The best is probably Hatfield Forest near Stanstead in Essex (Fig. 7.13). This was part of the royal forest of Essex, an area within which special laws protected remaining areas of common wood-pasture from encroachment or felling, in order to preserve deer

Fig. 7.13 Hatfield Forest, near Stanstead airport in Essex, *is the finest surviving clayland woodpasture in East Anglia. Most of the ancient pollarded trees are hornbeams.*

for the royal hunt. With its ancient pollards, mainly hornbeams, it is still a wonderful place, in spite of the proximity of Stanstead airport.

Commons, as we have already noted on a number of occasions, were particularly large and numerous towards the north of the clay plateau, in north Suffolk and Norfolk. Most were located on the most poorly draining soils, those classified by the soil survey as the Beccles Association, often in slight depressions in the plateau surface. Large commons could also be found along the flood plains of the major watercourses cutting through the plateau and, because the plateau depressions were often the sources of streams, ribbons of common land – sometimes interrupted by areas of privately owned meadow, sometimes continuous – frequently linked the 'high' commons with the 'low'. By the time the earliest maps were made, the larger commons were sometimes settled all around their margins, but more usually farms tended to cluster near to the entrances, where roads funnelled in to them. Smaller commons, in contrast – 'tyes' or 'greens' – generally had more continuous spreads of settlement around them. Whatever their size, most commons had characteristic curving, concave outlines, defined by deep ditches and banks, which narrowed towards the entrances; these were usually gated.

Much enclosure of, and encroachment onto, commons took place from late medieval times, but they remained extensive even at the end of the 18th century. When William Faden surveyed his map of Norfolk in 1794–5 great strings of them, linked end to end, rambled across the clay interfluves, and it was still possible to walk for 20km or more in central Norfolk without leaving one. Few, however, escaped the great wave of enclosure that spread through the region in the late 18th and early 19th centuries. Where still surviving they are an amazing sight, a reminder of what was lost from the landscape in the 'age of improvement'. Particularly good examples include Hales Green and Wacton Common in Norfolk, the latter still boasting some medieval farmhouses; and Chippenhall Green, and the various commons in the Elmhams and Ilketshalls in north Suffolk (Fig. 7.14). The smaller greens, which are particularly characteristic of the south of the clay plateau, have fared rather better. Their enclosure by Parliamentary act was seldom worth the effort or expense and they still form a prominent feature of the landscape, especially in Essex and east Hertfordshire. How far these often tiny parcels were still wooded when their margins were first settled in the 12th or 13th centuries remains uncertain. Most had probably already degenerated to open pasture. Like the larger commons, the majority occupy damp areas, especially at the headwaters of minor watercourses: places which were difficult to cultivate, but which provided good grass growth late into the summer.[39]

While the larger commons were more numerous in the area to the north and east of the Lark and Gipping valley, managed woods were – and still are – more common to the south and west – in south Suffolk, Essex and east Hertfordshire. This regional pattern seems, to some extent, to be related to topography, for woods and commons generally occupied rather different locations within the clayland landscape. Woods tended to cluster at the margins of clay plateaux, perhaps in order to limit the distance that wood and timber needed to be hauled down rutted clay roads, while the larger commons at least were normally to be found towards the centres of the main clay masses. Because the plateau becomes more dissected towards the south and west, woodland becomes a more dominant element in the landscape, large commons less so. However, this pattern may also reflect the fact that, in general, the strength of lordship was greater towards the south and the number of freemen rather less, so that lords were better able to enclose areas of 'waste' at the expense of their tenants.

OPPOSITE PAGE:

Fig. 7.14 Hales Green, Norfolk, *one of relatively few surviving examples of the kind of extensive common once ubiquitous on the claylands of northern East Anglia.*

PONDS AND MOATS

Clayland farmers were mainly concerned to remove water from the sodden fields, by means of ditches, under-drains and the rest, but water was also intentionally concentrated and maintained at certain points. Ponds are a particularly important, although often neglected, feature of the clayland landscape (Fig. 7.15). Cattle rather than sheep were always the most important livestock on this heavy land, and they require regular supplies of drinking water. Most watering ponds were dug in the corners of fields, where they could receive water flowing down perimeter ditches (as well as that draining directly off the adjacent land) and where they would not be in the way if the field was cultivated for a time. Sometimes they could be accessed by stock in adjacent fields. Ponds were a particular feature of common edges: these may also have served as a source of clay for the wattle and daub infill of medieval and later timber-framed

Fig. 7.15 Field ponds are one of the neglected details of the clayland landscape: some have medieval, or perhaps even earlier, origins.

Fig. 7.16 Tiptofts manor, Wimbish, Essex. An aisled hall of c.1350 which stands – like so many houses on the boulder clays – within a moat.

buildings. In Essex especially, but also elsewhere, field ponds often display a characteristically asymmetrical profile, steeper on one side than on the other, in order to facilitate access by stock. Some surviving field ponds are clearly 18th century or later in date, because they are associated with relatively recent field boundaries. But many examples are shown on 17th-century maps, and some have huge pollards growing on their margins, suggesting a medieval origin.

A particular and distinctive feature of the East Anglian claylands are moats – that is, rectangular or sub-rectangular enclosures defined by water-filled ditches. Some still surround large farms or manor houses, often of medieval or Tudor date – places such as the magnificent Tiptofts manor in Wimbish, erected in the early 13th century (Fig. 7.16). But many are now devoid of occupation. Like field ponds, they are usually connected to – and form a part of – the complex artificial drainage pattern of the clays. They enclose areas ranging in size from less than 400sq m to more than 6ha, but mostly in the range of 0.2–0.5ha.[40]

Sometimes two conjoined moats can be found, one perhaps for house and yards, the other surrounding orchard and garden. They vary greatly in width and depth, and at the lower end of the scale it is, indeed, difficult to distinguish a wide drainage ditch from a diminutive moat. In consequence, estimates of the numbers of moats in the region vary, although there is little doubt that the East Anglian claylands can boast a higher density than anywhere else in England (Fig. 7.17). They are especially numerous in central Suffolk and in western Essex.

Some moats only surround three sides of their central 'island', and many are too narrow and shallow to have served any serious defensive purpose. They are best interpreted as status symbols, their pseudo-defensive appearance proclaiming that their creators were members of the warrior rather than the labouring class, although some were clearly built by individuals who were little more than yeoman farmers. We should not, however, ignore the practical benefits that moats conferred on this wet land. Lateral drainage into perimeter ditches reduced the extent to which yards and gardens became a quagmire in the winter, while open water offered some protection against casual intruders, human or animal, and provided a source of fish and water.[41] Most moats were probably dug between the mid-12th and the late 13th centuries, and while some existing residences (such as manors mentioned in Domesday) were supplied with one, most surround later manors and sub-manors or small freehold properties

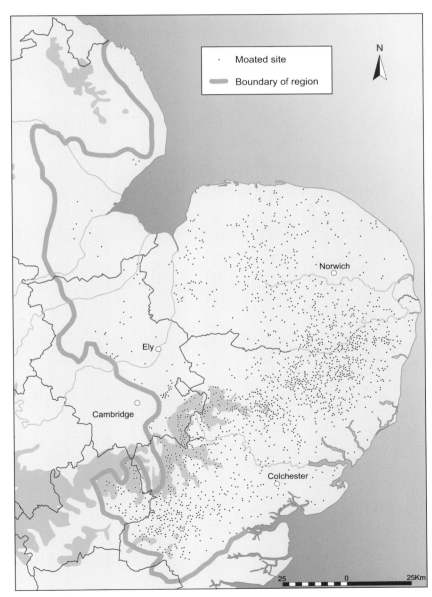

Fig. 7.17 East Anglia and the Fens: the distribution of medieval moated sites.

created during this age of expansion. Their location is interesting: a high proportion lie in relatively remote locations, towards or even on parish boundaries; many are positioned away from through roads; and while in south Norfolk and north Suffolk some lie on common edges, for the most part moats, and common- and green-edge settlement, are mutually exclusive. In the south of the region especially, moats evidently surrounded the homes of people who were socially superior from those dwelling on the margins of the common pastures.

CONCLUSION

In such a short chapter it is impossible to do justice to the rich, intricate complexity of the clayland landscapes of East Anglia. Nor is it possible to convey the appalling scale of the catastrophe which befell then in the second half of the 20th century. In what we can now see was a short-term need for security of food supplies, coupled with the lobbying power of the agricultural industry and a fashionable quest for modernity, thousands of hectares of ancient countryside – hedges, copses, green ways – were irrevocably destroyed. Some amends are now being made. However, the ersatz ancient hedges in their grow tubes, improbably planted with spindle, guelder rose and the like, the new copses in inconvenient corners of vast fields, and the 'conservation headlands', strangely but unconsciously mimicking the 'hedge greens' of earlier times, can only serve as a very partial recompense for what was lost in the space of a single generation.

NOTES

1 Hodge *et al.* 1984, 117–19, 132–5, 209–12.
2 Davison 1990; Martin 2001; Williamson 2003, 94–101; Roden 1973; Hunter 1999, 96–106, 115–17, 122–5; Postgate 1973, 315.
3 Newton 1960.
4 Hunter 1999, 115–16.
5 Davison 1990; Hardy & Martin 1986; Rogerson 1995; Williamson 1986.
6 Holderness 1985.
7 Hervey 1902, 29.
8 Rackham 1986b, 218–21.
9 Theobald 2000; West Suffolk Records Office, T1/1/6.
10 Norfolk Records Office, Beauchamp-Proctor 334; NRS 11126.
11 Tusser 1573.
12 West Suffolk Records Office, Acc. 1066.
13 Norfolk Records Office PD 80/90: NRS 12793 3F F8.
14 Theobald 2000.
15 Robinson 1949, 232.
16 Folkingham 1610, 48.
17 Wade-Martins & Williamson, 1999, 61–7.
18 Evans 1845.
19 Salmon 1728; Bradley 1727, 23.
20 Raynbird & Raynbird 1849, 112.
21 Turner 1993; Dymond 1999a.
22 Young 1795, 57.
23 Lambert 1977, 708, 724, 748.
24 Ibid, 748.
25 Ibid, 749.
26 Ibid, 776.
27 Cambridgeshire Records Office, CRO 124/P83a.
28 Brown 1996, 34.
29 Hooper *et al.* 1974.
30 Tusser 1573.
31 Young 1813, 49.
32 Rackham 1986b, 232–47; Richens 1977.
33 Richens 1967.
34 Rackham 1986b, 122–9; Hoppitt 1999a; Hoppitt 1992.
35 Rackham 1986a; Barnes 2002.
36 Barnes 2002, 214–15, 228–36, 294–307.
37 Public Records Office, IR 29/5937.
38 Martin 2001.
39 Williamson 2003, 160–79.
40 Rackham 1986b, 360–4; Hunter, 126–9.
41 Taylor 1972.

8

Light Lands

One of the most striking features of East Anglia is the contrast between the ancient, complex and many layered countryside of the claylands and the generally more recent landscapes of the light soil districts. It is a contrast made especially marked by the fact that the transition between the two is often quite rapid, the line of division cutting dramatically through the middle of parishes, most notably in south-eastern Cambridgeshire and north-west Essex. The largest area of light land runs in a broad band along the coast of north-west Norfolk, down through west Suffolk, and on into south-eastern Cambridgeshire and north-west Essex. It comprises a low chalk escarpment that is covered, to varying extents and to varying depths, with sandy, acid drift; at its foot in west Norfolk, on the edge of the Fens and the Wash, is another area of acid sands, derived not from glaciers but from rocks laid down before the formation of the chalk. Where the acid drift is thin or absent, on the slopes of the escarpment, arable land was extensive in medieval times and with careful management reasonable crops could be produced. But where the sands lie thicker, on the higher ground and (in west Norfolk) at the foot of the escarpment, much of the land lay uncultivated, as heathland. The thickest and most continuous deposits of sandy drift are in Breckland. Even at the end of 18th century, to judge from the county maps published by Faden (for Norfolk in 1797) and Hodskinson (for Suffolk in 1783), well over 40 per cent of Breckland was still occupied by heathland.[1] The worst parts were almost like a desert: when exposed to the wind by excessive grazing or cultivation, the sand was liable to blow and mobile dunes might form. William Gilpin, visiting the area in the 1760s, described 'sand, and scattered gravel, without the least vegetation; a mere African desert.' He continued:

> *In many places we saw the sand even driven into ridges; and the road totally covered; which indeed everywhere was so deep, and heavy, that four horses, which we were obliged to take, could scarce in the slowest pace, drag us through it. It was a little surprizing* [sic] *to find such a piece of absolute desert almost in the heart of England. To us it was a novel idea. We had not even heard of it.*[2]

The second main area of light land extends in a patchy band from Norwich northwards to the sea. It comprises various acid, sandy deposits of glacio-fluvial origin. This, like Breckland, was particularly poor land, and hard to reclaim. But the district also contained numerous ribbons of more loamy soil in the valleys cutting through it, and on the floors of which lush pastures and meadows could be found. Lastly, a broad belt of poor sandy soil, partly derived from the underlying Crag but mainly from glacial deposits, extends all along the Suffolk coast – the area traditionally known as the 'Sandlings' – and on intermittently into north-east Essex.[3] This, however, formed only a relatively narrow strip of land and most Sandlings parishes contained some areas of more fertile soil within their bounds. To the east lay rich coastal marshes, to the west the heavy but fertile soils of the boulder clay. Both these districts – the north Norfolk heathlands and the Suffolk Sandlings – carried a rather more dispersed settlement pattern than the light lands of western East Anglia, where settlement traditionally took the form of villages, albeit often small, or of an irregular, poorly nucleated variety.

These extensive areas of light land were mostly characterised, before the 18th and 19th centuries, by open fields and heathland mixed in varying proportions. Scattered throughout East Anglia, however, especially in the north of the region, much more limited areas of sandy drift could be found, surrounded by more fertile or heavier soils. These, for the most part, consisted entirely of heath, exploited by communities who used the adjacent areas of more favourable land for their arable farming.

HEATHS AND THEIR ORIGINS

In their natural state, the areas now occupied by heaths were largely covered in trees, sometimes in dense stands, sometimes more thinly scattered, and with only limited areas of more open ground where grazing ruminants kept the trees at bay. But because such areas were easy to cultivate, they were particularly attractive to farmers equipped with only a primitive technology, and many of them were comprehensively cleared at an early date for cultivation and by the intensive grazing of livestock. The acid soils, coupled with the continued pressure of grazing, then favoured the development of a characteristic undershrub vegetation, dominated by heather – called ling in East Anglia – (*Calluna vulgaris*), bell heather (*Erica cinerea*), gorse (furze in East Anglia) (*Ulex europaeus*) and broom (*Sarothamnus scoparius*) (Fig. 8.1). This is turn encouraged the development of a particular type of soil, the podzol, in which grey upper levels, leached of humus and iron, overlie hard layers called pan where these have been redeposited.[4] Characteristic grasses also thrive in such an environment, including sheep's fescue (*Festuca ovina*), wavy hair grass (*Deschampsia flexnosa*) and common bent (*Agrostis tenuis*), while some areas become dominated by bracken.

Fig. 8.1 Weather Heath, Eriswell, in the Suffolk Breckland.

Not all heaths have precisely the same kinds of vegetation. Those in East Anglia are mostly of the type categorised by the National Vegetation Classification scheme – the standard system used by British ecologists to classify different plant communities – as *H1 – Calluna vulgaris – Festuca ovina* heath.[5] Their main characteristic is the relatively limited number of species present. *Calluna* is the overwhelmingly dominant undershrub, *Erica cinerea* and gorse being limited by climatic factors – rainfall is too low, and the annual temperature range too great, for them to thrive. They are present in some numbers on the Sandlings heaths because the proximity of the sea serves to ameliorate these climatic factors, but even here usually as relatively limited stands. Such is the dominance of heather that usually even *Festuca ovina* is present only as scattered tussocks, and other grasses, such as *Agrostis cappilaris*, are even more confined (Fig. 8.2).[6]

Fig. 8.2 Heather (Calluna vulgaris) in bloom on Walberswick Heath in the Suffolk Sandlings.

Heaths do not constitute a stable 'climax' vegetation, but are a consequence of particular forms of management, especially intensive grazing by sheep. When grazing is reduced, or ceases altogether, they begin to change rapidly and become invaded by bracken and then by hawthorn, sloe and birch. It is difficult for trees and bushes to colonise dense stands of heather. But the older, more degenerate stands that develop once grazing is reduced provide more open ground. Once the trees become established they shade out the heather, leading eventually to the development of the *Quercus-Betula-Deschampsia* woodland, which is the natural climax vegetation – that is, the kind of plant community that would eventually come to dominate an area left to its own devices for long enough – on these poor soils.[7] Many surviving areas of heathland in the region are currently degenerating to scrub and woodland.

Although most East Anglian heaths are dominated by heather, chalk heath can be found in some places, normally where thin and intermittent sandy deposits overlie chalk. On chalk heath, grasses such as sheep's fescue are dominant and the various undershrubs, for example heather and gorse, constitute subsidiary elements. Heaths of this kind would have been extensive in north-west Norfolk before the great reclamations of the 18th century, and also on the chalk scarp of south-east Cambridgeshire.[8] Some still survive, usually interspersed in small patches with heath of normal type in Breckland – often as areas of 'patterned ground' (*see* p.14). The largest remaining tract is Newmarket Heath, where the constant mowing necessary to allow its use for horse racing ensures that ling and furze are virtually invisible – the area looks like chalk downland. A change in management, however, would certainly lead to their regeneration, although not their dominance.

Many East Anglian heaths became completely open landscapes in the Bronze or Iron Ages and have continued as such right up until the present.[9] Others appear to have been occupied by woods or wood-pastures in early medieval times, either because they had never been cleared of trees or because trees had reclaimed them in the immediate post-Roman period, when the population fell dramatically and land was used less intensively. Mousehold Heath near Norwich is a classic example.[10] Domesday implies that there was a substantial area of woodland here and the element 'hold' derives from *holt*, an Old English term for 'wood'. In the 13th century the agent of the bishop of Norwich complained of how it was proving difficult to restrain the tenants' use of the wood – which was common land – and that in consequence the trees were disappearing. By the end of the 13th century, documents refer to Mousehold *Heath*. In the Sandlings, evidence from Sutton Hoo suggests that extensive clearance occurred during the early Bronze Age, and that as a result the local landscape resembled 'open park-like countryside with mature oak

Fig. 8.3 Staverton Park, Wantisden, *in the Suffolk Sandlings is the only extensive area of wood-pasture now surviving on heath soils in East Anglia, although small fragments can still be found in a number of places.*

trees'.[11] Podzolisation occurred a little later, during the Iron Age, following a phase of intensive arable land use. Nevertheless, the names of parishes in the surrounding area – Shotley, Trimley, Hollesley, Hemley, Ramsholt, Waldringfield, Butley, Gedgrave and Hazelwood – all incorporate Anglo-Saxon words for woods, or for clearings within woodland (*leah, holt, feld, wudu*). One of the best surviving wood-pastures in East Anglia – Staverton Park – still exists only a few kilometres from Sutton Hoo, on soils which are identical to those of the neighbouring heaths (Fig. 8.3).[12] It was enclosed and managed as a hunting area in early medieval times and thus presumably saved from the indiscriminate grazing and felling that removed trees from adjacent areas. Elsewhere in East Anglia we have similar hints of relatively late clearance. A 17th-century map of North Creake in north-west Norfolk shows the higher ground of the parish occupied by a heath called The Frith (OE *Frið*, 'a wood'). And buried in the 18th-century estate woodland on the light sandy soils around Bayfield in the north of the same county are a number of huge oak pollards, some dating back to the 13th and 14th centuries, which appear to represent the last vestiges of once extensive heathland wood-pastures.

Some areas of East Anglian heathland may thus, in whole or part, have been occupied by woodland well into the medieval period or even beyond. Most, however, were largely open and treeless environments by the 13th century, and remained so because of their intensive exploitation by local communities.

THE USES OF HEATHLAND

In some parts of England, almost all heathland was common land, but in East Anglia large areas of *several* heath – that is, land held as private property – also existed. Numerous grants of private heath in the Suffolk Sandlings are thus mentioned in early charters. In *c.* 1157–74 William de Chesney granted various lands to Blythburgh Priory, including 'the heath called *Hulsatum*' in Blythburgh,[13] while in the early 13th century his daughter granted 12 acres of heathland in the significantly named *Westwood*.[14] In many Breckland vills, and in some in north-west Norfolk, the majority of the heathland similarly formed part of the lord's demesne. In certain Sandlings parishes even the smaller farmers held diminutive parcels: in Reydon in 1697 tenants such as Nicholas Lisle held portions covering less than 2 acres.[15]

Whether private or common, heaths had many uses. It was only later agricultural 'improvers' who viewed them as useless wastes. Bracken was used for fuel and for thatch, but mainly as animal litter, and it could raise significant sums (14 shillings at Staverton in 1274–5).[16] Ling or heather was also used as fuel, and perhaps as thatch, and during the medieval period certain areas seem to have been set apart for its cultivation and protected from grazing. It was certainly sold in large quantities, as again at Staverton where, in 1305–6, sales raised £2.12s.[17] Furze (or gorse) was also cut for fuel. It produces a rapid, intense heat suitable for kindling and bread ovens (it was the most common form of charcoal excavated at the Anglo-Saxon burial ground at Snape)[18] and was also used for fencing. John Norden, who had long experience of the Sandlings, described in his *Surveyors Dialogue* of 1618 how it was used 'to brew withall and bake, and to stoppe a little gap in a hedge'.[19] It, too, may have been grown in particular areas of heath. Certainly, if unprotected the intensity of grazing lessened its value. Norden noted that while in general he recommended the destruction of gorse, 'there is a kind of furze worth the preservation, if it grow in a Countrey barren of wood', and this supplied much of the fuel used in Devon and Cornwall. It grew 'very high, and the stalke great, whereof the people make faggots'. He continued:

> And this kind of Furse groweth also upon the Sea coast of Suffolke: But
> that the people make not the use of them, as in Devonshire and Cornwalle,
> for they suffer their sheep and cattell to browse and crop them when they
> be young, and so they grow too scrubbed and lowe tufts, seldome to that
> perfection that they might be.[20]

Another source of fuel was available: the turf could be stripped from the sheepwalks and used for domestic fires. The Suffolk poet George Crabbe, writing at the end of the 18th century, thus refers to the heath in his poem 'The Borough' as the source of 'the light turf that warms the neighbouring poor'.[21]

Sheep were the main animals grazed on the heaths, but in many places rabbits were also important. They were introduced into England soon after the Norman Conquest and by the 13th century warrens had been established in many areas of poor sand – poor for crops, but ideal for burrowing animals. In East Anglia the main concentrations were in Breckland and the Suffolk Sandlings, but they could be found almost anywhere that patches of heathland existed. In the area to the west of Thetford a great swathe of land was given over to the contiguous warrens of Westwick, Santon, High Lodge, Eriswell, Elveden, Lakenheath and Brandon.[22] Some warrens were operated directly by their owners but, from the 15th century especially, most were leased to professional warreners, with contracts stipulating the condition in which they should be left at the end of the lease. At Nacton in the Sandlings, for example, the lessee was to leave 'five hundred couple of coneys good, well conditioned and alive' when the lease expired in 1646.[23] The intensity of grazing gave many warrens a distinctive, desolate appearance. The rabbits stripped the turf, exposing the sand beneath to the force of the wind and leading to the formation of mobile dunes like those which, blown out of Lakenheath Warren, partly engulfed the village of Santon Downham in 1668 and blocked the Little Ouse.[24]

In many parts of England rabbits were kept in special ditched mounds. These were called 'pillow mounds' by archaeologists and 'burrows' or 'buries' by contemporaries, but few are known in East Anglia, the best example perhaps being that on Sutton Common in the Sandlings.[25] In part this is because it was less necessary to provide purpose-built accommodation on these deep, sandy soils, but also it reflects widespread destruction by later arable land use. When, during a court case in 1596 concerning the title to an area of heathland in Swainsthorpe, the judge enquired: 'Is there any great highe burrowes uppon the said pece of ground such as be commonly in warrens', a witness was able to reply 'yea my lorde'.[26] But if pillow mounds are rarely found, early warrens have left plenty of other traces in the landscape.

Warrens were often surrounded by banks, to prevent the rabbits from straying. In 1390 a colony of rabbits at Iken – descendants of escapees from Dunningworth warren, some 4km to the east – were already causing serious damage to crops. Perimeter banks and ditches existed in medieval times (a *fosse* is recorded at Lakenheath, for example, in the early 14th century), but they seem to have become more common in the course of the post-medieval period, as stocking levels were increased on many warrens through the use of fodder crops. The banks were of turf, between a metre and a metre and a half in height, and topped with faggots of gorse, which overhung the inner face of the bank in order to prevent escape (or, more rarely, by live bushes of gorse or thorn, below a capping of turf). The remains of numerous examples can still be seen in Breckland, running across heaths or (more usually) now buried within Forestry Commission plantations. The largest heathland warrens might be encompassed by banks as much as 20km in length. Some warrens also contained internal banks, some subdividing the area to allow better utilisation of the meagre grazing, others defining small enclosures in which fodder crops, such as turnips, were cultivated. Good examples of the latter survive on Lakenheath Warren in Breckland.[27]

Most warrens had special warren houses, or lodges, which provided accommodation for the warrener and a place to keep carcasses and skins, as well as all the nets, traps and other necessary equipment. Commercial warrens needed a resident keeper, not least to protect the rabbits from poachers. Hungry peasants must have looked with envy at well-stocked warrens, but many convicted poachers came from more affluent sections of the community. In the early 15th century Augustinian canons from Blythburgh Priory were regularly convicted of rabbit poaching in the warren at Westwood. One, Thomas Sherman by name, was actually described in 1425 as 'a poaching canon'.[28] The best surviving medieval warren lodges in England are in Breckland. That at Thetford, erected by the Prior of Thetford to serve Westwick Warren in the 15th century, is reminiscent of a small castle: a well-built tower house, constructed of local flint with some brick and limestone dressings (Fig. 8.4). The building was clearly designed with serious defence in mind. It has small windows, with those on the ground floor narrower than those above – little more than arrow slits – while above the single entrance is a *meurtriere*, a hole for dropping missiles onto attackers. These features indicate the high value of rabbit skins and the fact that attacks from armed intruders were expected, although to some extent the lodge may also have served as an expression of

Fig. 8.4 The fine 15th-century warren lodge at Thetford in Norfolk.

As well as serving to house carcasses and equipment, and providing accommodation for the warrener, this elaborate building may also have been used by its owner, the Abbot of Thetford, while on recreational hunting trips.

the power and status of its owner. Another, rather similar lodge exists at Mildenhall, some 12km to the south-west, and recent research by Anne Mason has shown that fragments of several others survive in the area, incorporated into later cottages or farm buildings.

Rabbits continued to be farmed into the 19th century, but on a declining scale, for agricultural improvers castigated warrens as wasteful and archaic, and large numbers were ploughed up. Nevertheless, as late as the 1920s nearly half the area of the Elveden estate near Thetford was given over to warrens. Thirty warreners were employed and 120,000 rabbits taken per annum.[29] Some of the warrens around Brandon continued to function into the 1950s, mainly to produce fur for making felt hats. Only the advent of myxamotosis in 1954 finally brought this ancient industry to an end.

Heaths supported a number of other distinctive local industries. In particular, the ancient tradition of flint-mining was revived in Breckland in the 18th century to supply gunflints for flintlock guns. The industry was centred on the Suffolk town of Brandon. The flint was extracted in large nodules from shallow pits, mainly on the area called Ling Heath to the south-east of the town. It was taken to the town to be knapped to the required shape and size. In the early 19th century Brandon was the sole supplier of gunflints for the British army, and 160 knappers produced more than one million gunflints each month. Ling Heath is still peppered with the kidney-shaped mounds of waste which surround the filled pit from which the flint was extracted.[30] The industry declined slowly from its early 19th-century peak, and although some knappers still work locally it had effectively come to an end by the middle decades of the 20th century.

THE TRADITIONAL FARMING OF THE LIGHT LANDS

Where heaths occurred as isolated incidents in more fertile country, they provided a useful resource for local inhabitants and were usually common, sometimes (as at Poringland in Norfolk or Tiptree in Essex) to several parishes. But where they formed part of more extensive areas of light, relatively infertile soil, their role in agriculture was crucial. Large flocks were grazed on them by day and by night folded on the neighbouring arable, where they 'tathed' it – that is, dunged it intensively. Only through regular inputs of manure could these light, easily leached lands be kept fertile. While the great sheep-flocks of Breckland, or the Sandlings, were certainly valued for their meat and wool they were most important as 'mobile muck-spreaders', and the principal local breed – the blackfaced Norfolk Horn – was a slow maturing, leggy animal that could 'breed and thrive upon open heath and barren sheep walks, where nine tenths of the breeds in the kingdom would starve'.[31] Nevertheless, it produced sweet mutton, and short, fine fleeces, particularly suitable for the local woollen industry.[32]

Until the 18th century the vast majority of the arable land comprised open fields, in which the strips of farmers were intermingled with varying degrees of regularity. As elsewhere in East Anglia, landscapes of intermingled strips had probably emerged during middle and later Saxon times through the division of land between coheirs and – perhaps – through the equitable allocation of land to colonists or freed slaves. But the extent of the continuous areas of open arable was much greater here than on the clays or more fertile loams. Settlement could not disperse freely across the landscape as population rose in the early medieval period. Because of the limited availability of water and damp grassland, so necessary to sustain the plough-oxen, it was hard to establish new, ring-fenced farms away from the existing settlements in the principal valleys. Moreover, the more fertile and calcareous soils were also to be found here. Equitable division of land therefore tended to generate particularly extensive areas of intermixed arable. But in addition, the area under cultivation expanded greatly on the lighter lands in the course of the medieval period, and as heaths were divided between those who had formerly exploited them as common grazing, the boundaries of the open fields extended still further.[33]

As holdings became increasingly intermingled, communal systems of agriculture of necessity developed to ensure the efficient dunging of the fields. Folding would have been prohibitively expensive in labour and time if every farmer had had to move his own diminutive flock each day to a small fold erected on one of his own scattered strips. This, together with lambing and shearing, would have taken most of his time.[34] Large communal flocks were the answer, folded across several contiguous strips at a time. But in many East Anglian vills, as already discussed, a particular form of sheep–corn husbandry – the 'fold course' system – developed in medieval times. The grazing on the fallows, and on some of the heaths, was reserved for a flock controlled by the manorial lord. Tenants usually contributed their sheep to these flocks; the demesne lands had first call on the fold, and received a majority of the dung, although various arrangements were made to ensure that the peasant lands also received a proportion. The movement of the great flocks would have been hampered by physical subdivisions and, while some of the major rights of way in these landscapes (and closes in the immediate vicinity of settlements) were evidently hedged, large areas – especially in Breckland – were completely devoid of physical barriers.

Fold courses were a distinctive feature of light land husbandry in East Anglia, although better attested in western areas – in Breckland and north-west Norfolk – than in eastern ones. Many Sandlings parishes, for example, lacked them. Another was the cultivation of temporary outfields, something which, like the fold course, probably became more systematic and organised with the passing of time.[35] A Parliamentary Survey of the Norwich Dean and Chapter manors in Sedgeford in north-west Norfolk, made in 1649, typically described how the arable lay in strips, 'intermixed and undivided with customary and other lands', which were divided between the 'infield lands' and the temporarily cropped 'brecks' occupying the higher and more acid ground. The fold course flock was:

> *kept in this manner, viz partly upon the common … partly upon the shack of all the arrable ground whether they be customary, freehold or demesne lands … and partly on the lands or unplowed ground of the said Brecks whereof five parts of the whole into eight being divided are every year to lye and lay for pasture ….*[36]

Here, as often in western East Anglia, regular rotations were imposed on the outfields: they were ploughed for a specified number of years and then allowed to tumble down to heath once more. But elsewhere, particularly in the Sandlings, a less organised system seems to have been employed. In times of rising prices portions of heath would be broken up and cultivated in an *ad hoc* manner before being allowed to revert to furze and ling. Indeed, at some times and in some places the majority of the heathland in a parish might be subject to such shifting cultivation. Witnesses to an enquiry in the late 16th century thus claimed that the lord of the manor of Blythburgh and Walberswick, or his steward:

> *Have used to plow such parte of the … walke or heath as they would; and where any parte thereof was sowen with corne, the inhabytants of Walberswick did not put their cattle upon such places soe sowen untill the corne was reaped; but if their cattle did stray and come on the corne, they were impounded. And that it appeares by the riggs and furrowes on most parte of the heath, that the same have usually byn ploughed.*[37]

Certainly, we should not posit too sharp or permanent a division between the open field arable and the heaths and sheepwalks.

THE LIGHT LANDS IN THE 'AGE OF IMPROVEMENT'

The 15th, 16th and 17th centuries saw much contraction of settlement on the light lands, especially in north-west Norfolk and Breckland. Some villages, as we have seen, experienced severe contraction. Wordwell in Suffolk was a distinct vill in medieval times, but by 1736 a single farm, 'the chief profits whereof arise from a flock of sheep, the soil being for the most part a barren dry heath, a very bleak place'.[38] In part these changes were associated with a shift in emphasis in the local economy, from grain to sheep, and with changes in the operation of the fold course. The institution increasingly became a way of keeping large commercial flocks on tenants' land, flocks from which the tenants' own sheep were excluded.[39] Nevertheless, there were few changes in the physical landscape of these districts. Some piecemeal enclosure occurred, especially in the Sandlings and in parts of north-west Norfolk, but in most districts the majority of the fields and heaths remained open. All this, however, changed rapidly in the period after *c.* 1660.

The classic 'Agricultural Revolution' of the textbooks was quintessentially a phenomenon of the light lands of East Anglia. The reclamation of heaths and sheepwalks, the enclosure of open fields and the adoption of the four-course rotation transformed the practice of agriculture. Yields rose, and the area under cultivation expanded, thus increasing significantly, although perhaps not dramatically, the output of wheat and barley. The output of meat was also increased, for sheep – and cattle, which became a more important part of the agrarian economy – were now fattened on hay, clover and root crops, rather than on the fallows and the rough heath grazing. Indeed, landowners – most notably Thomas Coke of Holkham – experimented with new breeds, more suitable for the new conditions. The old Norfolk Horn was steadily replaced, first by Bakewell's New Leicester, subsequently by South Downs and South-Down crosses ('Suffolks'), sheep better adapted to a more sedentary lifestyle, capable of producing more wool and meat when fed on a diet of improved grass and roots.[40] But as well as transforming the practice of farming, the Agricultural Revolution profoundly changed the appearance of the landscape. Reclamation and improvement were inextricably linked with enclosure, with the process of replacing open land under communal management with consolidated parcels, surrounded by hedges, under the control of individual farmers. Only in enclosed land could tenants freely plant turnips and clover, safe in the knowledge that they would not be eaten by the sheep.

Some hedges, complete with hedgerow trees, existed in light land areas before the late 17th century, planted around village closes and piecemeal enclosures from the open fields, and also – in some districts – beside the main tracks and lanes. Such hedges were rare in Breckland, but fairly common in north-west Norfolk and the Sandlings. In the latter district surviving examples often contain only a limited range of species and many are dominated by elm, a consequence of the district's exposed

Fig. 8.5 A ruler-straight, species-poor hedge at Warham in north Norfolk.

coastal location. But in north-west Norfolk they are more mixed and species-rich, in some places little different from the old hedges found in the claylands. Nevertheless, while few of these landscapes lay entirely open, the period after *c.* 1660 saw a steady increase in the numbers of hedges, particularly in the decades either side of 1800 when, as grain prices rose spectacularly during the Napoleonic Wars, a rash of Parliamentary enclosure swept away open land wholesale. Most of these recent hedges are ruler-straight and noticeably species-poor, usually

ABOVE: *Fig. 8.6 In a number of places in the area around Newmarket in Suffolk* *the rectilinear field boundaries created by late Parliamentary enclosure have been augmented by planting strips of trees in order to provide shelter for racehorses.*

RIGHT: *Fig. 8.7 A Breckland pine 'row'* – *an outgrown Scots pine hedge – near Elveden in west Suffolk.*

OPPOSITE PAGE:

TOP: *Fig. 8.8 The distribution of marl pits in north-west Norfolk: the majority are found on the high ground, away from the coast, where the chalk is masked by deposits of glacial sandy drift.*

BOTTOM: *Fig. 8.9 In parts of north-west Norfolk, as here between Flitcham and Houghton,* *nearly every field has a marl pit near its centre.*

consisting of hawthorn with small amounts of sloe, ash, elder and dog rose (Figs 8.5 and 8.6). But in Breckland, and sporadically in the Sandlings, some landowners planted hedges of Scots pine – a plant able to thrive in particularly harsh conditions – most of which have now grown into lines of mature, romantically twisted trees (Fig. 8.7). They were locally referred to as 'deal rows', deal being an all-purpose East Anglian word for a conifer, and have become an icon of Breckland. A few farmers and landowners also experimented with other hedging plants, such as the Duke of

Argyll's Tea Plant (*Lycignum halimifolium*).

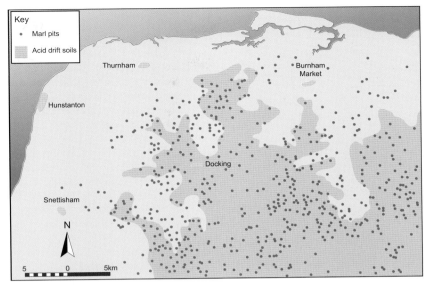

As the heaths and open fields came to be replaced by a mesh of rectilinear fields, new roads were often laid out and old ones terminated, tidied up or realigned. New farms were sometimes established on new sites, away from existing settlements, their names often testifying both to their late origins and their remote location: Botany Bay Farm, Waterloo Farm and the like. The farmhouses are usually symmetrical, double-pile, brick-built structures, sometimes with roofs of slate, sometimes pantiles. They were equipped with large barns and regular rows of cattle sheds, enclosing a yard in which bullocks could be over-wintered on turnips and clover, and their manure collected. Even where farms remained on the same sites, they were often comprehensively rebuilt. Existing buildings were poorly suited to the needs of the new husbandry in which farms functioned, in effect, as 'manure factories'. And they were often of insufficient size, for the area cultivated by each farm increased as the heathlands fell to the plough and as landlords engrossed holdings to make larger, more efficient units. On the Somerleyton estate, on the northern fringes of the Suffolk Sandlings, average farm size increased from 56 acres in 1663 to 106 in 1851;[41] on the Hunstanton estate in north-west Norfolk it rose from 17 acres in 1689 to over 220 in 1819.[42] By the middle of the 19th century, farms of 500 or even 1000 acres (200 or 400ha) were by no means uncommon on the poorest soils, especially in Breckland: few holdings of less than 100 acres remained.[43] Smart new farms were needed to attract tenants of sufficient wealth, for while the landlord supplied the fixed capital, the farmer supplied the working capital and the flocks and herds necessary to provide the manure required to keep the extensive ploughlands fertile.

Many other traces of the 'age of improvement' can be found in light land districts. In Breckland and north-west Norfolk, hundreds of marl pits were dug through the acid topsoil in

order to extract the more alkaline subsoil beneath, which was then assiduously spread on the surface to neutralise acidity (Figs 8.8 and 8.9).[44] This raised cereal yields and allowed turnips to be cultivated, which are highly sensitive to acidity and on particularly sour land are likely to fail altogether. Marling had been practised since at least medieval times, but its scale increased greatly during the 18th century, in part because it was easier to dig pits and spread the marl where land lay in large, privately owned fields rather than in a myriad of intermingled strips, in part because the reclamation of the acid heathlands would have been impossible without it. A map of Lodge Farm in Castle Acre, west Norfolk, surveyed in 1715 shows only a single communal marl pit, 'No Mans Pit', situated among the strips of West Field. A map surveyed c. 1840 shows no less than seven 'old pits' and 16 'new pits' within this same area.[45]

By 1752, the anonymous individual writing as 'N' in the *Gentleman's Magazine* put marling at the head of his list of practices which typified the 'improved' husbandry of Norfolk.[46] It was fortunate indeed that most acid soils in western East Anglia overlay chalk, or chalky clay, at no great depth. In the heathland areas to the north of Norwich, however, the chalk was deeply buried beneath Pliocene deposits. In some places, rafts of chalky material occurred within the glacial drift and were extensively quarried, but in addition major chalk quarries developed in the few places where the overlying deposits had been eroded, in the valleys of the River Yare at Whittlingham near Norwich and of the River Bure at Horstead and Coltishall. Their produce was then disseminated by wherry along the Broadland rivers.[47] In the Sandlings, similarly, pockets of chalk drift were exploited, but more important was a shelly, calcareous form of Crag, which occurs at no great depth in a number of districts, but especially in the area to the east of Woodbridge. This, like marl, was excavated from pits in the middle of fields and spread on the surface. Kirby reported that Crag had first been used in this way in 1718, by a farmer in Levington, but there are grounds for believing that the practice had been known for some time before this.[48] Either way, its use increased in the course of the 18th century and Arthur Young described in 1784 how, in the area around Ramsholt, 'pits are to be seen on every farm, some very large and deep'.[49] Crag pits are still a common sight in this part of the Sandlings, but this material was not everywhere available. Chalk was brought from Essex and Kent in ships returning from London, and some farmers carted calcareous clay many kilometres from the claylands to the west, However, an absence of suitable 'calcareous earths' remained a problem in many parts of the Sandlings.

In the period between 1700 and 1850, but especially in the decades either side of 1800, great swathes of landscape were thus transformed on the more extensive areas of light soil in East Anglia. The smaller patches of heathland scattered across the region, surrounded by heavier or more fertile soils, also generally disappeared in this period. Those in central Norfolk – including Foxley Heath, Belaugh Heath and Billingford Heath – were largely removed by Parliamentary enclosure acts during the Napoleonic Wars, while in Essex the great interconnected heaths around Colchester – Tiptree and its neighbours – disappeared in more diverse ways during the 18th and early 19th centuries.[50] All now survive only as islands of rectilinear boundaries in a landscape of older, generally more irregular fields.

So far I have discussed the transformation of the light lands in the 18th and 19th centuries entirely in terms of economics and agriculture. But here, more than anywhere else, the landscape was also moulded by the aesthetic preferences, and the recreational pursuits, of the class who owned it. These areas were dominated by large landed estates. They had already been strongly manorialised in medieval times, but in the course of the 16th, 17th and 18th centuries local lords had gobbled up the land of failing freeholders and copyholders, and squire had in turn acquired the lands of neighbouring squire. As a result, by the 19th century some estates extended, virtually without interruption, across huge areas

– more than 17,400ha in the case of Holkham in north-west Norfolk. The hold of big landowners was most absolute in areas of the poorest land, especially in the arid core of Breckland. Here, however, not all owners were from long-established local families. A significant proportion were outsiders, men who had made their wealth in government service or commerce, but who could not afford a sizeable property in more hospitable terrain. At Buckenham Tofts, for example, at the end of the 17th century one 'Mr Vincent', a retired officer in the Excise, erected an elaborate house, with elegant gardens, a fishpond on the roof and running water in every room. The house is now gone: the architect Roger North of Rougham ridiculed the pretension of the ambitious Vincent, describing him as 'one bred a servant, and by accident grew rich', and commenting that his lowly origins were reflected in the disproportionate size of the kitchen, services and servants' accommodation![51] A century and a half later nearby Lynford Hall was completely rebuilt by Mr Lyne Stevens, a London merchant and reputedly the 'richest commoner in England': his wife was a French Catholic ballet dancer.

Throughout the post-medieval period landowners – whether traditional and well-established or *parvenu* newcomers – built lavish houses, laid out landscape parks and indulged in extensive schemes of tree-planting. The late 18th-century owner of Riddlesworth in Norfolk, the appropriately named Sylvanus Bevan, reputedly planted 996,000 trees in and around the park.[52] New plantations were normally, as here, most extensive in the immediate vicinity of great houses, but by the early 19th century they were being established on some scale in the more remote parts of estates. Planting was a deeply symbolic activity, especially in areas which had traditionally been as devoid of trees as these.[53] It asserted both the ownership of land and the confidence of the family's continued enjoyment of possession: for why plant trees if your progeny will not enjoy the benefits, financial or otherwise? Planting proclaimed the fact that land was enclosed – for it was impossible to establish trees successfully where rights of common grazing still existed. It demonstrated patriotism, because there was recurrent concern that the nation possessed insufficient timber reserves to maintain the fleets upon which its security depended. Plantations also provided shelter for stock and, in particular, for game: in the course of the 18th century landowners took an increasing interest in preserving and shooting the pheasant, a bird which – unlike the partridge – thrives in a wooded environment.[54] Indeed, the shapes of many plantations – narrow belts and relatively small clumps – were ideally suited for maximising pheasant numbers, for the birds prefer to live close to the edges of woods, the lengths of which (relative to area) are maximised by adopting these shapes. East Anglia was never prime fox-hunting country, largely because of its increasingly arable character from the mid-18th century. But that other great predeliction of the gentry and aristocracy, pheasant shooting, has certainly left its mark on these light land districts.

It is also worth noting how the word 'improvement' was applied indiscriminately in the 18th century to both land reclamation and agricultural innovation *and* to such things as landscape gardening and afforestation. It summed up the 18th-century notion that existing arrangements, far from being God-given and immutable, were provisional, and could and should be changed for the better with verve and enthusiasm. Such a concept could be given particularly free reign on the relatively blank canvas of these open lands, large continuous tracts of which were often owned by individuals. Some forms of 'improvement' fall uncomfortably between the categories of 'agriculture' and 'garden design', such as the architect-designed 'model farms' erected on several estates in fashionable or whimsical style.[55] When the great agricultural improver Thomas William Coke expanded Holkham Park in the 1780s and 1790s, the centrepiece of the new landscape was the Great Barn; it was designed by the country-house architect Samuel Wyatt as a setting for Coke's agricultural shows, the famous 'sheep-shearings'. The surrounding parkland consisted of a mixture

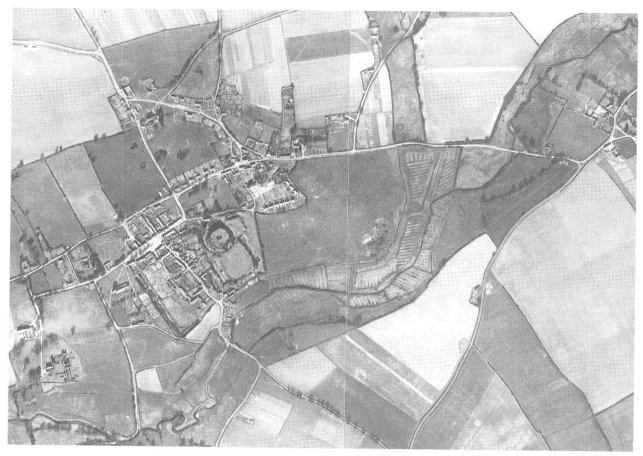

Fig. 8.10 The irrigated water meadows at Castle Acre in Norfolk, *as photographed in 1946 by the RAF. They were created around 1810 by a large tenant farmer on the Holkham estate.*

of sweeping turf, arable land and tree clumps, the latter carefully positioned both for aesthetic effect and for the benefit of game.[56]

> *What can be more beautiful than the diversified scenery which there presents itself?...The effects of order and industry, combined with abundance, must be gratifying to every spectator.*[57]

Some of the 'improvements' pioneered by large landowners and their tenants were simply fads, of more symbolic than practical significance. From the end of the 18th century, many 'improvers' constructed irrigated or 'floated' water-meadows, intended to force an early 'bite' for livestock by warming the grass in the early spring, as well as to produce a bumper hay crop in the dry summer months. The practice was long established on the chalklands of southern England, but had always been shunned by East Anglian landowners and farmers. Aristocratic improvers and their tenants thought they knew better, and a number of floated meadows – with 'bedworks', carriers and sluices – were constructed in the light lands in the years around 1800, when grain prices reached dizzying heights and money was available for this kind of improvement. The most striking remains are at Castle Acre in Norfolk, created around 1810 (Figs 8.10 and 8.11). Few of these systems were maintained for very long, however. The topographic and climatic characteristics of the region – the peaty soils of the valley floors and the sharp, late frosts – ensured that they simply did not work well. They were also expensive to create because the gentle gradients of local valleys meant that very long leats were required to provide a sufficient head of water. Several examples were located within or beside landscape parks, as at Lexham in Norfolk or Drinkstone in Suffolk: they were objects of fashionable display, as much as aspects of practical agriculture.[58]

Indeed, the more perceptive of contemporaries were well aware that 'improvements', and in particular the more spectacular reclamation schemes, might have complex motives. When in 1774 Thomas de Grey bemoaned the costs of enclosing the heaths at Tottington in Breckland, he observed that the 'great expense ... would but ill answer, unless there was a real satisfaction in employing the labourers and bringing forth a ragged dirty parish to neatness and cultivation'.[59] But most were more enthusiastic about the extension of cultivation. Arthur Young, for example, described how:

> All the country from
> Holkham to Houghton was a
> wild sheep walk before the
> spirit of improvement seized
> the inhabitants ... Instead
> of boundless wilds and
> uncultivated wastes inhabited
> by scare anything but sheep,
> the country is all cut up into
> enclosures, cultivated in a
> most husbandlike manner,
> well peopled, and yielding
> an hundred times the produce
> that it did in its former state.[60]

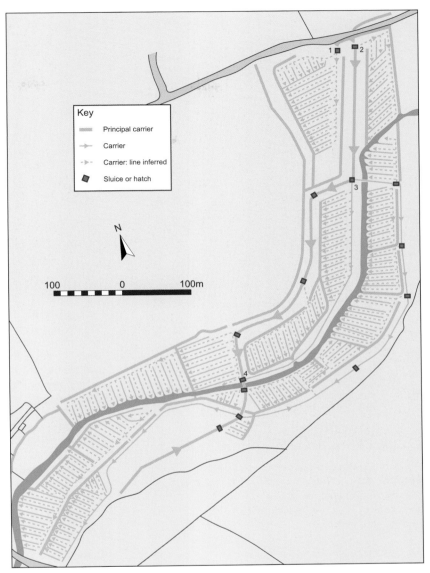

Fig. 8.11 Plan of the Castle Acre meadows, showing sluices, carriers and aqueducts. *The water flowed in narrow channels along the tops of low ridges, then down their sides, into drains, and back to the river.*

The area under arable cultivation in north-west Norfolk probably expanded by 50 per cent or more between *c.* 1720 and the 1840s: the tithe award maps surveyed at this time show that there was little permanent grass in the area, except on the floors of the major valleys. On the far poorer soils of Breckland, cultivation increased to a lesser, but nevertheless remarkable, extent (Fig. 8.12). The high point of heathland reclamation probably came during the Napoleonic Wars, when grain prices reached dizzying heights. Some of the reclaimed land went out of cultivation in the immediate aftermath of the war, but most continued to be cultivated until the end of the century. Nevertheless, large tracts of heathland were never reclaimed, and, as already noted, many rabbit warrens continued to function into the 20th century. However, it was in the Sandlings that inroads on the heaths were most limited, probably because of the limited supply of 'calcareous earths' with which soil acidity could be ameliorated.

In many ways the 'light land revolution' was a triumphant achievement. But it was also an ecological disaster, involving the destruction of thousands of hectares of ancient heathland. In Breckland the great bustard declined rapidly in numbers, and by the 1840s it was declared extinct. It still survives in parts of Spain and

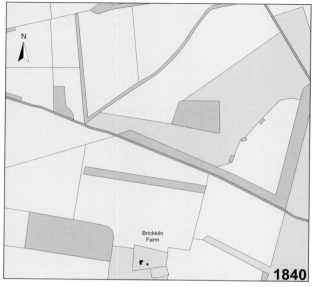

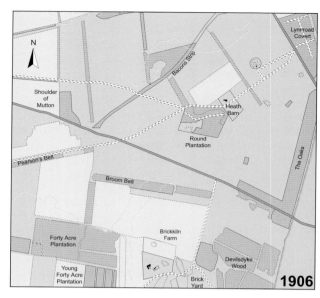

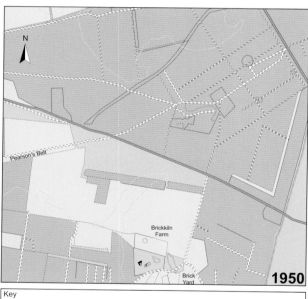

Key

f Building   Arable land   Heath and rough grazing   Woodland

200   0   200m

central Europe, thriving on treeless plains and grassy steppe, and the male is the heaviest bird in Europe. Reclamation and the adoption of more intensive forms of cultivation took their toll, but more important was the fact that the bustard was an open-country bird, and Breckland was now increasingly subdivided by hawthorn hedges, pine rows and tree belts:

> Not only entirely changing its aspect but rendering it entirely unsuitable to the wary habits of the bustard, which soon learned to become as jealous as any strategist of what might afford an enemy harbour.[61]

THE LIGHT LANDS IN THE 20th CENTURY

In the 'Good Sands' district of north-west Norfolk, and on the chalk scarp of the East Anglian Heights, the essential fabric of the landscape remains much as it was in the early 19th century. The neat rectilinear fields, the plantations and belts, the model farms and the great parks may not be very old, but they are of immense historical significance, quintessential landscapes of 18th- and 19th-century improvement. But in other light land areas the period after *c.* 1880 saw very significant changes to the landscape, so much so that in many places what we see today is largely, or even completely, a product of the 20th century.

With the onset of the agricultural depression in the 1880s, much of the heathland reclaimed during the previous century or so was abandoned. A comparison of the tithe award maps of *c.* 1840, and of the First and Second Edition OS 6-inch maps of *c.* 1885 and 1905, reveal numerous areas, especially in Breckland, which passed from arable back to rough grazing (Fig. 8.12). Further retrenchment occurred in the course of the 20th century and the Croxton Park estate in Norfolk was not unusual in being described in 1929 as comprising 'partly heath and partly low grade arable or pasture land which has passed, or is about to pass, out of cultivation'.[62] However, effective abandonment of farming in the heart of Breckland did not mean complete dereliction. Many large estates diversified, becoming in effect large game farms, profitably leased for the shooting season. Shooting was important in other areas of poor, light land: Edward Prince of Wales made Sandringham, on the Greensand soils of west Norfolk, the most famous shooting estate in England. But many landowners, their rent rolls falling dramatically, were in serious financial difficulties.

The recession had important effects upon the character of the heaths. The numbers of sheep being kept on farms often declined, so that land was less intensively grazed than before. The amount of bracken increased and so, more importantly, did the height of the heather. In the patches of bare ground between over-mature stands hawthorn, sloe and birch began to establish themselves as also, in places, did Scots pines, invading from adjacent plantations. Unchecked by grazing, these were able to grow into substantial bushes or trees. Iken Heath in 1920 was typically described as exhibiting 'very strong growths of heather, bracken etc with gorse and thorn bushes and a number of pine groups in scattered form'.[63]

The number of belts and plantations on the heaths also seems to have increased, partly because landowners wanted to provide more cover for pheasants but also because some felt that timber would make a better long-term investment than farming. However, it was from the 1920s that the area under trees really began to expand. The Forestry Commission was established in 1921 as a consequence of the severe timber shortages experienced during the First World War.[64] Two kinds of marginal land were chosen for planting – heathland and upland moor – and afforestation was also intended, in part, to relieve problems of rural unemployment. The Commission began to acquire land in Breckland in 1922, when *c.* 3,180 acres (1,275ha) of the Elveden estate were purchased. This was rapidly followed by the acquisition of the 4,944-acre (2,000ha) Downham Hall estate in 1923; and of the 6,208-acre (2,500ha) Lynford estate, and 822 acres (330ha) of the Beechamwell estate, in 1924. By 1929 the Commission owned some 40,000 acres (*c.* 16,200ha) in the district, mostly in the area to the north and west of Thetford. Almost all was purchased in the form of large continuous blocks of land – large pieces of, or the entire area of, impoverished landed estates. After a short pause, enforced by changes in government policy, acquisition of land resumed in 1934 with the purchase of the Culford estate between Bury St Edmunds and Thetford. By 1939, including land held on long leases, the Commission controlled no less than 59,000 acres (nearly 24,000ha) in Breckland.[65]

Planting this vast area with pine trees was an incredible achievement. All the work was done by hand, and no scheme of afforestation on this scale had ever been attempted before. The average planting rate between 1924 and 1929 was no less than 2,226 acres (900ha) per annum.[66] Rabbits were a major threat to the young trees – much of the forest was planted on former warrens – and prior to planting large areas had to be fenced and the rabbits within them systematically shot. At Santon Downham alone 500 rabbits a week were killed for most of the year preceding planting.[67] Originally a fairly mixed forest was planned, which would have included substantial numbers of beech, oak and other broadleaves as well as pines. However, experience soon showed that deciduous trees tended to do poorly in the face of late spring frosts and attacks by deer. Smaller numbers of other conifers, including Douglas fir and European larch, were also tried. Nevertheless, Scots pine remained the favoured tree by far, in part because the required seeds could be obtained with ease from the local landscape – from existing estate woodland and from the 'pine rows' (Fig. 8.13). It was only displaced in the mid-1930s by Corsican pine, which produces a higher volume of timber per hectare and is more resistant to insect pests and fungal diseases – especially *Fomes annosus*, a particular problem on the chalkier Breck soils.[68] The dominance of pines was never absolute, however, and strips of hardwoods were planted along the sides of the main public roads. In part this was for aesthetic

OPPOSITE PAGE:

Fig. 8.12 The Breckland landscape near Hockwold, Norfolk. *In 1840, much of the heathland had been reclaimed and was under arable cultivation. With the late 19th-century recession, however, a great deal reverted once more to heath or rough grazing, and the area of plantations and tree belts increased. By 1950, much of the heathland had been planted up as pine forest by the Forestry Commission. Note how the pattern of rides and tracks in the modern forest perpetuates, to some extent, the alignment of boundaries and features in the earlier landscape.*

Fig. 8.13 Only from the air *is it really possible to appreciate the vast scale of the Breckland pine forests.*

reasons, but mainly to act as fire breaks.[69] Conifers are particularly combustible when in the semi-mature, 'brushwood' stage; hardwoods, in contrast, do not ignite easily. The main potential sources of fire (other than sparks from the Norwich–Cambridge railway line) were steam-driven vehicles on the roads and cigarettes dropped by their drivers.

The changes wrought to the landscape as the pines matured were considerable. The forests have often been viewed in a largely negative light by ecologists because their establishment involved the destruction of so much ancient heath, yet much of the planted land was not virgin heathland, but rather fields abandoned to dereliction during the agricultural depression. Had it not been planted with conifers, the majority of the area would almost certainly have been ploughed up in the 1950s or 1960s, the fate which befell so many of the Sandlings heaths. From a landscape historian's point of view, one of the most interesting features of the Breckland forests is the way that the configuration of plantations – the boundaries between different compartments and the layout of access tracks – perpetuated in broad terms the pattern of roads and field boundaries which existed in the previous landscape (*see* Fig. 8.12).

Breckland contains the most extensive areas of conifer plantations in East Anglia, but there are others, for example on the Greensand soils in west Norfolk, on the former heaths around Horsford to the north of Norwich, and above all in the Sandlings. The Commission began to acquire land here in 1920 with the purchase of 1,878 acres (750ha) from Lord Rendlesham. By 1926, 2,307 acres (923ha) had been planted, rising to 3,817 (1,527ha) by 1930 and 4,905 (1,962ha) by 1938: the plantations were concentrated in three main blocks, the

'Forests' of Rendlesham, Tunstall and Dunwich.[70] The scale of afforestation was thus considerable. However, large areas of open heath, virgin or secondary, nevertheless survived in the Sandlings into the second half of the 20th century. Then, with the return of agricultural prosperity and improvements in agricultural technology, they came under renewed attack from farmers.

Small-scale attempts at reclamation had been made in the 1920s, and again in the 1940s.[71] From 1949 very large areas were ploughed, however, a development fuelled by government subsidies for liming, by the widespread use of artificial fertilisers and by the availability of cheap chemical treatments to rectify the potash, boron, manganese and copper deficiencies to which these acid, leached soils were prone.[72] Irrigation was first employed in the 1950s and was being practised on a significant scale by the end of the 1960s, significantly boosting yields and making it possible to grow potatoes and other vegetables on a large scale. Between 1949 and 1952, 1,533 acres (620ha) were ploughed at Wantisden Hall, at Iken Hall, at Lodge Farm in Sudbourne and on the Shotisham, Martlesham and Waldringfield heaths. By 1955 a further 1,120 acres (450ha) had been reclaimed around Sutton Hoo and on Sutton Hoo Common; at Methersgate Hall; and on the Kesgrave, Bromeswell, Hollesley, Nacton and Brightwell heaths. The years between 1955 and 1964 saw a further 207 acres (85ha) ploughed in Shottisham, Sutton and Hollesley. There were some losses further north, where some 490 acres (200ha) were brought into cultivation in the 1950s in Walberswick, Dunwich, Leiston, Aldringham and Snape, and 130 acres (53ha) on the Benacre estate. In all, some 3,640 acres (1,400ha) of heathland were lost to agriculture in the district between 1949 and 1970, although comparatively few areas disappeared after this date (Fig. 8.14).[73] In Breckland there was less reclamation: the largest areas of heathland had already been purchased by the Forestry Commission or by the War Office, to make their Battle Training Area, within which areas of heath are still maintained in fine condition.[74]

Heathland reclamation was an arduous business, probably more difficult than in the 18th and 19th centuries due to the overgrown and derelict condition of the land. Much of the heather had grown into 'tough woody plants standing up to 2 foot in height'.[75] The vegetation was broken down with a rotary cultivator or forage harvester and/or burnt, after which the land was ploughed, sometimes to a depth of a metre in order to destroy the 'pans' of iron and humus. Ground chalk was then applied at a rate of 10 or 20 tons per acre.[76]

Sadly, only fragments of the great East Anglian heaths now survive outside the Breckland Battle Training Area, mostly preserved as nature reserves; and even some of these are in danger of regenerating once more to secondary woodland. Yet this very instability is a reminder that they were not, in the strictest sense, 'natural' landscapes. Nor should we view the great conifer plantations, which have in many places replaced them, in entirely negative terms – aesthetically or ecologically. Such plantations are arguably the greatest contribution of the 20th century to the East Anglian landscape, and are themselves now becoming mature and diverse

Fig. 8.14 The contraction of the Sandlings heaths between 1906 (left) and 2000 (right).

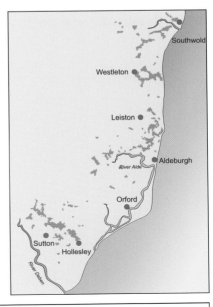

Key

● Town or village   ▨ Heath land

10   0   10km

environments. Many readers who mourn the loss of the heaths will also, as I do, relish that great panorama over the forests of Breckland from Gallows Hill near Thetford, in which the great pines recede, like a virgin wilderness, to the far horizon.

NOTES

1. Wade-Martins & Williamson 1999, 13.
2. Gilpin 1809, 28–9.
3. Chatwin 1961; Hodge *et al.* 1984, 272–3, 277–8.
4. Rackham 1986b, 286–91; Dimbleby 1962; Parry 2003.
5. Rodwell 1991, 372–8.
6. Ibid, 374–5.
7. Ibid, 377.
8. Grubb *et al.* 1969.
9. Dimbleby 1962.
10. Rackham 1986b, 299–302.
11. Carver 1998, 99.
12. Peterken 1968.
13. Harper-Bill 1980, charter 42.
14. Ibid, charter 43.
15. East Suffolk Records Office HA11: C2/10.
16. Rackham 1986b, 295.
17. Ibid, 295.
18. Filmer-Sankey & Pestell 2001.
19. Norden 1618, 234.
20. Ibid, 235.
21. Edwards 1991.
22. Bailey 1988; Hoppitt 1999b; Sheail 1971.
23. East Suffolk Records Office H93/3/48.
24. Wright 1668, **3**, 722–5.
25. Hoppitt 1999b.
26. Rutledge 1980.
27. Taylor & Crompton 1971.
28. Bailey 1988, 8.
29. Phillips 1909.
30. Sussams 1996, 123–8.
31. Marshall 1787.
32. Kerridge 1967, 312.
33. Williamson 2003, 127–32.
34. Kerridge 1992, 26–7.
35. Bailey 1989; Postgate 1962.
36. Norfolk Records Office LeStrange OC1: DCN 51/91.
37. East Suffolk Records Office V.50/22/3 (1).
38. Paine 1993.
39. Bailey 1990.
40. Wade-Martins & Williamson 1999, 128–9; Wade-Martins 1993.
41. East Suffolk Records Office, 194/A11/11, and 749/2/165.
42. Norfolk Records Office, Le Strange BH1 and BH9.
43. Wade-Martins & Williamson 1999, 76–81.
44. Mathew 1993.
45. Prince 1964, 22; Bacon 1844, 267–8.
46. Anon ('N') 1752.
47. Williamson 1997, 145–7.
48. Kirby 1735, 84.
49. Young 1795, 130.
50. Hunter 1999, 162–3.
51. Colvin & Newman 1985, 28.
52. Young 1804, 383.
53. Daniels 1988; Williamson 1995, 124–30.
54. Munsche 1981.
55. Robinson 1983.
56. Williamson 1998a, 100–4.
57. Curwen 1809, 238.
58. Wade-Martin & Williamson 1994.
59. Norfolk Records Office WLS XXLVII/19 415 X 5.
60. Young 1771.
61. Stevenson 1870, 17.
62. Forestry Commission Archives, Croxton Park *Acquisition Report*, 1928.
63. Forestry Commission Archives Iken Heath *Acquisition Report*, 1920.
64. Ryle 1969; Skipper & Williamson 1997.
65. Public Records Office FC 54386/4; FC 374/24; Forestry Commission Archives, FC L3/1/1; L3/3/9; L3/3/15; Skipper & Williamson 1997, 18–26.
66. Dannat 1996; Forestry Commission Archives *Annual Reports* 1927–9 and *Working Plan* 1959, sections 7, 8, 10.
67. Skipper & Williamson 1997, 34.
68. Forestry Commission Archives *Working Plan* 1959, sections 7, 8, 10.
69. Skipper & Williamson 1997, 64–6.
70. Butcher 1941, 331.
71. Trist 1971, 120.
72. Ibid, 120–3.
73. Ibid, 121.
74. Perry & Perry 1999, 264–85.
75. Trist 1971, 122.
76. Ibid, 122–3.

9

Wetlands

MARSHES AND FENS

Reclaimed wetlands account for nearly one-third of the area studied in this book. They are very varied in their extent, appearance and history, but a useful initial distinction may be made between marshes and fens. Today people tend to conflate and confuse the two, and to some extent they always have done so, but the distinction is nevertheless meaningful.[1] Marshes are areas of coastal silt and clay, usually located within former estuaries or behind spits of sand and shingle. They were embanked and reclaimed from tidal saltmarsh, usually in late Saxon or medieval times. Even in the medieval period most were occupied as private property, and they were exploited as either arable or pasture. Fens, in contrast, are areas of peat soil that, prior to drainage, were waterlogged for much of the year and did not contain any settlements, at least before the modern period.[2] They were, for the most part, used as common land by the communities living around them, grazed in the summer months and cut for a wide variety of products – fodder, animal bedding, thatching materials and peat – as well as being exploited for wildfowl and fish. Peatlands usually lay inland from marshes. In the Norfolk Broads, the great

level tract of Halvergate to the west of Yarmouth is a silt marsh, but the higher reaches of the valleys are fens or former fens. However, the junction between the two was often blurred, with areas of mixed soils often serving as areas of *common* grazing marsh.

Fig. 9.1 The higher silt Fens, just inland from the Wash, were colonised in Saxon times and by the 12th century could boast large, prosperous villages. Upwell in Norfolk is built on the firm ground provided by the levées on either side of the old River Nene.

MARSH LANDSCAPES

In medieval times marshes carried very varied landscapes. The largest area in eastern England, the district of silt soils which lies immediately inland from the Wash, contained substantial villages, large parish churches and extensive areas of arable land.[3] This area, called 'Marshland' in Norfolk and the 'Townlands' in Lincolnshire, was settled in Roman times, but subsequently abandoned, due to changes in the relative levels of land and sea. By middle Saxon times settlement had returned in the form of isolated ranches and salt-working sites, and in the late Saxon period a number of small

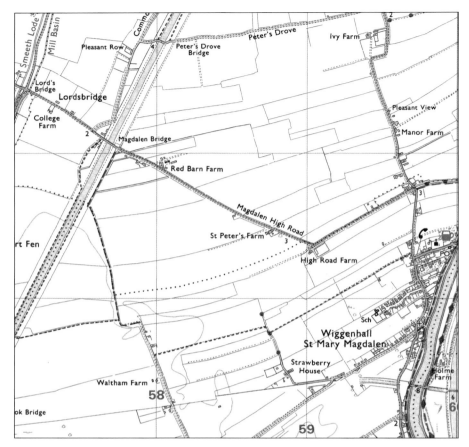

Fig. 9.2 The pattern of drainage dykes in Wiggenhall St Germans, in the Norfolk 'Marshland', preserves in simplified form the layout of the arable strips of the medieval landscape.

villages emerged here. They were associated with a pattern of small, irregularly shaped fields, protected from the sea by embankments.[4] The wealth and population of the district grew rapidly in the course of the 12th and 13th centuries, as expansion occurred inland onto the lower silt ground (Fig. 9.1). The new fields were protected by further 'walls' or banks and took the form of bundles of long parallel strips, seldom more than 20m in width, yet in some cases as much as 2km long. Subsequent piecemeal amalgamation has reduced the density of dykes, but the old pattern is still recognisable in many places (Fig. 9.2). The strips were oriented with the original, almost imperceptible gradient of the silt surface, running southwards towards the lower peat ground, or else in the direction of some lost natural watercourses which did so. Most Marshland strips, if not all, were under the plough, but they differed in a number of respects from the strips in 'upland' open fields. They were wider, and only limited rights of common grazing, and relatively few communal controls, were imposed upon them.[5] More importantly, their size meant that farmers usually held only a few strips – rather than, as in conventional open fields, large numbers, extensively scattered and intermingled with the property of others. These remarkable landscapes very closely resemble those created by 11th-, 12th- and 13th-century reclamation on the peat lands of Holland, especially North Holland. How far this was the consequence of parallel development, and to what extent the large landowners – especially monasteries – who directed much of the reclamation work actually brought in Dutch specialists is unclear. The spread of fields onto the lower silt grounds was accompanied by an expansion of settlement: archaeological fieldwork has revealed a massive increase in the number of farms and cottages here during the late 12th and 13th centuries. In typical East Anglian fashion, farms clustered along the edges of small commons and greens, and in particular beside the long, wide droveways which ran through the fields, southwards, to the great peat commons lying further inland.

Medieval Marshland was thus, in essence, an arable landscape. In post-medieval times, in contrast, the relative extent of grazing and arable fluctuated in accordance with market conditions, but pasture generally predominated, perhaps reaching its greatest extent during the recession of the late 17th and early 18th centuries, when population growth was sluggish and cereal prices relatively low. Thomas Cox in 1700 thought that the farms of the district 'turn to more Profit by Grazing than Ploughing', and tithe books and similar documents suggest that virtually all the silt soils were under grass.[6] Cattle were fattened here, but also large numbers of sheep, supplying much of the wool for the Norfolk textile industry.

Medieval Marshland was unusual in having such extensive areas of arable, and in containing substantial villages. It was also much larger than any of the other

areas of marsh scattered around the coast of Norfolk, Suffolk and Essex. Most of
these were exploited as rich pastures, and any settlements they contained took
the form of isolated farms. Halvergate Marsh, which forms the eastern seaward
portion of the Broads wetlands, was an open estuary in Roman times. Its mouth
was eventually closed by the accumulation of the shingle spit on which Yarmouth
now stands. By the 10th century the area had become dry enough for small
settlements to be established within it, on mounds raised on the low levees beside
the tidal creeks. Some were salt-working sites, some were sheep ranches, and
many survive today as isolated farms. Most of the area was parcelled up as
isolated blocks of demesne land, belonging to manors spread across a wide area
of east Norfolk. Indeed, until relatively recently much of the area comprised
detached portions of parishes, some of which, such as South Walsham or
Postwick, were located many kilometres away.[7] Domesday records large numbers
of sheep and saltpans in the area, and sheep and salt houses feature in various
documentary records dating to the 12th and 13th centuries. In 1147 Phillip
Basset granted the marsh of Fuelholme (in what is now the detached section of
Postwick parish) to St Benet's abbey, together with 300 sheep and saltpans for a
rent of 5 marks a year – a substantial sum. Around 1180 the same marsh was
granted to one Geoffrey, son of Master Nicholas, again with saltpans and
unspecified numbers of 'sheep'.[8] Medieval landowners grazed vast numbers of
sheep here: in 1343 the abbot of St Benets had over 1,500. In some cases, they
were penned up in folds at night and their dung carefully collected and taken by
boat to the 'upland', where it was spread on the arable fields to enhance fertility.[9]

Various portions of marsh were embanked in the course of the medieval
period, and – as sea levels rose – more systematically in the course of the 15th,
16th and 17th centuries. Banks were raised beside the principal watercourses,
streams such as the Pickerill Home draining off the upland, major creeks like the
Halvergate Fleet, and the principal
rivers (Figs 9.3 and 9.4). Late
medieval and early-modern leases were
at pains to stipulate the careful
maintenance of drainage works. When
in the 1550s Norwich Cathedral leased
out 'All those marshes and pastures
called Fowleholme and Sketeholme …
with all the ditches and stremys Fleetis
and Fysshyng to the same marryshes
and pastures belonging', the tenant
was responsible for 'drawynge
skowryng rearyng and matyng
[maintaining] off the diches ffences
stremes and Fleets and Bridges'.[10]
However, the dyke pattern on
Halvergate is very different from the
long, parallel strips of Marshland.
Many of the dykes are curving and
serpentine, representing fragments of
the original pattern of saltmarsh
drainage, utilised and fossilised as
embankment took place. Simple flap
sluices were constructed at the points
where these channels intersected with
the embankments, which were held
shut by the pressure of water when the
creek or river into which they
discharged filled at high tide, but

*Fig. 9.3 Halvergate Marshes, the finest
surviving tract of traditional grazing
marsh in East Anglia, and a landscape of
immense cultural importance. The Fleet Dyke,
a relict creek bounded by low embankments,
winds across the middle of the picture towards
Breydon Water, all that remains of the great
estuary that once occupied the whole of the
area shown. Beyond, in the far distance, lies
the town of Yarmouth, which occupies the spit
of sand and gravel that blocked the mouth of
the estuary in Saxon times. Drainage
windmills and marsh farms cluster along the
embankments beside the Fleet: many of the
latter were first established in late Saxon times.*

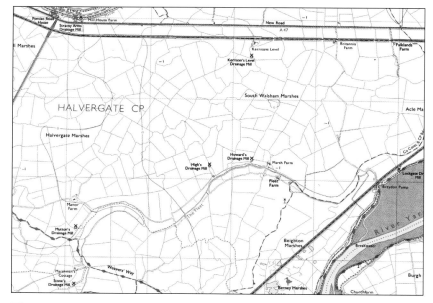

Fig. 9.4 The complex pattern of marsh dykes on Halvergate. *The irregular and serpentine watercourses are relics of the original pattern of channels that flowed across the saltmarshes, which were preserved after embanking and reclamation. The straight dykes are later additions or alterations of post-medieval date, created to improve the drainage.*

Fig. 9.5 A typical view across the Halvergate Marshes: *a green landscape, devoid of trees and hedges, but with a skyline peppered with the ruins of 18th- and 19th-century drainage mills.*

which opened to allow the outflow of water when the tide ebbed.

The Halvergate marshes continued, throughout the post-medieval period, to be a highly valued resource in a part of England in which good quality pasture was generally in short supply. They were used (and often owned) by people living, in some cases, far from the marsh edge. As Marshall explained in 1787:

> *The inclosures, or 'marshes', run from ten to fifteen to forty or fifty acres each; belong to a variety of owners; and are rented by a still greater number of occupiers; almost every farmer, within fifteen or even twenty miles, having his marsh.*[11]

Attempts were made to improve drainage, partly by adding straight dykes to the existing, serpentine network, partly (from *c.* 1700) by erecting drainage windmills. However, the marsh economy was no longer dominated by sheep. From the late medieval period, cattle were the most important stock grazed on the marsh. Young cattle, two or three years old, were brought to Norfolk by drovers from the northern and western areas of Britain – especially Skye, Galloway and the Highlands of Scotland, but also to some extent from Ireland – and were sold to local farmers at fairs, for example at Horsham St Faiths or Harleston. They were fattened (on the marshes in the summer and in yards during the winter) for between a year and 18 months before being sold in Norwich or London (Fig. 9.5).[12]

Other coastal marshes have a history broadly similar to that of Halvergate. Many of the Essex marshes were settled in late Saxon times by sheep-ranches, or *wics*, and salt-making sites, and here, too, a complex pattern of outlying demesne holdings and isolated parochial blocks developed.[13] Embankment, and more intensive draining, came in the course of the medieval period, partly as a response to rising sea levels. But along the Suffolk coast much embanking came rather later. Extensive reclamations were made in the area around Orford in the 1160s, and numerous portions of newly reclaimed marsh are described in 12th- and 13th-century documents relating to land in Bulcamp, Henham and elsewhere owned by the priories of Sibton and Blythburgh (Fig. 9.6).[14] However, embanking continued on a large scale into the post-medieval period. Leiston Abbey and Butley Priory reclaimed large areas in the saltmarshes in Alderton, Bawdsey and Butley, immediately before the Dissolution.[15] In the mid-1530s, 400 acres (*c.* 160ha) of the Duke of Norfolk's marsh at Hollesley were reclaimed, while John Norden's survey of the Stanhope estate, made in 1600–1, shows how marshes on the east side of the Butley river had recently been 'inned' with the construction of an embankment across the mouth of the Sudbourne Fleet.[16] In addition to these relatively extensive schemes, there were also innumerable small-scale and piecemeal encroachments on the saltmarshes. A survey of the manor of Walton cum Trimley, for example, made in 1613, describes 4 acres (1.6ha) of grazing marsh as 'a new improvement or enclosure latelie inclosed and taken in from the East Cliffe common or the salt marshes'.[17] As on Halvergate, the dyke patterns in all these areas of marsh are largely irregular and serpentine in character.

Most of the remaining coastal marshes along the East Anglian coast were embanked in the course of the 17th century, although in some places – for example, in the area around Wells and Holkham in north Norfolk – drainage activity continued into the 18th. In addition, during the late 17th and early 18th centuries, large landowners in Broadland managed to enclose areas of common grazing marsh lying on the wetter, more peaty soils in the lower reaches of the main river valleys immediately adjacent to, and inland from, long-drained Halvergate. These areas are today distinguished by much more rectilinear dyke patterns than those in the anciently enclosed areas of grazing marsh – patterns little different from those later created by Parliamentary enclosure of the peat fens higher up the valleys.

While most of the coastal marshes remained as pasture, some portions were sporadically ploughed. In 1781 the Norfolk historian M J Armstrong noted that parts of Halvergate were sometimes cultivated, and afforded 'greater crops of corn than any other land'.[18] John Kirby similarly observed in 1735 that the Suffolk marshes 'sometimes, when ploughed, afford the greatest crops of corn of any other land in this country'.[19] Numerous 17th- and 18th-century maps show areas called 'ploughed marsh' or 'wheat marsh'. Many landlords used prescriptive leases to prohibit or at least limit the extent of cultivation, however, fearing that this would damage and lessen the value of the land.

Fig. 9.6 Blythburgh church, Suffolk, viewed across the marshes and reedbeds. Large areas of the wetlands here were reclaimed in the 12th and 13th centuries.

THE TRADITIONAL LANDSCAPE OF THE FENS

Although fens were less valuable than grazing marshes, they nevertheless played an important role in the medieval and post-medieval rural economy as a source of grazing, fodder, thatching materials and fuel. Most were common land, but private fens also existed and were bought and sold by their owners. In the early 13th century Blythburgh Priory was granted an acre and a rood (*c.* half a hectare) of fen in Sandford in Henham by Robert son of Ulf, who had himself bought it from Geoffrey de Marci.[20] Where areas of common fen were relatively limited in area, moreover, they were often 'doled' to particular families, in order to ensure an equitable division of resources: specific areas were allotted in the form of narrow strips, similar to the 'lands' in arable open fields. The fen continued to be open for grazing for part of the year, but the holder of the dole was allowed the exclusive right to extract a range of commodities from it.[21] Doles gradually came to be treated as private property in many Broadland parishes. They were bought, sold and consolidated, and by the 19th century the dyke pattern in some of the valleys included large areas of 'consolidated doles' – that is, long parcels defined by parallel, slightly sinuous dykes ranged at right angles to the river. Sometimes (as in parts of the Yare valley) these served to demarcate what were still portions of unimproved fen, but elsewhere, especially in the Waveney valley, they defined areas of pasture and meadow that had been embanked and improved from damper ground (Fig. 9.7).

Doled or undoled, private or common, fens were exploited in diverse ways. Their drier areas were grazed for much of the year, but they were primarily valued for the materials cut from them (Fig. 9.8). Marsh hay was an important commodity, a mixture of fen grasses and rushes (principally *Juncus subnodulosus* and *Juncus effusus*) used for cattle fodder. It was usually mown on a yearly basis, but sometimes at longer intervals. Other areas were cut every other year, or occasionally every third or fourth, for 'litter', coarser herbage with a greater preponderance of rushes, which was principally used for cattle bedding. Some

Fig. 9.7 The dyke pattern in the Yare valley, near Surlingham. Many of the dykes were created when the common fens and marshes here were enclosed in the 19th century, but some (to the south) are of 17th-century origin and the distinctive parallel patterns, as around Rockland Broad, are the remnants of 'doles' of medieval date. Much land here reverted to fen and wet woodland, or 'carr', in the late 19th and 20th centuries. Note how the broads, flooded peat pits, lie a little way back from the river.

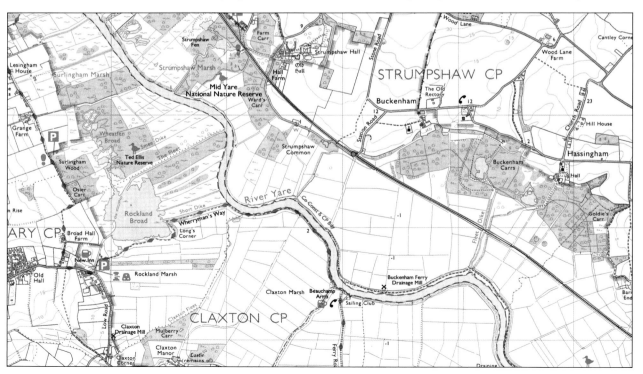

were cut for rushes alone, much in demand for covering domestic floors, a practice referred to at Beccles in 1544:

> *Also yt shalbe lawfulle to all*
> *women inh[abit]yng wythyne*
> *the seyd towne of Becclys att*
> *all tymes mete and convenyent*
> *to go into the sayd fen lands …*
> *to shere and gather wythe thyr*
> *sykkle … for the thyr dressyng*
> *up of thyr houses.*[22]

Fig. 9.8 The nature reserve at Wicken Fen, Cambridgeshire, is one of the last surviving fragments of undrained wetland in Fenland. It gives a good impression of the kind of environment destroyed by the great drainage schemes of the post-medieval period.

The damper areas were harvested for sedge (*Cladium mariscus*) and for reeds (*Phragmites australis*), both used for thatching. Reeds were always cut in the winter and early spring, beginning in early December and extending through to March or April: it was the dead stems of the plant that were harvested. The regulations for the commons of Ludham, Catfield and Potter Heigham drawn up in 1677 typically ordered that 'no reed be cut upon any of the said commons before the day after St Andrew under penalty of 6sh 8d for every fathom so cut'.[23] Sedge – more accurately saw sedge – was (and still is) principally used for thatching the ridges of roofs (it is extremely pliable when dry) and was usually cut at intervals of three or four years. Unlike reed, saw sedge was harvested in the summer. The two plants were cut from different areas of the fens, for the regular cutting of one tended, over time, to suppress the growth of the other, and indeed of other kinds of plant, leading to the emergence of ever purer stands.[24] In addition, there were a number of minor crops. Lesser reed-mace (*Typha angustifolia*) and yellow flag (*Iris pseudacorus*) were harvested for making mats, horse-collars and baskets; the bulrush was also cut for mat-making; while soft rush (*Juncus effusus*) and, to a lesser extent, compact rush (*Juncus conglomeratus*) were used to make 'rush lights'.[25]

As well as being harvested for this diverse range of crops, many fens were extensively cut for peat. It was used as a fuel and usually extracted from relatively shallow excavations, half a metre to one metre deep, often (like the other products of the common fens) within a framework of narrow 'doles'. Such shallow excavations filled quickly with water, vegetation and eventually with more peat, so that they are usually only just visible (if at all) as slight indentations in the surface of surviving fens. But in parts of Broadland, in the period between the 11th and the 13th centuries, cuttings were taken down to a greater depth in order to reach the more combustible 'brushwood peat', and the resultant pits eventually became the lakes locally known as 'broads' (Fig. 9.9). These were once thought to be natural features, but research in the 1960s showed that in most cases their sides consisted of almost vertical walls of peat, while within several of them steep-sided islands and narrow, well-defined peninsulas of solid peat could be found. The latter often continue out into the open water as submerged ridges, forming parallel lines that change direction where parish boundaries cross

Fig. 9.9 Barton Broad, Norfolk: one of the distinctive lakes created by large-scale medieval peat extraction.

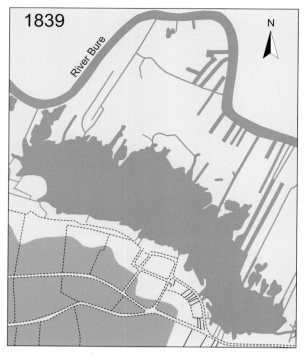

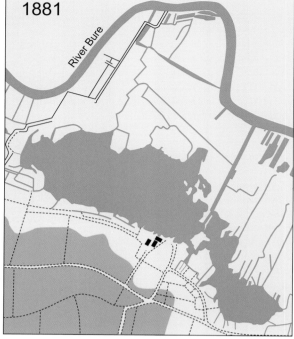

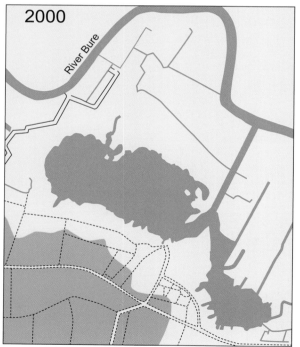

Fig. 9.10 Ranworth Broad, Norfolk. Like most of the broads, Ranworth has decreased in size during the post-medieval period. In 1839 there was a single large body of water, but encroachment by reedbeds and silting ensured that by the end of the century two distinct areas of water existed, Ranworth (to the west) and Malthouse (to the east).

the open water.[26] The scale of extraction was truly massive: CT Smith calculated that around 900 million cubic feet (26 million cubic metres) of peat must have been removed before the pits were abandoned.[27] Extraction on this scale is partly explained by the size of the market provided by Norwich and its populous hinterland; but it is also possible that much of the peat was used to smoke herring caught by the men of Yarmouth and other nearby coastal settlements. Abandonment and flooding came in the 14th century, partly because climatic changes and sea surges encouraged flooding, partly perhaps because the population collapse in the wake of the Black Death led to a declining market and escalating wage bills. Once flooded, the margins of the broads rapidly became colonised by reed, saw sedge and other emergent vegetation. As this died, peat began to fill the basins once more, ultimately leading in the case of the shallower broads to drastic shrinkage or even complete disappearance (Fig. 9.10). Sutton Broad, Carleton Broad, Dilham Broad and Strumpshaw Broad have all dwindled to nothing over the last century or so. Others disappeared in the more distant past, such as the lost Honing Broad, shown on a map of *c.* 1730. Its presence is still marked in the local landscape by the great loop taken by the road from Honing to East Ruston in order to avoid it.[28]

Fishing and wildfowling were important aspects of the traditional economy of the fens, and indeed of the marshes. Medieval fishing weirs have been discovered at a number of places in the inter-tidal mudflats, and examples of abandoned oyster pits are common, but the most characteristic feature of the eastern wetlands was the duck decoy. Decoys were introduced from Holland in the early 17th century as a method of trapping wildfowl.[29] They consisted of a number of curving 'pipes' – tapering channels covered by netting supported on a framework of hoops – leading off from an area of open water (Fig. 9.11). Each pipe terminated in a detachable bow-net. Along one side of each pipe screens of wood and reeds were erected, arranged *en echelon* (in an overlapping manner), behind which the decoy man would conceal himself. Wildfowl were lured into the net by using a combination of tame decoy ducks and a dog called a 'piper'. The former were trained to enter the pipe when commanded to do so by a low whistle; at the same time the dog would run around the screens, jumping over low boards or 'dog jumps' placed between them. The wildfowl gathered near the mouth of the pipe were attracted towards what – to them – must have looked like an appearing and disappearing dog. Encouraged by the behaviour of the decoy ducks, they swam towards it. When they had proceeded some way the decoy man would appear, waving his arms or a handkerchief and driving the birds in flight down the tapering pipe and into the bow-net.[30]

The wetlands and estuaries of the east coast teemed with wildfowl in the 17th and 18th centuries, particularly mallard, pintail, teal and widgeon. It is not surprising, then, that decoys became a prominent feature here: they were

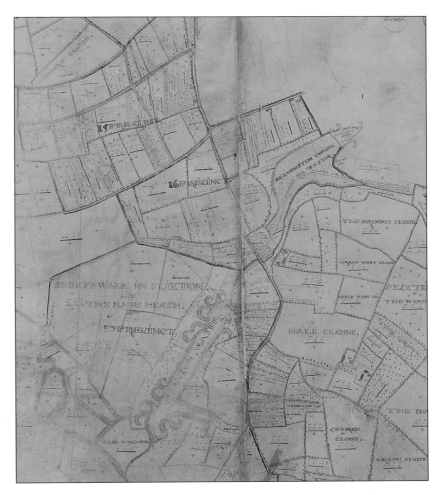

Fig. 9.11 Flixton Decoy, as shown on the 1653 map of Somerleyton.

valuable pieces of property, usually leased by their owners to professional operators. But the region's proximity to the Low Countries was also perhaps a factor in their early prominence. The earliest known example in England was at Waxham on the north-east cost of Norfolk where, as early as 1620, Sir William Wodehouse was reported to have constructed 'a device for catching DUCKS, known by the foreign name of a koye'.[31] The practice spread fast: other 17th-century examples are documented at Purdis Farm near Ipswich (in 1646);[32] at Acle and Hemsby in Norfolk; and at Flixton in north-east Suffolk, clearly shown on a map of 1653. By the early 18th century decoys had spread into the fens, where Defoe in 1720 described the 'abundance of those admirable pieces of art called decoys'. One near Ely, he claimed, sent 'three thousand couple a week' of wildfowl to London.[33]

The sites of more than 90 decoys are known in East Anglia, almost all in areas close to the coast, especially in the vicinity of major estuaries (Fig. 9.12). However, their numbers dwindled in the second half of the 19th century, partly because of changes in dietary habits, but mainly because their successful operation demanded peace and quiet, and as the century progressed the fens and marshes were increasingly disturbed by recreational shooting, tourists and railways. Nevertheless, Fritton decoy continued to operate into the 20th century, and in the winter of 1899–1900 no less than 2,721 wildfowl were caught there.[34] It was last worked in the 1950s. Most decoys have left only scant traces in the landscape. Once abandoned, the pipes – and often the open water of the pond itself – rapidly became colonised with vegetation and subsequently filled by peat.

Fig. 9.12 East Anglia and the Fens: the distribution of duck decoys
(those located outside the boundaries of the region are also included).

However, the decoy generally lives on in the names it has given to neighbouring features in the countryside, such as Decoy Farm, Decoy Plantation, Decoy Wood, Decoy Carr or Decoy Covert.

FEN DRAINAGE IN THE 17th CENTURY

The largest tract of peat fen in East Anglia, the southern part of the area we know today as Fenland, became the subject of large-scale drainage schemes in the 17th century. Some limited attempts at drainage (generally restricted to the peat margins) had occurred in the medieval period, most notably that which featured 'Morton's Leam', a drainage canal created by Bishop Morton in 1490. This canal collected the waters of the River Nene near Peterborough and took them across the fens to Guyhirn, to the south-west of Wisbech, there returning them to the river. But it was only in the late 16th and early 17th centuries that large landowners began to take a serious interest in comprehensive systems of improvement. They wanted to extend the grazing season on the lower peat ground, much of which was under water from autumn until late spring, and some also believed that the land could be made dry enough to allow the rich peat soils to be ploughed and cultivated. Not all landowners were enthusiastic about the prospect of reclamation, however. To small farmers, exploiting their rights to use the great wet commons, areas which lay regularly under water might be of real economic importance. As Lord Willoughby astutely pointed out in a letter to the Earl of Essex in 1597: 'a poor man may … make more commodity of a fen full of fish, fowl and reed, rented for little or nothing, than of ground made pasture and improved to high rent, as the charges of draining will require, for cattle and kine to feed on'.[35]

In 1585 the General Drainage Act was introduced into Parliament, eventually reaching the statute books in 1600. This established the principle that large landowners could overrule local proprietors and suppress any common rights that obstructed the path of drainage schemes, and that the investors (or 'adventurers') in such schemes might be rewarded with a share of the reclaimed land.[36] This, for the first time, created a mechanism that could finance large-scale schemes of improvement, although at the cost of local property rights and traditional lifestyles. Some limited attempts at drainage were made immediately after the passing of the act, most notably that headed by Sir John Popham, Lord Chief Justice, in the area around Upwell in Cambridgeshire. But far more ambitious schemes were mooted and submitted to the Privy Council by English speculators and various Dutch engineers, including William Mostart, Peter Morrice, Humphrey Bradley, Cornelius Liens and Cornelius Vereuil. All were rejected: but when at last a scheme was sanctioned, in 1629, to drain the 'Great Level' of the southern peat fens in Cambridgeshire, it was under the direction of yet another Dutchman, Cornelius Vermyden. Given the long and close contacts between England and the Low Countries, it is not surprising that Dutch engineers – the acknowledged experts in the field – should have been so prominent in fen drainage. The scheme was brought forward by a consortium of investors led by Francis, 4th Earl of Bedford.[37] He had considerable properties in the area, for he owned the extensive Thorney estate, purchased by his grandfather following the Dissolution of the monasteries. His involvement in the project was motivated less by a concern to improve his own property, however, than by a desire to benefit from the additional lands he would acquire as the principal 'adventurer'. Vermyden himself was both director of works and an important investor. Work on the various drainage works began in 1634.

Contemporary opinion was divided over the best way of improving drainage in the Fens. There was general agreement that the meandering, unembanked character of the rivers made them liable to spill out across the surrounding land during winter spate, and that this problem was worsened by the fact that their outfalls into the Wash were clogged with sediment. Some, including the Dutch engineer Jan Barents Westerdyke, believed that a thorough cleansing of the main rivers would be sufficient solution. This would assure that the waters flowed at greater speed, thus keeping the channels and outfalls scoured and open.[38] At the same time the rivers would be restrained within their courses, even during the winter, by the construction of embankments. Others advocated more radical improvements, based on the idea that increasing the velocity of water flowing down the watercourses, by straightening them or amalgamating them or both, would both reduce the risk of flooding and keep the outfalls open. Vermyden was of the latter opinion, and the principal feature of his scheme was the Seventy Foot or Bedford (later the 'Old Bedford') River: a stupendous piece of engineering that runs dead straight for some 32km (20 miles), is 70 feet (c. 22m) wide and served to divert the waters of the meandering River Ouse from Earith, just inside Huntingdonshire, to Denver in Norfolk. The old course of the Ouse was left as a minor drainage channel. In addition, a number of new arterial drains were constructed, the longest being Bevill's Leam and the Peakirk Drain, which ran from Glitton near Peterborough to Guyhirn, but which has now disappeared as a major channel (Fig. 9.13). There were innumerable smaller cuts, sluices and cut-off channels.[39] The embankments bordering the major channels were initially constructed of peat, together with some

Fig. 9.13 The main artificial watercourses created to drain the southern Fens in the 16th and 17th centuries.

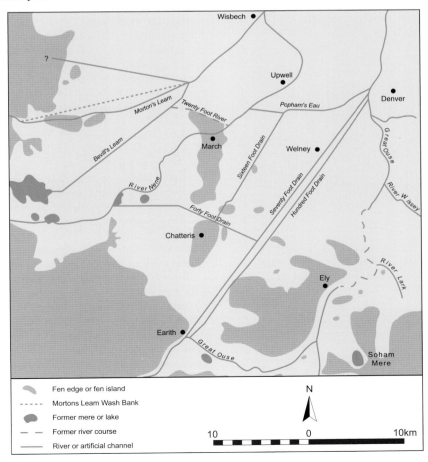

of the clay which lay beneath it, but the banks often burst under pressure as the peat dried out and extensive repairs had to be made later, using clay alone.[40]

In 1637, at a Session of the Court of Sewers at St Ives, it was declared that the project was completed and that the Great Level was drained. But the new works were only partially successful. There was sustained opposition from the local commoners, involving riots and sabotage. In 1638, for example, some 'forty or fifty men gathered in a fen called Whelpmoor … Common to Ely and Downham to throw down the ditches which the drainers had made for enclosing their fen grounds from the common'.[41] Their objection was less to the drainage works *per se* than to the fact that the allotments made to the 'adventurers' reduced the area of common land available to them. Large areas continued to be liable to flooding, and in general the situation was deemed unsatisfactory. Charles I therefore appointed a further Commission of Sewers to sit at Huntingdon in 1638, which ruled that the earl and his associates had not fulfilled their obligations. Charles himself took over as director of the scheme and Vermyden accepted office under him, shortly afterwards preparing his 'Discourse Touching the Draining of the Great Fennes', which contained his ideas for further improvements.

However, the outbreak of the Civil War suspended all further work, and it was only in 1649, with hostilities over and a Republic in place, that attention turned once more to drainage matters. An act of parliament authorised William, 5th Earl and 1st Duke of Bedford and his associates to resume drainage work. The stated intention was now to reclaim the land, not only for improved pasture, but also for arable. The Great Level was divided into three parts, the North, Middle and South Levels, each of which was given its own Board of Commissioners, and Vermyden was once more back in charge of the works. His main creation in this second phase of activity was the Hundred Foot Drain or New Bedford River, which ran parallel to the Old River. Substantial 'barrier banks' were created on the outer edges of each, thus creating a vast washland which could store the waters of the Ouse in time of winter flood (Fig. 9.14). More than 10,000 labourers were employed on this vast project. A number of other new watercourses were created, especially within the area of the Middle Level, most notably the Forty Foot or Vermyden's Drain (which ran from Ramsey in Huntingdonshire through Benwick, Doddington and Chatteris to the Old Bedford River at Welches Dam) and the Sixteen Foot or Thurlow's Drain (running north west from Chatteris through Wimblington to the Nene at Upwell). Improvements were also made to existing watercourses, including Bevill's Leam and Popham's Eau. A 'barrier bank' was raised parallel to the old medieval drainage cut of Morton's Leam to create another washland; Denver sluice was built in 1653, to prevent tides reaching up the old course of the River Ouse; and many new roads were laid out.[42] Less was done in the South Level, for Vermyden's main proposal for this area was never carried out in his lifetime. This was for a cut-off channel running around the eastern margin of the Fens, preventing the waters of the Little Ouse, Wissey and Lark rivers from reaching them. (The idea was revived on a number of subsequent occasions, but only finally implemented in 1964.)

In 1653 the works were completed and the Fens were again judged to be reclaimed. Following the Restoration of Charles II, the 1649 act, and the arrangements it put in place, were confirmed by a fresh act of Parliament. The agreed 95,000 acres were allotted to the 'adventurers' in the form of blocks of land of various sizes scattered across the Fens. Many can still be picked out on the modern map as distinct parcels of land with their drains oriented differently to those of the surrounding, later enclosures, and bearing the name Adventurer's Fen, Lands or Grounds. Occasionally the name Undertaker's Fen/Lands/Grounds appears as an alternative – the undertakers were the contractors who 'undertook' the drainage work.[43] Some of these dyked fields form patterns that seem to echo the regular, grid-like arrangements sometimes created by 17th-century drainage of lakes such as the Beemster in North Holland, as in the area of Burnt Fen near Littleport or at Adventurer's Fen near Haddenham (Fig. 9.15). Reclamation of

ABOVE: ***Fig. 9.14 The two great watercourses created by Cornelius Vermyden*** *in the middle of the 17th century, the Old and the New Bedford Rivers, run relentlessly across the level Fenlands. The embanked area in between them is a 'Washland', which still fills with water in winter and early spring.*

LEFT: ***Fig. 9.15 This grid-like pattern of dyked fields at Burnt Fen*** *near Littleport, Cambridgeshire, was created in the 17th century and is reminiscent of contemporary systems of land allotment in Holland.*

these damp lands was more than a matter of practical agrarian economics. These were abstract schemes of land division, imposed on the featureless fen surface, symbolic of the triumph of rational organisation over the chaos of nature. Indeed, a number of contemporary writers published much larger and more ambitious schemes of large-scale, systematic land division in the Fens.

Although the 'Great Level' comprised the most extensive area of the Fens, it did not include the smaller areas of peat lying further north: the North Holland Fens around Boston and Deeping Fen between Spalding and Stamford. Here, similar activities were taking place in the course of the 17th century, again under the direction of Dutch engineers. While some major drains were put in place, however, most notably the 38km (*c*. 24-mile) long South Forty Foot Drain, the engineering works here were on a less ambitious scale and the various schemes more fragmented in character, although similar in principle and execution.

Some drainage activity continued into the second half of the 17th century, but this phase of reclamation was effectively completed by the 1660s and the condition of the Fens was, in agricultural terms, greatly improved. Although most of the land was still used for grazing, some was now exploited as arable. There are, for example, records of cabbages and cereals being cultivated on newly reclaimed fen in 1683 at Thorney. Sir William Dugdale, who visited Willingham in 1657, reported that onions, peas and hemp were being grown there, while on fen ground to the north-east of Ely he saw flax, hemp, oats, wheat, coleseed and rape, and at Whittlesey fruit trees and extensive cornfields.[44] Walter Blith in 1652 described the practice of 'denshiring': ploughing off the turf with a light plough, burning it in heaps and spreading the ashes across the surface, in order to improve fertility.[45] The ashes were alkaline and thus helped to neutralise the natural acidity of the peat. Land so treated was usually cropped for a few years and then returned to grass, under a form of convertible husbandry.

However, the success of Vermyden's scheme, and of the similar projects in Lincolnshire, should not be exaggerated. The kinds of improvements and changes in land use noted above were largely restricted to privately owned land, but only a minority of the fens was actually enclosed at this time – those portions allotted to the undertakers and adventurers, and to some leading local landowners, or divided into 'severals' by the agreement of the commoners. The majority remained as open common grazing, although now often allocated to specific parishes rather than shared between many and, as a result of Vermyden's drainage works, less liable to serious inundation than before (Fig. 9.16). Some areas still lay entirely unreclaimed. As Dugdale emphasised in 1662, 'there are many great meres and lakes still continuing'.[46] Moreover, at a local level there were many problems with the drainage works, sometimes because of insufficient investment, sometimes because of continuing opposition and sabotage. In Deeping Fen 'a running fight between drainage projectors and fenmen lasted for over a century'.[47] Daniel Defoe described how, crossing the Gog Magog Hills in Cambridgeshire shortly before 1720, he saw 'the Fen country on our right, almost all covered with water like a sea, the Michaelmas rains having been very great this year'.[48] All this encouraged landowners to keep even the enclosed parcels under pasture. In short, 17th-century drainage left much of the Fens as common grazing, often only marginally improved. Some parts were completely undrained, and even within the enclosed and drained allotments, improved pasture seems to have predominated over tillage.

More importantly, towards the end of the century the condition of the reclaimed lands began to deteriorate.[49] Once water was removed from the absorbent peat it shrank steadily, while on land that was ploughed and burnt the peat blew away, and the surface was constantly degraded by microbial action. With remarkable speed the land surface fell below that of the adjacent rivers and channels. The only solution was to use horse mills or, more usually, drainage windmills, to lift water over the embankments and into the main watercourses. From the late 17th century onwards, drainage mills became a quintessential feature of East Anglia's wetland landscapes.

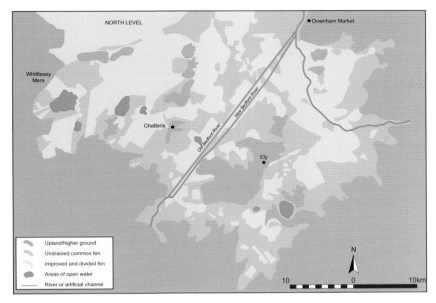

Fig. 9.16 The extent of drained land in the southern fens in c.1700. *The 'Great Level' was only partially drained by Vermyden. Large areas of unenclosed and only partially drained common fen survived: many remained until they were removed by Parliamentary act in the early 19th century.*

Map labels: NORTH LEVEL · Downham Market · Whittlesey Mere · Chatteris · Old Bedford River · New Bedford River · Ely

Legend:
- Upland/higher ground
- Undrained common fen
- Improved and divided fen
- Areas of open water
- River or artificial channel

10   0   10km

THE COMING OF THE WINDMILLS

The technology of wind drainage had been first developed in the Netherlands, where mills were widely established by the 15th century. They first appeared in the silt Fens of Lincolnshire and Norfolk in the 16th century, but it was only with the drainage and subsequent shrinkage of the peat that they began to be built on a large scale. References to the erection of 'engines' appear frequently in records of the Bedford Level Corporation from 1663. There were numerous complaints about the inundations which they caused to neighbouring land, and the deterioration of the embankments that they allegedly brought about. However, their numbers increased inexorably as the peat continued to contract. Almost all were simple wooden smock mills with four canvas sails, although some smaller structures, resembling the light *wipmolen* of the Netherlands, were also erected.[50] All drove scoop wheels which lifted water up from drainage ditches and into a higher level dyke or river. Not all drainage mills were erected by individuals. Some were established by groups of neighbours, and others by the various Drainage Commissions – local bodies of elected landowners who were responsible for drainage works in compact areas of wetland – which were established by parliamentary acts or by enclosure acts, although the latter continued to meet with opposition and few were successful before the end of the century.[51]

Drainage mills began to be constructed in Broadland slightly later than in the Fens – the earliest reference is on a map of 1700, of the Norwich Cathedral Dean and Chapter lands at St Benets Abbey. But they proliferated steadily and by *c.* 1800 there were around 50 of them (Fig. 9.17).[52] Most were erected by groups of local landowners, and a number of contracts drawn up for this purpose survive. In August 1769, for example, an agreement to erect a drainage mill was made between William Windham, John Berney of Bracon Ash, John Fowle of Broome and Dionissa his wife, all of whom owned substantial blocks of land in Thurlton Marsh. The lands in question were

> Subject to be overflowed and have been freqtly damaged by Floods and
> Inundations of water for want of a Mill or Engine and other proper Works
> Cuts Drains Dams Sluices and Outlets to carry off the same.[53]

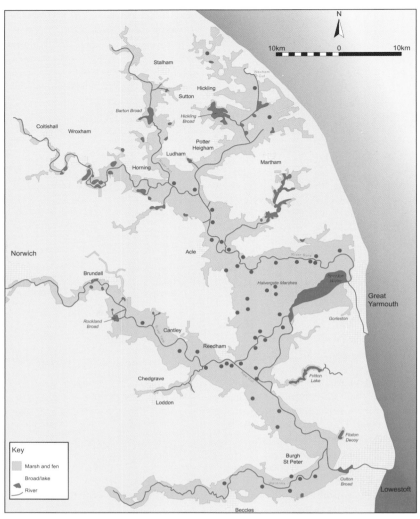

Others, however, were constructed by individual landowners. The Langley estate thus built one on the Round House Marshes in 1740, while William Windham had one erected in Norton in 1768.[54]

The earliest Broadland mills appear, like those in the Fens, to have been simple wooden smock mills with external scoop wheels (Fig. 9.18). By 1787, however, William Marshall was able to describe the standard mill as having a body 'built of brick, about twenty feet high, with sails similar to those of a corn mill, but somewhat smaller';[55] and the only surviving 18th-century examples are indeed small tower mills, like that on the Brograve Level in Hickling, which until recently carried a date stone of 1771, or Oby Mill, which bears the date 1753 (Fig. 9.19). All were rather low, squat structures. The proliferation of mills in the Broadland marshes was in part due to continuing changes in the relative levels of land and sea. Certainly, by 1803 one observer was able to assert that 'the marshes could not be kept dry from the water, were it not for the Engines – the water came thro' the banks every year, little or much'.[56] However, in addition, the enclosure by large landowners of areas of common marsh in the lower river valleys bordering on Halvergate in the late 17th century encouraged investment in the technology necessary

to improve them. Mills also appeared in other coastal marshes in East Anglia at this time. One is recorded in the Walberswick Marshes as early as 1743,[57] although all surviving examples along the Suffolk coast area appear to post-date 1800.

DRAINAGE IN THE 19th CENTURY

In spite of the erection of innumerable windmills, the peat Fens remained poorly drained throughout the 18th century, in part because large areas were still common land. No less than 40,000 acres (*c.* 1,620ha) in West, East and Wildmore Fens in Lincolnshire, for example, remained unenclosed until 1801 and lay largely under water in a wet winter (Arthur Young rowed across them in 1799).[58] The final and complete drainage of the Fens – and the creation of the arable landscape we see here today – only really occurred in the course of the 19th century.

Arable land use was increasing in the Fens by *c.* 1800, as the recovery in agricultural prices, fuelled by a resumption in population growth from *c.* 1760, was further stimulated by the blockade of the Napoleonic Wars. Initially it was the pastures on the silts of Marshland that fell to the plough, but soon the peat was beginning to be cultivated. Arthur Young in 1804 described the practice of burning and paring, or *den-shiring*, in terms very similar to those used by Blithe in 1658. Having stripped the surface turfs and burnt them in piles, farmers spread the ashes across the fields. 'Coleseed is then sown on one shallow ploughing', followed by oats. In earlier times, Young explained, the land had then been laid to grass for many years. But now, he noted, this traditional form of husbandry was being replaced by a more intensive course of cropping: 'the common conduct is to make this operation the preparation for successive corn crops, and perhaps in bad rotation'.[59]

The expansion of arable farming, which continued throughout the 19th century, was only possible because of major changes in the landscape and in drainage technology. The various fen commons were mainly eradicated in a great wave of Parliamentary enclosure, peaking during the Napoleonic War years. This filled the spaces between the adventurers' allotments, and other early divisions of the fen commons, with meshes of straight ditches, which are generally less grid-like than those found in the older allotments – long rectangles or attenuated rhomboids are dominant shapes. By the 1830s the fen districts lay almost entirely in severalty, and the resultant increase in drainage ditches allowed lower water levels to be maintained. More importantly, there were major changes to the arterial drainage channels,

OPPOSITE PAGE:

TOP: *Fig. 9.17 The distribution of drainage windmills in the Norfolk Broads: c.1800.*

BOTTOM: *Fig. 9.18 Herringfleet drainage mill, Suffolk, was erected in the 1820s but gives some idea of the kind of wooden smock mills used to drain the Norfolk Broads in the late 17th and early 18th centuries.*

THIS PAGE:

Fig. 9.19 Oby mill, erected in 1753, is one of the oldest surviving drainage windmills in Broadland.

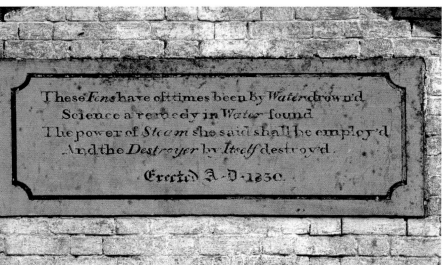

These *Fens* have oft times been by *Water* drown'd
Science a remedy in *Water* found
The power of *Steam* she said shall be employ'd
And the *Destroyer* by *Itself* destroy'd.

Erected A·D·1830.

TOP: ***Fig. 9.20 Stretham Old Engine, Cambridgeshire.*** *Built in 1831 and still containing much of its original equipment, this is the best-preserved steam pump in the Fens*

ABOVE: ***Fig. 9.21 This inscription on the gable of Littleport pumping engine,*** *built in 1830, neatly epitomises the overwhelming confidence of the 19th-century drainage engineers.*

including the construction of the Eau Brink Cut in 1821, the Ouse Cut between Ely and Littleport in 1827, the North Level Main Drain between 1831 and 1834 and the new outfall to the Nene in the late 1820s.[60] But above all, drainage was radically improved through the employment of steam pumps.

The use of steam drainage had been mooted by the engineer John Rennie as early as 1803, but the first engine was only erected, at Sutton St Edmund in Lincolnshire, in 1817. That at Ten Mile Bank, 5km south of Denver Sluice, was installed in 1819, followed by the engine at Borough Fen in the North Level in 1820 and by that at Upware in 1821.[61] In 1825 the two great engines in Deeping Fen were commissioned – the 60HP 'Kesteven' and the 80HP 'Holland'. They cost £17,000 to build and together drained some 30,000 acres (1,200ha). These in turn were followed by smaller engines at March West Fen in 1826 and at Pinchbeck in 1829.[62] Thereafter, during the 1830s and 1840s, steam drainage spread steadily into all parts of the fens (Figs 9.20 and 9.21).

The new machines had scoop wheels that were larger, and could rotate more quickly, than those of windmills, and they could lift more water through a greater vertical distance. Moreover, they continued to operate whatever the wind conditions. In 1852 J A Clarke estimated that there had once been around 700 drainage windmills between Cambridge and Lincoln, but the same area was now served by a mere 17 steam engines which collectively drained more than 222,000 acres (90,000ha).[63] The Duke of Bedford's agent on the Thorney estate, Tycho Wing, described in 1834 how the new steam engine was so successful that the eight drainage mills were now redundant. 'I am preparing to take down and sell as fast as I can dispose of them, the windmills formerly used for draining on this estate … it is impossible that they can ever be required again for the purposes of drainage'.[64]

All this investment and effort was amply rewarded by a phenomenal expansion of arable farming. By 1836, according to the documents called the Tithe Files, around 55 per cent of the peat fens were under cultivation.[65] However, there was another factor involved in this expansion of tillage. In many places the continued wastage of the surface was on such a scale that the underlying clay could now be excavated with relative ease and mixed with the peat. Better drainage allowed this to be carried out without the creation of permanently flooded trenches.[66] In 1830 the historian Samuel Wells described this as a practice 'still so very modern' that it was difficult to give 'an accurate account of its singular process',[67] but in 1858 C S Read stated how:

The clay is raised to the surface by means of deep trenches. It often happens that the peat, by being weighted and well drained, is so compressed that in a few years the clay is nearer the surface, and consequently more accessible for a second dressing.[68]

Claying neutralised acidity and encouraged the cultivation of wheat, rather than oats, the old mainstay of the fen farmer, for it ensured that the straw became firmer and the ears heavier and larger. In 1836 George Calthrop, a corn merchant from Spalding, could insist before a government inquiry that the price of wheat in England was being adversely effected by the 'immense tracts of land brought into cultivation in the fens of Lincolnshire, Cambridgeshire and Norfolk'.[69] And in the course of Victoria's reign the last remaining areas of open water and wet fen were enclosed and drained, including Grunty Fen in Cambridgeshire in 1857 and Holme Fen in Huntingdonshire in 1848. The Fen surface continued to shrink and erode: an iron column 22 feet (c.7m) in length was hammered into the fen surface at the latter place immediately after drainage began, and within 12 years 6 feet (c. 2m) were exposed; by 1890, this had increased to 10 feet (c. 3m).[70] There were further refinements in drainage technology with the use of light 'grasshopper' engines from the 1840s, and of centrifugal (or turbine) pumps from the 1850s. By the 1870s, around 75 per cent of the peat soils were under the plough. This was the most productive arable land in England, producing wheat yields of between 35 and 40 bushels an acre, on occasions reaching 50 bushels or more (compared with a national average of around 29 bushels an acre). But in addition, such was the fertility of the soil that it would stand far more intensive courses of cropping, with far less frequent fallowing or courses of root crops than any other in England.

The reclamation of the peat Fens was thus a more protracted and a more complex process than is sometimes assumed. As a consequence, the landscape itself is more varied and intricate than appears at first sight, with numerous different blocks of dyked fields aligned in different directions.[71] Some represent enclosures of fen ground dating to before the great schemes of Vermyden; others

Fig. 9.22 The pattern of drainage dykes in Borough Fen near Peterborough was largely created by Parliamentary enclosure in the early 19th century.

allotments given to adventurers, undertakers and wealthy landowners in the 17th century; most are portions of fen ground that were only enclosed and divided in the 18th and 19th centuries. Whatever their origins, almost all have a rigidly rectilinear layout that contrasts with the more sinuous dyke patterns of the old-enclosed silts of Marshland (Fig. 9.22). Most have farms scattered across them, erected soon after enclosure, often many kilometres from the 'upland'. These usually occupy the long, low ridges called 'roddons' – silt and gravel beds of lost rivers, now standing proud of the shrinking peat.[72]

THE BROADS IN THE 19th AND 20th CENTURIES

In the Broads, as in the coastal fens and marshes of Suffolk and Essex, 19th-century drainage developed along rather different lines. A spate of parliamentary acts, concentrated during the Napoleonic War years, enclosed almost all the remaining areas of damp peat common. In the course of the 19th century, many of these were embanked and drained, although significant areas continued to be cut – now as blocks of private ground – for reeds, sedge and peat. In the same period, the quality of drainage was further improved in the areas of long-enclosed marsh, although here there was little expansion of arable land. For the most part, the marshes continued to be used in the traditional way, for grazing. Moreover, although steam drainage was increasingly employed on the most extensive areas of wetland, wind continued to be of considerable importance and windmill technology improved steadily.[73]

The early 19th century saw a significant increase in the number of drainage mills in Broadland, partly as a result of the enclosure and drainage of the damp fen commons in the higher reaches of the river valleys. There were around 50 mills in Broadland at the end of the 18th century, but by *c.* 1825 this figure had nearly doubled (Fig. 9.23). To judge from surviving examples most of these mills, like their 18th-century predecessors, were rather low brick towers with canvas sails and external scoop wheels although a few, such as the one erected at Herringfleet in 1820, were wooden smock mills (*see* Fig. 9.18).[74] From *c.* 1830, however, landowners and drainage commissioners began to build more sophisticated structures, with self-regulating patent sails and fantails (*see* pp.70–1). These were much taller, and therefore more powerful, than earlier mills: many were more than 9m high (Berney Arms Mill, built in 1865, has a total height of 22m), and while most were equipped with a single scoop wheel some, such as Hunsett Mill and Turf Fen Mill on the River Ant, were provided with two (Fig. 9.24). From 1851 many

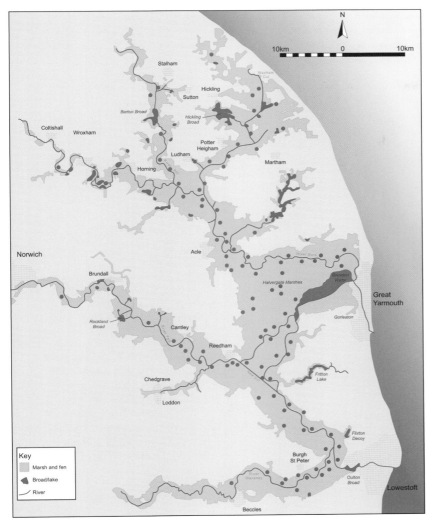

LEFT: *Fig. 9.23 The distribution of drainage windmills in the Norfolk Broads: c.1825.*

ABOVE: *Fig. 9.24 Turf Fen drainage mill on the River Ant: a typical mid-19th-century brick-built drainage windmill, with patent sails, fantail and self-winding mechanism. It originally drove two scoop wheels. The area which it drained, like many in the upper reaches of the Broadland valleys, has now reverted to fen.*

were fitted with turbine pumps (Fig. 9.25). These comprised sets of fans or vanes mounted in a cylindrical metal housing. It was said that such pumps could lift half as much again as a conventional scoop wheel, at least in a steady wind. Turbines were also added to many existing mills.[75]

Not all mills erected on the Broads in the middle and later decades of the 19th century were tall brick towers, however. Cheaper structures were built where small areas of fen were being reclaimed. Some were low brick towers, such as the diminutive Swim Coots mill in Catfield, a mere 5.6m high, built between *c.* 1816 and 1840. Others were quite different kinds of machine: 'skeleton' mills, comprising a low tower of open wooden framing; and 'trestle' mills, which consisted of a sturdy hollow upright post, held steady by diagonal wooden bracing, which contained a vertical iron driveshaft and carried a diminutive cap (Fig. 9.26). The latter was an old form, related to the Dutch *wipmolen*, but the former were probably invented by the millwright Edwin Daniel England as late as *c.* 1870.[76] Few examples of either type survive in Broadland today.

By the 1880s, to judge from First Edition Ordnance Survey 25-inch maps, there were around 110 drainage mills in Broadland (Fig. 9.27). They had now spread throughout the peat fens, yet their numbers had declined noticeably in the more extensive areas of silt marsh, especially in Halvergate. This was because

BELOW: *Fig. 9.25 The development of Broadland drainage windmills.* *The earliest mills were simple structures of wood, later brick, with common canvas sails and a long tailpole that was used to turn the sails to face the wind (left). Such mills drove a simple scoop wheel, which lifted water out of the marsh dykes into a river or other arterial watercourse. In the middle decades of the 19th century more sophisticated structures, with 'patent' sails, fantails and self-winding mechanisms, came into use (centre). By the second half of the century, some very tall brick tower mills were being constructed, and scoop wheels were often replaced by turbine pumps (right).*

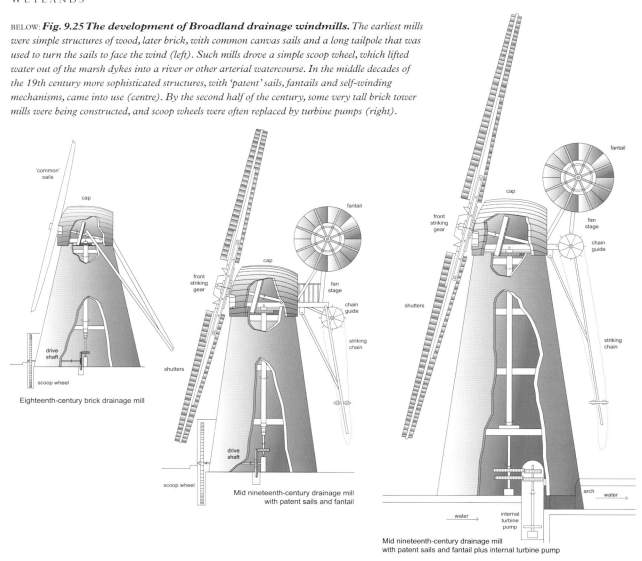

Eighteenth-century brick drainage mill

Mid nineteenth-century drainage mill with patent sails and fantail

Mid nineteenth-century drainage mill with patent sails and fantail plus internal turbine pump

Fig. 9.26 Not all late 19th-century drainage windmills were substantial, brick-built structures. *Where only restricted areas of land needed to be drained, smaller and simpler forms were often employed – like this trestle mill ('Boardman's Mill') erected at How Hill on the River Ant in 1897.*

steam drainage began to supplement wind power here as early as the 1840s.[77] By the 20th century there were more than 40 steam pumps in operation in the Broadland marshes, housed in sheds of brick and/or corrugated iron. Some, such as those at Hardley and Langley, were beam engines, but the majority were of more conventional horizontal or vertical type. Their chimneys, belching smoke out across the surrounding marshes, must once have been a familiar sight in Broadland. Remains of the sheds, in various states of ruin, can still be seen in a number of places, often beside pre-existing mills (as at Calthorpe Mill or Lambrigg Mill). Only at a few places, however, including Strumpshaw Mill, Black Mill on the Waveney near Somerleyton and Seven Mile House on the Yare, do more or less intact examples survive, complete with chimneys.[78]

Yet steam pumps never entirely replaced windmills. The latter were still being extensively refitted, and even constructed anew, into the early years of the 20th century. West Somerton Mill, for example, was built from scratch in 1900; Martham Mill was constructed in 1908 and extensively altered in 1912; while Horsey Mill was demolished, and entirely rebuilt, in the same year. Both drainage commissioners and private landowners often preferred to invest in the 'old' technology rather than the new. Both the initial building and the running costs of steam engines were much higher, and indeed, on occasions windmills replaced steam pumps. Only gradually, in the course of the 20th century, did mills fall into disuse. They were first, in the early decades of the century, supplemented by internal combustion engines, and then replaced wholesale by electric pumps, as the National Grid spread into the area. Nevertheless, many mills were still operating at the start of the Second World War. That at Ashtree Farm on the River Bure, 5km above Yarmouth, was only abandoned when its sails and part of its windshaft were blown off in February 1953.[79]

The drainage of the Broadland marshes thus developed along rather different lines from that of the Fens. In the latter, windmills were of marginal importance by the end of the 19th century and, in consequence, virtually none survive today. In the Broads, in contrast, they continued to be a major form of drainage and were developed in complex and sophisticated ways, and they still provide – although now usually in a ruined and derelict state – a major component of the landscape. The difference is partly due to the fact that the more fragmented nature of ownership, and of drainage responsibility, in Broadland ensured that only limited areas of marsh were drained as single units. Above all, however, it

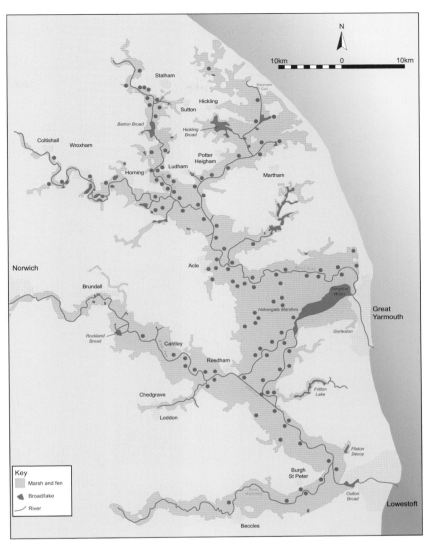

Fig. 9.27 *The distribution of drainage windmills in the Norfolk Broads:* c.1890.

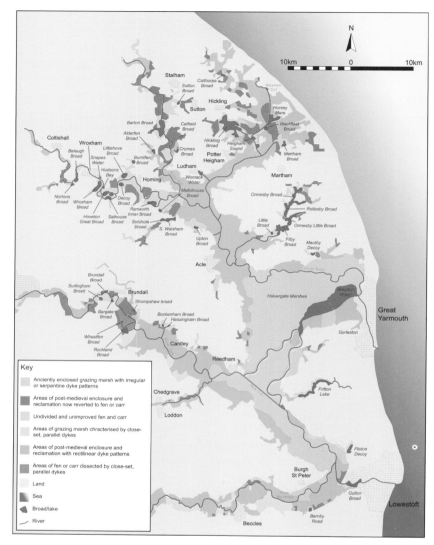

Fig. 9.28 The Norfolk Broadland has not one landscape, but many, as this complex map demonstrates.

was a consequence of the fact that arable land use on the Fens, and consequent wastage of the peat surface, made deep drainage indispensable. On the Broads, on the other hand, pasture predominated, shrinkage (especially on the silt soils) was much less and a far higher water-table, more easily maintained by wind drainage, could be tolerated.

RECENT HISTORY

The 20th century saw relatively few changes to the landscape of the Fens. Steam engines fell into disuse as they were gradually replaced, first by pumps driven by internal combustion engines, and then with electric pumps. Some were removed, while others survive as ruins or were converted to new uses. On the silts of Marshland, orchards and market gardens became more important as the agricultural recession encouraged a measure of diversification, but very little of this rich land went out of cultivation. Otherwise the arable landscape remained little changed, protected at vast expense from the waters – although not always with complete success: in the great floods of 1947, when high levels of precipitation and a rapid March thaw led the main Fen rivers to burst their banks, over 80,000ha were flooded and numerous farms were wrecked.[80]

In the smaller areas of peat fen, in contrast, and especially in Broadland, there was far more change in the course of the 20th century. Where fens had been reclaimed and turned into grazing marsh, large areas were gradually abandoned during the long periods of agricultural recession. Often this occurred as storms damaged drainage mills beyond repair, or as floods washed away embankments. The drainage mill on Minsmere Level, on the Suffolk coast, now stands somewhat incongruously within a vast sea of reeds. Where fens had continued to be managed in traditional ways, as in much of Broadland, there were also changes. The writer William Dutt in 1903 could still describe a landscape of managed reed-beds, of river banks 'almost covered' with reed-stacks in early spring, in which laden reed-craft were 'constantly being rowed or quanted down the dykes' and rafts heavy with marsh hay were still a common sight.[81] Not long after he wrote, however, many of these practices began to be abandoned. The First World War, when many local workers were sent off to die on the battlefields of Europe, marked a watershed, and decline continued steadily thereafter. Some reed and sedge cutting continues – precariously, in the face of foreign imports. But otherwise, except where deliberately kept open by conservation bodies, cessation of regular cutting has led to invasion by scrub, and ultimately wet woodland, dominated by alder and willow. Such woodland had always been a feature of the local landscape, but never such a dominant one, at least within recorded history. In the Ant valley there are still around 400ha of open fen, but nearly 700ha have tumbled to scrub or carr during the past 60 or 70 years.[82] The situation in the Bure valley above Ant Mouth is similar. What seems like a wild, primeval wilderness is in reality the consequence of relatively recent changes, which have added a further layer upon this intricate landscape (Fig. 9.28).

The grazing marshes on the alluvial silts of the Suffolk and Essex coast survived largely unchanged during the recession years. Agricultural recovery in the middle decades of the century, however, led to dramatic changes, in the form of wholesale conversion to arable. Some ploughing occurred during, and immediately after, the Second World War. But it was the disastrous floods of 1953 that proved the turning point. Unlike those of 1947, which were essentially caused by a rapid thaw and high volumes of water flowing down the main watercourses, these floods were caused by a sea surge. Abnormally high tides combined with onshore winds to inundate the coastal marshes, and much of the Broads, far more than the Fens.[83] Over 300 people were killed and large areas were inundated with salt water. In the aftermath the sea walls were raised along much of the Suffolk and Essex coast, often by as much as 0.6m, to prevent further incursions, and pumps were widely installed in places where there had formerly been only gravity sluices. After the flood, large areas of marsh lay in an unproductive, saline state for two years. With drainage conditions significantly improved, however, and with the post-war changes in the relative value of livestock as opposed to arable produce, conversion to arable began in earnest. Between 1955 and 1958 every marsh ditch on the 8,000 flooded hectares on the Suffolk marshes was excavated and large areas ploughed, and similar inroads were made in many of the Essex marshes. The new pumps allowed a lower freeboard to be maintained in the dykes, and this in turn made possible the installation of under-drains.[84] In most places the existing pattern of curvilinear dykes was retained, even where the ditches were deepened, but some new watercourses were installed and in parts of Sudbourne an entirely new rectilinear dyke pattern was created. Drainage improvements, and arable conversion, continued apace, and by the 1980s most of the Suffolk and Essex marshes were ploughed. In Norfolk, in contrast, the grazing marshes of Halvergate only came under serious threat in the 1980s. Some parts were then deep-drained and ploughed, but a well-publicised campaign of 'direct action' by Friends of the Earth and others culminated in the establishment of Broadland as the country's first Environmentally Sensitive Area (ESA), in which farmers are paid to follow 'traditional' agricultural practices, favourable to wildlife and landscape conservation.[85] Other coastal marshes survive in good condition on the north Norfolk coast, at Holkham and Wells, and – largely as a result of changes in farming subsidies – some of the Suffolk marshes have returned once more to grass.

Whether arable or pasture, however, all coastal marshes are now threatened by global warming, with its consequent sea level rise, and by the current fashion for 'managed retreat' involving the demolition of ancient embankments and reversion – in most cases, after many centuries – to tidal saltmarsh. Some nature conservationists welcome this last development because it provides more of this important, and increasingly scarce, resource. But reclaimed grazing marsh, where this has not been converted to arable, is itself an important habitat, and one which is also becoming scarce – in part because of this very policy of 'managed retreat'. And marshes are also vitally important *cultural* landscapes, with dykes which are often hundreds of years old and which, in the case of Halvergate, are still largely connected with their associated drainage windmills. Large areas of marsh are also currently threatened by the development of ports and industrial facilities, especially around Harwich and Ipswich, and moves are even afoot to make the A47 from Norwich to Yarmouth into a dual carriageway where it crosses the great, green, peaceful haven of Halvergate. The historic and cultural importance of our coastal wetlands is insufficiently appreciated by planners and policy-makers, or even by many conservationists. In East Anglia, as elsewhere, they deserve better.

NOTES

1   Reeves & Williamson 2000.
2   Taylor 2000.
3   Silvester 1999.
4   Silvester 1988, 160.
5   Hall 1999, 40.
6   Darby 1983, 138.
7   Williamson 1997, 43–5.
8   West 1932, 54, 87, 135.
9   Campbell 1983, 35.
10 Norfolk Records Office, DCN 49/66B.
11 Marshall 1787, 278.
12 Williamson 1997, 56–9.
13 Hunter 1999, 75–6.
14 Burrell 1960, 120.
15 Public Records Office E134 Eliz.27/28 M15.
16 Burrell 1960, 121–2.
17 Public Records Office, E 178 2190.
18 Armstrong 1786, **1**, 93.
19 Kirby 1735, 3.
20 Harper-Bill 1981, charter 316.
21 Williamson 1997, 82–4.
22 Beccles Borough Archives 1807, 4.
23 Norfolk Records Office, Ms 19424 103 X 4.
24 Williamson 1997, 78–83.
25 Bird 1909.
26 Lambert *et al.* 1952.
27 Ibid; George 1992, 79–98.
28 Norfolk Records Office MF/RO 389/17.
29 Payne Gallway 1886; Wentworth Day 1954, 115–17.
30 Heaton 2001, 12–16.
31 Payne Gallway 1886, 2.
32 East Suffolk Records Office, HA 93/3/48.
33 Defoe 1724, 79.
34 Patterson 1905, 56.
35 Harris 1953, 26–7.
36 Taylor 1999, 147.
37 Harris 1953 59–70.
38 Ibid, 19.
39 Darby 1983, 52–91; Taylor 1973, 193–4.
40 Ibid, 199–200.
41 Darby 1966, 61.
42 James 2000; Darby 1983, 71–91; Taylor 1973, 195–7.
43 Ibid.
44 Dugdale 1662, 151.
45 Darby 1983, 92.
46 Dugdale 1662, 267.
47 Holderness 1985, 205.
48 Defoe 1724, 79.
49 Darby 1983, 106.
50 Hills 1994, 138–7.
51 Taylor 1999, 196–205.
52 Williamson, 1997, 117–18.
53 NRO MEA 3/578, 659 X 2.
54 Williamson 1997, 111–12.
55 Marshall 1787, 282–3.
56 NRO EAW 2/118.
57 Warner 2000, 42.
58 Beastall 1978, 65.
59 Young 1804, 182–5.
60 Hills, 1967, 60–72.
61 Ibid, 78.
62 Ibid, 158.
63 Clarke 1848, 84.
64 Wade-Martins 1995, 128.
65 Williamson 2002b, 112.
66 Hills 1967, 130.
67 Wells 1830, 442.
68 Read 1858, 267–8.
69 British Parliamentary Papers 1836 VIII. I, 236.
70 Hills 1967, 128.
71 Taylor 1973, 196–205.
72 Ibid, 204.
73 Smith 1990.
74 Williamson 1997, 118–22.
75 Ibid, 122–5.
76 Norfolk Industrial Archaeology Society 1981.
77 Bacon 1844, 294.
78 Ward 1999; Ward 1999b.
79 Smith 1990, 52.
80 Ministry of Agriculture, Food and Fisheries 1948.
81 Dutt 1903, 140, 161.
82 George 1992, 229.
83 Pollard 1978.
84 Trist 1971, 130–2.
85 George 1992, 481–7.

10

The Imagined Landscape

THE STRUCTURES OF LANDSCAPE

Landscapes have so far been treated in this book primarily as physical by-products of past social and economic activities. However, they were, and are, also experienced and represented – and modified accordingly. They embody social and ideological meaning.[1] Moreover, the way we think about particular landscapes, and the way we decide which things about them we most value, often derives from how they have been described or illustrated, rather than from how they actually are, or indeed ever were. These representations are mainly contained in the art and literature produced over the last three centuries for, and in many cases by, a wealthy elite, many of whom lived outside the region itself. But local people have always read meanings in the landscape, and some of these can be recovered by historians.

Unconscious attitudes, as much as practical activities, structured the layout of the medieval and post-medieval landscape. Signs of social zoning are thus apparent in the pattern of rural settlement. In the south of the region, in particular, medieval moated sites were normally positioned away from public roads, while by the 17th century in some Norfolk parishes certain commons appear to have represented 'good' areas – and others 'bad' ones – in which to live. Large farms were often quite separate from clusters of mean cottages, which were in turn frequently associated with alehouses. Local communities had a mental image of the landscape, which determined the correct places in which certain activities or structures should be located. Although across much of East Anglia the church often lay isolated from other buildings, it nevertheless represented the notional core of the community. It was shared space, around and within which – through displays of heraldry, arrangements of seats or the placing of burials and monuments – the social organisation of the parish was displayed (Fig. 10.1).[2] The richest elements in the community were thus, from medieval times until the end of the 18th century, buried within the church. And outside, most churchyards display a clear pattern of spatial organisation, with the earliest gravestones (mainly, in East Anglia, of late 17th- or early 18th-century date) clustering on the south side, often close to

Fig. 10.1 This ornate 18th-century headstone at Brockdish in Norfolk stands in a highly visible position close to the main path to the church. Church and churchyard were important areas for social display.

219

the porch or the chancel end. In part, this is because the north side was darker, colder and associated with the Devil. However, numerous exceptions to this rule suggest that a more powerful factor was social display. Most churches were entered through the south door, and approached from the south, and where early graves cluster on the north side of the church, this pattern of access is reversed. Either way, those unable to afford permanent memorials – the majority – were relegated to less prominent, less prestigious locations.

If churches were central spaces, boundaries – especially those coinciding with areas of common land – were 'liminal' zones, where suicides or strangers might be buried. The course of parish boundaries was, throughout medieval and post-medieval times, re-affirmed by the annual ceremony of 'beating the bounds'. Distinctive features of the landscape – such as prehistoric barrows and ancient trees – provided key points along the processional route. The boundaries of Hundreds were invested with particular meaning. Well into the 19th century, gibbets – metal cages in which the bodies of executed criminals were hung, as a warning to the community – were usually located on areas of common land lying on Hundred boundaries, or at places where several parish boundaries converged.[3] Their sites often perpetuated those which, in medieval times, had been occupied by gallows – the wooden structures on which criminals were actually executed. Certainly, they were positioned in very similar places. 'Gallows Hill' in Quidenham, for example, marks the spot where three parishes met; those of Quidenham, Eccles and Hargham.[4]

The term 'hill' used here almost certainly refers to a round barrow, for many gallows, and subsequently gibbets, were placed on top of them. The tumulus known as 'Gallows Hill' in Thetford, for example was later re-used for a gibbet. The association of barrows with death in the popular mind may in part explain this pattern, but we can also pick up here continuities spanning immense periods of time. Saxon execution sites, or *cwealmstows*, were often placed on major boundaries and frequently at prehistoric barrows. Gallows Hill in Thetford, for example, seems to have been a Saxon execution site, while excavations near South Acre in Norfolk recovered a collection of 119 Saxon executions, focused on a cluster of six barrows, at the junction of three Hundreds: Freebridge Lynn, South Greenhoe and Launditch.[5] At Sutton Hoo, the great royal burial ground was also used as an execution site, and continued to function as such into the 11th century, long after the Wuffingas began to be buried elsewhere.[6]

Prehistoric monuments – principally, in East Anglia, round barrows – were also used in a variety of other ways by medieval and post-medieval communities. Lying on the boundaries between major Saxon estates, they often became the meeting places for Hundreds, many of which were named after them – South Greenhoe, North Greenhoe and Grimshoe in Norfolk, for example, all incorporate the Scandinavian term for a barrow. Barrows were frequently used in medieval times to mark the boundaries of manors and fold courses. The knowledge that these features were ancient and 'permanent' lent them particular authority in this respect, and the distribution of surviving examples is in part determined by this later function. The lost 'Gospel Hill' on the boundary between Great and Little Cressingham in Norfolk (the name implies that this is where readings were held during the annual ceremony of 'beating the bounds') seems to have been carefully preserved within the arable open fields, as was 'Threw Hill', a marker on a fold course boundary in Northwold.[7] In a similar way, some of the oldest 'veteran trees' in East Anglia lie on parish boundaries. 'Gospel oaks' and other trees might be carefully preserved because they gave sanction to the line of a boundary.

Court depositions from the 16th and 17th centuries show that local people's knowledge of the past in the landscape was intimate and extensive. Often they were able to remember the location of buildings or features swept away decades before, or the ways in which land had been used in the distant past – often drawing on archaeological argument, as in the case at Walberswick already discussed (*see* p.180), where the inhabitants confirmed the use of the common as periodic arable by pointing to 'the riggs and furrowes on most parte of the heath'. Minor place-names and field-names aided the preservation of memory. Some changed every generation or so, especially those given to land lying in severalty, in enclosed fields. Those given to communal spaces, however, such as commons and areas within open fields, seem to have altered more gradually. At the time of enclosure in 1805 one of the furlongs in the parish of Littlebury in north-west Essex was called 'Wheelbarrow shot'. Aerial photographs show the ring ditch that marks the site of the *hweol beorg*, the round barrow, which was presumably destroyed in Saxon times when the furlong was first laid out.[8]

Most field-names, however, refer to more mundane matters: to location; to the size of the parcel in question (Ten Acre Field); to the character of the soil within it (Clay Hill Furlong); to the land's productive potential (Great Gains in Rettendon (Essex); Starve Gut Field in Sible Hedingham (Essex)); or to the crops grown within it. A marked cluster of fields called Saffron Ground or Saffron Field thus recalls the importance of this industrial crop in western Essex and eastern Hertfordshire in the early-modern period.[9] In a world inhabited and named by farmers, such things mattered.

FROM PRODUCTIVE TO PICTURESQUE, 1500–1800

Most elite commentators in the 16th and 17th centuries similarly discussed the landscape primarily in terms of its agriculture and productive potential. Many emphasised the division between the early-enclosed 'woodland' areas on the heavier soils of the region, in which cattle-rearing and dairying were the mainstay of the economy, and the more open, treeless landscape of the 'champion', sheep-corn districts occupying the lighter land. One observer in 1595 typically described how 'Norfolk is compounded and sorted of soyles apt for grayne and sheepe and soyles apt for woode and pasture', the latter 'most apt and so employed to dayries and breeding of great cattell'.[10] The anonymous author of the *Chorography of Suffolk*, written in *c.* 1605, similarly distinguished between the enclosed landscape of 'Woodlande & High Suffolcke' running through the centre of the county; an area in the north-west (i.e. Breckland), which was 'mostly heathy and barren and fit only for sheepe and conyes'; and the coastal strip, which he considered 'fitte for sheep and corne'.[11] Most preferred 'woodland' country. Thomas Tusser, an Essex man writing in the 16th century with his native Essex in mind, was typical:

> The countrie enclosed I praise
> the tother delighteth not me
> For nothing the wealth it doth raise
> to such as inferior be.

– referring to the fact that, as we have noted, wealth was more evenly distributed in the 'woodland' than in arable districts. In open field country, Tusser emphasised, there were no hedges to prevent theft and trespass, nor to provide fuel for the inhabitants, in contrast to the situation in 'severall' land – he referred explicitly to Essex and Suffolk.[12] To 16th- and 17th-century writers, soils determined agriculture, and agriculture the extent of enclosure, as well as other aspects of landscape and even the character of the inhabitants. Another inhabitant of Essex, Thomas Harrison of Radwinter, thus emphasised in his *Description of England* of 1597 variations in the character of settlement:

> It is so, that our soile being divided into champaine ground and woodland, the houses of the first lie uniformelie builded in everie town togither, with streets and lanes; whereas in the woodland countries (except here and there,

*in great market towns) they stand scattered abroad, each one dwelling in
the midst of his owne occupieng.*[13]

Most 16th and 17th-century commentators were united in their dislike of the
Fens, universally held to be damp and unhealthy, and with inhabitants who were
difficult and unruly. One pamphleteer in 1630 described how the Fen air was 'for
the most part cloudy, gross, and full of rotten harrs [fogs]; the water putrid and
muddy, yea full of loathsome vermin'.[14] Yet even here some could wax lyrical about
the more productive aspects of the environment; Drayton in 1622, for example,
described livestock near Ely 'hid over head in grass'.[15] We should not, of course,
exaggerate the extent to which landscapes were simply appreciated in economic
and agrarian terms. People already visited the traces of antiquity in the landscape,
the remains of castles and abbeys. Harrison devoted large parts of his *Description*
to matters antiquarian; and Sir Thomas Browne published his *Hydriotaphia, Urne
Buriall, Or a Discourse on Sepulchrall Urnes Lately Found in Norfolk* as early as
1658. Nevertheless, the tradition of viewing landscapes primarily in terms of soils
and agriculture was paramount, and continued strongly into the 18th century
although, with an increasing interest in scientific agriculture, finer distinctions
began to be made between different kinds of countryside. In 1735 John Kirby thus
described the whole of the area 'from Landguard Fort to Yarmouth' as the
'Sandlands'.[16] But Arthur Young in 1797 noted that although the soils of the whole
of this coastal district were formed in sand, the term Sandlings was 'given
peculiarly to the country south of the line of Woodbridge and Orford, where a
large extent of poor, and even blowing sands is found'.[17] Moreover, in the writings
of Young, as in those of other 18th-century agriculturalists such as William
Marshall or Nathaniel Kent, we do not find the same sense that landscapes and
local character are determined and immutable. In this 'age of improvement', they
were considered capable of transformation. Young in 1797 typically praised the
recent drainage schemes in the area around Boston: 'Fens of water, mud, wild
fowl, frogs and ague have been converted to rich pasture and arable', adding that
'health was improved, morals corrected, and the community enriched'.[18]

In the course of the 18th century, however, other ways of looking at landscape
were becoming acceptable. Although, influenced in part by Classical writers such as
Virgil, people continued to find views across productive, settled countryside
particularly appealing, they began to think of them as paintings, ordered like the
representations of Italian countryside produced by artists such as Nicolas Poussin,
Claude Lorraine or Salvator Rosa – that is, with a well-defined foreground, middle
ground and distance. Lord Oxford was evidently thinking of these kinds of paintings
when he described the countryside between Blofield and Norwich as forming:

> *A most noble prospect and extremely beautiful ... the hills at a proper
> distance clothed with fine woods, and the other part cultivated, either grass
> ground or ploughed, the farmhouses scattered up and down, making all
> together a most beautiful landscape.*[19]

Such interests tended to reinforce existing preferences for enclosed countryside,
where trees and woods lent themselves to artistic composition, rather than open,
featureless, 'champion' land. However, they also served to increase the
importance placed on rolling landforms, and even when they enjoyed the
landscapes of Norfolk and north Suffolk, many visitors tended to qualify their
appreciation. Hannah Moore in the late 18th century, for example, noted how
the 'charms of nature' in Norfolk were 'of the middling, calm and pacific sort –
she does not put forth her bolder, stronger beauties'.[20] Areas valued for their
fertility might now be regarded as aesthetically displeasing, especially the
landscapes of improvement and reclamation on the light lands which, in spite of
extensive schemes of planting, remained relatively bare of trees. Mrs Delany,

visiting Holkham in 1756, thus joked that she could not see a tree or shrub that might shade the growing turnips.[21]

During the late 18th century the region's muted terrain became more of a problem because there was an increasing enthusiasm among the 'polite' for more dramatic scenery, of the kind provided by the English Lake District or the Alps. William Gilpin himself – arch-prophet of the new 'Picturesque' taste – undertook a tour of the eastern counties and his reactions to the scenery were mixed. The open 'champion' lands of the East Anglian Heights he thought 'chalky, bare, exposed, ridgy and unpleasant',[22] and the Fens he abhorred, comparing their appearance unfavourably with that of true lakes. The latter, he suggested, were the

> produce of a mountainous country, formed commonly by a rapid river, which carries off the superfluous waters in the continuance of the same stream, that introduced them. A Fen, on the contrary, is generated on a flat by land-springs or the exuberance of rain-waters; which, having no natural discharge, but by exhalation or through the pores of the earth, stagnate, and putrify upon the surface.[23]

He liked Breckland even less: 'We soon however found, that we were in the neighbourhood of a country still more disagreeable, at least for travelling, than a fenny one.' It was a 'wild, open and dreary' landscape, treeless, 'an absolute desert'.[24] The rolling 'champion' lands of north-west Norfolk were little better: 'sheep gave some life to a country otherwise but uninteresting'.[25] On the whole it was the old-enclosed 'woodland' landscapes that most appealed to Gilpin. These were more wooded, more varied, and had more views that could be interpreted in the manner of a painting, or rather a series of paintings. Travelling close to the Suffolk–Essex border, he thus described how the road was 'adorned with two or three beautiful dips, on the left, interspersed with cottages and a variety of fine wood. Beyond there is a good distance. Soon after the tower of Dedham-church makes a picturesque appearance.' Moving on into Essex, he described how:

> Ardley-woods, which in a manner surrounded us, afforded every where the most pleasing sylvan scenes – sometimes retiring to a distance, cometimes advancing – now incircling a common with it's [sic] cottages; and forming a back-ground behind them – then closing up the whole road, so as to leave the eye at a loss, where it could break out. Nor were these effects produced by copse-wood, or paltry trees; but by noble oaks, and elms; many of which, even single, had dignity enough to grace a scene.[26]

As these quotations suggest, the Picturesque taste was not in fact simply for wild mountains, waterfalls and upland scenery. It shaded off into a more general enthusiasm for irregularity, variety and intricacy, and in these terms much of the East Anglian countryside might indeed be considered appealing, even if – in the words of Samuel Jackson Pratt, visiting Norfolk in the 1790s – it displayed the 'unambitious beauties of nature'.[27] The late 18th and early 19th centuries saw, perhaps more than anything, an increasing regard for the particular character of places, as opposed to an earlier interest in simply making scenes fit into preconceived criteria derived from artistic representations of quite different places. This new enthusiasm is most clearly manifested in the paintings produced by John Constable and the members of the Norwich School.

THE 19th CENTURY – ARTISTS AND SCIENTISTS

Constable was born at East Bergholt, close to the Suffolk–Essex border, in 1776, the son of a prosperous local businessman, miller and corn merchant. He became

Fig. 10.2 **The Hay-wain,** *by John Constable (1821), one of the most popular and most frequently reproduced of English landscape paintings. By the 1890s, tours of 'Constable Country' were already being organised by Thomas Cook, the travel agents.*

an artist against the wishes of his father, who wanted him to take over the family business. Most of his paintings were made within a few kilometres of his place of birth, especially in Dedham Vale, part of the Stour valley (Fig. 10.2). Constable was little valued by contemporary critics, but his reputation grew steadily during the 19th century and by the 1890s tours of what was already being described as 'Constable Country' were being organised by Thomas Cook.[28] Constable's work has been variously assessed and interpreted by modern critics and academics. Some have read his obsessive focus on the area around his place of birth as a manifestation of his difficult relationships with his father, family and local society, and have suggested that his later paintings in particular are manifestations of a nostalgia for the countryside enjoyed in his childhood. Others have stressed the essentially unchanging nature of the rural scenes Constable depicts, arguing that they mask the true speed of change in the countryside.[29] But the Stour valley was not, in fact, changing very fast, at least in terms of the fabric of its landscape, even if the living and working conditions of the labourers who are often depicted as mere incidents within it were deteriorating rapidly at the time. True, Constable avoided painting the new landscapes created by enclosure on the light lands of East Anglia, but a predilection for old-enclosed countryside was, as we have seen, not novel; Gainsborough before him, painting scenes in west Suffolk, and the artists of the Norwich School also avoided the new landscapes of 'improvement'. Moreover, there is more modernity and realism in Constable's paintings than is sometimes suggested. The real subject of his *Spring: East Bergholt Common* is the ploughman in the foreground. The common was no more: it was being ploughed, for the first time ever, following its enclosure by parliamentary act in 1816 (Fig. 10.3).

Broadly contemporary with Constable were the artists of the 'Norwich School', members of the Norwich Society of Artists, which was founded in 1803

Fig. 10.3 **Spring: East Bergholt Common,** *by **John Constable.** We often miss the contemporary significance of Constable's paintings. The common is being ploughed, for the first time ever, following its enclosure in 1816.*

and held its first annual exhibition in 1805. It was the first of several societies and institutions concerned with promoting the visual arts – others appeared at Edinburgh and Bath in 1808 and at Leeds in 1809 – and its inception reflects in part the continuing economic vitality of the city and its hinterland in the early 19th century, and hence the market presented by wealthy businessmen who, as much as owners of country estates, were important collectors. Men such as the Norwich merchant and brewer John Patteson, for example, had a particular affection for Dutch art. This was a long tradition, for paintings by Flemish and Netherlandish artists, especially landscapes, had featured prominently on the walls of East Anglian country houses for more than a century.[30] In part, this local preference was yet another manifestation of the region's strong links with the Low Countries. However, it also reflected the similarity of the landscapes of Holland and East Anglia – the broad waterways, the prosperous yet ancient towns, the wide valleys and muted terrain – which made these paintings particularly appealing to local consumers.

Norwich School artist John Crome, and subsequently James Stark, Henry Bright and the Stannard family, produced paintings that are indeed sometimes closely comparable to those of Dutch 17th-century masters such as Hobbema, Hondecoeter or Cuyp.[31] However, the balance between influence and parallel development is a moot point: how far the artists in question were directly influenced by Dutch models, and catered for local patrons' taste for them, and how far resemblances in scale and subject matter reflected real similarities in the landscape of the two regions. Windmills were thus a common motif, and in the words of one art historian, one 'no doubt learnt from the Dutch'.[32] But, as we have seen, they were also a quintessential part of the East Anglian scene. Wide expanses of heath and valleys with wide and slow-flowing rivers are a feature of both regions. In both areas, too, level terrain ensured the overwhelming importance of the ever-changing sky as a major element in the scene (Fig. 10.4). Either way, John Sell Cotman, Crome and their fellows painted a wide variety of local views, mainly in Norwich and Yarmouth and the countryside around: landscapes, often featuring labourers at work; and buildings, especially medieval ruins. Many depicted the ruined gatehouse of St Benets Abbey on the Norfolk Broads, with the drainage mill that had been built into it in the middle of the previous century (Fig. 10.5).

***Fig. 10.4* View from Whittlingham Grove, *by James Stark (c.1840).* *Starks' view captures the gently rolling arable landscape of the Yare valley.*

BELOW: ***Fig. 10.5* Remains of Saint Benedict's Abbey on the Norfolk Marshes: storm coming on, *by Henry Bright (1847).* *The ruined abbey gatehouse, into which a drainage mill had been inserted in the middle of the 18th century, was a particularly popular subject for the Norwich School painters.*

When we think of the East Anglian landscape, we cannot avoid doing so through the eyes of Constable and the members of the Norwich School. The former remains perennially popular and – in the case of *The Hay-wain* in particular – endlessly reproduced. But we must not misunderstand the character of the scenes their paintings depict, concentrating on rural tranquility when what was often being presented was a vibrant, and modern, economic world. The wherries with their great black sails, which feature in so many of Crome's or Cotman's paintings, were not some picturesque and archaic form of local transport, but an efficient and routine craft carrying vital cargoes along the great economic arteries of eastern Norfolk. The features around Flatford so lovingly depicted by Constable include the great water-mill, one of several owned by his father and one of many processing the vast quantities of grain now pouring out of the surrounding claylands, and the locks designed to by-pass it on the busy Stour Navigation.

As the 19th century wore on, the East Anglian landscape began to be appreciated and interpreted not only by artists but also increasingly by scientists. Gentleman amateurs discussed the region's geological history and geomorphology. J W Robberds and R C Taylor thus argued about the changing levels of the North Sea; H B Woodward produced a series of articles and books (he was the first individual to suggest that some of the broads were not, in fact, natural, but the consequence of peat cutting); J B Phear wrote about the geological structure of Suffolk; while F W Harmer published his *Testimony of the Rocks in Norfolk: a Popular Description of the Geology of the County* in 1877.[33] Geology shaded easily into archaeology, interest in which also burgeoned. In 1846 the Norfolk and Norwich Archaeological Society was founded, followed in 1848 by the Suffolk Institute of Archaeology, in 1852 by the Essex Archaeological Society and in 1908 by the Prehistoric Society of East Anglia (which became the Prehistoric Society in 1934).[34] Above all, natural history, and especially botany, was an increasingly popular pastime among the middle classes, especially from around 1860. Trimmer's *Flora of Norfolk* was published in 1866, Henslow and Skepper's *Flora of Suffolk* in 1860, Gibson's *Flora of Essex* in 1862 and Babington's *Flora of Cambridgeshire* in 1860.[35] Henry Stevenson's *Birds of Norfolk* appeared in 1866, and the Norfolk and Norwich Naturalists Society was established in 1868. Increasing interest in archaeology and natural history thus coincided with the agricultural intensification of the 'high farming' period. Stevenson lamented the detrimental effects of recent changes in farming on bird populations, while Babington noted bitterly how, until the turn of the century, much of the East Anglian Heights in south Cambridgeshire had been covered by grass heath, but that this was now largely:

> *Converted into arable land, and its peculiar plants mostly confined to small waste plots … Even the tumuli, entrenchments, and other interesting works of the ancient inhabitants have seldom escaped the rapacity of the modern agriculturalist, who too frequently looks upon the native plants of the country as weeds, and its antiquities as deformities.*[16]

In Norfolk, Augustus Jessop similarly bemoaned in 1887 how:

> *The small fields that used to be so picturesque and so wasteful – where one could botanise with so much interest – are gone or are going; the tall hedges, the high banks, the scrub or the bottoms where a fox or weasel might hope to find a night's lodging … all these things have vanished.*[37]

People were beginning to think in terms of whole landscapes, rather than just about particular sites and buildings within them, and to value them for their archaeology and natural history as much as for their visual appeal.

THE LATE-19th AND 20th CENTURIES

The period between *c.* 1880 and *c.* 1950 saw important changes in the ways in which the East Anglian landscape was perceived and understood. The mid-19th century boom years of 'high farming' were followed, as we have seen, by a long period of recession. However, this was also a period in which England became increasingly urbanised, with the result that a large section of the population became divorced from the countryside and free to invest it with a range of meanings. Representations of the English landscape in this period have, Dennis Cosgrove has suggested, a recurrent structure – a kind of essential mythical geography. London, civilised and familiar, lay at its centre; outside were the 'heartlands' of the English landscape, an amalgam of the Home Counties, the Cotswolds and the familiar images of 'Constable Country'. Beyond this comfortable zone was the north and west, partly comprising the wild, picturesque and distant landscapes of the Lake District, Cornwall and Devon, and partly the less inviting industrial areas of northern England and South Wales.[38]

East Anglia fits somewhat awkwardly into this mental image. Essex and much of Suffolk, with gently rolling topography, village greens and thatched cottages, is a recognisable part of the English 'heartlands', and in the first half of the century villages such as Great Bardfield were repeatedly painted, and the Stour valley was once more lovingly evoked in paintings by John Nash, who settled there in 1929.[39] But the northern and eastern parts of the region were different. This was less picturesque country, rougher and more remote: 'I don't know any part of England where you feel so off the map as on the by-roads of Norfolk,' commented Bertram Wooster, shortly before the car breaks down: 'And there we were, somewhere in Norfolk, with darkness coming on and a cold wind that smelled of guano and dead mangel-wurzels playing searchingly about the spinal column.'[40] This was the land of great industrial farmers such as Trollope's Mr Cheesacre, proudly showing off his immense muck heap and boasting of Norfolk's ability to feed a third of the nation.[41] It was also – and increasingly, as the depression deepened – presented as a gloomy world, of hard toil by brutalised labourers in muddy fields: of 'gangs' of women working in the wide Fenlands, themselves and their children doped on opium. This is the land depicted by the Norfolk novelist and farmer's wife Mary Mann and by H Rider Haggard, and a generation later by Henry Williamson, trying to make a living as a farmer in the depths of the recession amidst a landscape of outgrown hedges and weed-covered fields.[42] By the middle of the 20th century, in a world increasingly dominated by educated, liberal, urban opinion, going to northern East Anglia was like going back in time, to a district of selfish squires, Victorian shooting parties and impoverished tenant farmers. In L P Hartley's novel *The Go Between*, the fictional Bradham Hall in Norfolk is physically remote for the younger Leo, but distant and alien in another sense for the older: 'The past is a foreign country, they do things differently there'.[43]

Moreover, these flat agricultural lands were not bounded by a mythical upland, whether industrialised or picturesque, but rather by the wild North Sea. From the end of the 19th century the landscape of the Suffolk coast, with its long, lonely beaches, its curious mixture of heaths and wetlands, was used as the evocative setting for several of the ghost stories of M R James, and artists began for the first time to paint its heaths, creeks and marshes, as well as villages such as Blythburgh and Southwold.[44] Several of James's stories dwell on the dangers of disturbing the dark forces lying dormant in barrows and the like, and this was a period in which the less dramatic prehistoric monuments of East Anglia, set in their evocative heathland landscapes, were first given particular attention by writers. In Breckland, the high tide of Victorian farming had now receded and writers such as W G Clarke waxed lyrical about its primeval beauty, conveniently forgetting that much of what they saw was the consequence of quite recent abandonment and recession.[45] Indeed, it can be said that Breckland was effectively invented in this period by Clarke. The term does not seem to have been used as a regional label before, only to describe particular fields under periodic cultivation. Others, for example H J Massingham in the 1920s, emphasised the lonely scale of the great heathlands:

> With the exception of Breckland, an area of 400 square miles, all, or nearly all, our wildernesses are pools, not lakes or inland seas of apartness. I once went for a walk on the Brecks with Clarke ... the Brecks that day gave me an inkling of what it meant to wander forty years in the Desert.[46]

This was clearly not a part of the English 'heartlands'. It was a much less cosy world.

Nevertheless, some parts of northern East Anglia did receive a more conventional treatment, especially districts in which the holiday industry was expanding, most notably the Broads. By the 1880s Norwich could be reached by London in less than four hours and the following decades saw a significant expansion in residential accommodation, and the proliferation of boatyards, at a number of places with railway stations, most notably Wroxham, Horning, Hoveton, Brundall and Oulton Broad. G Christopher Davies's *The Handbook to the Rivers and Broads of Norfolk and Suffolk* of 1882, and his *Norfolk Broads and Rivers* of 1885, were followed by numerous other volumes, most notably those of E R Suffling and John Payne Jennings.[47] Indeed, by 1897 one reviewer was able to comment wryly that:

> Surely no spot in the British Isles has been so 'be-guided' as the Norfolk
> Broads ... hardly a magazine exists which has not opened its pages to the
> flood of contributions on this apparently fascinating subject; and the whole
> has culminated in a shower of guide-books which enlivens the railway
> bookstalls with their gay exteriors.[48]

No less than 33 books on the Broads were received by the British Museum Library between 1880 and 1900.[49] Not all of Broadland was equally appreciated, however. The upper valleys, the broads themselves and especially the more wooded and undulating scenes were generally preferred to the level expanses of drained marshland. The parts most favoured, in other words, were those *least* like northern East Anglia. Davies thus praised the upper courses of the Bure and Yare rivers, 'bordered by pleasant woodlands, whose fresh green in early summer and glorious hues in autumn made them as lovely as many of the leafy backwaters of the upper Thames'. The 19km of the Bure between Acle and Yarmouth, however, across the Halvergate Marshes, was dismissed as 'very uninteresting'.[50]

Around the same time the beauties of the north Norfolk coast were being extolled by the journalist Clement Scott, whose *Poppy Land* (1883) described a landscape more gentle, less raw than that of James's Sandlings, but one nevertheless strangely remote and distant:

> Had I been cast on a desert island I could not have been more alone. Not a
> human being on the cliff, not a footfall on the beach ... and mile after mile
> of virgin sand, unsoiled by stone or pebble.[51]

The book did much to encourage the already burgeoning holiday industry in the area around Cromer and Sheringham, as the 'honest miller', Alfred Jermy, and his family became celebrities. China, postcards and much else liberally decorated with poppies were produced in quantities in the locality: which was ironic, given that the whole appeal of the district was supposed to be its remote, unspoilt character. Nevertheless, the frontispiece of Scott's book included a timetable for trains from London's Liverpool Street station. In a similar way, the Broads, having been 'discovered' by Davies in a book sponsored by the Great Eastern Railway, was soon full of visitors whom he was keen to criticise. In the 1880s he was woken at 7.00 in the morning, while moored on Wroxham Broad, by the occupants of a neighbouring boat loudly playing the piano.[52] Indeed, successive writers made similar complaints about the wrong 'kind' of holiday-maker.[53] In 1935 one commentator described how, on the Broads:

> Each year they had seen the crowds growing and the holiday season
> lengthening, until it seemed that the beautiful waterways would be turned
> into a Blackpool or a Brighton ... great fleets of tripper-boats ... hired

yachts, floating ice-cream vendors, bum-boats and craft of every description, largely in the hands of people who had not the slightest knowledge of how to manage them.[54]

Writers such as Scott and Davies exaggerated the slow and unchanging pace of life of the local residents which was threatened by this influx. In a similar way, P H Emerson's striking photographs, produced in the late 19th century, show Broadland labourers and reed-cutters standing as almost heroic figures in a level landscape, with receding panoramas behind – but with no steam-ploughs or threshing machines (Fig. 10.6). Middle-class commentators and visitors were in search of an archaic, untouched, 'natural' world, ever on the point of destruction by outsiders.[55]

Fig. 10.6 P H Emerson's carefully posed photographs of Broadland labourers *emphasise the timeless and unchanging character of rural life, suppressing any signs of modernity, or of the effects of the great late-19th-century agricultural recession.*

The Broads and parts of the coast were thus popular. However, large swathes of northern East Anglia continued to be rejected by visitors and largely ignored by artists and writers. The Fens were sporadically painted and had some admirers, in part the consequence of nostalgic memories of former undergraduates at Cambridge. Charles Kingsley described the 'vast height and width of the sky-arch ... the long, straight, silver dykes, with their gaudy carpets of strange floating water-plants', and suggested that the landscape here had 'an element of new and peculiar beauty'.[56] But for the most part the area was seldom visited, except by those making the journey out from Cambridge to see Ely's great cathedral, and its appearances in fiction were few. Dorothy L Sayers' detective story *The Nine Taylors*, published in 1936 and featuring Lord Peter

Wimsey, is one of the few exceptions: central to the story are the great church towers of Fenchurch, dominating a flat Lincolnshire landscape ever threatened with inundation. Sayers was the daughter of a Fenland rector and her descriptions of the landscape display an easy familiarity: 'I do wish everything wasn't so rectangular in this part of the world,' bemoans Wimsey at one point.[57]

EAST ANGLIA IN THE MODERN MIND

How have perceptions of the region's landscape changed over the last half century? To the former picture of East Anglia as, essentially, a flat land has been added the idea that it has been pretty thoroughly blitzed by modern agribusiness. The term 'East Anglian prairie' has entered the modern lexicon. The muddy fields in which the labourers scared crows or picked stones have been replaced by vast, empty prairies in which the machines of the barley-barons manoeuvre: '... the bulldozer rams at the old hedges, blots them out to make fields big and vacant enough for the machines of the new ranch-farming and the business-men farmers of five to ten thousand acres'.[58] However, in many ways mental geographies have developed along established lines. The north and east of the region continues to be perceived as more remote, more rural, than the south and south-west, even if that isolation is always in danger of being broken down by improved communications, and by the ripples of modernity spreading outwards from London and the south.

It was in the 1980s, for the first time, that the Fens received a full literary treatment. Indeed, in Graham Swift's novel *Waterland* they appear as a central feature, almost as a character. The landscape, which in the author's words 'of all landscapes approximates most closely to nothing', is repeatedly described:

> Flat, with an unrelieved and monotonous flatness ... it stretched away to the horizon, its uniform colour, peat-black, varied only by the crops that grew upon it – grey-green potato leaves, blue-green beet, yellow-green wheat; its uniform levelness broken only by the furrowed and dead-straight lines of the ditches and drains ...[59]

Other areas of northern East Anglia feature whenever authors require a lonely and remote setting, especially one in relatively easy reach of London. P D James used the writers' colony at the mythical Monksmere on the Suffolk coast in *Unnatural Causes*, and bleak Larksoken, on the north Norfolk coast, with its nuclear power station, in *Devices and Desires*.[60] But of all modern writers it is Ruth Rendell, and her alter ego Barbara Vine, who best captures the essence of the region's countryside, often with a strong sense that, in Essex and Suffolk especially, the truly rural has only just vanished, and exists within the reach of memory. This atmosphere of recent loss pervades the faded glory of Wyvis Hall in Suffolk in 1976 in her *Fatal Inversion* (1987); and, more keenly, in *Dark-Adapted Eye* (1986), looking back to the more distant past of the war years in north Essex:

> The loveliest houses in England are there, churches big as cathedrals, meadows that Constable painted and which had then changed very little since that day, before they pulled the hedges up and made a prairie of the fields.[61]

In the conclusion to *The Brimstone Wedding* (1996), the elderly Stella describes how, long ago, Gilda's body had been burnt in the debris of a recently stubbed hedge: 'an ancient hedge it had been, of oak and hawthorn, maple and rose, elder and dogwood'.[62] The remains were ploughed in as the adjacent fields were amalgamated:

The field which had been black was brown, the signs of burning gone, for all fifty acres of it were going under the plough. He had wasted no time, that farmer. His stubble was burnt, his hedge uprooted and burnt, and now the plough was turning and grinding and burying the burnt cornstalks and the ash and the cinders.[63]

The landscape of the south of the region is thus viewed in part through the lens of nostalgia for a recent past, but in a way that highlights its current, agriculturally blitzed character. Indeed, Rendell has a keen eye for the realities of modern rural life in East Anglia, as in *Gallowglass*, where the character Little Joe comments that 'These country towns are strange places. They aren't like what you'd think from the descriptions in guide books'. Instead of happy rural people and picturesque shops selling real country food there were peripheral industrial estates, 'about fifteen pubs', Indian and Chinese takeaways and 'every other shop is a bank or a building society'.[64] This is East Anglia in the modern world: and it is to this, and the future, to which we must finally turn.

NOTES

1   Ashmore & Knapp 1999; Bender 1993.
2   Finch, J 2000.
3   Whyte 2003.
4   Ibid, 31–2.
5   Wymer 1996.
6   Carver 1998, 137–43.
7   Whyte 2004.
8   Essex Records Office Q/DQy/27.
9   Field 1993, 100–1, 105–10.
10 Rye 1906, 180–3.
11 MacCulloch 1976, 19.
12 Tusser 1573.
13 Edelen 1968.
14 Darby 1983, 61–2.
15 Drayton 1876.
16 Kirby 1735, 1–2.
17 Young 1797, 3–5.
18 Young 1799, 245–6.
19 Historic Manuscripts Commission 1907, 155.
20 Ketton-Cremer 1957, 187.
21 Ibid.
22 Gilpin 1809, 10.
23 Ibid, 16–18.
24 Ibid, 28–9.
25 Ibid, 77.
26 Ibid, 87.
27 Ketton-Cremer 1957, 201.
28 Daniels 1991.
29 Whyte 2002, 118–20; Daniels 1993.
30 Moore 1988; Moore 1985.
31 Ibid, 58–9.
32 Howard 1991, 74.
33 Robberds 1826; Taylor 1827; Phear 1854; Woodward 1881; Harmer 1877.
34 Ashbee 1984.
35 Trimmer 1866; Henslow & Skepper 1860; Gibson 1862; Babington 1860.
36 Ibid.
37 Jessop 1887, 6.
38 Cosgrove 1993.
39 Howard 1991, 149, 165.
40 Wodehouse 1930, 322.
41 Trollope (1980 edn), 117.
42 Mann 1991; Williamson 1941; Haggard 1899.
43 Hartley 1953, 9.
44 Kneale 1973; Howard 1991, 111, 117, 144.
45 Clarke 1925.
46 Ibid, viii–ix.
47 Cleveland 1986.
48 Quoted in Malster 1993, 79.
49 Taylor 1986.
50 Davies 1890, 138.
51 Scott 1886, 18.
52 Davies 1890, 68.
53 Matless 1994.
54 Miller 1935, 12–13.
55 Knights 1986.
56 Kingsley 1877, 122.
57 Sayers 1934, 60–1; Kenney 1990, 53–80.
58 Hoskins 1955, 299.
59 Swift 1983, 2.
60 James 1967; James 1989.
61 Vine 1986, 47.
62 Vine 1995, 303.
63 Ibid, 309.
64 Vine 1990, 47.

11

Present and Future

In the course of this book we have examined some of the factors that have made the East Anglian landscape what it is today. Topography, geology, climate and soils have shaped patterns of farming and settlement over the centuries, culminating in a phase of intensive agriculture that has, across large tracts of the region, served to eradicate much of the earlier fabric of the landscape. In addition, networks of contact engendered by the region's location on the eastern edge of England, and on the margins of the North Sea, have also been crucial. Similar influences have shaped the various distinctive sub-regions within East Anglia. In particular, we have noted how soil districts have their own histories – their own particular trajectories of development. In each, the landscape was moulded by the attempts of successive generations of farmers to wrest a living from environments that presented a particular range of problems and possibilities: their endeavours created frameworks of fields, settlement and much else, which then helped to shape the activities of later generations, employing different technologies and living within very different economic circumstances.

Patterns of trade and communication, structured and channelled by the detailed configuration of rivers and coastline, have been vital in the generation of local character. Combined with topographic factors they have, above all, been responsible for the remarkable contrast that we have encountered again and again in the course of this enquiry – between the north and east of the region and the south and west. That divide has taken many forms over the centuries, but always seems to be defined by the same general line, running through the centre of Suffolk, roughly from Bury St Edmunds to Ipswich. It is a division which may, to some extent, have taken on a cultural aspect, as the styles of architecture or patterns of settlement found on either side came to be seen as the 'normal' way of living, and were thus replicated, or developed in particular ways, by the local inhabitants. Indeed, to some extent this may be true of the less pronounced idiosyncrasies of settlement, and architecture, associated with particular soil regions. But in the final analysis the character and form of any landscapes remains explicable – even if not yet fully explained – in terms of everyday, tangible factors: economic, agrarian, geographical, ideological and social. Landscapes were shaped by the ways in which people made a living – and by the methods they used to dominate or exploit their neighbours.

Yet at the same time landscapes are not only, or simply, reflections of economic and social processes. They possess meaning to those living within or passing through them. And their representation in literature, or in the visual arts, often determines how we think about them and their conservation as much as, if not more than, their 'real' appearance does. Indeed, the impact of the imagined and idealised landscape upon the real has never been greater than it is today.

Most of East Anglia remains rural and much of its built environment, whether in villages or towns, comprises buildings erected in the distant past. These have survived because of the region's gradual decline from medieval and early-modern greatness, as it lost its position as the most economically vibrant and populous

region in England. Succeeding generations lacked the means to replace them with something more fashionable. We are thus cursed, it sometimes seems, by too much history – by a plethora of structures, from innumerable medieval churches to landscape parks to farm buildings – which has been rendered redundant by social and economic change. There is so much 'heritage' – scenic, natural or historical – to be preserved here. However, there are also many people keen to preserve it. For East Anglia is a rural world in which fewer and fewer people are actually involved in farming, and therefore free to invest the landscape with new imaginings. Fields, to most residents of and visitors

Fig. 11.1 Dedham Vale, 'Constable Country', one of several Areas of Outstanding Natural Beauty in East Anglia in which planning controls are particularly tight.

to East Anglia, are components in a picturesque view, habitats for wildlife or part of the historic fabric of landscape – not a source of profit or a place of work. Moreover, this is a time in which a major restructuring of agriculture is under way, fuelled by the expansion of the European Union, over-production and falling prices, so that new uses need to be found for the rural environment. In a society in which more and more people are retired, and in which there are ever-higher disposable incomes among many sections of the middle class, leisure and tourism are becoming more economically important than farming.

Fig. 11.2 'California', near Scratby, Norfolk. The boundaries of designated landscapes are never clearly marked out on the ground, but are often obvious nevertheless. Here, where the Norfolk Coast AONB ends, the caravan parks and holiday chalets begin.

In such a climate conservation makes its own landscapes, and features which were once practical and functional are invested with new meanings. In spite of a popular perception that East Anglia is disappearing under concrete, development has largely been concentrated in such a way that most of the region remains extremely rural. In some areas particularly strong presumptions exist against change and development. The Norfolk Broads has recently, belatedly, become a National Park. The North Norfolk Coast, the Sandlings ('Suffolk Coast and Heaths') and Dedham Vale ('Constable Country') are Areas of Outstanding Natural Beauty – a label which most readers, given the manifestly man-made quality of all the landscapes described in this book, may find rather odd (Fig. 11.1). In these areas, planning restraints serve to fossilise the features that existed there by the middle of the 20th century, often for the benefit of populations largely composed of incomers and second-home owners. Planning controls, 'designations' and patterns of ownership by bodies such as the National Trust certainly have a major effect on the landscape: where the Norfolk Coast AONB ends, in the area to the north of Yarmouth, the caravan parks suddenly begin (Fig. 11.2). In some places attempts are even made to put the clock back, to recreate lost landscapes of the past. On the National Trust properties around Flatford Mill the concept of 'Constable Country' is taken to its ultimate, bizarre conclusion, as trees are cut back and features restored or excavated to ensure that they resemble, as much as possible, the scenes depicted in the great artist's paintings: the 'imagined' landscape structures the 'real' (Figs 11.3 and 11.4).

Observed from the perspective of landscape history, one of the oddest things about current attitudes to planning and conservation is the way in which attempts are made to celebrate, conserve or restore a landscape's 'character' without sufficient acknowledgement of just how complex such a thing really is. The paradox of curation then casts its curious shadow across the land: for to freeze a landscape at a single point in its development, for the benefit of posterity, can only be justified by constructing an image of an unchanging, ancient, 'traditional' landscape that is now being threatened by the forces of modernity. But in reality, as we have seen, the landscape has always been changing, responding to a complex interaction of social, economic and environmental influences. The countryside, 'natural' habitats, villages and historic towns that we enjoy today are not timeless entities, but an amalgam of numerous phases of development; and many of their 'characteristic' features are of no great antiquity. The Broadland drainage mills are not some timeless adornment of the rural scene, but pieces of quite recent industrial plant. The undulating clayland arable landscape, which conservationists understandably wish to save from housing and industrial development in east Hertfordshire or west Essex, is for the most part a recent creation. This is not an unspoilt, ancient countryside. The vast 'fields' of wheat and barley have often, as we have seen, absorbed as many of 50 of the enclosures that existed less than 50 years ago. Most of the renovated cottages with neat thatched roofs and carefully conserved architectural details would be unrecognisable to the people who dwelt in them less than a century ago, in what would then have been deemed 'mud-walled hovels'. If conservation implies an end to change it must fail: not only is further change inevitable, but today's eyesores are also, in many cases, tomorrow's heritage. Time hallows landscapes. The frightening horrors of Orford Ness – the military ranges and Cold War bunkers – are now owned by the National Trust, a magnet for

Fig. 11.3 **Boat Building,** *by John Constable (1814).*

Fig. 11.4 The diminutive dry dock, shown in use on Constable's painting, has been carefully excavated and recreated at Flatford by the National Trust, for no reason other than to make the landscape look as much as possible like the painting. It is one of several similar attempts around Flatford: the imagined landscape structures the real.

visitors (Fig. 11.5). Not far to the north, even the dome of Sizewell B nuclear power station, glistening in a winter sun, now seems curiously in harmony with its wild coastal setting (Fig. 11.6).

Perhaps we should pause here, however, for the logical conclusion of such an argument is a relativist position asserting that, because the landscape has always been changing, then all attempts to conserve and curate are doomed, pointless or ideologically suspect. To subscribe to anything approaching such a position would be to allow the past to be swept away and all local distinctiveness, all sense of place, to be steadily eroded. For changes are afoot, which could potentially undermine much of the region's distinctive character and threaten its historic landscapes.

Some of these threats are of such imponderable awfulness that they hardly bear consideration. Global warming and sea-level rise – if they come to pass – may eventually inundate not only Halvergate and our other coastal wetlands, returning them once more to tidal mudflats, but could even lead to the complete abandonment of the Fens. Drier summers and wetter winters would also have dire consequences for the region's vegetation and wildlife: will the ancient oaks of our woods, parks and hedgerows survive the resultant stress? However, most changes in the landscape will come, as they have always done, from patterns of economic and demographic development, fuelled in part by government policies and by changes in the geography of commerce

and communication. Agriculture has, for many centuries, been the single most important influence on the landscape – and over the last half century, largely a negative one. The threat of arable intensification has receded, and hedges and wood have begun to re-appear on the blitzed prairies. The greatest changes in the future will instead probably come from growing urbanisation. The region's population continues to increase, in large measure because of net in-migration – something which, together with the ubiquitous mass media, has largely eroded local accents from the south of the region (Fig. 11.7). It still threatens to do so over much of the north, although away from the coast the Norfolk accent manages to hang on, while that of Norwich, which is very different in character, continues to thrive.

The area discussed in this book, or the vast majority of it, now forms part of the East of England Region, with its own (unelected) assembly, its own government office and its own Development Agency. At the time of writing the assembly has, in response to government instructions, been drawing together a planning document that will chart the pattern of growth – and establish frameworks for conservation – over the next two decades across an area extending as far west as Bedfordshire. Growth is accepted as inevitable, if not desirable – growth in population, above all else. As many as half a million new houses are destined for this region over the next 20 years, as well as improvements to transport infrastructure. Some of this is to provide for indigenous population increase and some will take the form of 'social housing', sorely needed in rural areas where property prices climb inexorably. Much of the anticipated growth, however, is to cater for the continued movement of people from elsewhere in England, or from elsewhere in Europe, into an area predicted to expand as an economic 'hot spot', closely linked to London, the South East and the European mainland. Indeed, enhancement of direct links with the continent, through improvements to the 'Gateway Ports' at Harwich and Felixstowe, is a key element in present planning policies.

How far all this will impact upon the region discussed in this book – which, as I say, is considerably more limited than the 'East of England Region' – is a moot point. As ever, patterns of communication and contact seem destined to ensure that the north and east of the region will remain essentially rural, although the impact of better roads and railways may reduce its isolation. Most expansion will be on its southern and western fringes. Present plans will concentrate growth in the south of Essex – along the 'Thames Gateway' – and in the 'London-Stanstead-Peterborough Development Corridor'. The greatest impact will probably be felt in western Essex and eastern Hertfordshire, where Stanstead airport is set to expand in size, bringing in its train a wave of commercial, industrial and residential development in what is already a fairly populous district (Fig. 11.8).

Whether all this really happens remains to be seen. History is littered with the great schemes of planners, thrown off course by radical changes or unforeseen downturns in the economy. Moreover, current talk about the building of 'sustainable

OPPOSITE PAGE:

TOP: *Fig. 11.5 The 'Pagodas' on Orford Ness.* These sinister structures, designed to absorb the explosions from the conventional charges associated with nuclear bombs, are among the many striking features of the former military testing range on this bleak and isolated stretch of the Suffolk coast. It is now a National Trust property.

BOTTOM: *Fig. 11.6 The dome of Sizewell nuclear power station* seems curiously at one with its wild coastal setting. In the foreground, in a bizarre juxtaposition of features, are the ruins of the medieval Leiston Abbey.

Fig. 11.7 The Cam valley near Saffron Walden in Essex. On the right, the main line from Cambridge to Liverpool Street passes through two tunnels, to hide it from the great mansion of Audley End. To the left, the M11, opened in 1982. Improvements in transport continue to break down East Anglia's isolation.

communities' and numerous environmentally-friendly clauses in the great planning documents should ensure that new development is more carefully considered, and more in harmony with the character of the region, than some of the housing estates that have been built around our ancient market towns over the last four decades. There is now a much greater awareness of the importance of a 'sense of place' in society and culture: the current vogue for landscape history (of which this book is yet another manifestation) is part of this.

However, in this new climate, as conservation and 'sustainability' replace the quest for modernity and as government subsidies in the countryside switch towards conservation and away from over-production, there are also other, more subtle threats. For even apparently benign interventions in the landscape can erode aspects of local identity: and even among conservationists there is much potential for disagreement. Global warming means that more power must be generated by wind farms. Many would welcome this safe, 'green' form of electricity, and small groups of turbines make an interesting addition to the rural landscape. But there are currently hundreds of applications being made for wind farms in the region, and if only a proportion of these were agreed the impact on the countryside would be profound. Moreover, as agricultural policies have shifted towards 'stewardship' and other agro-environmental schemes there has been a resurgence in planting in the countryside. But the aims of nature conservation, and the conservation of historic landscapes, are not always the same – as we have seen most clearly in the case of coastal wetlands. Indeed, in pursuit of enhanced biodiversity some conservationists advocate the creation of 'large areas' for wildlife – effectively, the abandonment of farming completely across extensive tracts of countryside, allowing nature to reclaim the land and reducing, perhaps even removing, the rich complexity of the historic landscape.

Even minor interventions, if not carefully considered, can erode historic character, such as the planting of extensive woodlands on the open chalklands where none have existed since the early medieval period. Some purists might go further, arguing that planting new hedges with a standard 'ancient' mixture of dogwood, hazel, guelder rose and the rest within late-enclosed landscapes, otherwise dominated by species-poor hawthorn hedges, amounts to a significant erosion of a sense of place. Yet we can go too far, be too precious and too keen to protect and replicate the old. For this can be both a hopeless, and ultimately a pointless, task. The landscape cannot be entirely frozen in time and nor can it be made to develop simply along established lines. The ageing Scots pine rows of Breckland were never intended to be tall, romantically twisted trees, but were planted in the 19th century as low windbreaks and hedges. They are now redundant, unmanaged features of the landscape: yet when they are replanted it is with the intention of ultimately recreating that picturesque and over-mature appearance, not of establishing a dense, managed hedge. Perhaps we should not bother replacing them at all, but simply enjoy them while we can, and let them pass.

We cannot freeze the landscape, preserving it as a kind of huge, open-air museum. Nor should we react, with knee-jerk negativity, to every addition made by contemporary society. Everything once looked raw and new; and the various current

Fig. 11.8 Stansted airport *has already gobbled up many hundreds of hectares of Essex countryside, and is destined for further expansion – bringing in its wake additional development to the increasingly crowded south of the region.*

OPPOSITE PAGE:

TOP: **Fig. 11.9 The changing structure of the Breckland forests.** *In 1970 (top left) the forest was still dominated by the original planting of the 1920s and 1930s. There was little variation in age structure and the pattern of rides and divisions was highly rectilinear. By 1995 (below left) many of the original trees had been felled, a more varied age structure was developing, and a curvilinear pattern of divisions had begun to appear. By 2020 (right), if current policies continue, the forest will have a very diverse age structure, including stands of trees left beyond economic maturity, and a fragmented and highly curvilinear pattern of divisions.*

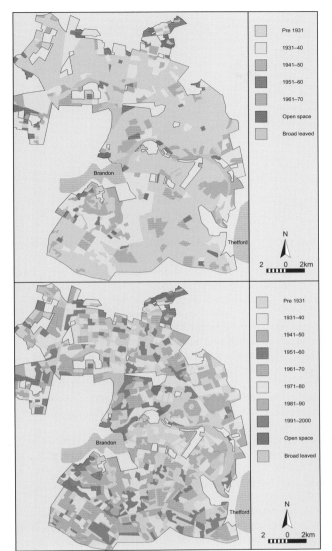

Fig. 11.10 Thetford Forest, near High Lodge: now one of the most visited parts of the East Anglian countryside.

developments that conservationists strive to prevent may themselves, one day, be accepted by future generations as a part of their historic landscape. Furthermore, we can appreciate some of the features appearing in the East Anglian countryside today as valuable additions, created with thought, care and consideration. The Forestry Commission, for most of its existence a body resolutely determined to limit public access to its Breckland forests, has over the past two decades begun to welcome visitors, greatly expanding recreational opportunities and wildlife conservation, and has shaped the appearance of its plantations accordingly. Stands of timber are retained well beyond their economic felling date and the rigid rectilinear layout of rides and compartments has been progressively softened by the instigation of 'organic coupe' cutting, creating bold, curving boundaries to the woodland edges (Figs 11.9 and 11.10). This is a new landscape, for new times, and one which is probably visited and enjoyed by more people than any other in East Anglia. We must understand, enhance and protect the old. But we can still celebrate and enjoy the new. For all landscapes were once so.

Bibliography

Addison, W 1982. *Local Styles in English Parish Churches*. London: Batsford

Aitkens, P 1998. 'Mid-Suffolk Houses, 1250–1550', *in* Stenning, D F and Andrews, D D (eds) *Regional Variation in Timber-Framed Buildings in England and Wales Down to 1550*. Chelmsford: Essex County Council

Alcock, L 1971. *Arthur's Britain*. London: Allen Lane

Allison, K J 1955. 'The Lost Villages of Norfolk'. *Norfolk Archaeology* **31**, 116–62

Allison, K J 1957. 'The Sheep-Corn Husbandry of Norfolk in the Sixteenth and Seventeenth Centuries'. *Agricultural History Review* **5**, 12–30

Anderson, O 1934. *The English Hundred Names*. Lund: University of Lund

Andrews, D and Ryan, P 1999. 'The Sixteenth and Seventeenth Centuries: manors, mansions, parks and fields', *in* Green, S, *The Essex Landscape: in Search of its History*. Chelmsford: Essex County Council

Andrews, D, Mundy, C and Walker, H 2002. 'Saffron Walden: the topography of the southern half of the town and the market place'. *Essex Archaeology and History* **33**, 221–73

Anon ('N') 1752. 'The Management of Three Farms in the County of Norfolk'. *Gentleman's Magazine* **22**, 502

Appleton, J 1986. 'Some Thoughts on the Geology of the Picturesque'. *Journal of Garden History* **6**(3), 270–91

Armstrong, M J 1781. *History and Antiquities of the County of Norfolk*. 10 Vols. Norwich

Ashbee, P 1984. 'Changing Prehistoric Configurations', *in* Barringer, C (ed.), *Aspects of East Anglian Prehistory*. Norwich: Geo Books, 2–9

Ashmore, W and Knapp, A B 1999. *Archaeologies of Landscape: Contemporary Perspectives*. Blakewell: Maddern

Ashwin, T 1996. 'Excavation of an Iron Age Site at Silfield, Wymondham, Norfolk, 1992–3'. *Norfolk Archaeology* **42**, 241–82

Ashwin, T 1999. 'Studying Iron Age Settlement in Norfolk', *in* Davies, J and Williamson, T (ed.), *Land of the Iceni: the Iron Age in Northern East Anglia*. Norwich: Centre of East Anglian Studies

Ashwin, T and Flitcroft, M 1999. 'The Launditch and its Setting: excavations at Beeston with Bittering'. *Norfolk Archaeology* **43**, 217–56

Ayers, B 1993. 'Planned Towns', *in* Wade-Martins, P (ed.), *An Historical Atlas of Norfolk*. Norwich: Norfolk Museums Service, 72–3

Ayers, B 1994. *Norwich*. London: English Heritage/Batsford

Babington, C C 1860. *Flora of Cambridgeshire*. Cambridge: Cambridge University Press

Bacon, R N 1844. *The Report on the Agriculture of Norfolk*. Norwich

Bailey, M 1988. 'The Rabbit and the Medieval East Anglian Economy'. *Agricultural History Review* **36**(1), 1–20

Bailey, M 1989. *A Marginal Economy? East Anglian Breckland in the Later Middle Ages*. Cambridge: Cambridge University Press

Bailey, M 1990. 'Sand into Gold: the evolution of the fold-course system in west Suffolk, 1200–1600'. *Agricultural History Review* **38**, 40–57

Baird, W and Tarrant, J 1973. *Hedgerow Destruction in Norfolk 1946–1970*. Norwich: Centre of East Anglian Studies

Banks, S J 1988. 'Nineteenth-Century Scandal or Twentieth-Century Model? A new look at open and close parishes'. *Economic History Review* **41**, 51–73

Barnes, G 2002. 'Woodlands in Norfolk: a landscape history', unpublished PhD thesis, University of East Anglia

Barnes, H D and Simpson, W D 1952. 'Caister Castle'. *Antiquaries Journal* **32**, 25–51

Barnes, P 1984. The Economic History of Landed Estates in Norfolk Since 1880, unpublished PhD thesis, University of East Anglia

Bassett, S R 1989. 'In Search of the Origins of Anglo-Saxon Kingdoms', *in* Bassett, S J (ed.), *The Origins of Anglo-Saxon Kingdoms*. Leicester: Leicester University Press, 3–27

Bassett, S R 1997. 'Continuity and Fission in the Anglo-Saxon Landscape: The Origins of the Rodings (Essex)'. *Landscape History* **19**, 25–42

Batcock, N 1991. 'The Ruined and Disused Churches of Norfolk'. *East Anglian Archaeology* **51**, 1

Beastall, T W 1978. *The Agricultural Revolution in Lincolnshire*. Lincoln: History of Lincolnshire Committee

Beccles Borough Archives 1808. 'An Account of the Corporation of Beccles Fen'. Beccles Town Hall

Beckett, J V 1990. *The Agricultural Revolution*. Oxford: Blackwell

Bender, B (ed.) 1993. *Landscape: Politics and Perspectives*. Oxford: Berg

Bennet, K 1983. 'Devensian Late-Glacial and Flandrian Vegetational History at Hockham Mere, Norfolk, England'. *New Phytologist* **95**, 457–87

Beresford, M and Hurst, J 1971. *Deserted Medieval Villages*. Woking: Lutterworth

Bird, M C H 1909. 'The Rural Economy, Sport and Natural History of East Ruston Common'. *Transactions of the Norfolk and Norwich Naturalists Society* **8**, 631–6

Blair, J 1988. 'Minsters in the Landscape', *in* Hooke, D (ed.), *Anglo-Saxon Settlements*. Oxford: Blackwell, 35–58

Boulton, G S, Cox, F, Hart, J and Thornton, M 1984. 'The Glacial Geology of Norfolk'. *Bulletin of the Geological Society of Norfolk* **34**, 103–22

Bowyer, M J F 1979. *Action Stations: military airfields of East Anglia*. London: Patrick Stephens

Boyes, J and Russell, R 1977. *The Canals of Eastern England*. Newton Abbot: David & Charles

Bradley, R 1727. *A General Treatise of Husbandry and Gardening*. London

Bradley, R 1993. 'Where is East Anglia? Themes in regional prehistory', *in* Gardiner, J P (ed.), Flatlands and Wetlands: current themes In East Anglian prehistory, *East Anglian Archaeology* **50**, 5–13

Britnell, R H 1981. 'Essex Markets Before 1350'. *Essex Archaeology and History* **13**, 15–21

Brown, A F J 1996. *Prosperity and Poverty: Rural Essex, 1700–1815*. Chelmsford: Essex Records Office

Brown, D 2001. 'Nathaniel Richmond (1724–84): "Gentleman Improver"', unpublished PhD thesis, Centre of East Anglian Studies, University of East Anglia

Brown, R Allen 1951. 'Framlingham Castle and Bigod, 1154–1216'. *Proceedings of the Suffolk Institute of Archaeology and History* **25**, 127–48

Brown, R Allen 1976. *English Castles*. London: Batsford

Brunskill, R W 1978. 'Distributions of Building Materials and Some Plan Types in the Domestic Vernacular Architecture of England and Wales'. *Transactions of the Ancient Monument Society* **23**, 46–7

Burrell, E 1960. 'An Historical Geography of the Sandlings before 1840', unpublished MSc Thesis, University of London

Butcher, R 1941. *The Land of Britain: Suffolk (East and West)*. London: Longman, Green & Co

Caird, J 1852. *English Agriculture 1851–2*. London

Campbell, B M S 1981. 'The Extent and Layout of Commonfields in East Norfolk'. *Norfolk Archaeology* **28**, 5–32

Campbell, B M S 1983. 'Agricultural Progress in Medieval England: some evidence from East Norfolk'. *Economic History Review Second Series* **36**, 24–46

Campbell, B M S 2000. *English Seigniorial Agriculture, 1250–1450*. Cambridge: Cambridge University Press

Campbell, L 1989. 'Sir Roger Townsend and His Family', unpublished PhD thesis, Centre of East Anglian Studies, University of East Anglia

Carver, M 1989. 'Pre-Viking Traffic in the North Sea', *in* McGrail, S (ed.), *Maritime Celts, Friesians and Saxons: papers presented at a conference at Oxford in November 1988*. London: Council for British Archaeology Research Report **71**, 117–26

Carver, M 1998. *Sutton Hoo: Burial Ground of Kings?* London: British Museum Press

Cathcart King, D J 1983. *Castellarium Anglicanum*. 2 vols. New York: Kraus

Catt, J A 1977. 'Loess and Coversands', *in* Shotton, F W (ed.), *British Quaternary Studies: Recent Advances*. Oxford: Clarendon Press, 221–9

Catt, J A 1978. 'The Contribution of Loess to Soils in Lowland Britain', *in* Limbrey, S and Evans, J G (eds), *The Effect of Man on the Landscape: the Lowland Zone*. London: Council for British Archaeology Research Report **21**, 12–20

Chambers, J D and Mingay, G E 1966. *The Agricultural Revolution 1750–1880*. London: Batsford

Chatwin, C P 1961. *British Regional Geology: East Anglia and Adjoining Areas*. London: HMSO

Clarke, J A 1848. 'On the Great Level of the Fens'. *Journal of the Royal Agricultural Society of England* **8**, 80–133

Clarke, R R 1935. 'Flint Knapping Industry at Brandon'. *Antiquity* **9**, 38–56

Clarke, W G 1925. *In Breckland Wilds*. London: Robert Scott

Clemenson, H 1982. *English Country Houses and Landed Estates*. New York: St Martin's Press

Cleveland, D 1986. 'Some Writers on the Norfolk Broads', *in* McWilliam, N and Sekules, V (eds), *Life and Landscape. P H Emerson: Art and Photography in East Anglia 1885–1900*. Norwich: University of East Anglia, 86–7

Coleman, S 1999. 'Crown Post Roofs', *in* Dymond, D and Martin, E (eds), *An Historical Atlas of Suffolk*. Ipswich: Suffolk County Council, 178–9

Coleman, S and Barnard, M 1999. 'Raised-Aisled Halls and Queen-Post Roofs', *in* Dymond, D and Martin, E (eds), *An Historical Atlas of Suffolk*. Ipswich: Suffolk County Council, 180–1

Colman, S and West, S E 1975. 'Edgar's Farm, Stowmarket: a re-appraisal'. *East Anglian Archaeology* **1**, 149–65

Colvin, H and Newman, J 1985. *Of Building: Roger North's Writings on Architecture*. Oxford: Clarendon Press

Cosgrove, D 1993. 'Myths: Gods and Humans', *in* Bender, B (ed.), *Landscape: Politics and Perspectives*. Oxford: Berg, 281–305

Cowell, F 1986a. 'Richard Woods (?1716–93) A Preliminary Account. Part 1'. *Garden History* **14**(2), 85–120

Cowell, F 1986b. 'Richard Woods (?1716–93) A Preliminary Account. Part 1'. *Garden History* **15**(2), 115–35

Cowell, F 1987. 'Richard Woods (?1716–93) A Preliminary Account. Part 2'. *Garden History* **15**(1), 19–54

Crummy, P 1997. *City of Victory.* Colchester: Colchester Archaeological Trust

Cunliffe, B 1995. *Iron Age Britain.* London: Batsford

Curwen, J C 1809. *General Hints on Agricultural Subjects.* London

Dallas, C and Sherlock, D 2002. 'Baconsthorpe Castle, Excavation and Finds, 1951–1972'. *East Anglian Archaeology* **102**

Daniels, S 1988. 'The Political Iconography of Woodland in Later Eighteenth-Century England', *in* Cosgrove, D and Daniels, S (eds), *The Iconography of Landscape.* Cambridge: Cambridge University Press, 51–72

Daniels, S 1991. 'The Making of Constable Country, 1880–1940'. *Landscape Research* **12**, 9–17

Daniels, S 1993. *Fields of Vision: Landscape and Identity in Europe and the United States.* Cambridge: Polity Press

Daniels, S 1999. *Humphry Repton: landscape gardening and the geography of Georgian England.* London and New Haven: Yale University Press

Dannat, N 1996. 'Thetford Forest: its history and development', *in* Ratcliffe, P and Calridge, J (eds), *Thetford Forest Park: the Ecology of a Pine Forest.* Edinburgh: Forestry Commission, 21–5

Darby, H C (ed.) 1952. *The Domesday Geography of Eastern England.* Cambridge: Cambridge University Press (reprinted 1971)

Darby, H C 1968. *The Draining of the Fens.* Cambridge: Cambridge University Press

Darby, H C 1983. *The Changing Fenland.* Cambridge: Cambridge University Press

Darley, G 1978. *Villages of Vision.* London: Architectural Press

Davies, G C 1890. *The Handbook to the Rivers and Broads of Norfolk and Suffolk.* London

Davies, J 1996. 'Where Eagles Dare: the Iron Age of Norfolk'. *Proceedings of the Prehistoric Society* **62**, 63–92

Davies, J 1999. 'Patterns, Power and Political Process', *in* Davies, J and Williamson, T (eds), *Land of the Iceni: the Iron Age in Northern East Anglia.* Norwich: Centre of East Anglian Studies

Davison, A 1988. 'Six Deserted Villages in Norfolk'. *East Anglian Archaeology* **44**

Davison, A 1990. 'The Evolution of Settlement in three Parishes in South East Norfolk'. *East Anglian Archaeology* **49**

Defoe, D 1724. *A Tour Through the Whole Island of Great Britain,* vol.1. London

Dimbleby, G W 1962. *The Development of British Heathlands and their Soils.* Oxford: Oxford University Press

Dodwell, B 1941. 'The Free Peasantry of East Anglia in Domesday'. *Norfolk Archaeology* **27**, 145–57

Drayton, M 1876. 'Pol-Obion', *in Works,* vol. 3. London, 32–3

Drury, P J 1978. *Excavations at Little Waltham.* Chelmsford: Chelmsford Excavation Committee

Drury, P J and Rodwell, W 1980. 'Late Iron Age and Roman settlement', *in* Buckley, D G (ed.), *The Archaeology of Essex to AD 1500.* London: Council for British Archaeology, 59–75

Dugdale, W 1662. *The History of Inbanking and Drayning of Diverse Fens and Marshes….* London

Dumville, D 1992. *Wessex and England from Alfred to Edgar: Six Essays in Political, Cultural and Ecclesiastical History.* Woodbridge: Boydell and Brewer

Dunmore, S and Carr, R 1976. 'The Late Saxon Town of Thetford'. *East Anglian Archaeology* **54**

Dutt, W A 1903. *The Norfolk Broads.* London: Methuen

Dyer, C 1980. 'Deserted Medieval Villages in the West Midlands'. *Economic History Review* **35**, 19–34

Dymond, D 1985. *The Norfolk Landscape.* London: Hodder and Stoughton

Dymond, D 1999a. 'Enclosure and Reclamation', *in* Dymond, D and Martin, E (eds), *An Historical Atlas of Suffolk.* Ipswich: Suffolk County Council, 104–5

Dymond, D 1999b. 'The Woollen Cloth Industry', *in* Dymond, D and Martin, E (eds), *An Historical Atlas of Suffolk.* Ipswich: Suffolk County Council, 140–1

Eddy, M R 1979. *Historic Towns in Essex: an Archaeological Survey of Saxon and Medieval Towns, with Guidance for their Future Planning.* Chelmsford: Essex County Council

Ede, J, Virgoe, N and Williamson, T 1994. *Halls of Zion: Chapels and Meeting-houses in Norfolk.* Norwich: Centre of East Anglian Studies

Edelen, G (ed.) 1968. *William Harrison: the Description of England.* Washington: Folger Shakespeare Library edn

Eden, P 1968. 'Smaller Post-Medieval Houses in East Anglia', *in* Munby, L (ed.), *East Anglian Studies.* Cambridge: Heffer, 71–93

Edwards, D and Williamson, T 2000. *Norfolk Country Houses from the Air.* London: Sutton

Edwards, G (ed.) 1991. *George Crabbe: Selected Poems.* Harmondsworth: Penguin

Edwards, J K 1984. 'Industrial Development 1800–1900', *in* Barringer, C (ed.), *Norwich in the Nineteenth Century.* Norwich: Gliddon Books, 136–59

Elliott, B 1986. *Victorian Gardens.* London: Batsford

Ellis, P H (ed.) 1840. *Speculi Britanniae Pars: an Historical and Chorographical Description of the County of Essex by John Norden.* London: Camden Society

Ernle, Lord (R E Prothero) 1912. *English Farming, Past and Present.* London: Hutchinson

Evans, H 1845. 'Norfolk Draining'. *Journal of the Royal Agricultural Society of England* **4**, 43–4

Evans, N 1993. 'Worsted and Linen Weavers', in Wade-Martins, P (ed.), *An Historical Atlas of Norfolk.* Norwich: Norfolk Museums Service, 150–1

Evans, N 1999. 'The Linen Industry', *in* Dymond, D and Martin, E (eds), *An Historical Atlas of Suffolk.* Ipswich: Suffolk County Council, 142–3

Evans, R 1972. 'Air Photographs for Soil Survey in Lowland England: soil patterns'. *Photogrametric Record* **7**, 302–22

Everitt, A 1977. 'River and Wold: reflections on the historical origin of regions and pays'. *Journal of Historical Geography* **3**, 1–19

Eyre, S R 1955. 'The Curving Ploughland Strip and its Historical Implications'. *Agricultural History Review* **3**, 80–94

Faith, R 1997. *The English Peasantry and the Growth of Lordship*. Leicester: Leicester University Press

Fernie, E 1983. *The Archaeology of the Anglo-Saxons*. London: Batsford

Field, J 1993. *A History of English Field Names*. London: Longman

Filmer-Sankey, W and Pestell, T 2001. 'Snape Anglo-Saxon Cemetery: excavations and surveys 1824–1992'. *East Anglian Archaeology* **95**

Finch, J 2000. *Church Monuments in Norfolk Before 1850: An Archaeology of Commemoration*. Oxford: *British Archaeological Reports* **317**

Folkingham, W 1610. *Feudographica*. London

Freeman, R A 1999. 'Airfields of the Two World Wars', *in* Dymond, D and Martin, E (eds), *An Historical Atlas of Suffolk*. Ipswich: Suffolk County Council, 188–9

Funnell, B 1993a. 'Recent Geology', *in* Wade-Martins, P (ed.), *An Historical Atlas of Norfolk*. Norwich: Norfolk Museums Service, 12–13

Funnell, B 1993b. 'Glaciers Change the Landscape', *in* Wade-Martins, P (ed.), *An Historical Atlas of Norfolk*. Norwich: Norfolk Museums Service, 14–15

Gage, J 1822. *History and Antiquities of Hengrave*. London

Gage, J 1831. 'On the Ecclesiastical Round Towers of Norfolk and Suffolk'. *Archaeologia* **23**, 10–17

Garmondsway G (ed.) 1953. *The Anglo-Saxon Chronicle*. London: Everyman

George, M 1992. *The Land Use, Ecology and Conservation of Broadland*. Chichester: Packard Publishing

Gibson, G S 1862. *The Flora of Essex, Or A List of the Flowering Plants and Ferns Found in the County of Essex*. London: Pamplon

Gilpin, W 1809. *Observations On Several Parts of the Counties of Cambridge, Norfolk, Suffolk and Essex. Also on Several Parts of North Wales; Relative Chiefly to Picturesque Beauty, in Two Tours, the Former Made in the Year 1769, The Latter in the Year 1773*. London

Girouard, M 1978. *Life in the English Country House*. New Haven: Yale University Press

Girouard, M 1979. *The Victorian Country House*. London and New Haven: Yale University Press

Godwin, H 1968. 'Studies in the Post-Glacial History of British Vegetation 15. Organic Deposits of Old Buckenham Mere, Norfolk'. *New Phytologist* **67**, 95–107

Godwin, H and Tallantire, P 1951. 'Studies in the Post-Glacial History of British Vegetation 12. Hockham Mere, Norfolk'. *Journal of Ecology* **39**, 285–307

Going, C J 1996. 'The Roman Countryside', *in* Bedwin, O (ed.), *The Archaeology of Essex: Proceedings of the Writtle Conference*. Chelmsford: Essex County Council, 95–108

Goode, W J 1982. *East Anglian Round Towers and their Churches*. Lowestoft: Round Tower Church Society

Gordon, D L 1977. *Regional History of the Railways of Great Britain*. Newton Abbot: David & Charles

Grace, F 1999. 'The Growth of Modern Ipswich', *in* Dymond, D and Martin, E (eds) *An Historical Atlas of Suffolk*. Ipswich: Suffolk County Council, 160–1

Gray, H L 1915. *English Field Systems*. Cambridge, Mass.

Green, B and Young, R 1986. *Norwich: the Growth of a City*. Norwich: Norfolk Museums Service

Gregory, T 1992. 'Excavations at Thetford 1980–82: Fisons Way'. *East Anglian Archaeology* **53**

Grubb, P J, Green, H E and Merrifield, R C J 1969. 'The Ecology of Chalk Heath: its relevance to the calciole-calcifuge and soil acidification problems'. *Journal of Ecology* **57**, 175–212

Gurney, D 1986. 'Settlement, Religion and Industry on the Fen Edge: three Romano-British sites in Norfolk'. *East Anglian Archaeology* **31**, 146–8

Haggard, H Rider 1899. *A Farmer's Year*. London: Cresset Library

Hall, D 1999. 'The Drainage of Arable Land in Medieval England', *in* Cook, H and Williamson, T (eds), *Water Management in the English Landscape: Field, Marsh and Meadow*. Edinburgh: Edinburgh University Press, 28–40

Hardy, M and Martin, E 1986. 'Archaeological Fieldwork: South Elmham St Cross and South Elmham St James'. *Proceedings of the Suffolk Institute of Archaeology and History* **36**, 147–50

Harmer, F W 1877. *The Testimony of the Rocks in Norfolk: a Popular Description of the Geology of the County*. London

Harper-Bill, C (ed.) 1980. *Blythburgh Priory Cartulary Part One*. Woodbridge: Suffolk Record Society

Harris, J 1961. 'Raynham Hall, Norfolk'. *Arch J* **118**, 180–7

Harris, L E 1953. *Vermuyden and the Fens: a Study of Cornelius Vermuyden and the Great Level*. London: Cleaver-Hume

Harrison, S 2002. 'Open Fields and Earlier Landscapes: six parishes in south-east Cambridgeshire'. *Landscapes* **3**(1), 35–54

Harrison, S 2004. 'The Icknield Way: some queries'. *Arch J* **160**, 1–23

Hartley, J P 1953. *The Go-Between*. London: Hamish Hamilton

Haselgrove, C 1982. 'Wealth, Prestige and Power: the dynamics of Late Iron Age political centralisation in England', *in* Renfrew, C and Shennan, S (eds), *Ranking, Resource and Exchange: Aspects of the Archaeology of Early European Society*. Cambridge: Cambridge University Press, 79–88

Haslam, J 1982. 'The Development and Topography of Saxon Cambridgeshire'. *Proceedings of the Cambridge Antiquarian Society* **72**, 13–29

Hassell Smith, A 2002. 'Concept and Compromise: Sir Nicholas Bacon and the buildings of Stiffkey Hall', *in* Harper-Bill, C, Rawcliffe, C and Wilson, R G (eds), *East Anglia's History: Studies in Honour of Norman Scarfe*. Woodbridge: Boydell, 159–88

Heaton, A 2001. *Duck Decoys*. Princes Risborough: Shire

Henslow, J S and Skepper, E 1860. *Flora of Suffolk: a Catalogue of Plants found in a Wild State in the County of Suffolk*. London: Simpkin & Marshall

Hervey, Lord F 1902. *Suffolk in the Seventeenth Century: the Breviary of Suffolk by Robert Reyce*. London

Hesse, M 1992. 'Fields, Tracks and Boundaries in the Creakes, North Norfolk'. *Norfolk Archaeology* **41**, 305–24

Hewett, C A 1968. 'Aisled Timber Halls and Related Buildings, Chiefly in Essex'. *Transactions of the Ancient Monuments Society* **16**, 45–99

Hewitt, C 1980. *English Historic Carpentry*. Chichester: Phillimore

Heywood, S R 1988. 'The Round Towers of East Anglia', *in* Blair, J (ed.), *Minsters and Parish Churches: the Local Church in Transition 950–1200*. Oxford: Blackwell, 169–77

Heywood, S 1993. 'Round Towered Churches', *in* Wade-Martins, P (ed.), *An Historical Atlas of Norfolk*. Norwich: Norfolk Museums Service, 56–7

Hill, D 1988 'Towns as Structures and as Functioning Communities Through Time: the development of central places from 600 to 1066', *in* Hooke, D *Anglo-Saxon Settlements*. Oxford: Blackwell, 192–202

Hill, D 2000. 'Sulh – the Anglo-Saxon Plough *c*.1000 AD'. *Landscape History* **22**, 7–19

Hill, D and Cowie, R (eds) 2001. *Wics: the Early Medieval Trading Centres of Northern Europe*. Sheffield: Sheffield Archaeological Monographs **14**

Hill, J D 1999. 'Settlement, Landscape and Regionality: Norfolk and Suffolk in the pre-Roman Iron Age of Britain and beyond', *in* Davies, J and Williamson, T (eds), *Land of the Iceni: the Iron Age in Northern East Anglia*. Norwich: Centre of East Anglian Studies

Hills, R L 1967. *Machines, Mills and Uncountable Costly Necessities: a Short History of the Drainage of the Fens*. Norwich: Goose & Son

Hills, R L 1994. *Power from Wind*. Cambridge: Cambridge University Press

Hines, J 1992. 'The Scandinavian Character of Anglian England: an update', *in* Carver, M (ed.), *The Age of Sutton Hoo*. Woodbridge: Boydell Press, 315–40

Hinton, D 1997. 'The "Scole-Dickleburgh Field System" Examined'. *Landscape History* **19**, 5–13

Hinton, D 1990. *Archaeology, Economy and Society*. London: Seaby

Historic Manuscripts Commission 1907. *Fifteenth Report, Appendix, Part VI. The Manuscripts of the Earl of Carlisle Preserved at Castle Howard*. London

Hodge, C, Burton, R, Corbett, W, Evans, R and Scale, R 1984. *Soils and their Uses in Eastern England*. Harpenden: Soil Survey of England and Wales

Hodges, R 1982. *Dark Age Economics*. London: Duckworth

Holderness, B A 1972. '"Open" and "Close" Parishes in England in the Eighteenth and Nineteenth Centuries'. *Agricultural History Review* **20**, 126–39

Holderness, B A 1985. 'East Anglia and the Fens', *in* Thirsk, J (ed.), *The Agrarian History of England and Wales, part 2*. Cambridge: Cambridge University Press, 119–245

Homans, G C 1969. 'The Explanation of English Regional Differences'. *Past and Present* **42**, 18–34

Home, M 1946. *Spring Sowing*. London: Methuen

Hooper, M D, Pollard, E and Moore, N W 1974. *Hedges*. London: Collins

Hoppitt, R 1992. 'The Development of Parks in Suffolk from the Eleventh to the Seventeenth Centuries', unpublished PhD thesis, Centre of East Anglian Studies, University of East Anglia, 63–95

Hoppitt, R 1999a. 'Deer Parks, 1086–1600', *in* Dymond, D and Martin, E (eds), *An Historical Atlas of Suffolk*. Ipswich: Suffolk County Council, 66–7

Hoppitt, R 1999b. 'Rabbit Warrens', *in* Dymond, D and Martin, E (eds), *An Historical Atlas of Suffolk*. Ipswich: Suffolk County Council, 68–9

Hoskins, W G 1955. *The Making of the English Landscape*. London: Hodder and Stoughton

Howard, P 1991. *Landscapes: the Artists' Vision*. London: Routledge

Hunter, J 1999. *The Essex Landscape: a Study of its Form and History*. Chelmsford: Essex Records Office

Imray, Laurie, Norie and Wilson 2002. *Marine Charts* C28, Harwich to Wells; Y6, The Wash; C1, Thames Estuary. (St Ives)

James, N 2000. 'The Transformation of the Fens', *in* Kirby, T and Oosthuizen, S (eds), *An Atlas of Cambridgeshire and Huntingdonshire History*. Cambridge: Anglia Polytechnic University, 47

James, P D 1967. *Unnatural Causes*. Harmondsworth: Penguin

James, P D 1989. *Devices and Desires*. Harmondsworth: Penguin

Jessop, A 1887. *Arcady: For Better, For Worse*. London

Joby, R 1993. 'Waterways', *in* Wade-Martins, P (ed.), *An Historical Atlas of Norfolk*. Norwich: Norfolk Museums Service, 146–7

Johnson D E (ed.) 1977. *The Saxon Shore*. London: Council for British Archaeology Research Report **18**

Johnson, M 1993. *Housing Culture*. London: UCL Press

Jones, R L and Keen, D H 1993. *Pleistocene Environments in the British Isles*. London: Chapman & Hall

Kenney, C 1990. *The Remarkable Case of Dorothy L Sayers*. Kent, Ohio: Kent State University Press

Kent, P 1999. 'Fortifications of the Two World Wars', *in* Dymond, D and Martin, E (eds), *An Historical Atlas of Suffolk*. Ipswich: Suffolk County Council, 186–7

Kerridge, E 1967. *The Agricultural Revolution*. London: Allen & Unwin

Kerridge, E 1985. *Textile Manufactures in Early Modern England*. Manchester: Manchester University Press

Kerridge, E 1992. *The Common Fields of England*. Manchester: Manchester University Press

Ketton-Cremer, R W 1957. *Norfok Assembly*. London: Faber

Kiln, R J and Partridge, C R 1995. *Ware and Hertford: the Story of two Towns from Birth to Middle Age*. Welwyn Garden City: Castlemead

Kingsley, C 1877. *Alton Locke*. London

Kirby, J 1735. *The Suffolk Traveller*. London

Kneale, N (ed.) 1973. *The Ghost Stories of M R James*. London: Folio Society

Knights, S 1986. 'Change and Decay: Emerson's Social Order', *in* McWilliam, N and Sekules, V (eds), *Life and Landscape. P H Emerson: Art and Photography in East Anglia 1885–1900*. Norwich: University of East Anglia, 12–20

Knowles, D and Hadcock, R M 1971. *Medieval Religious Houses, England and Wales*. London: Longman

Laird, M 1999. *The Flowering of the Landscape Garden: English Pleasure Grounds 1720–1800*. Philadelphia: University of Pennsylvania Press

Lambert, J M, Jennings, J N, Smith, C T, Green, C and Hutchinson, J N 1952. *The Origins of the Broads*. London: Royal Geographical Society Research Series B2B

Lambert, S (ed.) 1977. *House of Commons Sessional Papers of the Eighteenth Century: George III; Reports of the Commissioners of Land Revenue, 8–11, 1792*. Delaware

Langdon, J 1986. *Horses, Oxen and Technological Innovation*. Cambridge: Cambridge University Press

Liddiard, R 1999. 'The Distribution of Ridge and Furrow in Norfolk: ploughing practice and subsequent land use'. *Agricultural History Review* **47**, 1–6

Liddiard, R 2000a. *'Landscapes of Lordship': Norman Castles and the Countryside in Medieval Norfolk 1066–1200*. Oxford: British Archaeological Reports **309**

Liddiard, R 2000b. 'Population Density and Norman Castle-Building: some evidence from East Anglia', *Landscape History* **22**, 37–46

Lilley, K 2002. *Urban Life in the Middle Ages 1000–1450*. Basingstoke: Palgrave

Longcroft, A 2002. 'Plan-Forms in Smaller Post-Medieval Houses: a case study from Norfolk'. *Vernacular Architecture* **33**, 34–56

Lucas, R 1993. 'Studwork, Early Brick and Clay-Brick Chimneys in Norfolk and Suffolk'. *Vernacular Architecture* **24**, 18–19

Mabey, R 1980. *The Common Ground*. London: Hutchinson

MacCulloch, D (ed.) 1976. *The Chorography of Suffolk*. Ipswich: Suffolk Record Society

Malim, T 1996. 'New Evidence on the Cambridgeshire Dykes and Worstead Street Roman Road'. *Proceedings of the Cambridgeshire Antiquarian Society* **85**, 27–122

Malster, R 1993. *The Broads*. Chichester: Philimore

Mann, M E 1991. *Tales of Victorian Norfolk*. Bungay: Morrow & Co

Margeson, S 1996. 'Viking Settlement in Norfolk: a study of new evidence', *in* Margeson, S, Ayers, B and Heywood, S (eds), *A Festival of Norfolk Archaeology: in Celebration of the 150th Anniversary of the Norfolk and Norwich Archaeological Society*. Norwich: Norfolk and Norwich Archaeological Society, 47–57

Markham, S 1984. *John Loveday of Caversham, 1711–1789: the Life and Times of an Eighteenth-century Onlooker*. Salisbury: Michael Russel

Marshall, W 1787a. *The Rural Economy of Norfolk*, vol.1. London: G. Nicol, G. G. & J. Robinson, and J. Debrett

Marshall, W 1787b. *The Rural Economy of Norfolk*, vol.2. London: G. Nicol, G. G. & J. Robinson, and J. Debrett

Martin, E 1999. 'Suffolk in the Iron Age', *in* Davies, J and Williamson, T (eds), *Land of the Iceni: the Iron Age in Northern East Anglia*. Norwich: Centre of East Anglian Studies, 45–99

Martin, E 2001. 'Rural Settlement Patterns in Medieval Suffolk'. *Annual Report of the Medieval Settlement Research Group* **15**

Martin, E 2002. 'Garden Canals in Suffolk', *in* Harper-Bill, C, Rawcliffe, C and Wilson, R G (eds), *East Anglia's History: Studies in Honour of Norman Scarfe*. Woodbridge: Boydell, 213–42

Mathew, W 1993. 'Marling in British Agriculture: a case of partial identity'. *Agricultural History Review* **41**, 97–110

Matless, D 1994. 'Moral Geography in Broadland'. *Ecumene* **1**(2), 127–56

McCann, J 1987. 'Is Clay Lump a Traditional Building Material?'. *Vernacular Architecture* **18**, 1–16

McCann, J 1997. 'The Origins of Clay Lump in England'. *Vernacular Architecture* **28**, 57–67

Mercer, E 1975. *English Vernacular Houses: a study of traditional farmhouses and cottages*. London: Royal Commission on Historical Monuments

Miller, D 1935. *Seen From a Windmill: a Norfolk Broads Revue*. London: Heath Cranton Ltd

Mingay, G E 1997. *Parliamentary Enclosure in England: an Introduction to its Causes, Incidence and Impact*. London: Longman

Ministry of Agriculture, Food and Fisheries 1948. *Harvest Home: the Official Story of the Great Floods of 1947 and their Sequel*. London: Central Office of Information

Moore, A 1985. *The Norwich School*. Norwich: Norfolk Museums Service

Moore, A 1988. *Dutch and Flemish Painting in Norfolk: a History of Taste and Influence, Fashion and Collecting*. London: HMSO

Moore, A (ed.) 1996. *Houghton Hall: the Prime Minister, the Empress, and the Heritage*. Norwich: Norfolk Museums Service

Munby, L 1977. *The Hertfordshire Landscape*. London: Hodder and Stoughton

Munsche, P B 1981. *Gentlemen and Poachers: the English Game Laws 1671–1831*. Cambridge: Cambridge University Press

Muthesius, S 1984. 'Nineteenth Century Norwich Houses', *in* Barringer, C (ed.), *Norwich in the Nineteenth Century*. Norwich: Gliddon Books, 94–117

Newsome, S 2003. 'The Coastal Landscapes of Suffolk During the Second World War'. *Landscapes* 4(2), 42–58

Newton, K C 1960. *Thaxted in the Fourteenth Century*. Chelmsford: Essex Records Office

Newton, S 1993. *The Origins of Beowulf and the Pre-Viking Kingdom of East Anglia*. Cambridge: Cambridge University Press

Nicolson, N 1998. 'Oxburgh Hall', *in* Ford, B (ed.), *The Cambridge Guide to the Arts in Britain*, vol.2, 88–95. Cambridge: Cambridge University Press

Norden, J 1618. *The Surveyor's Dialogue*. London

Norfolk Industrial Archaeology Society 1981. 'A Survey of Ludham'. *Journal of the Norfolk Industrial Archaeology Society* 3(1), 34–51

North, R 1713. *A Treatise on Fish and Fish Ponds*. London

O'Donell, R 1978. 'W J Donthorne'. *Architectural History* 21, 83–92

Oosthuizen, S 2000. 'The Cambridgeshire Lodes', *in* Kirby, T and Oosthuizen, S (eds), *An Atlas of Cambridgeshire and Huntingdonshire History*. Cambridge: Anglia Polytechnic University, 32

Owen, D 1980. 'Bishop's Lynn: the first century of a new town?', *in* Allen Brown, R (ed.), *Proceedings of the Battle Conference 1979*. Woodbridge: Boydell and Brewer

Paine, C (ed.) 1993. *The Culford Estate 1780–1935*, Bury St Edmunds

Parker, V 1971. *The Making of King's Lynn: secular buildings from the 11th to the 17th century*. Chichester: Philimore

Parry, J 2003. *Heathland*. London: The National Trust

Patten, J 1978. *English Towns 1500–1700*. Folkstone: Dawson

Patterson, A H 1905. *Nature in Eastern Norfolk*. London: Methuen

Payne Gallway, R 1886. *The Book of Duck Decoys*. London

Pearson, A 2003. *The Construction of Saxon Shore Forts*. Oxford: British Archaeological Reports 349

Peglar, S, Fritz, S and Birks, J 1989. 'Vegetation and Land Use History at Diss, Norfolk'. *Journal of Ecology* 77, 203–32

Penn, K 1993a. 'Early Unplanned Towns', *in* Wade-Martins, P (ed.), *An Historical Atlas of Norfolk*. Norwich: Norfolk Museums Service, 70–1

Penn, K 1993b. 'Anglo-Saxon Thetford', *in* Wade-Martins, P (ed.), *An Historical Atlas of Norfolk*. Norwich: Norfolk Museums Service, 46–7

Perry, H and Perry, E 1999. *Tottington: a Lost Village in Norfolk*. Wymondham: George Reeves

Perry, P J 1974. *British Farming in the Great Depression*. Newton Abbot: David & Charles

Pestell, T 1999. 'An Analysis of Monastic Foundation *c*.650–1200', unpublished PhD Thesis, Centre of East Anglian Studies, University of East Anglia

Peterken, G F 1968. 'The Development of Vegetation in Staverton Park'. *Field Studies* 2, 1–39

Pevsner, N 1961. *The Buildings of England: Suffolk*. Harmondsworth: Penguin

Pevsner, N 1965. *The Buildings of England: Essex*. Harmondsworth: Penguin

Pevsner, N and Wilson, B 2002a. *Norfolk I: Norwich and North East*. London: Yale University Press

Pevsner, N and Wilson, B 2002b. *Norfolk II: North West*. London: Yale University Press

Phear, J B 1854. 'On the Geology of Some Parts of Suffolk'. *Transactions of the Cambridge Philosophical Society* 9

Phillips, M 1909. 'Two Industries Connected with Flint at Ling Heath, Brandon'. *Proceedings of the Society of Antiquaries* 23, 102–4

Phythian Adams, C 1987. *Rethinking English Local History*. Leicester: Leicester University Press

Phythian Adams, C 1993. *Societies, Cultures and Kinship 1580–1850: Cultural Provinces and English Local History*. Leicester: Leicester University Press

Pollard, M 1978. *North Sea Surge: the Story of the East Coast Floods of 1953*. Lavenham: T Dalton

Postgate, M R 1962. 'The Field Systems of Breckland'. *Agricultural History Review* 10, 80–101

Postgate, M R 1973. 'Field systems of East Anglia', *in* Baker, A R H and Butlin, R A (eds), *Studies of Field Systems in the British Isles*. London: Cambridge University Press

Prince, H 1964. 'The Origins of Pits and Depressions in Norfolk'. *Geography* 49, 15–32

Rackham, O 1986a. 'The Ancient Woods of Norfolk'. *Transactions of the Norfolk and Norwich Naturalists Society* 27(3), 161–77

Rackham, O 1986b. *The History of the Countryside*. London: Dent

Raynbird, W and Raynbird, H 1849. *On the Farming of Suffolk*. London

Read, C S 1858. 'Recent Improvements in Norfolk Farming'. *Journal of the Royal Agricultural Society of England* 19, 265–310

Reeves, A and Williamson, T 2000. 'Marshes', *in* Thirsk, J (ed.), *The English Rural Landscape*. Oxford: Oxford University Press, 150–60

Reid, A 1986. *Cromer and Sheringham: the Growth of the Holiday Trade 1877–1904*. Norwich: Centre of East Anglian Studies

Richens, R H 1967. 'Studies on *Ulmus*. VII. Essex Elms'. *Forestry* **40**, 184–206

Richens, R H 1977. *Elm*. Cambridge: Cambridge University Press

Riches, N 1937. *The Agricultural Revolution in Norfolk*. Chapel Hill: North Carolina

Rickett, R and Rose, E 1993. 'Monastic Houses', *in* Wade-Martins, P (ed.), *An Historical Atlas of Norfolk*. Norwich: Norfolk Museums Service, 64–5

Ridgeway, C 1993. 'Williams Andrews Nesfield: between Uvedale Price and Isambard Kingdom Brunel'. *Journal of Garden History* **13**, 69–89

Robberds, J W 1826. *Geological and Historical Observations on the Eastern Vallies* [sic] *of Norfolk*. London

Roberts, B K and Wrathmell, S 1998. 'Dispersed Settlement in England: a national view', *in* Everson, P and Williamson, T (eds), *The Archaeology of Landscape: Studies Presented to Christopher Taylor*. Manchester: Manchester University Press, 95–116

Roberts, B K and Wrathmell, S 2000a. *An Atlas of Rural Settlement in England*. London: English Heritage

Roberts, B K and Wrathmell, S 2000b. 'Peoples of Wood and Plain: an exploration of national and local regional contrasts', *in* Hooke, D (ed.), *Landscape: the Richest Historical Record*. London: Landscape History Society, 85–96

Robertson, A 1999. 'Rivers and Navigations', *in* Dymond, D and Martin, E (eds), *An Historical Atlas of Suffolk*. Ipswich: Suffolk County Council, 130–1

Robinson, D H 1949. *Fream's Elements of Agriculture*, 13 edn. London: John Murray

Robinson, J M 1983. *Georgian Model Farms: a Study of Decorative and Model Farm Buildings in the Age of Improvement, 1700–1846*. Oxford: Clarendon Press

Roden, D 1973. 'Field Systems of the Chiltern Hills and their Environs', *in* Baker, A R H and Butlin, R A (eds), *Studies of Field Systems in the British Isles*. Cambridge: Cambridge University Press, 325–74

Rodwell, J S 1991. *British Plant Communities Volume 2: Mires and Heaths*. Cambridge: Cambridge University Press

Rodwell, W 1978. 'Relict landscapes in Essex', *in* Bowen, H C and Fowler, P J (eds), *Early Land Allotment*. Oxford: British Archaeological Reports **48**, 89–98

Rogerson, A 1995. 'Fransham: an archaeological and historical study of a parish on the Norfolk boulder clay', unpublished PhD Thesis, Centre of East Anglian Studies, University of East Anglia

Rogerson, A and Dallas, C 1984. 'Excavations in Thetford, 1948–59 and 1973–80'. *East Anglian Archaeology* **22**

Rogerson, R 1993. 'Castles', *in* Wade-Martins, P (ed.), *An Historical Atlas of Norfolk*. Norwich: Norfolk Museums Service, 68–9

Rowe, A 1998. 'Country House Chameleon: the story of Hamels Mansion'. *Hertfordshire's Past* **43**(4), 44–54

Rowley, N 1972. *Town Life and Improvement in Essex, 1730–1908*. Chelmsford: Essex County Council

Rowley, T and Wood, J 2000. *Deserted Villages*, 3rd edn. Princes Risborough: Shire

Rutherford Davis, K 1973. *The Deserted Medieval Villages of Hertfordshire*. Chichester: Phillimore

Rutledge, P 1980. 'A Rabbit Warren at Swainsthorpe'. *Norfolk Research Council Bulletin* **23**, 7–8

Rye, W (ed.) 1906. *State Papers Relating to Musters Beacons and Ship Money &c in Norfolk from 1626*. Norwich: Norfolk and Norwich Archaeological Society

Ryle, G 1969. *Forest Service: the First Forty-five Years of the Forestry Commission in Great Britain*. Newton Abbot: David & Charles

Salmon, N 1728. *The History of Hertfordshire*. London

Sandon, E 1977. *Suffolk Houses: a Study of Domestic Architecture*. Woodbridge: Baron Publishing

Sayers, D L 1934. *The Nine Taylors*. London: Coronet

Scarfe, N 1972. *The Suffolk Landscape*. London: Hodder & Stoughton

Scarfe, N 1986. *Suffolk in the Middle Ages*. Woodbridge: Boydell & Brewer

Scarfe, N (ed.) 1988. *A Frenchman's Year in Suffolk: French Impressions of Suffolk Life in 1784*. (Suffolk Records Society **30**) Woodbridge: Boydell Press, 34–5

Scarfe, N 1999. 'Medieval and Later Markets', *in* Dymond, D and Martin, E (eds), *An Historical Atlas of Suffolk*. Ipswich: Suffolk County Council, 76–7

Schmidt, L 1980. 'Holkham Hall, Norfolk', *Country Life*

Scott, C S 1886. *Poppyland: Papers Descriptive of Scenery on the East Coast*. London: Carson & Comerford

Scull, C 2002. 'Ipswich: development and contexts of an urban precursor in the seventh century', *in* Hardh, B and Larson, L (eds), *Central Places in the Migration and Merovingian Periods*. Lund: *Acta Archaeologica Lundensia* **8**, **39**, 303–16

Sheail, J 1971. *Rabbits and Their History*. Newton Abbot: David & Charles

Shoard, M 1980. *The Theft of the Countryside*. London: Temple Smith

Short, D 1988. 'Braughing: a possible Saxon estate'. *Hertfordshire's Past* **23**, 8–15

Silcoxe-Crowe, N 1985. 'Roger Pratt 1620–1685: the ingenious gentleman architect', *in* Brown, R (ed.), *The Architectural Outsiders*. London: Waterstone

Silvester, R 1988. 'The Fenland Project No 3: Norfolk Survey, Marshland and the Nar Valley'. *East Anglian Archaeology* **45**, 154–6

Silvester, R 1999. 'Medieval Reclamation of Marsh and Fen', *in* Cook, H and Williamson, T (eds), *Water Management in the English Landscape: Field, Marsh and Meadow*. Edinburgh: Edinburgh University Press, 122–40

Sims, R 1978. 'Man and Vegetation in Norfolk', *in* Limbry, S and Evans, J G (eds), *The Effect of Man on the Landscape: the Lowland Zone*. London: Council for British Archaeology Research Report **21**, 57–62

Skipper, K and Williamson, T 1997. *Thetford Forest: Making a Landscape, 1922–1997*. Norwich: Centre of East Anglian Studies

Smith, A C 1990. *Drainage Windmills of the Norfolk Marshes: a Contemporary Survey*, 2nd edn. Stevenage: Stevenage Museum

Smith, J T 1958. 'Medieval Roofs: a classification'. *Arch J* **115**, 111–49

Smith, J T 1992. *English Houses 1200–1800: the Hertfordshire evidence*. London: Royal Commission on Historical Monuments

Spencer, H E P 1970. 'A Contribution to the Geological History of Suffolk'. *Transactions of the Suffolk Naturalists' Society* **13**, 197–209, 290–313, 366–89

Stamp, L Dudley 1950. *The Land of Britain: its Use and Misuse*. London: Longmans, Green & Co

Stenning, D F 1985. 'Timber-Framed Shops 1300–1600: comparative plans'. *Vernacular Architecture* **16**, 35–8

Stenning, D F 1996. 'Standing Timber-Framed Buildings', *in* Bedwin, O (ed.), *The Archaeology of Essex: Proceedings of the Writtle Conference*. Chelmsford: Essex County Council

Stenton, F M 1947. *Anglo-Saxon England*. Oxford: Oxford University Press

Stevenson, H 1870. *The Birds of Norfolk*. London

Sussams, K 1996. *The Breckland Archaeological Survey*. Ipswich: Suffolk County Council

Swift, G 1983. *Waterland*. London: Heinneman

Taylor, C 1972. 'Medieval Moats in Cambridgeshire', *in* Fowler, P J (ed.), *Archaeology and the Landscape*. London: John Baker

Taylor, C 1973. *The Cambridgeshire Landscape*. London: Hodder & Stoughton

Taylor, C 1999. 'Post-medieval Drainage of Marsh and Fen', *in* Cook, H and Williamson, T (eds), *Water Management in the English Landscape*. Edinburgh: Edinburgh University Press, 237–49

Taylor, C 2000. 'Fenlands', *in* Thirsk, J (ed.), *The English Rural Landscape*. Oxford: Oxford University Press, 167–87

Taylor, C and Crompton, G 1971. 'Earthwork Enclosures on Lakenheath Warren'. *Proceedings of the Suffolk Institute of Archaeology and History* **32**, 13–20

Taylor, H M and Taylor, J 1965. *Anglo-Saxon Architecture*. Cambridge: Cambridge University Press

Taylor, J 1986. 'Landscape and Leisure', *in* McWilliam, N and Sekules, V (eds), *Life and Landscape. P H Emerson: Art and Photography in East Anglia 1885–1900*. Norwich: University of East Anglia, 73–82

Taylor, R C 1827. *On the Geology of East Norfolk*. London

Theobald, J 2000. 'Changing Landscapes, Changing Economies: holdings in woodland high Suffolk 1600–1850, unpublished PhD Thesis, Centre of East Anglian Studies, University of East Anglia

Thirsk, J 1987. *England's Agricultural Regions and Agrarian History 1500–1750*. London: MacMillan

Trimmer, K 1866. *Flora of Norfolk: a Catalogue of the Plants Found in Norfolk*. London: Hamilton-Adams

Trist, P J O 1971. *A Survey of the Agriculture of Suffolk*. Royal Agricultural Society of England County Agriculture Surveys **7**. London: Royal Agricultural Society

Trollope, A 1980. *Can You Forgive Her?* London: Penguin

Turner, M 1980. *English Parliamentary Enclosure*. Folkestone: Dawson

Turner, M 1993. 'Parliamentary Enclosure', *in* Wade-Martins, P (ed.), *An Historical Atlas of Norfolk*. Norwich: Norfolk Museums Service, 124–5

Tusser, T 1573. *Five Hundred Pointes of Good Husbandrie, as Well for the Champion of Open Countrie as Also for the Woodland, or Seuerall*. London

Vine, B 1986. *A Dark-Adapted Eye*. Harmondsworth: Penguin

Vine, B 1990. *Gallowglass*. Harmondsworth: Penguin

Vine, B 1995. *The Brimstone Wedding*. Harmondsworth: Penguin

Wade, K 1980. 'A Settlement Site at Bonhunt Farm, Wicken Bonhunt, Essex', *in* Buckley, D (ed.), *The Archaeology of Essex to AD1500*. London: Council for British Archaeology, 96–102

Wade, K 1988. 'Ipswich', *in* Hodges, R and Hobley, B (eds), *The Rebirth of Towns in the West, AD 700–1050*. London: Council for British Archaeology Research Report **68**, 93–100

Wade, K 1993. 'The Urbanisation of East Anglia: the Ipswich Experience', *in* Gardiner, J (ed.), *Flat Lands and Wetlands: Current Themes in East Anglian Archaeology*. *East Anglian Archaeology* **50**, 144–51

Wade, K and Dymond, D 1999. 'Smaller Medieval Towns', *in* Dymond, D and Martin, E (eds), *An Historical Atlas of Suffolk*. Ipswich: Suffolk County Council, 162–3

Wade-Martins, P 1974. 'The Linear Earthworks of West Norfolk'. *Norfolk Archaeology* **36**, 23–38

Wade-Martins, P 1980. 'Village Sites in the Launditch Hundred'. *East Anglian Archaeology* **10**

Wade-Martins, S 1993. 'From Black Face to White Face. An Aspect of the Agricultural Revolution in Norfolk'. *Agricultural History Review* **41**, 20–30

Wade-Martins, S 1995. *Farms and Fields*. London: Batsford

Wade-Martins, S and Williamson, T 1994. 'Floated Water-Meadows in Norfolk: a misplaced innovation'. *Agricultural History Review* **42**, 20–37

Wade-Martins, S and Williamson, T 1999. 'Roots of Change: farming in the landscape in East Anglia 1700–1870'. Exeter: British Agricultural History Society

Ward, A J 1999a. 'Smoke Drifting Over the Reeds Part 1: the simple engines of the River Bure'. *Journal of the Norfolk Industrial Archaeology Society* **6**(2), 46–63

Ward, A J 1999b. 'Smoke Drifting Over the Reeds Part 1: the River Yare – Norwich to Hardley Cross'. *Journal of the Norfolk Industrial Archaeology Society* **6**(3), 40–56

Warner, P 1986. 'Shared Churchyards, Freemen Church Builders and the Development of Parishes in Eleventh-Century East Anglia'. *Landscape History* **8**, 39–52

Warner, P 1996. *The Origins of Suffolk.* Manchester: Manchester University Press

Warner, P 2000. *Bloody Marsh: a Seventeenth-century Village in Crisis.* Macclesfield: Windgather Press

Way, T 2000. 'Open and Close Parishes', *in* Kirby, T and Ousthuizen, S (eds), *An Atlas of Cambridgeshire and Huntingdonshire History.* Cambridge: Anglia Polytechnic University, 66

Webster, G 1978. *Boudicca: the British revolt against Rome.* London: Batsford

Wells, S 1830. *The History of the Drainage of the Great Level of the Fens.* London

Wentworth Day, J 1954. *A History of the Fens: being some Account of their Swamps, Meres, Men, Sports, Duck Decoys, Drainage, Riots, Floods, Legends, Fish and Fowl.* London: Harrap

West, J R (ed.) 1932. *St Benet of Holme 1020–1210: the Eleventh and Twelfth Century Sections of Cott.Ms Galba E ii, the Register of the Abbey of St Benet of Holme.* Norwich: Norfolk Record Society **2**

Whittock, M 1986. *The Origins of England 410–600.* London: Croom Helm

Whyte, I 2002. *Landscape and History Since 1500.* London: Reaktion

Whyte, N 2003. 'The Deviant dead in the Norfolk landscape'. *Landscapes* **4**(1), 24–39

Whyte, N 2004. 'The After Life of Barrows'. *Landscape History* **28**, 5–16

Wickendon, N P 1996. 'The Roman Towns of Essex', *in* Bedwin, O (ed.), *The Archaeology of Essex: Proceedings of the Writtle Conference.* Chelmsford: Essex County Council

Williamson, H 1941. *The Story of a Norfolk Farm.* London: Faber & Faber

Williamson, T 1986. 'The Development of Settlement in North West Essex: the results of a recent field survey'. *Essex Archaeology and History* **17**, 120–32

Williamson, T 1987. 'Early Co-axial Field Systems on the East Anglian Boulder Clays'. *Proceedings of the Prehistoric Society* **53**, 419–31

Williamson, T 1993. *The Origins of Norfolk.* Manchester: Manchester University Press.

Williamson, T 1995. *Polite Landscapes: Gardens and Society in Eighteenth-century England.* Stroud: Alan Sutton

Williamson, T 1996. 'Roger North at Rougham: a lost house and its landscape', *in* Rawcliffe, C, Virgoe, R and Wilson, R G (eds), *Counties and Communities: Essays on East Anglian History Presented to Hassell Smith.* Norwich: Centre of East Anglian Studies, 275–90

Williamson, T 1997. *The Norfolk Broads: a Landscape History.* Manchester: Manchester University Press

Williamson, T 1998a. *The Archaeology of the Landscape Park: Garden Design in Norfolk, England, 1680–1840.* Oxford: British Archaeological Reports

Williamson, T 1998b. 'The Scole-Dickleburgh Field System Revisited'. *Landscape History* **20**, 19–28

Williamson, T 2000a. *The Origins of Hertfordshire.* Manchester: Manchester University Press

Williamson, T 2000b. *Suffolk's Gardens and Parks: Designed Landscapes from the Tudors to the Victorians.* Macclesfield: Windgather Press

Williamson, T 2000c. 'Understanding Enclosure'. *Landscapes* **1**, 56–79

Williamson, T 2002a. 'Shrubland Before Barry: a house and its landscape 1660–1880', *in* Harper-Bill, C, Rawcliffe, C and Wilson, R G (eds), *East Anglia's History: Studies in Honour of Norman Scarfe.* Woodbridge: Boydell

Williamson, T 2002b. *The Transformation of Rural England: Farming and the Landscape 1700–1870.* Exeter: Exeter University Press

Williamson, T 2003. *Shaping Medieval Landscapes: Settlement, Society, Environment.* Macclesfield: Windgather Press

Wilton, J W 1980. *Monastic Life in Norfolk and Suffolk.* Fakenham: Acorn

Wiltshire, P and Murphy, P 1999. 'Current Knowledge of the Iron Age Environment and Agrarian Economy of Norfolk and Adjacent Areas', *in* Davies, J and Williamson, T (eds), *Land of the Iceni: the Iron Age in Northern East Anglia.* Norwich: Centre of East Anglian Studies, 132–61

Wodehouse, P G 1930. *Very Good, Jeeves!* (Republished in *Life With Jeeves*, 1986). London, Penguin

Woodward, H B 1881. *The Geology of the Country Around Norwich.* London

Wright, T 1668. 'A Curious and Exact Relation of a Sand-Floud'. *Philosophical Transactions* **3**, 722–5

Wymer, J 1984. 'East Anglian Palaeolithic Sites and Their Settings', *in* Barringer, C (ed.), *Aspects of East Anglian Prehistory.* Norwich: Geo Books, 16–32

Wymer, J 1996. 'Barrow excavations in Norfolk, 1984–1988'. *East Anglian Archaeology* **77**

Wymer, J 1999. 'Surface Geology', *in* Dymond, D and Martin, E (eds), *An Historical Atlas of Suffolk.* Ipswich: Suffolk County Council, 16–19

Yaxley, D 1994. 'The Tower of Houghton St Martin Church'. *Annual Bulletin of the Norfolk Archaeological Research Group* **3**, 46–50

Yelling, J A 1977. *Common Field and Enclosure in England 1450–1850.* London: Macmillan, 11–29

Young, A 1771. *The Farmer's Tour Through the East of England.* 4 vols. London, Vol **2**(1)

Young, A 1795. *General View of the Agriculture of the County of Suffolk.* London

Young, A 1797. *General View of the Agriculture of the County of Suffolk.* London

Young, A 1799. *General View of the Agriculture of the County of Lincolnshire.* London

Young, A 1804. *General View of the Agriculture of Norfolk.* London

Young, A 1813. *General View of the Agriculture of Hertfordshire.* London

Index

Page numbers in *italic* refer to illustrations.

Picture Credits

Images on the following pages © Crown copyright.NMR or © English Heritage: 14 (NMR 23503/10); 15b (NMR 23397/32); 16 (NMR 23623/02); 18 (NMR 23502/20); 19t (NMR 23296/24); 19b (NMR 23920/05); 20 (NMR 23500/15); 22 (NMR 23664/34); 23 (NMR 23297/14); 24 (NMR 24036/21); 26 (NMR 23298/21); 28 (NMR 23498/05); 32t (NMR 23354/31); 32b (NMR 23912/18); 33t (NMR 23726/08); 34 (NMR 23503/16); 39 (NMR 23665/25); 40b (NMR 23504/20); 44 (NMR 21831/19); 53t (NMR 23499/15); 53b (NMR 23280/06); 58 (NMR 23729/03); 59 (NMR 23630/12); 63 (NMR 23281/23); 67 (BB93/10627); 68 (NMR 23524/03); 81 (NMR 23503/22); 82 (NMR 23725/24); 86 (NMR 23281/24); 87 (NMR 23495/24); 90–1 (NMR 23498/24); 92b (BB93/10415); 110 (NMR 23727/23); 111t (NMR 23285/18); 111b (NMR 23297/21); 112b (NMR 23525/05); 115 (NMR 23497/09); 125 (NMR 20403/01); 128t (NMR 23492/07); 128b (NMR 23286/01); 130b (NMR 23493/24); 132 (NMR 23502/03); 133 (NMR 23217/18); 137b (BB97/10608); 139b (NMR 23504/04); 146b (NMR 24038/02); 148 (NMR 23525/18); 150 (NMR 23435/33); 154b (NMR 23630/18); 169 (NMR 23728/16); 182t (NMR 23524/08); 183b (NMR 23504/17); 190 (NMR 23969/12); 193 (NMR 23285/04); 195 (NMR 23501/04); 199b (NMR 23437/10); 205t (NMR 23216/17); 205b (NMR 23624/16); 234b (NMR 23501/09); 236b (NMR 23495/08); 237b (NMR 23384/22).

English Heritage ground photography was taken by Alun Bull, Derek Kendall and Peter Williams. Additional English Heritage photography by Steve Cole, Patricia Payne and Bob Skingle.

Additional photographs: Alamy: Michael Juno: 197; The Bridgeman Art Library: National Gallery, London: 224; National Gallery of Art, Washington DC: 141, Norwich Castle Museum and Art Gallery: 120t, 226b, Private Collection/The Stapleton Collection: 230, Victoria and Albert Museum: 235t; reproduced by permission of the British Geological Survey. © NERC. All rights reserved. IPR/62-03C: 12; The British Library: 160; courtesy of Lord Coke: 140b; Corbis: Philippa Lewis/Edifice: 88t; courtesy of Tom and Diana Dring: 120b; Doug Atfield and East Suffolk Record Office: 135t; Essex County Council: photo by David Strachan: 31; reproduced by courtesy of Essex Record Office: 54, 140t; James Fielding/Digital Atlas of England: 88b; The Francis Frith Collection: 73; Sarah Harrison: 175; courtesy of Philip Judge: 149; Faden's Map of Norfolk: digitally redrawn by Andrew Macnair: 52; Norfolk Museum and Archaeology Service: 15t, 18b, 112b, 123, 139, 147t, 186; Norfolk Record Office/reference DN/TA 527: 155; Norwich Castle Museum and Art Gallery: 226t; reproduced by permission of Ordnance Survey on behalf of HMSO. © Crown copyright 2006. All rights reserved. Ordnance Survey licence number 100017771: 194, 196, 198, 212; courtesy of The Pratt Family: 137; Sarah Roberts Architects Ltd: photo by Mr B Roberts: 105; courtesy of Lord de Saumarez: 146t, c; Suffolk Record Office: 136t, 201; © Tate, London, 2006: 75; Victoria and Albert Museum: 225; Matt Williamson: 17; Tom Williamson: 62t, 69t, 89, 100, 121l, 136b, 138t, b, 143, 147b, 154t, 163, 164, 168, 170, 181, 196b, 219, 239b.

Aerial survey acknowledgements

New English Heritage aerial photographs were taken by Damian Grady. The Aerial Reconnaissance team would like to thank the following people for their help: a special note of thanks must go to the skills and patience of the pilots Mick Webb and Marten White; the aircraft owner David Sanders; the NMR cataloguing team Rose Ogle, Katy Groves, Catherine Runciman, Cinzia Bacilieri, Philip Daniels, Geoff Hall; Jon Proudman for all the publication scanning; and Sarah Prince for laser copying thousands of aerial photographs to send to the authors.